INTERMITTENT EXPLOSIVE DISORDER

INTERMITTENT EXPLOSIVE DISORDER

Etiology, Assessment, and Treatment

Edited by

EMIL F. COCCARO
MICHAEL S. MCCLOSKEY

ELSEVIER

ACADEMIC PRESS
An imprint of Elsevier

Academic Press is an imprint of Elsevier
125 London Wall, London EC2Y 5AS, United Kingdom
525 B Street, Suite 1650, San Diego, CA 92101, United States
50 Hampshire Street, 5th Floor, Cambridge, MA 02139, United States
The Boulevard, Langford Lane, Kidlington, Oxford OX5 1GB, United Kingdom

Library of Congress Cataloging-in-Publication Data
A catalog record for this book is available from the Library of Congress

British Library Cataloguing-in-Publication Data
A catalogue record for this book is available from the British Library

ISBN 978-0-12-813858-8

For information on all Academic Press publications
visit our website at https://www.elsevier.com/books-and-journals

Publisher: Nikki Levy
Acquisition Editor: Nikki Levy
Editorial Project Manager: Karen Miller
Production Project Manager: Omer Mukthar Moosa
Cover Designer: Mark Rogers

Typeset by SPi Global, India

Contents

Contributors

Madj Alsayed
Clinical Neuroscience & Psychopharmacology Research Unit, Department of Psychiatry and Behavioral Neuroscience, Pritzker School of Medicine, University of Chicago, Chicago, IL, United States

Mitchell E. Berman
Department of Psychology, Mississppi State University, Starkville, MS, United States

Linda Booij
Department of Psychology, Concordia University; Sainte-Justine Hospital Research Centre, Montreal, QC, Canada

Emil F. Coccaro
Clinical Neuroscience & Psychopharmacology Research Unit, Department of Psychiatry and Behavioral Neuroscience, Pritzker School of Medicine, University of Chicago, Chicago, IL, United States

Sylvana M. Côté
University of Montreal, Montreal, QC, Canada; University of Bordeaux, Bordeaux, France

Jennifer R. Fanning
Center for Depression, Anxiety and Stress Research, McLean Hospital, Belmont, MA, United States

Alan R. Felthous
Forensic Psychiatry Division, Department of Psychiatry and Behavioral Neuroscience, Saint Louis University School of Medicine, Saint Louis, MO, United States

Louise Frogner
Örebro University, School of Law, Psychology and Social Work/Criminology, Örebro, Sweden

Cédric Galera
University of Bordeaux, Bordeaux, France

Maureen Hanlon
Supreme Court of Missouri, Jefferson City, MO, United States

Sarah K. Keedy
Clinical Neuroscience & Psychopharmacology Research Unit, Department of Psychiatry and Behavioral Neuroscience, Pritzker School of Medicine, University of Chicago, Chicago, IL, United States

Jacqueline Landess
Forensic Psychiatry Division, Department of Psychiatry and Behavioral Neuroscience, Saint Louis University School of Medicine, Saint Louis, MO, United States

Royce J. Lee
Clinical Neuroscience & Psychopharmacology Research Unit, Department of Psychiatry and Behavioral Neuroscience, Pritzker School of Medicine, University of Chicago, Chicago, IL, United States

Michael S. McCloskey
Mechanisms of Affect Dysregulation Laboratory (MAD LAB), Department of Psychology, Temple University, Philadelphia, PA, United States

Massimiliano Orri
McGill University, Montreal, QC, Canada

Lauren Pasetes
Clinical Neuroscience and Research Psychopharmacology Unit, Department of Psychiatry & Behavioral Neuroscience, Pritzker School of Medicine, University of Chicago, Chicago, IL, United States

Kristin A. Ridder
Clinical Neuroscience & Psychopharmacology Research Unit, Department of Psychiatry and Behavioral Neuroscience, Pritzker School of Medicine, University of Chicago, Chicago, IL, United States

Mari Sild
Department of Psychology, Concordia University; Sainte-Justine Hospital Research Centre, Montreal, QC, Canada

Richard E. Tremblay
University of Montreal, Montreal, QC, Canada; University College Dublin, Dublin, Ireland

Catherine Tuvblad
Örebro University, School of Law, Psychology and Social Work/Criminology, Örebro, Sweden; Department of Psychology, University of Southern California, Los Angeles, CA, United States

Jennifer Wang
Clinical Neuroscience & Psychopharmacology Research Unit, Department of Psychiatry and Behavioral Neuroscience, Pritzker School of Medicine, University of Chicago, Chicago, IL, United States

Preface

We are excited and honored to have the opportunity to edit and help write this book, *Intermittent Explosive Disorder.* We have both worked on the etiology and treatment of Intermittent Explosive Disorder (IED) for the majority of our careers, and have bemoaned the lack of information available about IED in academic texts, despite the prevalence and severity of the disorder. I (MSM) remember reviewing textbooks for my undergraduate psychopathology and not being able to find any that has more than a paragraph or two on IED (most had nothing on IED). This led me to look at graduate textbooks where sadly, the same pattern emerged. Therefore, the ability to have a book devoted to the etiology and treatment of IED represents an important step in educating individuals about this disorder, and we are proud to be a part of that step.

Aggression is all around us in our daily lives. It is verbal and physical in nature and is characteristic of up to 7%–8% of the population over the lifetime. While not all of such individuals have aggressive outbursts related to identifiable issues, up to 3%–4% display recurrent, problematic, impulsive, aggressive behaviors not secondary to other psychiatric disorder, medical conditions, or psychopharmacologic substances. Instead, these individuals have Intermittent Explosive Disorder (IED), a psychological condition increasingly understood as common, chronic, and complex. The essence of IED, as a disorder of impulsive aggression, has been included in the Diagnostic and Statistical Manual (DSM) from the beginning in 1956. It has gone through a variety of changes since then but is now operationalized as a disorder of primary impulsive aggression.

Research using research criteria and DSM-5 (adapted from research) criteria has shown that IED is straightforward to diagnose and that IED is the categorical expression of a dimension of impulsive aggression. Taxometric studies suggest a discontinuity at the extreme right side (higher scores) of the aggression spectrum, likely due to the presence of impairment and distress, and that individuals with IED represent a discrete population with a clinically relevant behavioral disorder. Not surprisingly, those with IED appear to demonstrate anomalies of psychological and pathophysiological function associated with high levels of impulsive aggression. Other studies demonstrate that targeted treatments may reduce impulsive aggression in those with IED.

This all said, there has been reluctance for the field to recognize the validity of IED for a variety of reasons. First, isn't impulsive aggression just "bad behavior"? Won't the existence of such a diagnosis be used to exonerate those committing aggressive acts? Second, since aggression is observed across the spectrum of psychiatric disorders, is there a need for a disorder of impulsive aggression? Is it possible that what is observed in IED is simply a product of other behavioral disorders comorbid with IED? These are all valid questions that have now been explored, and generally refuted, as will be seen in this book.

One of the editors (EFC) has been engaged in the psychobiology of mood, anxiety, and personality disorders for close to 35 years. When he first began, the biology of aggression was focused on aggression as a dimension, not as a disorder. Early studies showed consistent inverse correlations between dimensional measures of brain serotonin (5-HT) function and dimensional measures of aggression. These studies suggested that as 5-HT function declined across individuals, history, and dispositional measures, of aggression went up. This led to treatment studies to determine if increasing brain 5-HT with pharmacologic agents, such as 5-HT uptake inhibitors (e.g., fluoxetine) would reduce impulsive aggression. Not surprisingly, treatment with such agents did reduce impulsive aggression. However, that then led to the question of how to define and identify such impulsive aggressive individuals for further study and treatment.

At that time, more than 20 years ago, no diagnostic criteria appropriately described individuals with recurrent, problematic, impulsive aggression. The DSM-III included IED as a disorder but criteria for IED excluded individuals with a history of aggressiveness and impulsivity between major aggressive outbursts. Psychobiological research suggested, however, that impulsive aggressive individuals frequently display aggression, though some at relatively low levels, between extreme impulsive aggressive outbursts. This led the DSM-IV to remove the exclusion criteria for IED ruling out individuals with frequent interepisode impulsive aggressive behavior. This was an important change and it fostered increasingly greater research in this area, including the development of highly operationalized research diagnostic for IED.

The development of improved criteria of IED (DSM-IV or Research Diagnostic Criteria - RDC) allowed an estimate of how many in the community had IED, something critical to demonstrating the extent of the problem. While the initial epidemiological surveys of DSM-IV IED suggested a fairly high lifetime incidence (7.3%), application of Research or DSM-5 criteria recently revised this estimate downward to 3.6% lifetime. While still substantial, this figure represents those with IED displaying frequent serious impulsive aggressive outbursts at least three times per year (Mean ± SEM Outbursts/Year = 11.8 ± 1.4) rather than those with simply three serious outbursts over the lifetime (Mean ± SEM Outbursts/Year = 1.3 ± 0.1). Not surprisingly, those with IED by RDC or DSM-5 criteria also report substantial impairment in function (Mean ± SEM on Sheehan Disability Scale: 40.4 ± 3.6) compared with those with IED by DSM-IV criteria only (Mean ± SEM on Sheehan Disability Scale: 19.6 ± 6.5).

Despite increasing data of the validity of IED, this disorder of impulsive aggression continues to escape the measured attention of clinicians and researchers, alike. Worse, governmental, and private foundation, funding agencies have not prioritized research in aggression, especially of the psychobiological kind. The lack of support by funding agencies has consequences beyond the declination of funding for some fundable projects. Most importantly, the lack of funding leads to fewer investigators conducting research in aggression and fewer investigators with the knowledge to review grant applications in the area of aggression. This creates a downward spiral where research in this area can only stay at low levels, despite the societal consequences of impulsive aggression

This is the first scientific book we are aware of focusing on IED, and as such, includes and integrates virtually all of the extant research on IED (much of which was conducted by the two editors). For the purpose of this volume, we are defining human aggression as behavior by one individual directed at another person or object in which either verbal force or physical force is used to express anger and/or frustration. As such, we focus on anger-based, reactive, impulsive aggression as opposed to aggression occurring in the context of a socially sanctioned role (e.g., soldiers or law enforcement), or a medical condition affecting mental status, or aggression that is premeditated or instrumental in nature.

This volume is divided into three sections. The first section is on basic aspects of impulsive aggression and IED. It contains chapters on the developmental aspects of aggression, the behavioral and molecular genetics of aggression, the phenomenology of IED, and the comorbidity of IED. The second section focuses on the psychobiologic and psychocognitive aspects of IED including chapters on neurotransmitters, neuroimaging, biomedical aspects, social cognition, and relevance of trauma to aggression and IED. The last section focuses on the more clinical aspects of IED and includes chapters on the clinical approach to IED, the pharmacologic and psychosocial treatment of IED, and the forensic issues involved with working with individuals with IED.

We hope this book can serve as a tool for both clinicians and researchers working in the mental health field. For those who read this book, we hope you find it helpful to you in your understanding of aggression, particularly impulsive aggression, in your patients and others in your life.

Emil F. Coccaro*, Michael S. McCloskey†
*Clinical Neuroscience & Psychopharmacology Research Unit, Department of Psychiatry and Behavioral Neuroscience, Pritzker School of Medicine, University of Chicago, Chicago, IL, United States
†Mechanisms of Affect Dysregulation Laboratory (MAD LAB), Department of Psychology, Temple University, Philadelphia, PA, United States

PART I

Aggression and IED: Basic Aspects

CHAPTER ONE

Developmental Trajectories of Aggression and Other Problematic Behaviors Associated With IED☆

Richard E. Tremblay[*,†], **Cédric Galera**[‡], **Massimiliano Orri**[§], **Sylvana M. Côté**[*,‡]
[*]University of Montreal, Montreal, QC, Canada
[†]University College Dublin, Dublin, Ireland
[‡]University of Bordeaux, Bordeaux, France
[§]McGill University, Montreal, QC, Canada

Contents

Historical Perspective

In their invitation to write the present chapter, the volume editors wrote: "We very much want to have a chapter in our book on Intermittent Explosive Disorder (IED) covering the topic of 'Developmental Trajectories of Aggression' because we believe that many of the children you and your colleagues study grow up to have IED."

In making this request the volume editors were following in the steps of Aristotle who wrote, some 2600 years ago, that: *He who considers things in their first growth and origin, … will obtain the clearest view of them.* (Politics, Book 1 chap 2). Similarly, 19th century investigators of animal and human behavior explicitly stated that understanding a given behavior required the description

☆ Adapted from the following: Tremblay (2000), Tremblay (2010), and Tremblay (2018).

Intermittent Explosive Disorder
https://doi.org/10.1016/B978-0-12-813858-8.00001-2

of that behavior's development from conception onwards (Cairns, 1983). But not all scientists agreed! One of the fiercest debates concerning the origins of species in the 1820s, described at the time by Goethe as a volcano eruption, was sparked by the decision of a French naturalist, Etienne Geoffroy Saint-Hilaire, to compare the development of fetuses rather than continue comparing only the anatomy of adult animals (Appel, 1987). Some 30 years later, Charles Darwin cited this early work on the differences in the development of fetuses as one of the best support for his theory (Darwin, 1859, p. 409). In his history of developmental psychology, Robert Cairns (1983) reminded his readers that the father of experimental psychology in the 19th century, Wilhelm Wundt, rejected the developmental perspective arguing that the adult mind could be understood independently from the mind of the child.

This refusal to take a developmental perspective has largely prevailed in the study of aggressive behavior over the 20th century. Aggressive behavior problems during adulthood, as well as during adolescence, were generally studied without reference to childhood aggressive behavior problems.

One debate on the developmental origins of aggression among humans reached its peak in the late 1960s and early 1970s. It centered on the nature vs nurture origin of aggression. Konrad Lorenz's book 'On Aggression' (Lorenz, 1966) was based on Lorenz's observations of animal behavior and concluded that humans, like all other animals, inherit an 'aggressive instinct' which could lead to the destruction of humanity. The nurture side of the debate was highlighted by the social psychologist Albert Bandura in his book 'Aggression: A social learning perspective' published 7 years later (Bandura, 1973). Bandura's book was based on studies of children in a laboratory situation where they were shown to spontaneously imitate an adult hitting a Bobo doll. Bandura concluded from these observations: "People are not born with preformed repertories of aggressive behaviors; they must learn them in one way or another" (Bandura, 1973, p. 61). His work led to numerous studies that were partly driven by the hypothesis that children were becoming more aggressive because of violence on television (e.g., Eron, Walder, Toigo, & Lefkowitz, 1963; Huesmann, Lagerspetz, & Eron, 1984).

The social learning hypothesis of aggression essentially dominated the fields of criminology, education, child psychiatry, psychology, public health, and sociology. For example, in 1993 the US National Academy of Science Panel 'On understanding and control of violent behavior' concluded: "Modern Psychological perspectives emphasize that aggressive and violent behaviors are learned responses to frustration, that they can also be learned as instruments for achieving goals, and that the learning occurs by observing models of such behavior. Such models may be observed in the family, among peers, elsewhere in the neighborhood, through the mass media ..." (Reiss & Roth, 1993, p. 7). As recently as 2002, the World Health Organization's 'World Report on Violence and Health' concluded: "The majority of young people who become violent are adolescent-limited offenders who, in fact, show little or no evidence of high levels of aggression or other problem behaviors during their childhood" (World Health Organization, 2002, p. 31). They attributed this conclusion to the following source: 'Youth violence: a report of the Surgeon General. Washington, DC United States Department of Health and Human Services' (US Surgeon General, 2001).

Developmental Trajectories of Physical Aggression From Early Childhood to Old Age

In the last half of the 20th century, there was a strong interest in the stability of aggressive behavior. In one of the most often cited reviews, Olweus (1979) concluded that aggressive behavior was as stable as intelligence because of a high correlation between assessments at two points in time in 16 samples of males. Two studies starting toward the end of infancy also indicated that stability of physical aggression was high during the preschool years (Cummings, Iannotti, & Zahn-Waxler, 1989; Keenan & Shaw, 1994). However, it is important to remember that a high correlation between two assessments only indicates that individuals retain a relatively consistent placement within the group at two points in time. Correlational analyses of aggressive behavior with longitudinal data do not provide information on intraindividual change in aggressive behavior over time.

In 1984 we initiated the first large prospective longitudinal study of boys' physical aggressions from kindergarten onwards. The study made annual assessments of a sample of 1031 boys from 53 schools of low socioeconomic neighborhoods in Montreal (Canada). Results surprisingly showed that the mean frequency of physical aggressions decreased from early childhood to adolescence. To rule out the hypothesis that a subgroup of children were increasing their frequency of physical aggressions with age, while most others decreased their frequency of aggressions, we used semiparametric trajectory analyses. Results showed (see Fig. 1 from Nagin & Tremblay, 1999) that no significant group of children went from low frequency of physical

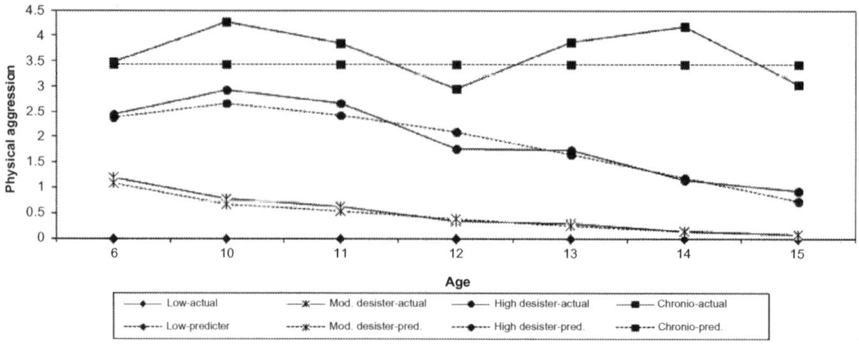

Fig. 1 Trajectories of physical aggression between 6 and 15 years of age. *(From Nagin, D., & Tremblay, R. E. (1999). Trajectories of boys' physical aggression, opposition, and hyperactivity on the path to physically violent and nonviolent juvenile delinquency.* Child Development, *70(5), 1181–1196.)*

aggressions during childhood to high frequency during adolescence. Those who frequently aggressed in adolescence were those who frequently aggressed during childhood. These results were replicated with longitudinal studies in Italy, New Zealand, and the United States (Broidy et al., 2003; Di Giunta et al., 2010).

The results of these longitudinal studies in many countries suggested that if children learn to aggress from their environment, this must happen before school entry. With the first data collection of a nation-wide accelerated longitudinal study in Canada, we showed that, for boys and girls, the frequency of hitting, kicking, and biting substantially decreased from 2 to 11 years of age (see Fig. 2 from Tremblay et al., 1999).

We then traced the developmental trajectories of physical aggressions from 17 to 60 months with a prospective longitudinal study of a representative sample of births in the Canadian province of Quebec (Fig. 3 from Côté et al., 2007). Results indicated that there were three developmental trajectories that had the same shape, but with significant differences in the frequencies of physical aggressions. The three groups increased their frequency of physical aggressions from 17 to 42 months followed by a decrease in the frequency from 42 to 60 months. However, a third of the sample had low frequencies of physical aggressions, 50% had a medium frequency of physical aggressions, while 17% had the highest frequency of physical aggressions at all assessment points. This high physical aggression group was different from the rest of the sample on numerous characteristics: there were more boys; the families had low income and was described by the mother as dysfunctional; the mothers

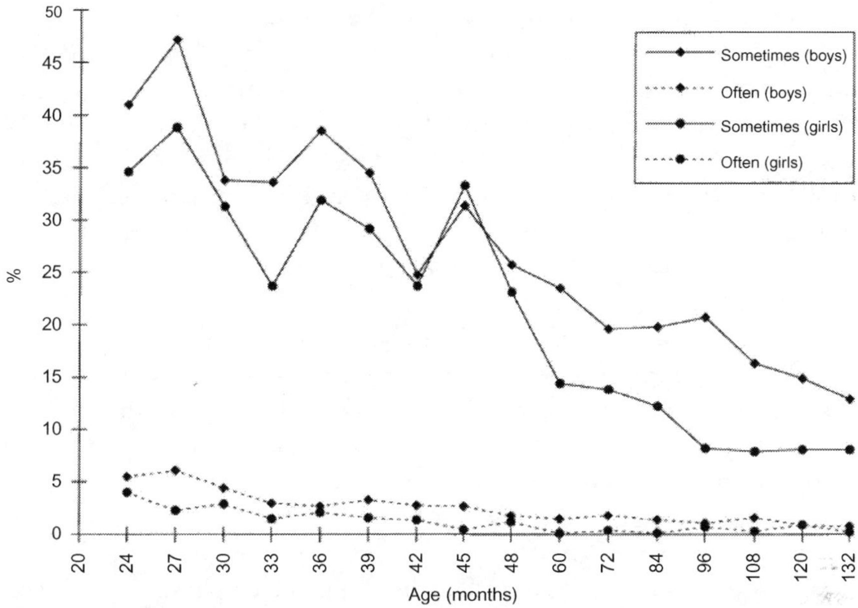

Fig. 2 Hitting, biting, and kicking (boys and girls aged 2–11 years). *(From Tremblay, R. E., Japel, C., Pérusse, D., McDuff, P., Boivin, M., Zoccolillo, M., & Montplaisir, J. (1999). The search for the age of "onset" of physical aggression: Rousseau and Bandura revisited.* Criminal Behavior and Mental Health, *9(1), 8–23.)*

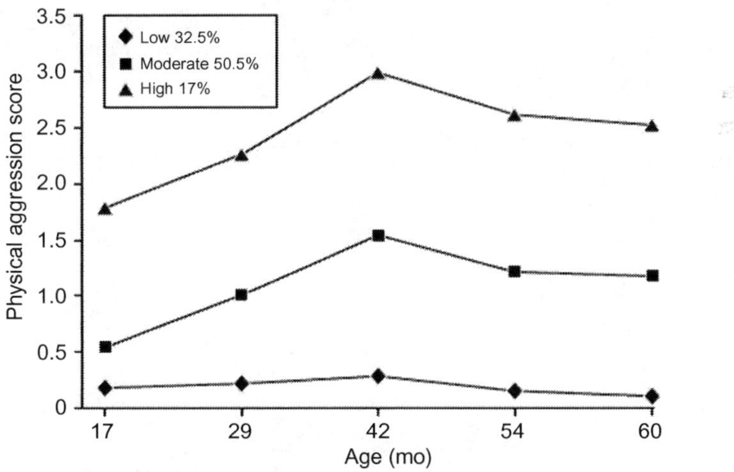

Fig. 3 Trajectories of physical aggression between 1.5 and 5 years of age ($n = 1758$). *(From Côté, S. M., Boivin, M., Nagin, D. S., Japel, C., Xu, Q., Zoccolillo, M., & Tremblay, R. E. (2007). The role of maternal education and non-maternal care services in the prevention of children's physical aggression.* Archives of General Psychiatry, *64(11), 1305–1312.)*

had a history of depression, of conduct problems during adolescence, and of alcohol consumption (see also Tremblay et al., 2004). More recent studies in Great Britain and Norway have confirmed the early onset of physical aggression and the decreasing developmental trajectories as children learn to control their behavior (e.g., Hay et al., 2014; Naerde, Ogden, Janson, & Zachrisson, 2014; Tremblay et al., 1999) (Campbell, Spieker, Burchinal, Poe, & NICHD Early Child Care Research Network, 2006; Côté, Vaillancourt, LeBlanc, Nagin, & Tremblay, 2006; Dearing, Zachrisson, & Naerde, 2015; Naerde et al., 2014).

The longitudinal studies of physical aggression which have continued to follow children during adolescence and early adulthood showed that the frequency of physical aggression continues to decline with age for the majority (Tremblay & Côté, 2009). However, among the most physically aggressive individuals, there is often a slight increase of physical aggression during mid-adolescence followed by a decline (see Fig. 4) (Lacourse et al., 2002; van Lier, Vitaro, Barker, Koot, & Tremblay, 2009, see Fig. 3).

Few studies have monitored the development of physical aggression from adolescence throughout adulthood with longitudinal studies. The best data comes from court records of a sample of male juvenile delinquents living in Boston in the 1940s (Sampson & Laub, 2003). The results showed a clear decline in arrests for violent crimes from early adulthood to old age. Similar results were obtained for physical aggressions among couples from cross-sectional and short-term longitudinal studies (Bookwala, Sobin, & Zdaniuk, 2005; O'Leary & Woodin, 2005; Suitor, Pillemer, & Straus, 1990; Vickerman & Margolin, 2008).

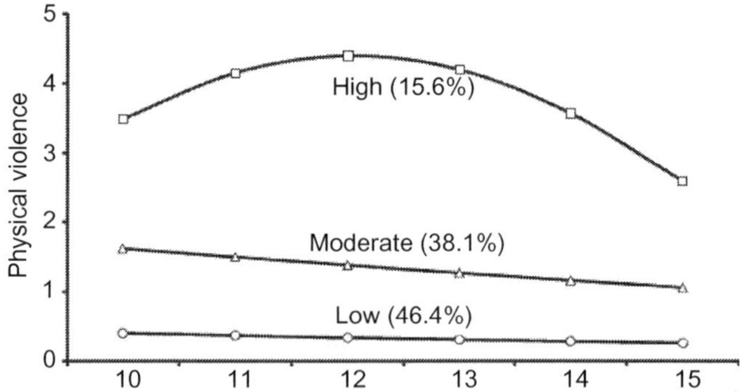

Fig. 4 Developmental trajectories of physical violence. *(From van Lier, P. A. C., Vitaro, F., Barker, E. D., Koot, H. M., & Tremblay, R. E. (2009). Developmental links between trajectories of physical violence, vandalism, theft, and alcohol-drug use from childhood to adolescence.* Journal of Abnormal Child Psychology, 37*(4), 481–492. doi:10.1007/s10802-008-9289-6.)*

Thus research on the development of physical aggression from infancy to old age indicates that (a) humans start to physically aggress before the end of their first year after birth; (b) the frequency of physical aggression reaches a peak during the first 3 to 4 years after birth; and (c) from that infancy peak, the frequency of physical aggressions then decreases until old age. A small group of individuals, mainly males, tend to use physical aggression more frequently than others throughout life and they are more likely to increase the frequency of their physical aggressions during mid-adolescence.

The Development of Other Forms of Aggression

Up to now, the focus of this chapter has been on physical aggressions. That choice was made because physical aggression is the more lethal form of aggression and the easiest to observe, partly because of its obvious negative consequences. However, in the context of the present book's focus on IED, it is important to understand that the history of research on human aggression has clearly shown that the major problem with the field has long been with the definition of aggression (see, e.g., Berkowitz, 1962; Burt, 1925; Buss, 1961).

The definition of aggression problem can be clearly seen when the content of the « aggression » scales for children is examined. We see a mix of behaviors that range from physical aggressions to attention seeking and disobedience. For example, the frequently used Child Behavior Checklist "Aggression" scale contains « argues, brags, demands attention, disobeys, poor peer relations, jealous, lies, shows off, stubborn, moody, sulks, loud » (Achenbach & Edelbrock, 1983). The common denominator of these items appears to be that they can be annoying. The total score for this "aggression" scale is clearly mixing children who are annoying and disruptive with those who physically attack. In fact, only 2 of the 23 items refer clearly to physical aggressions, and two others which could be interpreted as physical aggression. These items are regularly used to identify either « aggressive », « externalizing », « conduct problem », or « antisocial » individuals in clinical practice. They are also used to identify genetic influences on phenotypes which are alternatively referred to as « aggressive », « externalizing », « conduct disordered », or « antisocial » (e.g., Eley, Lichenstein, & Stevenson, 1999; O'Connor, McGuire, Reiss, Hetherington, & Plomin, 1998; Slutske et al., 1997; van Beijsterveldt, Bartels, Hudziak, & Boomsma, 2003).

The definition of IED clearly includes both physical and verbal aggression, while the 3rd criterion (behavior is not premeditated) clearly excludes proactive aggression and possibly indirect aggression (relational aggression), a form of aggression which involves a delayed response to frustration (Côté et al., 2007; Crick, 1995). From this perspective, research on the developmental origins of IED needs to distinguish proactive from reactive aggression.

Much work has been done on differentiating proactive and reactive aggression with children and adolescents. For example, Vitaro, Brendgen, and Tremblay (2002) used longitudinal data from a large population sample of children between 6 and 13 years of age to differentiate the reactively and proactively aggressive children between 10 and 12 years of age and identify their antecedent and subsequent characteristics. The study showed that the children who were rated by their teachers as the most reactively aggressive between 10 and 12 years of age had been rated the most reactive by their mothers on a reactive temperament scale (Lerner, Palermo, Spiro, & Nesselroade, 1982) at 6 years of age. With reference to IED, it is important to note that this reactivity scale includes items concerning reactivity to physical phenomena such as light and pain. At age 6, the physically reactive children were also rated by their mothers as more inattentive, hyperactive-impulsive, withdrawn, and physically aggressive. At age 13 the reactively aggressive children were less likely to report delinquent behavior than the proactively aggressive, but more likely to report depressive feelings.

These results suggest that reactively aggressive preadolescents have had problems with reactive aggression at least since kindergarten, but they also have a more general reactivity profile that includes reactivity to physical stimuli such as light and pain, as well as social withdrawal problems, impulsivity, hyperactivity, and inattention.

The Early Development of Hyperactivity-Impulsivity

It would be a major surprise if IED was not in some way related to the early development of the well-studied hyperactivity-impulsivity disorder. Its development from 18 months to 8 years was described (Galéra et al., 2011) with maternal ratings of 2057 children from the Quebec Longitudinal Study of Child Development (QLSCD) at the following ages: 1 ½, 2 ½, 3 ½, 4 ½, 5, 6, and 8 years. Five items were used to assess hyperactivity-impulsivity: "can't sit still, is restless or hyperactive," "fidgets," "is impulsive, acts without thinking," "has difficulty waiting for his/her turn in games," "cannot settle down to do anything for more than a few moments." The three hyperactivity-impulsivity trajectories were high (16.1%), moderate (52.7%),

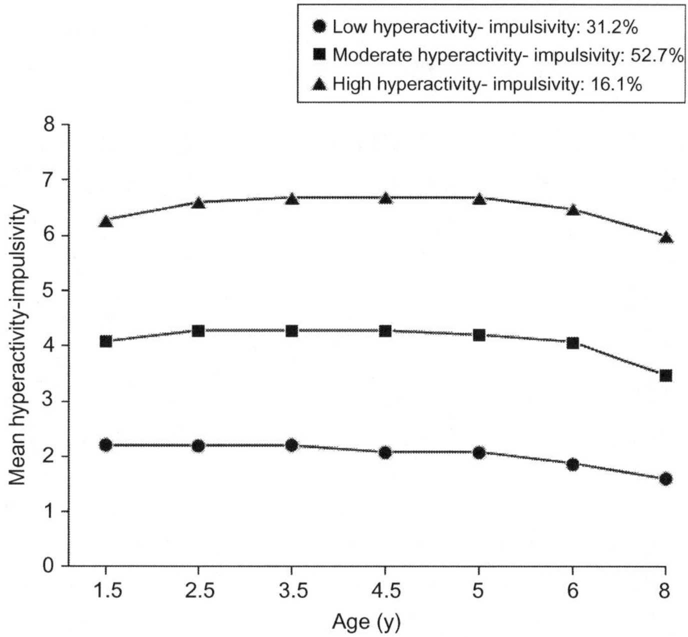

Fig. 5 Developmental trajectories of hyperactivity-impulsivity. *(From Galéra, C., Côté, S. M., Bouvard, M. P., Pingault, J. B., Melchior, M., Michel, G., … Tremblay, R. E. (2011). Early risk factors for hyperactivity-impulsivity and inattention trajectories from age 17 months to 8 years.* Archives of General Psychiatry, *68(12), 1267–1275. doi:10.1001/archgenpsychiatry.2011.138.)*

and low (31.2%). Fig. 5 clearly shows that the level of hyperactivity-impulsivity was stable for the three groups from early childhood to mid childhood. In a longitudinal study from 6 to 12 years of age, with a representative sample ($N=2000$) of Canadian children, the results showed that those on high as well as low trajectories of hyperactivity-impulsivity did not substantially increase nor decrease their level of hyperactivity-impulsivity between 6 and 12 years of ages, while those in the middle showed a little bit more variability (Pingault et al., 2011). Thus levels of hyperactivity-impulsivity remain fairly stable from early childhood to adolescence and they are good predictors of numerous mental health, educational and social problems (Pingault, Côté, Galéra, et al., 2013; Pingault, Côté, Lacourse, et al., 2013; Pingault et al., 2011). It is easy to imagine that such an accumulation of problems, from early childhood to adulthood, could be involved in IED development.

The Early Development of Irritability and its Link to Suicidality

A recent study on the development of irritability during elementary school, as a predictor of suicidal ideations and suicidal attempts during adolescence, may also be an important contribution to understanding IED development. Orri et al. (2018) used the Quebec Longitudinal Study of Child Development, first to describe the developmental trajectories of irritability between 6 and 12 years of age, based on teacher ratings; second to investigate their associations to suicidal thoughts and attempts. Three of the four items that were used in the study related to reactive aggression: reacted in an aggressive manner when teased, reacted in an aggressive manner when contradicted, reacted in an aggressive manner when something was taken away from him/her. The fourth item was had temper tantrums or hot temper. Children with high irritability and anxious mood between 6 and 12 years of age compared to those with low symptom levels had higher rates of suicidal ideation and attempts.

Conclusions

Longitudinal studies of behavior development which start during infancy systematically show that the behavior problems we observe during adolescence and adulthood were present in early childhood. In fact, the frequency of physical aggressions, loss of control, and hyperactive and impulsive behaviors are at their highest during early childhood. Learning to gain control over one's behavior is probably the main task of childhood and this has been clear for centuries to the wisest observers of human behavior. For example, some 2400 years ago Aristotle wrote in his book on politics that *"anger and will and desire are implanted in a child from their very birth, but reason and understanding develop as they grow older."* More recently, Thomas Hobbes, in his book On the Citizen (Hobbes, 1641), was more explicit when he wrote: *"Unless you give infants everything they want, they cry and get angry, they even beat their own parents … Thus, an evil man is rather like a sturdy boy, or a man of childish mind, and evil is simply want of reason at an age when it normally accrues to men by nature governed by discipline and experience of harm."*

By referring to nature and discipline and experience, as the causal factors of behavior problems during adulthood, Hobbes appears to have been more insightful than many "modern" investigators of mental health who tend to attribute behavior problems to either genes or environment or experience. We suggest that the next step in understanding the developmental origins of IED, would involve using longitudinal studies that have assessed large cohorts of children throughout their development, to assess their IED during adulthood. These studies would help trace the pathway from pregnancy to IED in adulthood, and thus identify preventive interventions that can be implemented from pregnancy onwards.

References

Achenbach, T. M., & Edelbrock, C. (1983). *Manual for the child behavior checklist and revised child behavior profile. Burlington*. VT: University of Vermont, Department of Psychiatry.

Appel, T. A. (1987). *The Cuvier-Geoffroy debate: French biology in the decades before Darwin*. New York, NY: Oxford University Press.

Bandura, A. (1973). *Aggression: A social learning analysis*. New York, NY: Holt.

Berkowitz, L. (1962). *Aggression: A social psychological analysis*. New York: McGraw-Hill.

Bookwala, J., Sobin, J., & Zdaniuk, B. (2005). Gender and aggression in marital relationships: a life-span perspective. *Sex Roles*, *52*(11 – 12), 797–806. https://doi.org/10.1007/s11199-005-4200-1.

Broidy, L. M., Nagin, D. S., Tremblay, R. E., Bates, J. E., Brame, B., Dodge, K. A., et al. (2003). Developmental trajectories of childhood disruptive behaviors and adolescent delinquency: a six site, cross national study. *Developmental Psychology*, *39*(2), 222–245.

Burt, C. L. (1925). *The young delinquent*. London: University of London Press.

Buss, A. H. (1961). *The psychology of aggression*. New York: Wiley.

Cairns, R. B. (1983). The emergence of developmental psychology. In: P. H. Mussen (Ed.), Vol. 1. *Handbook of child Psychology* (pp. 41–102). Toronto, ON: John Wiley & Sons.

Campbell, S. B., Spieker, S., Burchinal, M., Poe, M. D., & NICHD Early Child Care Research Network (2006). Trajectories of aggression from toddlerhood to age 9 predict academic and social functioning through age 12. *Journal of Child Psychology and Psychiatry, and Allied Disciplines*, *47*(8), 791–800.

Côté, S. M., Boivin, M., Nagin, D. S., Japel, C., Xu, Q., Zoccolillo, M., et al. (2007). The role of maternal education and non-maternal care services in the prevention of children's physical aggression. *Archives of General Psychiatry*, *64*(11), 1305–1312.

Côté, S. M., Vaillancourt, T., LeBlanc, J. C., Nagin, D. S., & Tremblay, R. E. (2006). The development of physical aggression from toddlerhood to pre-adolescence: a nation wide longitudinal study of Canadian children. *Journal of Abnormal Child Psychology*, *34*(1), 71–85.

Crick, N. R. (1995). Relational aggression: the role of intent attributions, feelings of distress, and provocation types. *Development and Psychopathology*, 7(2), 313–322.

Cummings, E. M., Iannotti, R. J., & Zahn-Waxler, C. (1989). Aggression between peers in early childhood: individual continuity and developmental change. *Child Development*, *60*(4), 887–895.

Darwin, C. (1859). *On the origin of species*. London, United Kingdom: John Murray. reprinted by Gryphon Edition.

Dearing, E., Zachrisson, H. D., & Naerde, A. (2015). Age of entry into early childhood education and care as a predictor of aggression: faint and fading associations for young Norwegian children. *Psychological Science*, *26*(10), 1595–1607. https://doi.org/10.1177/0956797615595011.

Di Giunta, L., Pastorelli, C., Eisenberg, N., Gerbino, M., Castellani, V., & Bombi, A. S. (2010). Developmental trajectories of physical aggression: prediction of overt and covert antisocial behaviors from self- and mothers' reports. *European Child & Adolescent Psychiatry, 19*(12), 873–882. https://doi.org/10.1007/s00787-010-0134-4.

Eley, T. C., Lichenstein, P., & Stevenson, J. (1999). Sex differences in the etiology of aggressive and nonaggressive antisocial behavior: results from two twin studies. *Child Development, 70*(1), 155–168.

Eron, L. D., Walder, L. O., Toigo, R., & Lefkowitz, M. M. (1963). Social class, parental punishment for aggression, and child aggression. *Child Development, 34*(4), 849–867. https://doi.org/10.1111/j.1467-8624.1963.tb05159.x.

Galéra, C., Côté, S. M., Bouvard, M. P., Pingault, J. B., Melchior, M., Michel, G., et al. (2011). Early risk factors for hyperactivity-impulsivity and inattention trajectories from age 17 months to 8 years. *Archives of General Psychiatry, 68*(12), 1267–1275. https://doi.org/10.1001/archgenpsychiatry.2011.138.

Hay, D. F., Waters, C. S., Perra, O., Swift, N., Kairis, V., Phillips, R., et al. (2014). Precursors to aggression are evident by 6 months of age. *Developmental Science, 17*(3), 471–480. https://doi.org/10.1111/desc.12133.

Hobbes, T. (1641). *On the citizen*. Cambridge: Cambridge University Press.

Huesmann, L. R., Lagerspetz, K., & Eron, L. D. (1984). Intervening variables in the TV violence–aggression relation: evidence from two countries. *Developmental Psychology, 20*(5), 746–775. https://doi.org/10.1037//0012-1649.20.5.746.

Keenan, K., & Shaw, D. S. (1994). The development of aggression in toddlers: a study of low-income families. *Journal of Abnormal Child Psychology, 22*(1), 53–77.

Lacourse, E., Côté, S., Nagin, D. S., Vitaro, F., Brendgen, M., & Tremblay, R. E. (2002). A longitudinal-experimental approach to testing theories of antisocial behavior development. *Development and Psychopathology, 14*(4), 909–924. https://doi.org/10.1017/S0954579402004121.

Lerner, R. M., Palermo, M., Spiro, A., & Nesselroade, J. R. (1982). Assessing the dimensions of temperament indivuality across the life-span: the dimensions of temperament survey (DOTS). *Child Development, 53*, 149–159.

Lorenz, K. (1966). *On aggression*. New York, NY: Harcourt, Brace and World.

Naerde, A., Ogden, T., Janson, H., & Zachrisson, H. D. (2014). Normative development of physical aggression from 8 to 26 months. *Developmental Psychology, 50*(6), 1710–1720. https://doi.org/10.1037/a0036324.

Nagin, D., & Tremblay, R. E. (1999). Trajectories of boys' physical aggression, opposition, and hyperactivity on the path to physically violent and nonviolent juvenile delinquency. *Child Development, 70*(5), 1181–1196.

O'Connor, T. G., McGuire, S., Reiss, D., Hetherington, M. E., & Plomin, R. (1998). Co-occurrence of depressive symptoms and antisocial behavior in adolescence: a common genetic liability. *Journal of Abnormal Psychology, 107*(1), 27–37.

O'Leary, K. D., & Woodin, E. M. (2005). Partner aggression and problem drinking across the lifespan: how much do they decline? *Clinical Psychology Review, 25*(7), 877–894. https://doi.org/10.1016/j.cpr.2005.03.004.

Olweus, D. (1979). Stability of aggressive reaction patterns in males: a review. *Psychological Bulletin, 86*(4), 852.

Orri, M., Galera, C., Turecki, G., Forte, A., Renaud, J., Boivin, M., et al. (2018). Association of childhood irritability and depressive/anxious mood profiles with adolescent suicidal ideation and attemps [online]. *JAMA Psychiatry 75*(5), 465–473.

Pingault, J. -B., Côté, S. M., Galéra, C., Genolini, C., Falissard, B., Vitaro, F., et al. (2013). Childhood trajectories of inattention, hyperactivity and oppositional behaviors and prediction of substance abuse/dependence: a 15-year longitudinal population-based study. *Molecular Psychiatry, 18*(7), 806–812. https://doi.org/10.1038/mp.2012.87.

Pingault, J. -B., Côté, S. M., Lacourse, E., Galéra, C., Vitaro, F., & Tremblay, R. E. (2013). Childhood hyperactivity, physical aggression and criminality: a 19-year prospective population-based study. *PLoS One*, *8*(5), 1–7.

Pingault, J. B., Tremblay, R. E., Vitaro, F., Carbonneau, R., Genolini, C., Falissard, B., et al. (2011). Childhood trajectories of inattention and hyperactivity and prediction of educational attainment in early adulthood: a 16-year longitudinal population-based study. *The American Journal of Psychiatry*, *168*(11), 1164–1170. https://doi.org/10.1176/appi.ajp.2011.10121732.

Reiss, A. J., & Roth, J. A. (Eds.), (1993). *Understanding and preventing violence*. Washington, DC: National Academy Press.

Sampson, R. J., & Laub, J. H. (2003). Life-course desisters? Trajectories of crime among delinquent boys followed to age 70. *Criminology*, *41*(3), 555–592.

Slutske, W. S., Heath, A. C., Dunne, M. P., Statham, D. J., Dinwiddie, S. H., Madden, P. A. F., et al. (1997). Modeling genetic and environmental influences in the etiology of conduct disorder: a study of 2,682 adult twin pairs. *Journal of Abnormal Psychology*, *106*(2), 266–279.

Suitor, J. J., Pillemer, K., & Straus, M. A. (1990). Marital violence in a life course perspective. In M. A. Straus & R. J. Gelles (Eds.), *Physical violence in American families: Risk factors and adaptations to violence in 8,145 families* (pp. 305–317). New Brunswick, NJ: Transaction.

Tremblay, R. E. (2000). The development of aggressive behaviour during childhood: what have we learned in the past century? *International Journal of Behavioral Development*, *24*(2), 129–141.

Tremblay, R. E. (2010). Developmental origins of disruptive behaviour problems: the 'original sin' hypothesis, epigenetics and their consequences for prevention. *Journal of Child Psychology and Psychiatry*, *51*, 341–367.

Tremblay, R. E. (2018). Anger and aggression. In *Reference module in neuroscience and Biobehavioral Psychology*. Elsevier.

Tremblay, R. E., & Côté, S. M. (2009). Development of sex differences in physical aggression: the maternal link to epigenetic mechanisms [comment]. *Behavioral and Brain Sciences*, *32*(3–4), 290–291. https://doi.org/10.1017/S0140525X09990951.

Tremblay, R. E., Japel, C., Pérusse, D., McDuff, P., Boivin, M., Zoccolillo, M., et al. (1999). The search for the age of "onset" of physical aggression: Rousseau and Bandura revisited. *Criminal Behavior and Mental Health*, *9*(1), 8–23.

Tremblay, R. E., Nagin, D., Séguin, J. R., Zoccolillo, M., Zelazo, P. D., Boivin, M., et al. (2004). Physical aggression during early childhood: trajectories and predictors. *Pediatrics*, *114*(1), e43–e50.

US Surgeon General. (2001). *Youth violence: A report of the Surgeon General*. Washington, DC: US Department of Health and Human Services.

van Beijsterveldt, C. E. M., Bartels, M., Hudziak, J. J., & Boomsma, D. I. (2003). Causes of stability of aggression from early childhood to adolescence: a longitudinal genetic analysis in dutch twins. *Behavior Genetics*, *33*(5), 591–605.

van Lier, P. A. C., Vitaro, F., Barker, E. D., Koot, H. M., & Tremblay, R. E. (2009). Developmental links between trajectories of physical violence, vandalism, theft, and alcohol-drug use from childhood to adolescence. *Journal of Abnormal Child Psychology*, *37*(4), 481–492. https://doi.org/10.1007/s10802-008-9289-6.

Vickerman, K. A., & Margolin, G. (2008). Trajectories of physical and emotional marital aggression in midlife couples. *Violence and Victims*, *23*(1), 18–34.

Vitaro, F., Brendgen, M., & Tremblay, R. E. (2002). Reactively and proactively aggressive children: antecedent and subsequent characteristics. *Journal of Child Psychology and Psychiatry*, *43*(4), 495–505.

World Health Organization. (2002). *World report on violence and health*. Geneva, Switzerland: WHO.

CHAPTER TWO

Behavioral Genetics of Aggression and Intermittent Explosive Disorder

Catherine Tuvblad*,†, Mari Sild‡,§, Louise Frogner*, Linda Booij‡,§
*Örebro University, School of Law, Psychology and Social Work/Criminology, Örebro, Sweden
†Department of Psychology, University of Southern California, Los Angeles, CA, United States
‡Department of Psychology, Concordia University, Montreal, QC, Canada
§Sainte-Justine Hospital Research Centre, Montreal, QC, Canada

Contents

Intermittent Explosive Disorder
https://doi.org/10.1016/B978-0-12-813858-8.00002-4

Aggressive Behavior

Aggressive behavior is commonly defined as a behavior that is intended to cause pain or harm to another person who is motivated to avoid that harm (Bushman & Huesmann, 2010). This harm can take many forms and aggressive behavior is divided into various subtypes, based on in what way and situation this behavior is carried out. Subtypes include (but are not limited to) reactive, hostile, or affective aggressive behavior; proactive or instrumental aggressive behavior; indirect or relational aggressive behavior and verbal aggression (Allen & Anderson, 2017). Violence is considered a more extreme form of aggressive behavior that has severe physical harm as its goal. Aggressive behavior and violence are considered to be on the same continuum, where aggressive behavior is at the less severe and violence at the more severe end (Allen & Anderson, 2017). Thus aggressive behavior is not only common, but it is also a very complex phenomenon that can come in various forms.

This chapter will review evidence of genetic and *epi*genetic contributions to aggressive behavior. Specifically, we will review findings from behavioral genetic studies (i.e., twin and adoption studies) and molecular (epi)genetic studies. We will first consider the behavioral genetic research design and its assumptions, followed by findings from metaanalyses, systematic reviews, and recent studies using a behavioral genetic research design. Lastly, we review genome-wide, candidate gene and epigenetic studies on human aggressive behavior. Since empirical studies focusing on Intermittent Explosive Disorder (IED) (or in any other specific diagnostic category) are scarce, our focus is aggressive behavior in general.

Behavioral Genetic Research Design

Behavioral genetic research relies on the different levels of genetic relatedness between family members in order to estimate the relative contribution of heritable and environmental factors to individual differences in a phenotype of interest, in this case aggressive behavior. Behavioral genetic research designs include (1) studies of twins, and (2) studies of adopted individuals and their biological and adoptive family members. However, in the past three decades adoption samples have become less accessible (Moffitt, Caspi, & Rutter, 2005).

In the classical twin design, monozygotic (identical) twins share their common environment and they are assumed to share 100% of their genetic makeup. Dizygotic (fraternal) twins are assumed to share on average 50% of their genes. Both monozygotic and dizygotic twins are assumed to share their common environment. By comparing the resemblance for aggressive behavior between monozygotic and dizygotic twins, the total phenotypic variance of aggression can be divided into additive genetic factors (or heritability, h^2), shared environmental factors (c^2), and nonshared environmental factors (e^2). Shared environmental factors refer to nongenetic influences that contribute to similarity within pairs of twins. Nonshared environmental factors refer to individual experiences that make siblings differ in their levels of aggressive behavior. Heritability is the proportion of total phenotypic variance due to genetic variation. Heritability is time- and population-specific, and it is a population parameter, rather than an individual one (Neale & Cardon, 1992). Genetic influences may also be divided into those that are additive (i.e., allelic effects add up across loci) and those that are nonadditive (i.e., due to dominance or epistasis). However, data from twins reared together do not contain sufficient information to permit evaluation of the contrasting effects of dominant genetic and shared environmental influences. To estimate dominant genetic and shared environmental influences simultaneously would, for example, require an adoptive sibling design.

In sibling adoption studies, the correlation between adoptive siblings is compared with the correlation between biological siblings to estimate the influence of genetic and environmental factors on aggressive behavior (Plomin, DeFries, Knopik, & Neiderhiser, 2013). Resemblance between adoptive siblings for measures of aggression is indicative of shared (or common) family environment, while the extent to which biological sibling resemblance exceeds that of adoptive siblings is taken as evidence of heritable genetic influences for aggressive behavior.

Behavioral Genetic Research Design: Generalizability and Assumptions

Generalizability From Twin Studies to the General Population

Studies examining whether twins differ from singletons on aggressive behavior show that findings from twin research can be generalized to nontwins (Barnes & Boutwell, 2013).

The Equal Environment Assumption (EEA)

The most controversial assumption in behavior genetics is the equal environment assumption. If the equal environment assumption is not met, higher correlations among MZ twins may be due to environmental factors rather than genetic factors and heritability may be overestimated. However, studies examining the equal environment assumption generally report that this assumption tends to hold and that the resulting bias is likely modest (for an extensive review: (Felson, 2014)).

Random Mating

Random mating in the parent generation can lead to increased resemblance for dizygotic but not monozygotic twin pairs, and thereby bias shared environmental estimates upward and additive genetic effects downward. A significant correlation between spouses for a particular trait is usually interpreted as assortative mating (Maes et al., 1998). However, most behavior genetic studies report finding no or very modest influence from the shared environment on aggressive behavior, suggesting that the influence of assortative mating may be minimal.

Gene–Environment Interaction and Correlation

It is also assumed that genetic and environmental influences do not interact and are uncorrelated. Regardless, certain environmental experiences have been found to moderate the genetic influences on aggressive behavior (i.e., GxE), (Dick, 2011). It is also possible that some genetic predispositions may be associated with certain environmental experiences, resulting in a correlation between genes and environments. Gene–environment correlations (r_{ge}) can arise in three different ways (Scarr & McCartney, 1983), (1) Passive r_{ge} occur when genes overlap between parents and their offspring. (2) Evocative/reactive r_{ge} arises when a person's characteristic elicits a particular response from the environment. For example, O'Connor, Deater-Deckard, Fulker, Rutter, and Plomin (1998) found that children at genetic risk (based on the biological mother's characteristics) received more negative parenting from their adoptive parents than children not at genetic risk (O'Connor et al., 1998). (3) Active r_{ge} is defined as the process whereby an individual actively seeks out environmental situations that are more closely matched to the person's genotype. If the assumption of no gene–environment correlation is violated, heritability estimates for aggressive behavior in twin studies could include both additive genetic effects *and* the effects of gene–environment correlation, which in turn means that the heritability estimate would be inflated.

Generalizability From Adoption Studies to the General Population

Adoptive parents commonly tend to be in good health and from higher socioeconomic backgrounds (Rutter, 2006). Also, adopted children may be at greater risk to display aggressive behavior compared to nonadoptees, since birth parents may have increased rates of externalizing behaviors, including substance use, criminal behavior, and aggression (Lewis, Yeager, Gidlow, & Lewis, 2001). Further, selective placement (i.e., similarities between adoptive and biological parents) for certain traits would result in overestimated correlations between adoptive siblings and thereby overestimated shared environmental effects (Plomin et al., 2013). However, it is unlikely that children with antisocial biological parents are being placed into homes where the adoptive parents are more antisocial. Regardless, results from adoption studies may not be generalizable to the larger population.

Metaanalyses and Systematic Reviews Summarizing Studies Examining the Influence of Genetic and Environmental Factors on Aggressive Behavior

There have been a few metaanalyses and systematic reviews of twin and adoption studies of aggressive behavior and the wider construct of antisocial behavior. Antisocial behavior is broader in scope than aggression as it also includes nonaggressive behaviors, e.g., littering, vandalism, and lying which are considered antisocial behaviors, which are not necessarily aggressive. These studies are summarized in Table 1. Together these studies show that about half or more of the variance in aggressive behavior is explained by heritable influences (Burt, 2009; Ferguson, 2010; Mason & Frick, 1994; Miles & Carey, 1997; Rhee & Waldman, 2002). Two metaanalyses have examined nonadditive genetic effects. Only one found significant nonadditive genetic effects for broader concept of antisocial behavior, but not for aggressive behavior (Burt, 2009; Rhee & Waldman, 2002) It is important to note that genetic influences are consistently found across these reviews, while shared environmental influences are relatively small or nonexistent. Family similarity in aggressive behavior therefore seems to primarily be the result of shared genes, not environment.

Table 1 Summary of Metaanalysis and Systematic Reviews: Aggressive Behavior

Author, Year	**Measure**	**Estimates**
(Mason & Frick, 1994) 12 twin studies (3795 twin pairs); 3 adoption studies (338 adoptees)	Antisocial behavior	a^2 48%
(Miles & Carey, 1997) 20 twin studies (1757 twins); 4 adoption studies 3157 adoptees)	Aggressive behavior	a^2 50%
(Rhee & Waldman, 2002) 41 twin studies; 10 adoption studies	Antisocial behavior	a^2 32% d^2 9% c^2 16% e^2 43%
(Rhee & Waldman, 2002) 41 twin studies; 10 adoption studies	Aggressive behavior	a^2 44% c^2 6% e^2 50%
(Burt, 2009) 15 twin studies; 4 adoption studies	Aggressive behavior	a^2 65% c^2 5% e^2 30%
(Ferguson, 2010) 38 twin studies	Antisocial behavior	a^2 56% c^2 11% e^2 31%
(Tuvblad & Baker, 2011) 33 twin studies; 4 adoption studies	Aggressive behavior	a^2 50% c^2 0% e^2 50%

Note. a^2, genetic effects; c^2, shared environmental effects; d^2, dominant effects; e^2, nonshared environmental effects.

Some of the metaanalyses examined whether moderators influenced the magnitude of genetic and environmental influences on aggressive behavior. Mason and Frick (1994) did not find that different definitions of antisocial behavior, i.e., criminality, aggression, and antisocial personality varied across effect sizes (Mason & Frick, 1994). Rhee and Waldman (2002) found that effect sizes varied across different definitions of antisocial behavior, i.e., criminal behavior, delinquency, psychopathy, conduct disorder, and antisocial personality disorder, as well as aggressive behavior (Rhee & Waldman, 2002). Assessment method, zygosity determination method, and age were also significant moderators of the magnitude of genetic and environmental influences on antisocial behavior, but there were no significant differences in the magnitude of genetic and environmental influences for males and females. Burt (2009) found that effect sizes varied across age, with heritable influences being more important at older ages. Estimates were similar for males and females. Type of informant (i.e., self, parent, teacher) was also a significant moderator (Burt, 2009). Ferguson (2010) reported that effect sizes varied across different definitions of antisocial behavior, with broader measure of aggression obtaining higher effect sizes than measures limited to DSM-IV criteria for antisocial personality disorder (Ferguson, 2010). Finally, Tuvblad and Baker (2011) found that form of aggressive behavior (reactive, proactive, direct /physical, indirect/relational), method of assessment (laboratory observation, self-report, ratings by parents and teachers), and age of the participants were significant moderators of the magnitude of genetic and environmental influences on aggressive behavior (Tuvblad, Narusyte, Grann, Sarnecki, & Lichtenstein, 2011). Neither study design (twin vs. sibling adoption design) nor sex (male vs. female) seemed to impact the magnitude of the genetic and environmental influences on aggressive behavior.

Recent Studies Using a Behavioral Genetic Research Design

There have been several papers published examining the influence of genetic contributions to aggressive behavior since the last metaanalysis was published in 2011. Some notable findings include a recent study showing that the variance in relational aggression is largely explained by additive genetic effects (0.15–0.77) (Slawinski, Klump, & Burt, 2018). Another large study included longitudinal data from a large sample of twins participating in the Netherlands Twin Register (N=42,827, age range 3–16) (Lubke, McArtor, Boomsma, & Bartels, 2018). The study showed that the *overt* and more physical aspects of childhood *aggression* (OA) are highly heritable between ages 3 and 16. Additive genetic effects explained between 50% and 68% of the variance. The study also showed that OA is largely affected by the same genes throughout childhood. Environmental effects shared by children from the same family typically account for 20% of the variance of OA early in childhood, but they are negligible in adolescence. Nonshared environmental effects on OA are comparatively smaller in childhood (20% variance explained) than in adolescence (40%). Another recent study compared the development of aggressive behavior between Dutch and English population samples and showed that the stability and heritability of aggressive behavior was high for both samples, with longitudinal genetic correlations being the main reason for stability of aggressive behavior (Porsch et al., 2016). Harden et al. (2015) reported that genetic influences specific to rule-breaking increased as a function of pubertal development controlling for age (a gene × puberty interaction), but did not vary as a function of age controlling for pubertal status. There were no developmental differences in the genetic etiology of aggression. Family level environmental influences common to aggression and rule-breaking decreased with age, further contributing to the differentiation between these subtypes of antisocial behavior from childhood to adolescence (Harden et al., 2015).

Neurobiology of Aggression—Where to Look for the Relevant Genes?

As aggressive behavior is not a uniform behavioral construct and likely comprises several neurobiological mechanisms, pinpointing specific genetic components of aggression is challenging (Waltes, Chiocchetti, & Freitag, 2016). Aggression varies in its extent over the lifespan and progresses nonlinearly (Petersen, Bates, Dodge, Lansford, & Pettit, 2015). Additionally, pathological aggression is highly comorbid with psychiatric disorders such as major depression, posttraumatic stress disorder, borderline personality disorder, schizophrenia, autism spectrum disorder, attention deficit hyperactivity disorder (ADHD) and is often accompanied by phenotypic traits such as negative emotionality, greater affective instability, and impulsive decision-making (Fettich, McCloskey, Look, & Coccaro, 2015). This suggests possible shared or overlapping underlying mechanisms for aggression and other psychiatric conditions/phenotypes as well as interactions between aggression and developmental processes.

Various studies in populations characterized by high aggression have reported alterations in neurotransmitter systems (involving serotonin (5-HT), dopamine, glutamate, GABA, and noradrenaline) and neuroendocrine processes (e.g., cortisol, testosterone) (Rosell & Siever, 2015), leading to the design of specific candidate gene studies. Additionally, genome-wide and epigenetic studies have advanced the field by identifying other possible candidate genes and potential relevant physiological processes. Following, we will discuss some of the relevant literature. Additional detailed discussions can be found in several excellent reviews (e.g., Fettich et al., 2015; Petersen et al., 2015; Rosell & Siever, 2015; Waltes et al., 2016).

Candidate Gene Studies

The candidate gene approach focuses on investigating genetic variations based on a priori hypotheses about the roles of the selected genes or pathways in a phenotype or disease. Commonly, polymorphisms are tested for the association by comparing their occurrence in groups of cases with the disease/phenotype and controls. Candidate genes in aggression research have been mainly selected based on their relation to monoaminergic neurotransmitter systems. The first systematic metaanalysis of 185 candidate gene studies (31 genes) in relation to aggression did not derive any significant associations (Vassos, Collier, & Fazel, 2014).

Regulation of Monoamine Level: MAOA and MAOB

Monoamine oxidases *MAOA* and *MAOB* are X-linked genes encoding enzymes that regulate the levels of monoamines by catabolizing 5-HT, norepinephrine, and dopamine in the brain. 5-HT is mostly degraded by MAOA (Shih, Chen, & Ridd, 1999). Since the association of a missense mutation in *MAOA* with familial impulsive aggression (Brunner syndrome) (Brunner, Nelen, Breakefield, Ropers, & van Oost, 1993), *MAOA* has become a target of many candidate gene studies. A common nucleotide tandem repeat (VNTR) polymorphism upstream of the *MAOA* coding sequence (also known as MAOA-uVNTR) was found to affect transcription, with certain alleles being transcribed 2–10 times more efficiently. "High-activity" but more often "low-activity" alleles have been reported to be associated with aggression in different studies (Kolla & Vinette, 2017; Smeijers, Bulten, Franke, Buitelaar, & Verkes, 2017; Waltes et al., 2016). MAOA-uVNTR genotype has been reported to interact with environment (Waltes et al., 2016), affecting the outcome of adulthood aggressive behavior in individuals who suffered various extents of childhood adversity (Gorodetsky et al., 2014). Furthermore, the MAOA-uVNTR x childhood adversity interaction may be moderated by sex (Holz et al., 2018). The less studied *MAOB* gene does not appear to be significantly involved in aggressive behavior, but lack of MAOB may exacerbate the severity of MAOA dysfunction (Bortolato, Floris, & Shih, 2018).

Serotonin Transporter 5-HTT (SLC6A4)

The 5-HTT (also known as SERT; 5-HT transporter; SLC6A4) regulates extracellular levels of 5-HT by transporting it from the synaptic cleft to the presynaptic neuron. The most extensively studied polymorphism of the *SLC6A4* gene is 5HTTLPR (5-HT transporter-linked polymorphic region) that is located in the promoter area and constitutes "long" and "short" 5HTTLPR variants due to a 44-bp insertion. The "long" (L) variant leads to higher expression of 5-HTT than the "short" (S). The S allele has more often than the L allele been associated with increased aggressive behavior and impulsivity in children (Haberstick, Smolen, & Hewitt, 2006) and adults (Retz, Retz-Junginger, Supprian, Thome, & Rösler, 2004). 5-HTT includes other gene variations that have been studied in the context of aggression, including a polymorphism within the 5HTTLPR "long" version that can alter the 5-HTT expression level to more similar of that of the S allele (Praschak-Rieder et al., 2007). This accentuates the importance of considering the polymorphism–polymorphism interactions. A metaanalysis of 31 studies concluded that the "low-activity" allele of the MAOA-uVNTR and the "short" allele of the 5HTTLPR (both variants thought to increase the availability of synaptic 5-HT and considered risk alleles) were both significantly associated with aggressive or antisocial behavior (Ficks & Waldman, 2014).

5-HT Receptors and Tryptophan Hydroxylases

Type 1 5-HT receptors are involved in the negative control of 5-HT signaling, whereas type 2 5-HT receptors are positive mediators of 5-HT transmission (Waltes et al., 2016). Various tested *HTR2C* or *HTR1A* gene variants were not found to contribute to aggression-related behaviors in a sample of suicide attempters and controls, despite there may be a sex-by-genotype interaction effect on trait anger. However, the functional *HTR1A* polymorphism C(−1019)G has been associated with impulsivity (Benko et al., 2010; Waltes et al., 2016).

HTR1B polymorphisms have been associated with childhood aggression, impulsive–aggressive behaviors in adults, and conduct disorder (Hakulinen et al., 2013; Zouk et al., 2007). The "risk polymorphisms" in *HTR1B* are generally thought to be related to lower gene expression levels, either through functional modifications or via linkage disequilibrium with other variants. There is also evidence for sex-by-genotype interactions for *HTR1B* in the context of aggression (Waltes et al., 2016). Polymorphism rs6313C > T in *HTR2A* may be associated with increased aggression in Alzheimer's disease whereas *HTR2A* rs6311 C > T has been found associated with impulsive behavior in healthy controls and aggression-related traits in suicide attempters. Furthermore, a potentially functional *HTR2A* SNP rs7322347 T allele was associated with hostility, anger, and physical aggression in healthy individuals (Waltes et al., 2016). Several other *HTR2A* polymorphisms have been suggested to be associated with impulsive behavior in psychiatric patients (Bruce et al., 2005; Tsuang et al., 2013). A stop codon variant of the *HTR2B* gene (*20) was identified exclusively in Finnish population and found to cosegregate with psychiatric diseases marked by impulsivity (Bevilacqua et al., 2010). However, an association with aggression was not found in a study of Finnish violent offenders (Tiihonen et al., 2015).

Tryptophan hydroxylases (TPH) are the rate-limiting enzymes for 5-HT synthesis, with TPH1 primarily operating in the peripheral and TPH2 exclusively in the central nervous system. Despite their importance in 5-HT synthesis, only a few association studies have been performed in relation to aggression. *TPH1* A218C was studied twice and yielded opposing results, possibly because one of the studies was in a healthy sample and other investigated patients with Alzheimer's disease. A *TPH2* "risk haplotype" was found associated with borderline personality disorder diagnosis, aggression, and affective instability scores (Waltes et al., 2016).

Components of the Dopaminergic System

COMT (catechol-*O*-methyltransferase) is an enzyme inactivating catecholamine neurotransmitters including dopamine. The most studied polymorphism in *COMT* Val158Met (rs4680G>A) Met variant reduces the enzymatic activity almost fourfold. The studies of Val158Met in relation to aggression have yielded inconsistent results (Qayyum et al., 2015). A recent metaanalysis did not find a significant association of this polymorphism with aggression in general (Vassos et al., 2014). However, the low or high activity *Val158Met* polymorphisms may be associated with aggression in schizophrenia or conduct problems in ADHD patients, respectively (Qayyum et al., 2015). A VNTR in the dopamine transporter *DAT1* has been associated with aggression in a cohort of heroin users. Polymorphisms in different dopamine receptor genes have been reported associated with aggression in children (*DRD2*), patients with Alzheimer's disease (*DRD1*), and patients with schizophrenia (*DRD4*). A 7 repeat (7-R) risk allele of a VNTR in *DRD4* may interact with 5HTTLPR "short" variant to increase the level of externalizing behavior in adolescents (Fresan et al., 2007; Waltes et al., 2016). DRD4 may also be involved in a GxE interaction whereby prenatal stress correlates with higher levels of aggression and attenuated cortisol secretion in young adults with the *DRD4 7-R* risk allele (Buchmann et al., 2014).

Oxytocin and Arginine Vasopressin Systems

Oxytocin and arginine vasopressin (also known as AVP, antidiuretic hormone) are highly conserved neuropeptides that mediate the regulation of complex social behaviors. A SNP rs35369693 in arginine vasopressin receptor

1B (*AVPR1B*) has been associated with childhood aggression (Waltes et al., 2016). Possible interaction between *AVPR1A* and *RS3* genes may occur in impulsive aggression in patients with borderline personality disorder (Vogel et al., 2012). In the largest study exploring children's aggressive behavior to date ($N = 18{,}988$), *AVPR1A* was the only gene which variations were found significantly associated with childhood aggression in the gene-based analysis (Pappa et al., 2016). Polymorphisms rs6770632G > T and rs1042778C > A in the oxytocin receptor gene (*OXTR*) have been suggested to play a role in pervasive childhood aggression (Malik et al., 2014).

Other Candidate Genes of Interest

Various other polymorphisms have been investigated in relation to aggression, including variations in genes related to stress response, cholesterol metabolism, nitric oxide, and BDNF signaling. There is evidence suggesting involvement of genes relevant for hormonal regulation, e.g., the androgen receptor, in aggression (Rosell & Siever, 2015; Waltes et al., 2016).

Genome-Wide Association Studies (GWASs)

Genome-wide association studies (GWASs) enable a hypothesis-free approach whereby a large number of polymorphic markers (such as Single Nucleotide Polymorphisms (SNPs)) from all over the genome are tested for association with a disease or phenotype. Genome scan results of cases with the disease/phenotype are compared with these of the controls.

GWASs of Aggression

Despite some promising leads, GWASs in aggression have not reported any conclusively significant association. In addition, a recent metaanalysis comprising genome-wide data from five large population-based cohorts in association with antisocial behavior ($N = 16{,}400$) did not reveal any significant markers (Tielbeek et al., 2017). A GWAS of aggressive behavior in children (the EAGLE consortium) included 18,988 participants and measured aggressive behavior in childhood and early adolescence. Metaanalysis of the total cohort identified a near genome-wide significant region on chromosome 2p12, near the gene *LRRTM4* that is involved in excitatory synapse development (Pappa et al., 2016). A GWAS in 8747 European adults investigated associations with an aggression-related trait—proneness to anger. This study reported a nominally significant finding on the chromosome 6q21 in the gene coding for the nonreceptor protein-tyrosine kinase Fyn. Fyn participates in signaling pathways important for memory, learning, and neuronal survival and may therefore be involved in cognitive regulation in aggression (Mick et al., 2014). A GWAS in two cohorts of violent offenders imprisoned in Finland revealed a suggestive polymorphism rs11649622 on chromosome 16q23.3 inside the intron of a gene coding for a neural adhesion protein cadherin 13 (*CDH13*) (Tiihonen et al., 2015) that has previously been associated with various psychiatric diseases including ADHD. Another GWAS investigating genetic etiology of adult antisocial behavior did not detect genome-wide significance, but the most associated gene *DYRK1A* encodes for an enzyme considered important for synaptic plasticity and brain development (Tielbeek et al., 2012). Finally, a study in children with ADHD found an ADHD-related polygenic risk score including 46,156 alleles to correlate positively with the number of aggressive conduct disorder symptoms (Hamshere et al., 2013), despite no significant variation has been detected in GWASs investigating aggression in ADHD (Aebi et al., 2016; Brevik et al., 2016). In summary, several markers in loci related to genes that are important for neuronal function have been found to reach near significance in GWASs investigating aggression. Notably, GWASs on aggression did not find significant associations for the genes that are mostly being studied in candidate gene studies.

Epigenetics of Aggression

Epigenetic modifications, such as DNA methylation or histone acetylation, can change the activity of the genes in the absence of DNA sequence changes. Epigenetic modifications may occur in response to environmental influences, e.g., early life adversity, and are potentially reversible (Nestler, Peña, Kundakovic, Mitchell, & Akbarian, 2016). DNA methylation is the most studied epigenetic modification in the context of human aggression, with epigenetic changes mainly measured in peripheral blood cell DNA. 5-HT system components may be affected by epigenetic regulation. For example, women who had been sexually abused during childhood were found to exhibit hypermethylation of the *5-HTT* promoter that in turn associated with increased symptoms of antisocial behavior in comparison to controls. Furthermore, 5-HTTLPR polymorphism seemed to affect the outcome, whereby *5-HTT* promoter methylation in individuals homozygous for the "long" variant of 5-HTTLPR was not significantly associated with antisocial behavior symptoms (Beach, Bordy, Todorov, Gunter, & Philibert, 2011).

Higher *5-HTT* promoter methylation levels were also found in adult males with higher levels of childhood aggression which correlated with lower in vivo 5-HT synthesis in orbitofrontal cortex (Wang et al., 2012). In line with that, *MAOA* promoter region was found hypermethylated in incarcerated individuals with antisocial personality disorder. Functional studies indicated that such increased promoter methylation contributes to decreased expression of MAOA (Checknita et al., 2015). As alterations in cytokine levels have been found correlated with physical aggression, epigenetic profiles of the loci of numerous cytokines were analyzed in a longitudinal sample of adult males with chronic physical aggression trajectory in comparison to males with normal aggression trajectory. Differentially methylated regions between groups were found in the loci of *IL-6, IL-1α, IL-8, IL-4, IL-10* and their transcriptional regulators *NFkB1*, *NFAT5*, and *STAT6* (Provencal et al., 2013).

Epigenome-wide promoter-targeting studies have uncovered similar DNA methylation signatures (over 400 distinct differentially methylated promoter regions) for adult males and females who have exhibited childhood chronic physical aggression, in comparison to individuals with normal aggression levels (Guillemin et al., 2014; Provencal et al., 2014), also pinpointing some genes that have previously been associated with aggressive phenotypes using other approaches, such as *AVPR1A*, *HTR1D*, and *SLC6A3* (Provencal et al., 2014). In the first *epi*genome-wide association study (EWAS) in relation to aggressive behavior, no epigenome-wide significance was detected. Areas close to the trichorhinophalangeal syndrome I (*TRPS1*) gene and activity-dependent neuroprotective protein 2 (*ADNP2*) gene were among the most promising loci. Gene ontology enrichment analyses suggested the involvement of pathways implicated in development, metabolism, and central nervous system/neural function-related processes (van Dongen et al., 2015). Another recent EWAS in a small group of individuals with IED and controls also revealed numerous suggestive loci, despite none with epigenome-wide significance. Functional enrichment analysis pointed toward the importance of the immune system, endocrine system, and components of the neuronal differentiation pathways in IED (Montalvo-Ortiz, Zhang, Chen, Liu, & Coccaro, 2018). In a study examining prospective associations between epigenome-wide methylation patterns at birth and trajectories of early onset conduct problems, differential methylation was detected at seven loci across the genome, with additional subthreshold associations close to the typical candidate genes in aggression—*MAOA*, *BDNF*, and *FKBP5* (Cecil et al., 2018).

Conclusion

Aggression has been consistently shown to have a large genetic component based on findings from behavioral genetic studies. However, candidate gene and GWA studies on aggression have not identified a significant genetic marker. This does not mean that there are no genes relevant for aggression, but possibly indicates a complex interplay between various genetic components and environmental factors/triggers in aggression. Additionally, distinct forms of aggressive behavior (e.g., reactive, proactive, direct/physical, indirect/relational) may differ in their underlying neurobiological mechanisms. The extent to which environment affects epigenetic processes may depend on genotype, as well as other factors such as age, sex, and developmental history. The nonlinear occurrence of aggression over the lifetime (Petersen et al., 2015) hints the involvement of developmental processes in the manifestation of aggression. Also, pathological aggression is highly comorbid with numerous psychiatric disorders and the concept of aggression is very heterogeneous, which further increases the complexity in the search for genetic and epigenetic markers. Notably, while most clinical studies focus on antisocial personality disorder, (epi) genetic research in psychiatric disorders that have aggression as a core symptom (such as IED) is scarce. Multidisciplinary collaborative research of genetic and epigenetic factors at various ages throughout the lifespan in well-characterized clinical and nonclinical study samples is needed to further shed light on the specific genetic and epigenetic contributions to (different types of) aggression including IED.

References

Aebi, M., van Donkelaar, M. M., Poelmans, G., Buitelaar, J. K., Sonuga-Barke, E. J., Stringaris, A., et al. (2016). Gene-set and multivariate genome-wide association analysis of oppositional defiant. Behavior subtypes in attention-deficit/hyperactivity disorder. *American Journal of Medical Genetics. Part B, Neuropsychiatric Genetics*, *171*(5), 573–588.

Allen, J. J., & Anderson, C. A. (2017). Aggression and violence: Definitions and distinctions. In P. Sturmey (Ed.), *The Wiley handbook of violence and Aggression*: John Wiley & Sons.

Barnes, J. C., & Boutwell, B. B. (2013). A demonstration of the generalizability of twin-based research on antisocial behavior. *Behavior Genetics*, *43*(2), 120–131.

Beach, S. R., Bordy, G. H., Todorov, A. A., Gunter, T. D., & Philibert, R. A. (2011). Methylation at 5HTT mediates the impact of child sex abuse on women's antisocial behavior: an examination of the Iowa adoptee sample. *Psychosomatic Medicine*, *73*(1), 83–87.

Benko, A., Lazary, J., Molnar, E., Gonda, X., Tothfalusi, L., Pap, D., et al. (2010). Significant association between the C(−1019)G functional polymorphism of the HTR1A gene and impulsivity. *American Journal of Medical Genetics. Part B, Neuropsychiatric Genetics. Part B, Neuropsychiatric Genetics*, *153B*(2), 592–599.

Bevilacqua, L., Doly, S., Kaprio, J., Yuan, Q., Tikkanen, R., Paunio, T., et al. (2010). A population-specific HTR2B stop codon predisposes to severe impulsivity. *Nature*, *468*(7327), 1061–1066.

Bortolato, M., Floris, G., & Shih, J. C. (2018). From aggression to autism: new perspectives on the behavioral sequelae of monoamine oxidase deficiency. *Journal of Neural Transmission (Vienna, Austria: 1996)*. *125*, 1589–1599.

Brevik, E. J., van Donkelaar, M. M., Weber, H., Sánchez-Mora, C., Jacob, C., Rivero, O., et al. (2016). Genome-wide analyses of aggressiveness in attention-deficit hyperactivity disorder. *American Journal of Medical Genetics. Part B, Neuropsychiatric Genetics*, *171*(5), 733–747.

Bruce, K. R., Steiger, H., Joober, R., Ng Ying Kin, N. M., Israel, M., & Young, S. N. (2005). Association of the promoter polymorphism -1438G/a of the 5-HT2A receptor gene with behavioral impulsiveness and serotonin function in women with bulimia nervosa. *American Journal of Medical Genetics. Part B, Neuropsychiatric Genetics*, *137B*(1), 40–44.

Brunner, H. G., Nelen, M., Breakefield, X. O., Ropers, H. H., & van Oost, B. A. (1993). Abnormal behavior associated with a point mutation in the structural gene for monoamine oxidase A. *Science*, *262*(5133), 578–580.

Buchmann, A. F., Zohsel, K., Blomeye, D., Hohm, E., Hohmann, S., Jennen-Steinmetz, C., et al. (2014). Interaction between prenatal stress and dopamine D4 receptor genotype in predicting aggression and cortisol levels in young adults. *Psychopharmacology*, *231*(16), 3089–3097.

Burt, A. S. (2009). Are there meaningful etiological differences within antisocial behavior? Results of a meta-analysis. *Clinical Psychology Review*, *29*, 163–178.

Bushman, B. J., & Huesmann, L. R. (2010). Aggression. In S. T. Fiske, D. T. Gilbert, & G. Lindzey (Eds.), *Handbook of social psychology* (pp. 833–863). Hoboken, New Jersey: John Wiley & Sons.

Cecil, C. A. M., Walton, E., Jaffee, S. R., O'Connor, T., Maughan, B., Relton, C. L., et al. (2018). Neonatal DNA methylation and early-onset conduct problems: a genome-wide, prospective study. *Development and Psychopathology*, *30*(2), 383–397.

Checknita, D., Maussion, G., Labonté, B., Comai, S., Tremblay, R. E., Vitaro, F., et al. (2015). Monoamine oxidase A gene promoter methylation and transcriptional downregulation in an offender population with antisocial personality disorder. *The British Journal of Psychiatry*, *206*(3), 216–222.

Dick, D. M. (2011). Gene-environment interaction in psychological traits and disorders. *Annual Review of Clinical Psychology*, 7, 383–409.

Felson, J. (2014). What can we learn from twin studies? A comprehensive evaluation of the equal environments assumption. *Social Science Research*, *43*, 184–199.

Ferguson, C. J. (2010). Genetic contributions to antisocial personality and behavior: a meta-analytic review from an evolutionary perspective. *The Journal of Social Psychology*, *150*(2), 160–180.

Fettich, K. C., McCloskey, M. S., Look, A. E., & Coccaro, E. F. (2015). Emotion regulation deficits in intermittent explosive disorder. *Aggressive Behavior*, *41*(1), 25–33.

Ficks, C. A., & Waldman, I. D. (2014). Candidate genes for aggression and antisocial behavior: a meta-analysis of association studies of the 5HTTLPR and MAOA-uVNTR. *Behavior Genetics*, *44*(5), 427–444.

Fresan, A., Camarena, B., Apiquian, R., Aguilar, A., Urraca, N., & Nicolini, H. (2007). Association study of MAO-A and DRD4 genes in schizophrenic patients with aggressive behavior. *Neuropsychobiology*, *55*(3–4), 171–175.

Gorodetsky, E., Bevilacqua, L., Carli, V., Sarchiapone, M., Roy, A., Goldman, D., et al. (2014). The interactive effect of MAOA-LPR genotype and childhood physical neglect on aggressive behaviors in Italian male prisoners. *Genes, Brain, and Behavior*, *3*(6), 543–549.

Guillemin, C., Provençal, N., Suderman, M., Côté, S. M., Vitaro, F., Hallett, M., et al. (2014). DNA methylation signature of childhood chronic physical aggression in T cells of both men and women. *PLoS One*, *9*(1)e86822.

Haberstick, B. C., Smolen, A., & Hewitt, J. K. (2006). Family-based association test of the 5HTTLPR and aggressive behavior in a general population sample of children. *Biological Psychiatry*, *59*, 836–843.

Hakulinen, C., Jokela, M., Hintsanen, M., Merjonen, P., Pulkki-Råback, L., Seppälä, I., et al. (2013). Serotonin receptor 1B genotype and hostility, anger and aggressive behavior through the lifespan: the Young Finns study. *Journal of Behavioral Medicine*, *36*(6), 583–590.

Hamshere, M. L., Langley, K., Martin, J., Agha, S. S., Stergiakouli, E., Anney, R. J., et al. (2013). High loading of polygenic risk for ADHD in children with comorbid aggression. *The American Journal of Psychiatry*, *170*(8), 909–916.

Harden, K. P., Patterson, M. W., Briley, D. A., Engelhardt, L. E., Kretsch, N., Mann, F. D., et al. (2015). Developmental changes in genetic and environmental influences on rule-breaking and aggression: age and pubertal development. *Journal of Child Psychology and Psychiatry*, *56*(12), 1370–1379.

Holz, N. E., Zohsel, K., Laucht, M., Banaschewski, T., Hohmann, S., & Brandeis, D. (2018). Gene x environment interactions in conduct disorder: implications for future treatments. *Neuroscience and Biobehavioral Reviews*, *91*, 239–258.

Kolla, N. J., & Vinette, S. A. (2017). Monoamine oxidase A in antisocial personality disorder and borderline personality disorder. *Current Behavioral Neuroscience Reports*, *4*(1), 41–48.

Lewis, D. O., Yeager, C. A., Gidlow, B., & Lewis, M. (2001). Six adoptees who murdered: neuropsychiatric vulnerabilities and characteristics of biological and adoptive parents. *The Journal of the American Academy of Psychiatry and the Law*, *29*(4), 390–397.

Lubke, G. H., McArtor, D. B., Boomsma, D. I., & Bartels, M. (2018). Genetic and environmental contributions to the development of childhood aggression. *Developmental Psychology*, *54*(1), 39–50.

Maes, H. H. M., Neale, M. C., Kendler, K. S., Hewitt, J. K., Silberg, J. L., Foley, D. L., et al. (1998). Assortative mating for major psychiatric diagnosis in two population-based samples. *Psychological Medicine*, *28*, 1389–1401.

Malik, A. I., Zai, C. C., Berall, L., Abu, Z., Din, F., Nowrouzi, B., et al. (2014). The role of genetic variants in genes regulating the oxytocin-vasopressin neurohumoral system in childhood-onset aggression. *Psychiatric Genetics*, *24*(5), 201–210.

Mason, D. A., & Frick, P. J. (1994). The heritability of antisocial behavior: a meta-analysis of twin and adoption studies. *Journal of Psychopathology and Behavioral Assessment*, *16*, 301–323.

Mick, E., McGough, J., Deutsch, C. K., Frazier, J. A., Kennedy, D., & Goldberg, R. J. (2014). Genome-wide association study of proneness to anger. *PLoS One*, *9*(1).

Miles, D. R., & Carey, G. (1997). Genetic and environmental architecture of human aggression. *Journal of Personality and Social Psychology*, *72*(1), 207–217.

Moffitt, T. E., Caspi, A., & Rutter, M. (2005). Strategy for investigating interactions between measured genes and measured environments. *Archives of General Psychiatry*, *62*(5), 473–481.

Montalvo-Ortiz, J. L., Zhang, H., Chen, C., Liu, C., & Coccaro, E. F. (2018). Genome-wide DNA methylation changes associated with intermittent explosive disorder: a gene-based functional enrichment analysis. *The International Journal of Neuropsychopharmacology*, *21*(1), 12–20.

Neale, M. C., & Cardon, L. R. (1992). *Methodology for genetic studies of twins and families*. Dordrecht, The Netherlands: Kluwer Academic Publications.

Nestler, E. J., Peña, C. J., Kundakovic, M., Mitchell, A., & Akbarian, S. (2016). Epigenetic basis of mental illness. *The Neuroscientist*, *22*(5), 447–463.

O'Connor, T. G., Deater-Deckard, K., Fulker, D., Rutter, M., & Plomin, R. (1998). Genotype-environment correlations in late childhood and early adolescence: antisocial behavioral problems and coercive parenting. *Developmental Psychology*, *34*, 970–981.

Pappa, I., St Pourcain, B., Benke, K., Cavadino, A., Hakulinen, C., Nivard, M. G., et al. (2016). A genome-wide approach to children's aggressive behavior: the EAGLE consortium. *American Journal of Medical Genetics. Part B, Neuropsychiatric Genetics*, *171*(5), 562–572.

Petersen, I. T., Bates, J. E., Dodge, K. A., Lansford, J. E., & Pettit, G. S. (2015). Describing and predicting developmental profiles of externalizing problems from childhood to adulthood. *Development and Psychopathology*, *27*(3), 791–818.

Plomin, R., DeFries, J. C., Knopik, V. S., & Neiderhiser, J. M. (2013). *Behavioral genetics* (6th ed.). New York: Worth Publishers.

Porsch, R. M., Middeldorp, C. M., Cherny, S. S., Krapohl, E., van Beijsterveldt, C. E., Loukola, A., et al. (2016). Longitudinal heritability of childhood aggression. *American Journal of Medical Genetics. Part B, Neuropsychiatric Genetics*, (5), 697–707.

Praschak-Rieder, N., Kennedy, J., Wilson, A. A., Hussey, D., Boovariwala, A., Willeit, M., et al. (2007). Novel 5-HTTLPR allele associates with higher serotonin transporter binding in putamen: a [(11)C] DASB positron emission tomography study. *Biological Psychiatry*, *62*(4), 327–331.

Provencal, N., Suderman, M. J., Caramaschi, D., Wang, D., Hallett, H., Vitaro, F., et al. (2013). Differential DNA methylation regions in cytokine and transcription factor genomic loci associate with childhood physical aggression. *PLoS One*, *8*(8).

Provencal, N., Suderman, M. J., Guillemin, C., Vitaro, F., Côté, S. M., Hallett, M., et al. (2014). Association of childhood chronic physical aggression with a DNA methylation signature in adult human T cells. *PLoS One*, *9*(4), e89839.

Qayyum, A., Zai, C. C., Hirata, Y., Tiwari, A. K., Cheema, S., Nowrouzi, B., et al. (2015). The role of the catechol-o-methyltransferase (COMT) GeneVal158Met in aggressive behavior, a review of genetic studies. *Current Neuropharmacology*, *13*(6), 802–814.

Retz, W., Retz-Junginger, P., Supprian, T., Thome, J., & Rösler, M. (2004). Association of serotonin transporter promoter gene polymorphism with violence: relation with personality disorders, impulsivity and childhood ADHD psychopathology. *Behavioral Sciences & the Law*, *22*(3), 415–425.

Rhee, S. H., & Waldman, I. D. (2002). Genetic and environmental influences on antisocial behavior: a meta-analysis of twin and adoption studies. *Psychological Bulletin*, *128*, 490–529.

Rosell, D. R., & Siever, L. J. (2015). The neurobiology of aggression and violence. *CNS Spectrums*, *20*(3), 254–279.

Rutter, M. (2006). *Genes and behavior. Nature-nurture interplay explained*. Oxford, UK: Blackwell Publishing Ltd.

Scarr, S., & McCartney, K. (1983). How people make their own environments: a theory of gneotype-environment effects. *Child Development*, *54*, 425–435.

Shih, J. C., Chen, K., & Ridd, M. J. (1999). Monoamine oxidase: from genes to behavior. *Annual Review of Neuroscience*, *22*, 197–217.

Slawinski, L., Klump, K. L., & Burt, S. A. (2018). *The etiology of social aggression: A nuclear twin family study*. [Psychological Medicine Epub ahead of print].

Smeijers, D., Bulten, E., Franke, B., Buitelaar, J., & Verkes, R. J. (2017). Associations of multiple trauma types and MAOA with severe aggressive behavior and MAOA effects on training outcome. *European Neuropsychopharmacology*. July 1, (EPub Ahead of Print).

Tielbeek, J. J., Johansson, A., Polderman, T. J., Rautiainen, M. R., Jansen, P., Taylor, M., et al. (2017). Genome-wide association studies of a broad Spectrum of antisocial behavior. *JAMA Psychiatry*, *74*(12), 1242–1250.

Tielbeek, J. J., Medland, S. E., Benyamin, B., Byrne, E. M., Heath, A. C., Madden, P. A., et al. (2012). Unraveling the genetic etiology of adult antisocial behavior: a genome-wide association study. *PLoS One*, 7(10).

Tiihonen, J., Rautiainen, M. R., Ollila, H. M., Repo-Tiihonen, E., Virkkunen, M., Palotie, A., et al. (2015). Genetic background of extreme violent behavior. *Molecular Psychiatry*, *20*(6), 786–792.

Tsuang, H. C., Chen, W. J., Lin, S. H., Chen, T. Y., Chang, Y. L., Huang, K. H., et al. (2013). Impaired impulse control is associated with a 5-HT2A receptor polymorphism in schizophrenia. *Psychiatry Research*, *208*(2), 105–110.

Tuvblad, C., & Baker, L. A. (2011). Human aggression across the lifespan: Genetic propensities and environmental moderators. In R. Huber, P. Brennan, & D. Bannasch (Eds.), *Vol. 75 of Advances in Genetics (Agression)*. *75*, pp. 171–214.

Tuvblad, C., Narusyte, J., Grann, M., Sarnecki, J., & Lichtenstein, P. (2011). The genetic and environmental etiology of antisocial behavior, from early adolescence to emerging adulthood. *Behavior Genetics*, *41*(5), 629–640.

van Dongen, J., Nivard, M. G., Baselmans, B. M., Zilhão, N. R., Ligthart, L., Heijmans, B. T., et al. (2015). Epigenome-wide association study of aggressive behavior. *Twin Research and Human Genetics*, *18*(6), 686–698.

Vassos, E., Collier, D. A., & Fazel, S. (2014). Systematic meta-analyses and field synopsis of genetic association studies of violence and aggression. *Molecular Psychiatry*, *19*(4), 4711–4717.

Vogel, F., Wagner, S., Başkaya, O., Leuenberger, B., Mobascher, A., Dahmen, N., et al. (2012). Variable number of tandem repeat polymorphisms of the arginine vasopressin receptor 1A gene and impulsive aggression in patients with borderline personality disorder. *Psychiatric Genetics*, *22*(2), 105–106.

Waltes, R., Chiocchetti, A. G., & Freitag, C. M. (2016). The neurobiological basis of human aggression: a review on genetic and epigenetic mechanisms. *American Journal of Medical Genetics. Part B, Neuropsychiatric Genetics*, *171*(5), 650–675.

Wang, D., Szyf, M., Benkelfat, C., Provençal, N., Turecki, G., Caramaschi, D., et al. (2012). Peripheral SLC6A4 DNA methylation is associated with in vivo measures of human brain serotonin synthesis and childhood physical aggression. *PLoS One*, 7(6)e39501.

Zouk, H., McGirr, A., Lebel, V., Benkelfat, C., Rouleau, G., & Turecki, G. (2007). The effect of genetic variation of the serotonin 1B receptor gene on impulsive aggressive behavior and suicide. *American Journal of Medical Genetics, Part B, Neuropsychiatric Genetics*, *155*, 996–1002.

CHAPTER THREE

Phenomenology of Impulsive Aggression and Intermittent Explosive Disorder

Emil F. Coccaro*, Michael S. McCloskey†
*Clinical Neuroscience & Psychopharmacology Research Unit, Department of Psychiatry and Behavioral Neuroscience, Pritzker School of Medicine, University of Chicago, Chicago, IL, United States
†Mechanisms of Affect Dysregulation Laboratory (MAD LAB), Department of Psychology, Temple University, Philadelphia, PA, United States

Contents

Intermittent Explosive Disorder
https://doi.org/10.1016/B978-0-12-813858-8.00003-6

Aggression as a Behavioral Dimension

Human aggression occurs when individual assaults/attacks another in the context of defense or in the context of securing access to resources needed for survival. As such, aggression represents a fundamental aspect of human behavior. Over the course of civilization, however, human aggression has become less advantageous, with the use of aggression, for reasons other than self-defense, generally viewed as unacceptable.

Aggressive behavior can vary in both form and type. With respect to form, aggression can be verbal (e.g., snapping, name-calling, arguments, and threats) and/or physical (e.g., throwing things, to breaking things, to pushing/hitting to physically injuring someone). The aggression can also be direct (yelling at/hitting a person) or indirect (gossiping about a person, damaging an object). Indirect aggression aimed at damaging a person's interpersonal relationships is called relational aggression (Murray-Close, Ostrov, Nelson, Crick, & Coccaro, 2010). What all forms of aggression have in common is intent to harm and/or to forcibly defend oneself in the setting of a perceived social threat, though the function or "type" of aggression may differ.

Aggression can be socially sanctioned (e.g., soldiers, law enforcement) or medically related. Neither type of aggression is typically the focus of aggression interventions, as in the former case the aggression is not seen as problematic and in the latter there is clear medical cause for the behavior. Other, more "primary" types of aggression are premeditated (i.e., instrumental, proactive) aggression, and impulsive (e.g., affective, angry, or reactive) aggression (Dodge, Bates, & Pettit, 1990; Barratt, Stanford, Felthous, & Kent, 1997).

The critical difference between these types of aggression is that in premeditated aggression, the harm caused by the aggressive behavior is a merely a means to an end (e.g., punching someone to steal their wallet), whereas in the case of impulsive aggression the desire to harm to another, in response to a social threat, or frustration, is a primary goal of the aggressive act.

Though aggressive acts can include both aspects instrumental and impulsive facets, the large majority of aggression is predominately impulsive (Fanning, Coleman, Lee, & Coccaro, 2019). Furthermore, primary aggression can be viewed as both along a continuum (i.e., dimensionally) and as a dichotomy between normative and pathological aggression (i.e., diagnostically). In this chapter we will examine the nature and phenomenology of primary aggression reflected by the clinical diagnosis of Intermittent Explosive Disorder.

Relevance of Anger to Impulsive Aggression

There are at least three, related, dysphoric affects: depression, anxiety, and anger. While the first two have been the subject of much study, anger has been less extensively studied. Built into the definition of impulsive aggression is the idea that the aggressive behavior is manifest in the context of anger. That said, dimensional measures of depression and anxiety may also be related to aggressive behavior through their relationship with anger. In examining our own clinical research data of more than 300 study participants, we found that measures of these three trait dysphoric affects are highly correlated with each other (i.e., depression with anger: $r = 0.50$; anxiety with anger: $r = 0.60$; depression with anxiety: $r = 0.73$; all $P < .001$). However, when entered into the same regression model, trait anger emerges as the strongest correlate of lifetime aggression ($\beta = 0.55$, $P < .001$) compared with trait anxiety ($\beta = 0.19$, $P = .003$) and trait depression ($\beta = 0.10$, $P = .114$). Thus attention to the presence of anger in psychiatric patients is critical in predicting aggression at some time in the future.

Not surprisingly, the presence of anger in psychiatric patients appears to be far more prevalent and meaningful than previously thought. For example, a recent study by Judd, Schettler, Coryell, Akiskal, and Fiedorowicz (2013) reported that more than half of the acutely depressed patients had at least a "mild" degree of overt anger (i.e., quick to express annoyance) during their current or worst week of depression. More importantly, the presence of anger was associated with increased depressive severity, longer duration of the index major depressive episode, poorer impulse control, a more chronic and severe long-term course of illness, higher rates of lifetime comorbid substance abuse and anxiety disorder, antisocial personality disorder, greater psychosocial impairment before evaluation and during follow-up, and reduced life satisfaction. A more recent study (Genovese, Dalrymple, Chelminski, & Zimmerman, 2017) reported that nearly half of a large ($n=3800$) general sample of psychiatric outpatients reported moderate-to-severe levels of current subjective anger, and that one-fifth reported moderate-to-severe levels of current overt aggression. The frequency of anger was similar to the frequencies of depressed mood and psychic anxiety. Anger and aggression were elevated across all diagnoses except adjustment disorder. Anger and aggression were most elevated in patients with major depressive disorder, panic disorder with agoraphobia, posttraumatic stress disorder, intermittent explosive disorder, and cluster B personality disorders.

Intermittent Explosive Disorder

When sufficiently frequent and severe, individuals with expressed anger and impulsive aggression can meet the DSM-5 diagnosis of Intermittent Explosive Disorder (IED; Coccaro, 2012). While impulsive aggression is also observed in other diagnostic conditions, where aggression is not directly due to another psychiatric disorder, a diagnosis of IED may be made. In this way, IED represents a disorder of primary impulsive aggression while other behavioral disorders in which aggression may occur (e.g., psychosis, mania, etc.) can be referred to disorders of secondary aggression.

Diagnostic Criteria for IED in DSM-5

The essence of recurrent, problematic, impulsive aggression has been in the DSM since its first edition. Despite this, criteria for IED did not unequivocally require impulsive aggression as its hallmark characteristic until its fifth edition (DSM-5). IED in the DSM-5 is characterized by one, or both, types of impulsive aggressive outbursts (Coccaro, 2011). First (Criterion A), frequent, but low intensity, outbursts occurring twice weekly for at least 3 months (A_1 Criterion) and/or infrequent, but high intensity, outbursts occurring three times per year (A_2 Criterion). Second (Criterion B), outbursts are out of proportion to stressors and, thus, do not reflect normative reactions to extreme provocation (i.e., otherwise healthy individuals would not respond to the "stressor" with an aggressive outburst). Third (Criterion C), aggressive outbursts are impulsive (i.e., not premeditated), anger based in nature, and not displayed in order to reach some tangible goal (i.e., not instrumental). Fourth (Criterion D), aggressive outbursts are associated with distress and impairment. Fifth (Criterion E), individuals are 6 years old or older before the diagnosis is made. Sixth (Criterion F), aggressive outbursts are not better accounted for by another disorder (i.e., aggressive outbursts do not occur only during the presence of another disorder).

Relevance of the A_1 Criteria for DSM-5 IED

In preparation for the update of DSM-IV IED criteria for DSM-5, we conducted a series of analyses to see if individuals with recurrent, problematic, impulsive aggression (i.e., IED) could be effectively identified if both high frequency but low intensity impulsive aggressive outbursts (A_1 in DSM-5) were used to define IED [in addition to low frequency but high intensity impulsive aggressive outbursts (A_2 in DSM-5) that was already part of the DSM-IV criteria for IED]. We found that those who met (at the time) research diagnostic criteria for IED due only to A_1 outbursts did not differ from those with only A_2 outbursts as a function of aggression severity measures, presence of familial IED, biological characteristics (e.g., platelet binding of 5-HT Transporters, hormonal responses to 5-HT pharmaco-challenge), and treatment response to fluoxetine (Coccaro, 2012). Considering all with a lifetime diagnosis of IED in our early studies we found that about 70% met both A_1 and A_2 criteria, 20% met A_2 criteria only, and 10% met A_1 criteria only for IED (Coccaro, 2011). We reexamined this issue in our present studies of individuals with current DSM-5 IED and found that, while a similar proportion met both A_1 and A_2 criteria for IED, the proportion meeting A_1-Only and A_2-Only was reversed. Overall, it appears that most individuals who meet current DSM-5 criteria for IED have both forms of the "A" criteria for aggressive behavior.

Relevance of the A_2 Criteria for DSM-5 IED

We also examined our data regarding how to best operationalize the A_2 criteria. In this analysis we looked at those with current DSM-5 IED who had reported physical aggression that was not destructive or injurious, physical aggression that was moderately destructive/injurious (i.e., damage to items worth less than $50, bodily injury not requiring medical attention), and physical aggression that was more seriously destructive/injurious (i.e., damage to items worth $50 or more, bodily injury requiring medical attention). Compared with healthy controls, psychiatric controls, and those meeting the A_1 criteria only (i.e., no reported physical aggression), we found a stepwise increase in aggression severity that was statistically significant only for those with serious physical aggression. These data suggest that, perhaps, only serious physical aggressive behavior should meet criteria for A_2 aggressive outbursts. If so, this would increase the proportion of those meeting the A_1 criteria alone. Regardless of how individuals met the DSM-5 criteria for IED, all study participants with IED (i.e., A1-Only, A2-No Damage/Injury, A2-Moderate Damage/Injury, A2-Serious Damage/Injury) had significantly higher aggression scores compared with both healthy and psychiatric controls. Thus even those with less than serious physical aggression are more aggressive than other individuals without recurrent, problematic, impulsive aggressive behavior.

Community Survey Studies of IED

Though early versions of the DSM characterized IED as a "rare" disorder (DSM-I through DSM-IIIR), recent studies indicate that IED is much more common than previously thought up through the publication of the DSM-IV in 1994. Since the mid-2000s a number of community surveys have been conducted that included an assessment of DSM-IV IED. These include a small "add-on" IED assessment to an Epidemiological Catchment Area follow-up study in Baltimore (ECA-B; Coccaro, Schmidt, Samuels, & Nestadt, 2004); the National Comorbidity Study—Replication (NCS-R; Kessler et al., 2006); the National Latino and Asian American Study (NLAAS; Ortega, Canino, & Alegria, 2008); the NCS-R Adolescent Supplement Study (McLaughlin et al., 2012); the Army STAARS Study (Knock et al., 2014); the National Survey of American Life, Adolescent Supplement Study (NSAL-AS; Oliver et al., 2016) which reported on black adolescents; the Mental Health Surveillance Study (MHSS; Karg et al., 2014); as well as a series of other community surveys conducted in a number of non-US countries included in a recent summary of 17 national surveys in the World Mental Health Survey (WMHS; including the United States; Scott et al., 2016). Below, we review these data in terms of nature of diagnosis, prevalence (lifetime and 12 month), age of onset, male/female ratio, type of aggressive behavior in those with IED, persistence of IED over time, impairment, and severity. Comorbidity data from these studies will be reviewed in the next chapter of this volume.

Nature of IED Diagnosis in Community Survey Studies

No community survey has yet employed DSM-5 criteria for IED due to the fact that the DSM-5 has been available only since May 2013. While all community studies employed DSM-IV criteria, one small study also included the Research Criteria for IED (Coccaro et al., 2004). For all community surveys using DSM-IV criteria, the diagnosis of IED used either a "broad" and/or a "narrow" definition of IED. The broad definition simply required cases to have at least three "anger attacks" over the course of their life. These anger attacks had to be out of proportion to provocation and not due to medical or pharmacologic reasons for aggressive behavior. The narrow definition was similar but required the presence of three anger attacks in any given year. Twelve-month prevalence required that there be at least one anger attack in the past year. This distinction is important because, on most relevant parameters, those diagnosed IED by the narrow definition are more severely affected compared with diagnosed IED by the broad definition only in terms of severity, persistence, and impairment related to IED (Coccaro, 2012). In addition, the narrow definition is much closer to the definition outlined in DSM-5 which requires at least three aggressive outbursts in a single year rather than across the lifetime.

Prevalence of IED in Community Survey Studies

The first comprehensive survey including IED as a disorder of interest was the NCS-R study including 9282 adult individuals in the United States (Kessler et al., 2006). This study reported a lifetime and 12-month prevalence of "Broad IED" of 7.3% and 3.9%, respectively, and 5.4% and 2.7% for "Narrow IED," respectively. An independent analysis of the NCS-R study data, performed by our group, including the new DSM-5 criteria (i.e., presence of A_2 outbursts, presence of substantial anger during aggressive outbursts, presence of distress and/or psychosocial impairment, and age of onset $\geq$6 years) reported that the prevalence of IED in the United States may be somewhat lower at 4.0% and 2.6% for lifetime and 12-month prevalence, respectively. That said, the true prevalence of IED by DSM-5 cannot be known based on existing data because DSM-5 criteria for IED require either low intensity (but high-frequency) impulsive aggressive outbursts (A_1 Criteria) or high intensity (but low frequency) outbursts (A_2 Criteria). Since the data instrument used in the NCS-R (Kessler et al., 2006) and the multinational (Scott et al., 2016) study only sought information primarily about A_2, not A_1, type of aggressive outbursts, the prevalence of those meeting only the A_1 criteria in any of the existing community survey studies is unknown at this time. This absence of data referable to A_1 outbursts is important because data from our own studies suggest that more than one-fifth of those with current DSM-5 IED meet the A_1 criteria only (i.e., have frequent verbal and/or nondestructive/injurious outbursts only) but not the A_2 criteria for DSM-5 IED. If so, our revised numbers for the prevalence of DSM-5 IED likely constitute an underestimate.

In the NCS-AS study of 6493 adolescents (McLaughlin et al., 2012), lifetime and 12-month prevalence of "Broad" IED were somewhat lower at 5.3% and 1.7%, respectively. Among 1170 Black adolescents in the NSAL study (Oliver et al., 2016), lifetime and 12-month prevalence of "Narrow IED" were in a similar range at 6.2% and 4.1%, respectively. Among 2554 Latino adults (NLAAS study; Ortega et al., 2008), lifetime and 12-month prevalence of "Narrow IED" were 5.8% and 4.1%, respectively. Notably, IED was more prevalent in Latinos born in the United States compared with those born outside the United States (9.5% vs. 3.2% for lifetime; 6.7% vs. 2.3% for 12 months). This was also true for those whose parents were born in the United States compared with those born outside the continental United States (9.4%–9.7% vs. 3.2%), suggesting that there may be something about the culture of the United States that facilitates the expression of impulsive aggression. Finally, the Army STAARS study of 5428 nondeployed army soldiers (Knock et al., 2014) reported a lifetime pre- and post-enlistment diagnosis of "Broad IED" of 15.7% and 4.8%, respectively. If so, it appears that the prevalence of IED among those entering the military in the United States may be twice than of the general population, suggesting that those who seek military service may already be more impulsive aggressive than the general population. The Army STAARS study, however, did not apply hierarchical rules (as did NCS-R) to the diagnosis of IED and, thus, its prevalence estimate is, naturally, higher compared with the results from other community surveys. That said, if one takes a rate of 4.0%, as representing the prevalence of individuals who met the DSM-IV "A" and "B," but not "C," for IED from the NCS-R study, one could estimate the preenlistment rate of DSM-IV "Broad IED," in Army STAARS as 11.7%, a figure still higher than that in the general US population as assessed in the NCS-R study (7.4%).

In contrast to the earlier are results from the MHSS study (Karg et al., 2014) involving 5653 US adults and from the WMHS survey (Scott et al., 2016) involving 88,063 adults in 16 countries (including the

NCS-R study in the United States). Unlike the earlier studies, the 12-month prevalence of "Narrow IED" was 0.4% in the MHSS study. This may have been due to the fact that this study used the Structured Clinical Interview for DSM Disorders (SCID; First, Williams, & Gibbon, 1997) which contained a very limited module for IED compared with the Composite International Diagnostic Interview (CIDI; Kessler & Ustün, 2004) used for most of the community surveys including the NCS-R, NCS-R-AS, and the WMH surveys, which included more than 30, compared with three, questions regarding anger attacks and that the MHSS study employed telephone rather than face-to-face interviews. The WMHS survey (Scott et al., 2016), involving 16 countries, also reported a 12-month prevalence of 0.4% (0.8% for lifetime). In this study, 12 of the individual surveys reported a lifetime prevalence of "Narrow IED" of less than 1.0%, while four reported a lifetime prevalence of 1.1 (Northern Ireland, Ukraine) or 1.2 (Columbia, South Africa), and one reported a lifetime prevalence of 2.7% (USA). Reasons for these cross-national differences are not known but are likely related to variation in general risk factors, cultural factors that impact on willingness to disclose information about one's own psychopathology, and other methodological factors. That said, even the prevalence of DSM-IV "Narrow IED" in the United States, which was initially published as 5.4% and 2.7% for lifetime and 12-month prevalence, respectively, was reported at 2.7% and 1.5%, respectively. This is because the WMHS survey algorithm for DSM-IV IED included impairment as a criterion (based on a single CIDI item) and this reduced prevalence estimates by 50% for lifetime and by 56% for 12-month prevalence. In our own reanalysis of the NCS-R data (Coccaro, Fanning, Fisher, Couture, & Lee, 2017; Coccaro, Fanning, & Lee, 2017), we included impairment and distress as a criterion (DSM-5 Criterion D) based on eight, rather than one, CIDI item and found the lifetime and 12-month prevalence to be 4.0% and 2.6%, respectively.

Even if the worldwide lifetime prevalence is truly 0.8%, IED by "Narrow" DSM-IV criteria would not be considered rare because "rare disorders" (in the United States) are defined as affecting less than 1 in 1500 individuals (<0.066%; Rare Disease Act of 2002). For the United States, however, the 12-month prevalence of IED (2.7% in Kessler et al., 2006; 1.5% in Scott et al., 2016; 2.6% in our NCS-R reanalysis) is relatively common, especially in comparison to the 12-month prevalence estimates for schizophrenia (0.3%; McGrath, Saha, Chant, & Welhan, 2008), autism spectrum disorder (1.5%; Christensen et al., 2016), and all forms of bipolar disorder (2.6%; Kessler, Chiu, Demler, Merikangas, & Walters, 2005).

Other Characteristics of IED Explored in Community Survey Studies

Age of Onset (AOO)

Across community survey studies, the mean AOO is reported as early to middle adolescence. In the NCS-R study (Kessler et al., 2006), mean age of onset (AOO) was similar for both "Broad IED" (14.8 years) and "Narrow IED" (13.5 years). In the NCS-AS study (McLaughlin et al., 2012) mean AAO was 12.5 years and in the ECA-B study (Coccaro et al., 2004) mean AOO was 18.3 years. In the NSAL study (Oliver et al., 2016) mean AOO was 10 years.

Type of Aggression

In the NCS-R study (Kessler et al., 2006), type of aggression was similar between "Broad" and "Narrow" IED with about two-thirds of anger attacks involving physical aggression with the rest involving threat, but not acts, of physical aggression.

Severity of IED

No IED-specific severity measures have been used in the community surveys conducted to date. That said, the NCS-R study reported that those with "Narrow IED" had nearly 10 times the number of anger attacks in the previous year compared with those with "Broad IED" (11.8 vs. 1.3 incidents); this was also true for number of weeks with at least one anger attack (19.6 vs. 1.5 weeks). In addition, the NCS-R study noted that the mean value of property damage was three times greater for those with "Narrow IED" compared with "Broad IED" ($1603 vs. $447). This was also true for the mean number of times in the lifetime that someone was physically hurt and required medical attention (233 vs. 37 incidents).

Persistence of IED

Persistence of a disorder can be assessed by dividing the 12-month prevalence by the lifetime prevalence. For the NCS-R study (Kessler et al., 2006), the persistence figure for "Narrow IED" was 64% compared with 24% for "Broad IED." For the WMHS survey (Scott et al., 2016), the persistence figure was 50% for all countries and the persistence figure for the NLAAS Latino study was 71% (Ortega et al., 2008). For adolescents, the persistence figure for the NSAL Black Adolescent study (Oliver et al., 2016) was 66%, though the persistence figure for the NCS-R-AS study (McLaughlin et al., 2012) was 32%.

Impairment Associated With IED

In the studies utilizing the CIDI, impairment was assessed using the Sheehan Disability Scale (SDS; Sheehan, Harnett-Sheehan, & Raj, 1986). In the NCS-R study, reported SDS scores associated with IED were twice as high among those with "Narrow IED" compared with those with "Broad IED (40.4 vs. 19.6).

Association With Suicidal Behavior

In our reanalysis of the NCS-R data set, we found that history of a suicide attempt (SA) was fourfold higher in those with lifetime DSM-5 IED compared with those without IED [19.0% vs. 4.5%; Odds Ratio: 4.69 (95% CI: 3.51–6.29), $P<.001$]. Adding relevant comorbid diagnoses (i.e., mood, anxiety, substance use, and posttraumatic stress disorders) lowered the odds ratio for history of a past SA to about twofold, but still at a highly statistically significant level [Odds Ratio: 2.11 (95% CI: 1.53–2.91), $P<.001$]. Thus the relationship between suicidal behavior and IED is present even after accounting for the presence of other relevant disorders.

Treatment Seeking in IED

In the NCS-R study, only 13.2% of those with "Narrow" IED in the past year received treatment for their impulsive aggressive behavior compared with 33.2% for treatment of any psychiatric disorder. This trend was similar for those with lifetime "Narrow" IED (32.4% for treatment for IED and 61.6% for treatment of any psychiatric disorder) indicating that IED is far less recognized for treatment than other psychiatric disorders.

Relationship With Age

The inverse relationship between age and aggression is well known. Accordingly, it is important to explore the prevalence of IED as a function of age (Olweus, 1979). The NCS-R study reported a significantly higher prevalence of lifetime "Broad IED" in individuals 59 years and younger compared to individuals 60 years and older and revealed a stepwise reduction in the odds ratios going from the youngest to the oldest of individuals [OR for 18–29 years of age: 4.3 (2.1–9.0); OR for 30–44 years of age: 2.9 (1.3–6.3);

OR for 45–59 years of age: 1.6 (0.8–3.5)]. Our reanalysis of these data using DSM-5 criteria revealed a similar finding for past year IED but with much larger odds ratios for the younger age groups compared to the oldest age group [OR for 18–29 years of age: 15.9 (7.4–34.6); OR for 30–44 years of age: 9.2 (4.2–20.1); OR for 45–59 years of age: 6.0 (2.7–13.5)]. Thus IED emerges early in life with the greatest prevalence before 30 years of age and becomes increasing less prevalent approaching late middle age.

Relationship With Biological Sex

Clinical studies (McElroy, 1999) have suggested that males are much more likely to have IED than females. While recent community survey data suggests the same this ratio is lower than previously thought. This is consistent with observations that females are generally less physically, though not verbally, aggressive than males (Eagly & Steffen, 1986). However, in our clinical research studies, we have found that such sex differences are modest in magnitude: between a small- ($d=0.10$) and medium- ($d=0.30$) sized effect. For example, in our studies, males in our studies have a significantly greater degree of lifetime history of aggression (Life History of Aggression: LHA; Coccaro, Berman, & Kavoussi, 1997); a greater degree of a disposition to physical, but not verbal, aggression (Buss-Perry Aggression Questionnaire: BPA); and a greater degree of aggressive responding on a laboratory assessment of physical aggression (Taylor Aggression Paradigm: TAP). The effect sizes for these differences range from small ($d=0.09$ for Buss-Perry Verbal Aggression) to medium ($d=0.23$ for mean shock in the TAP which is a type of physical aggression). In contrast, females have higher trait anger scores than males on the BPA ($d=0.21$). Given that trait anger is a very strong correlate of IED, the lower rate of IED in females suggests that other factors must be working to constrain females from behaving aggressively. Such factors may be both biological and cultural.

In the NCS-R study, the sex ratio was reported for lifetime "Broad IED" only and this ratio was 1.66–1.00 suggesting a 66% greater prevalence of IED in males compared with females. In our reanalysis of the NCS-R data, we found a 1.52–1.00 ratio for past year DSM-5 IED. In contrast, the NCS-AS study found no significant difference in the prevalence of IED as a function of sex while other community studies report mixed results. The NLAAS (Ortega et al., 2008) and NSAL (Oliver et al., 2016) studies report a 1:35–1.00, and a 1.94–1.00, male-female ratio, respectively, while the

MUSS study (Karg et al., 2014) reports a threefold increase in prevalence among males compared with females. In summary, while IED is more prevalent in males than in females the difference in prevalence of IED as a function of sex is not as large as previously thought.

Ethnic Differences in IED

The NCS-R study reported only modest effects for differences in ethnicity as a function of lifetime "Broad IED"; note that the published data did not break this down as a function of "Narrow IED." Our reanalysis of these data using DSM-5 criteria for lifetime IED revealed no significant difference in prevalence of IED as a function of ethnicity (i.e., White, Black, Latino, Other); for past year IED, however, those with "Other" ethnicity had a greater prevalence of IED compared to those who self-identified as non-Latino-White.

Relationship With Education

Similar to age, the NCS-R study reported a significantly higher prevalence of lifetime "Broad IED" in individuals with less than a full college education compared with those with a college education or more [OR for "less than high school": 2.0 (1.4–3.0); OR for "high school graduates": 1.4 (1.0–1.8); OR for "partial college": 1.6 (1.2–2.2)]. Our reanalysis of these data revealed a similar finding for past year DSM-5 IED with odds ratios of about two (2) for each comparison [OR for "less than high school": 2.2 (1.4–3.6), $P=.001$; OR for "high school graduates": 1.7 (1.1–2.5), $P=.022$; OR for "partial college": 1.46 (0.9–2.2), $P=.083$]. Accordingly, the presence of higher education (i.e., 16 plus years) may be a protective factor in the case of IED. This may be partly accounted for by the higher intelligence of those who go on to graduate college (Ceci & Williams, 1997), and the development of cognitive skills that reduce the risk of aggression since greater intelligence is associated with problem-solving skills that limit aggressive responding in social interaction (Huesmann, Eron, & Yarmell, 1987).

Relationship With Household Income

Also, similar to age, the NCS-R study reported a significantly higher prevalence of lifetime "Broad IED" in individuals with lower incomes compared with those with "high" incomes [OR for "low income": 1.5 (1.4–3.6); OR for "low average income": 1.3 (1.3–3.0); OR for "high average income": 1.3 (1.2–2.9)] though only the comparison for "low" vs. "high income" was statistically significant. While our reanalysis of these data found a similar odds ratio, comparing the prevalence of past year IED for the "low income" group with the "high income" group [OR: 1.3 (0.9–1.9), $P=.209$], group differences did not reach statistical significance ($P=.119$).

Clinical Research Studies of IED

Clinical research studies are quite different from community/epidemiologic studies in that study participants are drawn from the community either through public service announcements regarding the participation in research studies of IED ("symptomatic volunteers") or through clinical referral for treatment. An advantage of clinical research studies is that investigators are able to collect much more data on study participants and the assessments are done by research psychiatrists and/or clinical psychologists. The disadvantage is that the study participants may not reflect all the characteristics of those with IED in the community because study participants are not necessarily representative of the full population with the disorder of interest.

The first such clinical research study in IED was performed in the DSM-III era and reported that very few individuals reporting "anger issues" actually met DSM-III criteria for IED (Felthous, Bryant, Wingerter, & Barratt, 1991). This result was due to the fact that the "B" criterion of DSM-III IED prohibited the diagnosis of IED in individuals with interoutburst aggressiveness and/or impulsivity and because of the exclusionary "C" criteria which prohibited the diagnosis in those with antisocial and/or borderline personality disorder. The DSM-IV revised IED criteria so that generalized aggressiveness/impulsiveness was not exclusionary for diagnosing IED and that impulsive aggressive individuals with AsPD/BPD could be given the diagnosis if the impulsive aggressive behavior was not explained, simply by the presence of AsPD and/or BPD.

Prevalence of IED in Clinical Research Studies

For the DSM-IV diagnosis of IED, we found a lifetime and current prevalence of IED of 6.6% and 3.1%, respectively, in a university outpatient clinic population of 1800 individuals (Coccaro et al., 2005). An updated study adding another 2000 individuals to this data set reported a similar current prevalence of DSM-IV IED at 3.6% (Genovese et al., 2017); lifetime prevalence was not reported. The most recent study (Gelegen & Tamam, 2018) reported on the prevalence of IED by DSM-5 criteria in 406 patients consecutively evaluated in a Turkish outpatient psychiatry clinic and found a lifetime and 12-month prevalence of IED of 16.7% and 11.3%. To our knowledge, no other clinical studies have been conducted as a consecutive series of individuals coming for treatment in which the presence of IED was assessed.

Biological Sex and Ethnic Differences in IED

In a clinical survey study of psychiatric disorders in which the presence of DSM-IV IED was assessed (Coccaro et al., 2005), no significant differences were observed for the male-to-female ratio for current (1.17–1.00) or lifetime IED, though the sex ratio for lifetime IED (1.40–1.00) was in the same range as that reported in many of the community surveys. In contrast to this result, a recent study in Turkey (Gelegen & Tamam, 2018) reported a much higher male-to-female ratio for lifetime DSM-5 IED (2.97–1.00). In the first clinical survey study (Coccaro et al., 2005), the prevalence of DSM-IV IED, as a function of ethnicity, was significantly higher for nonwhites compared to whites for both current (2.7–1.0) and lifetime DSM-IV IED (1.9–1.0); subgroups of nonwhites did not differ from each other. These findings should be taken with caution, however, because the number of those with IED (current: 40; lifetime: 82) was relatively small. The recent clinical survey of Turkish psychiatric outpatients did not report data on ethnicity.

Type of Aggression in IED

The frequency of verbal assault (>100 events/year), during aggressive outbursts, is an order of magnitude greater than that for physical assault (>10 events/year (Kulper, Kleiman, McCloskey, Berman, & Coccaro, 2015); these frequencies are much greater than that seen in psychiatric (<5.0, and 0.1, events/year), or healthy (<0.1, and< 0.01, events/year), controls. Like both psychiatric and healthy controls, the vast majority of aggressive behavior in those with is impulsive, rather than instrumental or premeditated, in nature (Fanning, Coleman et al., 2019).

Psychometric Characteristics of Aggression in IED

Examination of all our clinical research data comparing study participants with IED to those with nonaggressive psychiatric disorders (Psychiatric Controls) and nonaggressive Healthy Controls, document clear separation between the three groups with respect to both state (Overt Aggression Scale—Modified) and trait (LHA, BPA, and laboratory assessments of aggression such as the Taylor Aggression Paradigm and the Point Subtraction Aggression Paradigm) measures of aggression. While separation from Healthy Controls is expected, it is important to note that the high levels of aggression in IED are not due to the presence of general psychopathology since the IED and Psychiatric Control groups share that feature (Table 1).

Table 1 Mean Aggression and Impulsiveness Scores in Healthy Controls (HC), Psychiatric Controls (PC), and in Current IED Study Participants

	HC	PC	Current-IED	Group Differences
State Measures (±SD)				
OAS-M Total Aggression	1.8 ± 3.9	12.1 ± 26.1	101.1 ± 136.9	IED > PC > HC
OAS-M Global Anger and Aggression	0.9 ± 1.1	2.0 ± 2.5	5.9 ± 1.8	IED > PC > HC
Trait Measures (±SD)				
LHA Aggression	4.6 ± 3.4	7.7 ± 5.1	18.5 ± 4.0	IED > PC > HC
BPAQ Aggression	27.7 ± 8.9	32.0 ± 9.8	47.9 ± 11.2	IED > PC > HC
BPAQ Anger	12.0 ± 4.7	14.9 ± 6.0	25.1 ± 6.0	IED > PC > HC
LHIB Impulsivity	24.3 ± 16.6	34.5 ± 19.9	52.9 ± 19.7	IED > PC > HC
BIS Impulsivity	54.3 ± 8.9	61.9 ± 11.5	68.2 ± 11.1	IED > PC > HC
Laboratory Measures (±SD)				
Taylor Aggression (Mean Shock)				
(Low Provocation)	2.34 ± 2.13	2.44 ± 2.56	3.43 ± 3.39	IED > PC = HC
(High Provocation)	4.99 ± 3.85	5.23 ± 4.38	7.35 ± 5.04	IED > PC = HC
Point Subtraction Aggression (% Aggressive/All Presses)	4.98 ± 9.24	6.55 ± 9.53	10.02 ± 11.31	IED > PC = HC

Association With Suicidal and Self-Injurious Behavior

Analysis of our clinical research data set revealed that history of a SA and history of self-injurious behavior (SIB) was two- to fourfold higher in those with lifetime DSM-5 IED compared with those without IED [SA: 21.3% vs. 5.6%; Odds Ratio: 3.46 (95% CI: 2.4–5.0), $P<.001$; SIB: 16.4% vs. 5.7%; Odds Ratio: 2.5 (95% CI: 1.7–3.7), $P<.001$]. Adding relevant comorbid diagnoses (i.e., mood, anxiety, substance use, and posttraumatic stress disorders) lowered the odds ratio for both by about half (as was observed in the reanalysis of the NCS-R data set, see previously) to an Odds Ratio of 1.66 (95% CI: 1.1–2.5); $P<.015$) for SA and 1.4 (95% CI: 0.9–2.2, $P<.09$) for SIB. Adding Life History of Aggression (LHA) scores, however, completely eliminated the relationship between SA and SIB with DSM-5 IED [Odds Ratio for SA: 1.2 (95% CI: 0.7–2.1), $P=.839$; Odds Ratio for SIB: 1.1 (95% CI: 0.6–1.9), $P=.924$] indicating that the relationship between IED and risk of SA (and SIB) is fully explained by history of aggression.

Subjective Experience of Impulsive Aggressive Outbursts in IED

As part of our initial studies in IED we developed a semistructured research module to assess for the presence of IED as well as other aspects regarding the emotions and sensations felt before and during impulsive aggressive outbursts (IED-Module; IED-M). In an analysis comparing those with IED to healthy and psychiatric controls (Kulper et al., 2015; Fig. 1), we found that the vast majority of IED and psychiatric controls reported being angry (or irritated) compared with healthy controls. Much larger differences between the groups were seen for "feeling enraged" with those with IED endorsing this feeling compared with both psychiatric and healthy controls. Though less prevalent, nearly 40% of those with IED reported "feeling detached/unreal" or "feeling fearful/panicky" before/during outbursts, though this was also true for psychiatric, but not healthy, controls. IED and psychiatric controls also reported being less "clear-headed" before/during outbursts compared with healthy controls. For physical sensations, about three-quarters of IED and psychiatric controls reported having a racing heart, about half of both groups reported feeling "tremulous," and up to a third of both groups reported "hot flashes," before/during outbursts, proportions that were significantly greater compared with healthy controls. Other sensations, such as shortness of breath, did not differ among the groups. In contrast, feelings after impulsive aggressive outbursts

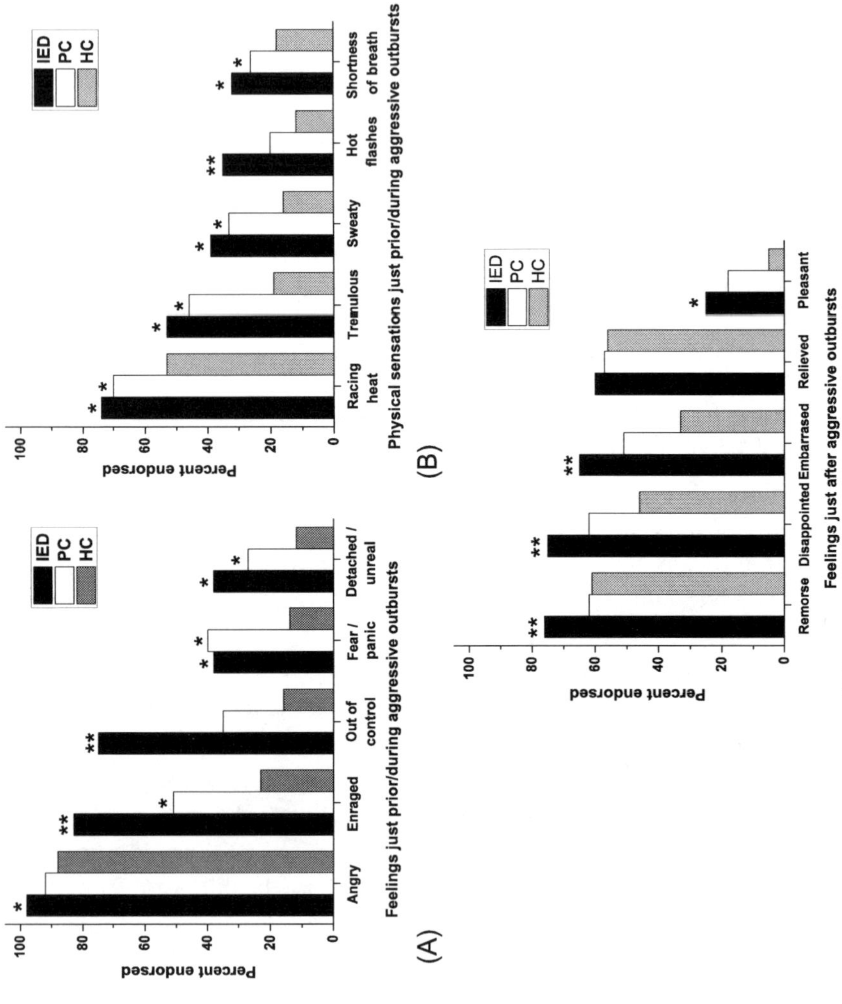

Fig. 1 Percent endorsing the emotions/sensations prior to and after aggressive outbursts as a function of group. *HC*, healthy control; *PC*, psychiatric control; *IED*, Intermittent Explosive Disorder. Asterisks indicate statistically significant differences from other groups.

distinguished those with IED from both psychiatric and healthy controls in most cases. Nine of ten of those with IED reported being "upset" after outbursts compared with about half for psychiatric controls and a third for healthy controls. Three-quarters of those with IED felt "remorseful" or "disappointed" after outbursts compared with about two-fifths to three-fifths for the control groups. Two-thirds of those with IED reported feeling "embarrassed" after outbursts compared to half for psychiatric controls and a third for healthy controls. Finally, one-quarter of those with IED reported feeling "pleasure" after outbursts compared with less than a fifth for psychiatric and healthy controls.

Psychosocial Consequences

Not surprisingly, individuals with IED experience significant psychosocial consequences as a result of recurrent, impulsive, aggressive behavior. First, global psychosocial function is reduced in IED compared with both healthy and psychiatric controls as is quality of life experience, even when differences in global psychosocial function are accounted for (Rynar & Coccaro, 2018). Examined more closely (Kulper et al., 2015), individuals with IED report large differences with psychiatric and healthy controls with regard to dysfunction with family (82% vs. 23% vs. 13%), with friends (75% vs. 24% vs. 6%), at work (56% vs. 16% vs. 4%), and in legal matters (39% vs. 11% vs. 0%). A second study in this area (Rynar & Coccaro, 2018) reported that those with IED had been more episodes of unemployment (1.57 vs. 0.96 vs. 0.93), and had been fired due to aggressive behavior in the workplace more often (17.5% vs. 7.0% vs. 4.0%), compared with psychiatric and healthy controls.

Treatment Seeking in IED

In a clinical survey study of psychiatric disorders in which the presence of DSM-IV IED was assessed (Coccaro et al., 2005), only 20% of those with IED were primarily in treatment to reduce their impulsive aggressive behavior, though an additional 60% would have been interested in such treatment. The remaining individuals were either unsure or uninterested in treatment.

Psychological Correlates

Consistent with the broad and significant impairments associated with the disorder, individuals with IED also demonstrate deficits across several psychological areas. Not surprisingly, those with IED report higher rates of relational aggression (Murray-Close et al., 2010). They also endorse greater levels of immature defensive styles (i.e., acting out) and less use of mature defensive styles (i.e., sublimation; Puhalla, McCloskey, Brickman, Fauber, & Coccaro, 2016), which may contribute to the reduced emotional intelligence found among those with IED (Coccaro, Solis, Fanning, & Lee, 2015). Further, several studies have found cognitive-affective deficits among those with IED including a hostile attribution bias and related socio-emotional information-processing deficits (e.g., Coccaro, Fanning, Keedy, & Lee, 2016, also see the chapter on Social Cognition). Another area of focus has been impulsivity, as IED is often characterized as a clinical manifestation of "impulsive" aggression. This was supported by several studies in which those with IED self-reported greater impulsivity relative to non-psychiatric and psychiatric comparison groups (e.g., McCloskey, Lee, Berman, Noblett, & Coccaro, 2008). However, studies using behavioral measures of impulsivity were more equivocal (e.g., Coccaro, 1998). A recent study that may shed light on this discrepancy (Puhalla, Ammerman, Uyeji, Berman, & McCloskey, 2016) showed that, though individuals with IED reported greater impulsivity across several domains relative to a nonpsychiatric comparison group, only the impulsivity domain of negative urgency (the tendency to act out impulsively when experiencing a negative emotion) discriminated between those with IED and those with other psychiatric disorders. Furthermore, negative urgency uniquely predicted both increased anger and problems with aggression control among those with IED (; Puhalla, McCloskey, et al., 2016). Thus it seems that impulsivity problems in IED may be limited to "hot" periods of negative affect (e.g., anger). This is also consistent with research showing that IED is associated with poor emotion regulation that extends beyond anger problems to global problems with increased affect lability and negative affect intensity, though anger dysregulation is most prominent (Fettich, McCloskey, Look, & Coccaro, 2015). These emotion regulation problems may be linked to dysregulation of corticolimbic brain circuitry, as individuals with IED demonstrate increased amygdala and, to a lesser extent, decreased orbitomedial activation to threatening stimuli (i.e., angry faces; Coccaro, McCloskey, Fitzgerald, & Phan, 2007; McCloskey et al., 2016). Difficulties with emotion regulation and impulsivity may also be facilitated by the tendency of individuals with IED to engage in angry rumination (Fahlgren, Puhalla, Sorgi, & McCloskey, 2019). Finally, though individuals with IED may have difficulty identifying their own emotion, early evidence suggests they do not have problems identifying and/or empathizing with the emotions of others (Fahlgren et al., 2019). Thus IED appears to be linked to socioemotional deficits that both facilitate, and are exacerbated by, negative affect, rather than the lack of empathy often found in psychopathy (Coccaro, Lee, & McCloskey, 2014).

Criticisms of IED and Commentary

IED is an Unnecessary "Medicalization" of Human Aggression

There is no doubt that impulsive aggressive behavior is dimensional in nature and that individuals manifest aggression along dimensions of severity and frequency. If so, what are the reasons to have a categorical disorder of impulsive aggression? First, distributions of aggression scores are highly skewed to the left. In a population-based study we conducted (Coccaro & Jacobson, 2006), the vast majority of individuals (80.9%) had life history of aggression (LHA; Coccaro et al., 1998) scores in the normative range (e.g., LHA scores $\leq$11), while a smaller proportion (15.7%) had aggression scores in the moderate range (LHA scores from 12 to 17), and a much smaller proportion (3.5%) had aggression scores in the high range (LHA scores from 18 to 25), suggesting the possibility of a discontinuity in aggression scores. Second, in the context of medical models, therapeutic intervention is guided by the identification of a "disorder" as a target for treatment. While one could use the score on an aggression assessment in making this decision, valid cutoff scores on rating scales are difficult to establish and, more importantly, do not necessarily reflect on the degree of distress and/or impairment due to aggressive behavior. Third, sophisticated taxometric analyses (Meehl & Yonce, 1994) have shown that IED (Ahmed, Green, McCloskey, & Berman, 2010), unlike many other behavioral disorders (Haslam, Holland, & Kuppens, 2012), is categorical (taxonic) rather than dimensional in nature. This is in contrast to 80% of behavioral disorders in which aggression is a feature (Haslam et al., 2012). In a community study of over 20,000 individuals (Alegria, Jackson, Kessler, & Takeuchi, 2007), Ahmed et al. (2010) mapped seven behavioral indicators (derived from 28 IED-related items) onto both DSM-IV and Research Criteria for IED (Coccaro, 1998). Analysis yielded a statistical profile consistent with a taxonic, rather than dimensional, structure for IED. Taxon group membership was also associated with treatment seeking, family history of aggressive outbursts, lower age of onset of these outbursts, and male gender, factors that characterize individuals with IED. Recently, we replicated this finding for DSM-5 IED in a clinical research sample (unpublished data). In this sample of those with IED ($n=344$) and healthy ($n=174$) and psychiatric ($n=295$) controls, a taxon for IED was identified in both the whole sample and in the sample after removing healthy controls. Among the IED and psychiatric control groups, the taxon displayed a sensitivity of 89.8% and a specificity of 81.4% (and a positive predictive value of 84.5% and a negative predictive value of 87.3%) for the DSM-5 diagnosis of IED. Not surprisingly, members of the taxon group had significantly higher scores on assessments of aggression, impulsivity, and related measures. This is in contrast to other disorders, in which aggression is frequently observed, such as post-traumatic stress disorder (Forbes, Haslam, Williams, & Creamer, 2005), antisocial personality disorder (Marcus, Ruscio, Lilienfeld, & Hughes, 2008), and borderline personality disorder (Fossati, Raine, Borroni, & Maffei, 2007; Rothschild, Cleland, Haslam, & Zimmerman, 2003).

IED is Just "Bad Behavior"

There has been increasing concern that the field of psychiatry is medicalizing "normative" behavior, especially, in the context of aggressive behavior. However, recurrent, problematic, impulsive aggressive behavior, as defined by DSM-5 IED, does not represent a variant of normal human behavior. Data from both community surveys and clinical research studies clearly indicate that the impulsive aggressive behavior of those with IED is aberrant when compared with both healthy controls and others with nonaggressive psychiatric disorders (psychiatric controls). Not only are dimensional measures of aggression, anger, and impulsivity higher in those with IED compared with controls, but this behavior is associated with objective assessments of distress and impairment. Further, those with IED display significant differences from controls on a number of biological parameters, including indices of serotonin function, gray matter volume in fronto-limbic circuits, shape of subcortical structures, amygdala activation to anger faces, and white matter integrity in selected brain areas (see relevant chapters in this volume). Accordingly, it is difficult to claim that there is "nothing there" when it comes to the validity of IED.

IED is Due to the Presence of Other Disorders and Conditions

In general, IED begins early in life (see the Age of Onset sections), typically earlier than the onset of many other psychiatric disorders such as mood, anxiety, and substance use disorders. [The one exception being that of phobic (social, and simple, phobic) disorders for which the onset precedes that of

IED by a few years in most individuals with both types of disorders.] Accordingly, it is difficult to argue that IED is due to other comorbid disorders. Rather, it is likely that IED increases the risk of other psychiatric disorders rather than the other way round. A more detailed discussion regarding comorbidity in IED is the focus of the next chapter in this volume.

IED is Due to "Psychopathy"

Psychopathy is a critical, though often misunderstood, cognitive-behavioral concept related to, but not identical to, antisocial behavior. Research over several decades has shown that there are at least two components to psychopathy. First, "callous-unemotionality" (i.e., superficial emotionality, grandiosity, lack of remorse, lack of empathy, deceitfulness, denial of responsibility) and second, "social deviance" (i.e., antisocial behavior, impulsivity, lack of clear goals, lack of behavioral controls, general irresponsibility). When we examine the presence of psychopathy in those with IED (Coccaro et al., 2014) we find that while dimensional scores of this factor are higher among those with IED, compared with psychiatric and healthy controls, only a small proportion of those with IED are likely to be psychopathic (20% total: 14% possibly psychopathic and 6% highly likely to be psychopathic) using the Psychopathy Checklist-Screening Version (Hart, Cox, & Hare, 2003). More importantly, scores for "social deviance" were significantly higher than those of "callous/unemotional" scores by about 71% in those with IED without psychopathy and by about 35% in those with IED with possible psychopathy. Accordingly, IED appears to be far less related to "callous-unemotionality" than to "social deviance" in general. This is also consistent with the fact that the form of aggression observed in IED is impulsive rather than premeditated in nature (Fanning, Coleman, et al., 2019).

Data on IED are Unreliable Because Those With Impulsive Aggressive Outbursts are Inherently Unreliable

This critique is driven by the assumption that those with recurrent, problematic, impulsive aggressive outbursts are in denial about their behavior and/or deliberately seek to minimize it. While there is little data regarding this specific issue, it is likely that those who seek evaluation and treatment for IED are different from those who are forced into to evaluation and treatment. When we examine our own data we have two separate findings of relevance (Steakley-Freeman, Lee, McCloskey, & Coccaro, 2018). First, compared with healthy and psychiatric controls, those with DSM-5 IED score significantly lower on measures of social desirability (Social Desirability Scale) and deceptive self-reporting (Lie scale on the Eysenck Personality Questionnaire), and score significantly higher on "readiness to change" their aggressive behavior. Second, the use of first degree family informants did not increase the proportion of those meeting DSM-5 criteria for IED. In fact, out of 70 study participants in a family study of DSM-5 IED, only one study participant was identified by a family member as having IED when the study participant denied it. These data suggest that it is unlikely that denial, or the minimalization, of impulsive aggressive behavior is an important factor when studying those interested in evaluation and/or treatment of impulsive aggressive/angry behavior.

Summary

Anger is a common human emotion and, consequently, many behavioral disorders show some elevation in levels of anger and corresponding aggression that is secondary to the focus of that disorder. However, when excessive levels of anger and aggression are the core pathology, then IED is appropriate diagnosis. A disorder of primary aggression, IED is defined by excessive/disproportionate aggressive acts either in the form of frequent minor aggression (i.e., twice a week for 3 months or more) or more severe, damaging acts of aggression that can occur less frequently (i.e., three or more times a year), though most individuals with IED will show both over their lifetime. Research shows that IED is common (~3%–4%), persistent (typically beginning in adolescence and continuing throughout much of adulthood), and highly impairing across most domains of functioning. Though highly comorbid, IED tends to precede other psychiatric diagnoses. IED occurs in both men and women, though slightly more often in men, across racial and ethnic groups. Aggressive outbursts in IED are differentiated by their extreme level of anger, rage, and lack of subjective control, as well as the strong negative (and to some extent positive) feeling after the outbursts. This feeling of dyscontrol is also reflected in several cognitive-affective deficits among those with IED including hostile attributional biases, poor emotion regulation, and increased impulsivity when experiencing negative affect. However, unlike psychopathy, those with IED demonstrate a normal capacity for empathy, and despite the common symptom of aggression, the two disorders are not highly comorbid. In sum, IED is a distinct and common disorder of primary aggression that is poorly understood (or even known) by much of the public as well as by many practitioners, resulting in the undertreatment of this serious disorder.

References

Ahmed, A., Green, B., McCloskey, M. S., & Berman, M. E. (2010). Latent structure of intermittent explosive disorder in an epidemiological sample. *Journal of Psychiatric Research, 44*, 663–672.

Alegria, M., Jackson, J. S., Kessler, R. C., & Takeuchi, D. (2007). *Collaborative Psychiatric Epidemiology Surveys (CPES), 2001–2003 [United States]*. Computer file ICPSR20240-v5. Ann Arbor, MI: Institute for Social Research, Survey Research Center.

Barratt, E. S., Stanford, M. S., Felthous, A. R., & Kent, T. A. (1997). The effects of phenytoin on impulsive and premeditated aggression: a controlled study. *Journal of Clinical Psychopharmacology, 17*, 341–349.

Ceci, S. J., & Williams, W. M. (1997). Schooling, intelligence, and income. *The American Psychologist, 52*(10), 1051–1058.

Christensen, D. L., Baio, J., Van Naarden Braun, K., Bilder, D., Charles, J., Constantino, J. N., et al. (2016). Centers for disease control and prevention (CDC). *MMWR Surveillance Summaries, 65*(3), 1–23.

Coccaro, E. F. (1998). Impulsive aggression: a behavior in search of clinical definition. *Harvard Review of Psychiatry, 5*, 336–339.

Coccaro, E. F. (2011). Intermittent explosive disorder: development of integrated research criteria for Diagnostic and Statistical Manual of Mental Disorders, Fifth Edition. *Comprehensive Psychiatry, 52*(2), 119–125.

Coccaro, E. F. (2012). Intermittent explosive disorder as a disorder of impulsive aggression for DSM-5. *The American Journal of Psychiatry, 169*, 577–588.

Coccaro, E. F., & Jacobson, K. C. (2006). PennTwins: A population-based cohort for twin studies. *Twin Research and Human Genetics, 9*(6), 998–1005.

Coccaro, E. F., Berman, M. E., & Kavoussi, R. J. (1997). Assessment of life history of aggression: Development and psychometric characteristics. *Psychiatry Research, 73*(3), 147–157.

Coccaro, E. F., Fanning, J. R., Fisher, E., Couture, L., & Lee, R. J. (2017). Social emotional information processing in adults: development and psychometrics of a computerized video assessment in healthy controls and aggressive individuals. *Psychiatry Research, 248*, 40–47.

Coccaro, E. F., Fanning, J. R., Keedy, S. K., & Lee, R. J. (2016). Social cognition in intermittent explosive disorder and aggression. *Journal of Psychiatric Research, 83*, 140–150.

Coccaro, E. F., Fanning, J. R., & Lee, R. (2017). Intermittent explosive disorder and substance use disorder: analysis of the National Comorbidity Study-Replication sample. *The Journal of Clinical Psychiatry, 78*, 697–702.

Coccaro, E. F., Lee, R., & McCloskey, M. S. (2014). Relationship between psychopathy, aggression, anger, impulsivity, and intermittent explosive disorder. *Aggressive Behavior, 40*, 526–536.

Coccaro, E. F., McCloskey, M. S., Fitzgerald, D. A., & Phan, K. L. (2007). Amygdala and orbitofrontal reactivity to social threat in individuals with impulsive aggression. *Biological Psychiatry, 62*, 168–178.

Coccaro, E. F., Posternak, M. A., & Zimmerman, M. (2005). Prevalence and features of intermittent explosive disorder in a clinical, setting. *The Journal of Clinical Psychiatry, 66*(10), 1221–1227.

Coccaro, E. F., Schmidt, C. A., Samuels, J. F., & Nestadt, G. (2004). Lifetime and 1-month prevalence rates of intermittent explosive disorder in a community sample. *Journal of Clinical Psychiatry, 65*(6), 820–824.

Coccaro, E. F., Solis, O., Fanning, J., & Lee, R. (2015). Emotional intelligence and impulsive aggression in intermittent explosive disorder. *Journal of Psychiatric Research, 61*, 135–140.

Dodge, K. A., Bates, J. E., & Pettit, G. S. (1990). Mechanisms in the cycle of violence. *Science, 250*(4988), 1678–1683.

Eagly, A. H., & Steffen, V. J. (1986). Gender and aggressive behavior: a meta-analytic review of the social psychological literature. *Psychological Bulletin, 100*(3), 309–330.

Fahlgren, M. K., Puhalla, A. A., Sorgi, K. M., & McCloskey, M. S. (2019). Emotion processing in intermittent explosive disorder. *Psychiatry Research, 273*, 544–550.

Fanning, J. R., Coleman, M., Lee, R., & Coccaro, E. F. (2019). Subtypes of aggression in intermittent explosive disorder. *Journal of Psychiatric Research, 109*, 164–172.

Felthous, A. R., Bryant, S. G., Wingerter, C. B., & Barratt, E. (1991). The diagnosis of intermittent explosive disorder in violent men. *Bulletin of the American Academy of Psychiatry and the Law, 19*(1), 71–79.

Fettich, K. C., McCloskey, M. S., Look, A. E., & Coccaro, E. F. (2015). Emotion regulation deficits in intermittent explosive disorder. *Aggressive Behavior, 41*(1), 25–33.

First, M. B., Williams, J. B. W., & Gibbon, M. (1997). *Structured clinical interview for DSM-IV patient edition (SCID-P)*. Washington, DC: American Psychiatric Press.

Forbes, D., Haslam, N., Williams, B. J., & Creamer, M. (2005). Testing the latent structure of posttraumatic stress disorder: a taxometric study of combat veterans. *Journal of Traumatic Stress, 18*(6), 647–656.

Fossati, A., Raine, A., Borroni, S., & Maffei, C. (2007). Taxonic structure of schizotypal personality in nonclinical subjects: issues of replicability and age consistency. *Psychiatry Research, 152*(2–3), 103–112.

Gelegen, V., & Tamam, L. (2018). Prevalence and clinical correlates of intermittent explosive disorder in Turkish psychoatric outpatients. *Comprehensive Psychiatry, 83*, 64–70.

Genovese, T., Dalrymple, K., Chelminski, I., & Zimmerman, M. (2017). Subjective anger and overt aggression in psychiatric outpatients. *Comprehensive Psychiatry, 73*, 23–30.

Hart, R. D., Cox, D. N., & Hare, R. D. (2003). *The hare psychopathy checklist-screening version*. Toronto, ON, Canada: Multi Heath Systems.

Haslam, N., Holland, E., & Kuppens, P. (2012). Categories versus dimensions in personality and psychopathology: a quantitative review of taxometric research. *Psychological Medicine, 42*(5), 903–920.

Huesmann, L. R., Eron, L. D., & Yarmell, P. W. (1987). Intellectual function and aggression. *Journal of Personality and Social Psychology, 52*(1), 232–240.

Judd, L. L., Schettler, P. J., Coryell, W., Akiskal, H. S., & Fiedorowicz, J. G. (2013). Overt irritability/anger in unipolar major depressive episodes: Past and current characteristics and implications for long-term course. *JAMA Psychiatry, 70*(11), 1171–1180.

Karg, R. S., Bose, J., Batts, K. R., Forman-Hoffman, V. L., Liao, D., Hirsch, E., et al. (2014). Past year mental disorders among adults in the United States: Results from the 2008–2012 Mental Health Surveillance Study. CBHSQ Data Review. Rockville (MD): Substance Abuse and Mental Health Services Administration (US).

Kessler, R. C., & Ustün, T. B. (2004). The World Mental Health (WMH) Survey Initiative Version of the World Health Organization (WHO) Composite International Diagnostic Interview (CIDI). *International Journal of Methods in Psychiatric Research, 13*(2), 93–121.

Kessler, R. C., Chiu, W. T., Demler, O., Merikangas, K. R., & Walters, E. E. (2005). Prevalence, severity, and comorbidity of 12-month DSM-IV disorders in the National Comorbidity Survey Replication. *Archives of General Psychiatry, 62*(6), 617–627.

Kessler, R. C., Coccaro, E. F., Fava, M., Jaeger, S., Jin, R., & Walters, E. (2006). The prevalence and correlates of DSM-IV intermittent explosive disorder in the National Comorbidity Survey Replication. *Archives of General Psychiatry, 63*, 669–678.

Knock, M. K., Stein, M. B., Heeringa, S. G., Ursano, R. J., Colpe, L. J., Fullerton, C. S., et al. (2014). Prevalence and correlates of suicidal behavior among soldiers: results from the army study to assess risk and resilience in servicemembers (Army STAARS). *JAMA Psychiatry, 71*(5), 514–522.

Kulper, D. A., Kleiman, E. M., McCloskey, M. S., Berman, M. E., & Coccaro, E. F. (2015). The experience of aggressive outbursts in Intermittent Explosive Disorder. *Psychiatry Research, 225*(3), 710–715.

Marcus, D. K., Ruscio, J., Lilienfeld, S. O., & Hughes, K. T. (2008). Converging Evidence for the Latent Structure of Antisocial Personality Disorder. *Criminal Justice and Behavior, 35*(3), 284–293.

McCloskey, M. S., Lee, R., Berman, M. E., Noblett, K. L., & Coccaro, E. F. (2008). The relationship between impulsive verbal aggression and intermittent explosive disorder. *Aggressive Behavior, 34*, 51–60.

McCloskey, M. S., Phan, K. L., Angstadt, A., Fettich, K. C., Keedy, S., & Coccaro, E. F. (2016). Amygdala hyperactivation to angry faces in intermittent explosive disorder. *Journal of Psychiatric Research, 79*, 34–41.

McElroy, S. L. (1999). Recognition and treatment of DSM-IV intermittent explosive disorder. *The Journal of Clinical Psychiatry, 60*, 12–16. Suppl 15.

McGrath, J., Saha, S., Chant, D., & Welhan, J. (2008). Schizophrenia: a concise overview of incidence, prevalence, and mortality. *Epidemiologic Reviews, 30*, 67–76.

McLaughlin, K. A., Green, J. G., Hwang, I., Sampson, N. A., Zaslavsky, A. M., & Kessler, R. C. (2012). Intermittent explosive disorder in the National Comorbidity Survey Replication Adolescent Supplement. *Archives of General Psychiatry, 69*, 1131–1139.

Meehl, P. E., & Yonce, L. J. (1994). Taxometric analysis: I. Detecting taxonicity with two quantitative indicators using means above and below a sliding cut (MAMBAC procedure). *Psychological Reports, 74*, 1059–1274.

Murray-Close, D., Ostrov, J. M., Nelson, D. A., Crick, N. R., & Coccaro, E. F. (2010). Proactive, reactive, and romantic relational aggression in adulthood: measurement, predictive validity, gender differences, and association with Intermittent Explosive Disorder. *Journal of Psychiatric Research, 44*(6), 393–404.

Oliver, D. G., Caldwell, C. H., Faison, N., Sweetman, J. A., Abelson, J. M., et al. (2016). Prevalence of DSM-IV intermittent explosive disorder in Black adolescents: Findings from the National Survey of American Life, Adolescent Supplement. *American Journal of Orthopsychiatry, 86*(5), 552–563.

Olweus, D. (1979). Stability of aggressive reaction patterns in males: A review. *Psychological Bulletin, 86*(4), 852–875.

Ortega, A. N., Canino, G., & Alegria, M. (2008). Lifetime and 12-month intermittent explosive disorder in Latinos. *American Journal of Orthopsychiatry, 78*(1), 133–139.

Puhalla, A. A., Ammerman, B. A., Uyeji, L. L., Berman, M. E., & McCloskey, M. S. (2016). Negative urgency and reward/punishment sensitivity in intermittent explosive disorder. *Journal of Affective Disorders, 201*, 8–14.

Puhalla, A. A., McCloskey, M. S., Brickman, L. J., Fauber, R., & Coccaro, E. F. (2016). Defense styles in Intermittent Explosive Disorder. *Psychiatry Research, 238*, 137–142.

Rothschild, L., Cleland, C., Haslam, N., & Zimmerman, M. (2003). A taxometric study of borderline personality disorder. *Journal of Abnormal Psychology, 112*(4), 657–666.

Rynar, L., & Coccaro, E. F. (2018). Psychosocial impairment in DSM-5 intermittent explosive disorder. *Psychiatry Research, 264*, 91–95.

Scott, K. M., Lim, C. C., Hwang, I., Adamoswki, T., Al-Hamzawi, A., Bromet, E., et al. (2016). The cross-national epidemiology of DSM-IV intermittent explosive disorder. *Psychological Medicine, 46*(15), 3161–3172.

Sheehan, D. V., Harnett-Sheehan, K., & Raj, B. A. (1986). The measurement of disability. *International Clinical Psychopharmacology, 11*, 89–95. Suppl, 3.

Steakley-Freeman, D. M., Lee, R. J., McCloskey, M. S., & Coccaro, E. F. (2018). Social desirability, deceptive reporting, and awareness of problematic aggression in intermittent explosive disorder compared with non-aggressive healthy and psychiatric controls. *Psychiatry Research, 270*, 20–25.

Further Reading

Brown, G. L., Ebert, H., Goyer, F., Jimerson, D. C., Klein, W. J., Bunney, W. E., et al. (1982). Aggression, suicide, and serotonin: relationships to CSF amine metabolites. *The American Journal of Psychiatry, 139*, 741–746.

Brown, G. L., Goodwin, F. K., Ballenger, J. C., Goyer, P. F., & Major, L. F. (1979). Aggression in humans correlates fluid amine metabolites with cerebrospinal. *Psychiatry Research, 1*, 131–139.

Coccaro, E. F. (2010). A family history study of intermittent explosive disorder. *Journal of Psychiatric Research, 44*, 1101–1105.

Coccaro, E. F., Bergeman, C. S., Kavoussi, R. J., & Seroczynski, A. D. (1997). Heritability of aggression and irritability: a twin study of the buss-durkee aggression scales in adult male subjects. *Biological Psychiatry, 41*(3), 273–284.

Coccaro, E. F., Fitzgerald, D. A., Lee, R., McCloskey, M., & Phan, K. L. (2016). Frontolimbic morphometric abnormalities in intermittent explosive disorder and aggression. *Biological Psychiatry: Cognitive Neuroscience and Neuroimaging, 1*, 32–38.

Coccaro, E. F., Lee, R., & Kavoussi, R. J. (2009). Inverse relationship between numbers of 5-HT transporter binding sites and life history of aggression and intermittent explosive disorder. *Journal of Psychiatric Research, 44*, 137–142.

Coccaro, E. F., Lee, R., & Kavoussi, R. J. (2010). Aggression, suicidality, and intermittent explosive disorder: serotonergic correlates in personality disorder and healthy control subjects. *Neuropsychopharmacology, 35*, 435–444.

Coccaro, E. F., Lee, R., McCloskey, M., Csernansky, J. G., & Wang, L. (2015). Morphometric analysis of amygdala and hippocampus shape in impulsively aggressive and healthy control subjects. *Journal of Psychiatric Research, 69*, 80–86.

Coccaro, E. F., Siever, L. J., Klar, H. M., Maurer, G., Cochrane, K., Cooper, T. B., et al. (1989). Serotonergic studies in patients with affective and personality disorders. *Archives of General Psychiatry, 46*, 587–599.

Duke, A. A., Bègue, L., Bell, R., & Eisenlohr-Moul, T. (2013). Revisiting the serotonin-aggression relation in humans: a meta-analysis. *Psychological Bulletin, 139*, 1148–1172.

Fanning, J. R., Meyerhoff, J. J., Lee, R., & Coccaro, E. F. (2014). History of childhood maltreatment in intermittent explosive disorder and suicidal behavior. *Journal of Psychiatric Research, 56*, 10–17.

Frankle, W. G., Lombardo, I., New, A. S., Goodman, M., Talbot, P. S., Huang, Y., et al. (2005). Brain serotonin transporter distribution in subjects with impulsive aggressivity: a positron emission study with [11C]McN 5652. *The American Journal of Psychiatry, 162*, 915–923.

Haslam, N. (2003). Categorical versus dimensional models of mental disorder: the taxometric evidence. *The Australian and New Zealand Journal of Psychiatry, 37*(6), 696–704.

Lee, R., Arfanakis, K., Evia, A. M., Fanning, J., Keedy, S., & Coccaro, E. F. (2016). White Matter Integrity Reductions in Intermittent Explosive Disorder. *Neuropsychopharmacology, 41*(11), 2697–2703.

Lee, R., Meyerhoff, J., & Coccaro, E. F. (2014). Intermittent explosive disorder and aversive parental care. *Psychiatry Research, 220*, 477–482.

Linnoila, M., Virkkunen, M., Scheinin, M., Nuutila, A., Rimon, R., & Goodwin, F. K. (1983). Low cerebrospinal fluid 5-hydroxyindoleacetic acid concentration differentiates impulsive from nonimpulsive violent behavior. *Life Sciences, 33*, 2609–2614.

Miles, D. R., & Carey, G. (1997). Geentic and environmental architecture of human aggression. *Journal of Personality and Social Psychology, 72*(1), 207–217.

Montalvo-Ortiz, J. L., Zhang, H., Chen, C., Liu, C., & Coccaro, E. F. (2018). Genome-wide DNA methylation changes associated with intermittent explosive disorder: a gene-based functional enrichment analysis. *The International Journal of Neuropsychopharmacology, 21*(1), 12–20.

New, A. S., Trestman, R. F., Mitropoulou, V., Goodman, M., Koenigsberg, H. H., Silverman, J., et al. (2004). Low prolactin response to fenfluramine in impulsive aggression. *Journal of Psychiatric Research*, *38*, 223–230.

Nickerson, A., Aderka, I. M., Bryant, R. A., & Hofmann, S. G. (2012). The relationship between childhood exposure to trauma and intermittent explosive disorder. *Psychiatry Research*, *197*, 128–134.

Rosell, D. R., Thompson, J. L., Slifstein, M., Xu, X., Frankle, W. G., New, A. S., et al. (2010). Increased serotonin 2A receptor availability in the orbitofrontal cortex of physically aggressive personality disordered patients. *Biological Psychiatry*, *67*, 1154–1162.

Seroczynski, A. D., Bergeman, C. S., & Coccaro, E. F. (1999). Etiology of the impulsivity/aggression relationship: genes or environment? *Psychiatry Research*, *86*, 41–57.

Siever, L. J., Buchsbaum, M. S., New, A. S., Spiegel-Cohen, J., Wei, T., Hazlett, E. A., et al. (1999). d,l-fenfluramine response in impulsive personality disorder assessed with [18F] fluorodeoxyglucose positron emission tomography. *Neuropsychopharmacology*, *20*, 413–423.

Tremblay, R. E. (2013). Early development of physical aggression and early risk factors for chronic physical aggression in humans. In K. Miczek & A. Meyer-Lindenberg (Eds.), *Vol. 17. Neuroscience of Aggression. Current Topics in Behavioral Neurosciences*. Berlin, Heidelberg: Springer.

van de Giessen, E., Rosell, D. R., Thompson, J. L., Xu, X., Girgis, R. R., Ehrlich, Y., et al. (2014). Serotonin transporter availability in impulsive aggressive personality disordered patients: a PET study with [11C]DASB. *Journal of Psychiatric Research*, *58*, 147–154.

Virkkunen, M., De Jong, J., Bartko, J., Goodwin, F. K., & Linnoila, M. (1989). Relationship of psychobiological variables to recidivism in violent offenders and impulsive fire setters. A follow-up study. *Archives of General Psychiatry*, *46*, 600–603.

Virkkunen, M., Nuutila, A., Goodwin, F. K., & Linnoila, M. (1987). Cerebrospinal fluid monoamine metabolite levels in male arsonists. *Archives of General Psychiatry*, *44*, 241–247.

CHAPTER FOUR

Psychiatric Comorbidity in Intermittent Explosive Disorder

Emil F. Coccaro
Clinical Neuroscience & Psychopharmacology Research Unit, Department of Psychiatry and Behavioral Neuroscience, Pritzker School of Medicine, University of Chicago, Chicago, IL, United States

Contents

Impulsive aggressive behavior appears in psychiatric patients with diagnoses ranging from schizophrenia and other psychotic disorders as well as bipolar, depressive, anxiety, substance use, posttraumatic stress, and personality disorders, among others. Accordingly, clinicians have been reluctant to make the diagnosis of IED in the presence of other psychiatric diagnoses. In the DSM-III (American Psychiatric Association, 1980), the diagnosis of IED was, essentially, a disorder of exclusion. That is, if any other behavioral disorder was present to (possibly) explain impulsive aggressive, the diagnosis of IED was often not given.

DSM-IV (American Psychiatric Association, 1994) revised the IED criteria so that it could be more widely applied. This included relaxing the comorbidity exclusions such that IED could be diagnosed as long as another psychiatric disorder did not "better explain" the impulsive aggressiveness of the individual in question. Later, Research Diagnostic Criteria (Coccaro, 2011; Coccaro, Kavoussi, Berman, & Lish, 1998) and DSM-5 (American Psychiatric Association, 2013) criteria sets took this a step further and proposed that IED could be diagnosed along with other disorders (in most cases) as long as the individual also met criteria for IED at times when another disorder was not present. While this is true in general, IED is typically not diagnosed in the context of lifetime schizophrenia and lifetime bipolar

Intermittent Explosive Disorder
https://doi.org/10.1016/B978-0-12-813858-8.00004-8

disorder so as to be diagnostically conservative and because the underlying presence of schizophrenia or bipolar disorder often, but not always, better explains impulsive aggressiveness than IED in such individuals.

In this chapter, we will review the issue of comorbidity in IED in adults based on available empiric data. Consideration is given to the co-occurrence of IED in the context of lifetime and current comorbid psychiatric disorders, the temporal sequence for the age of onset of IED and comorbid disorders, and the effect of comorbidity on measures of aggression in those with and without IED and the comorbid disorder in question. In analyzing our own clinical research, and reanalyzing published [e.g., the National Comorbidity Study-Replication (NCS-R); Kessler et al., 2004] data sets, we sought to examine, where possible, the relationships between current (past year), and lifetime, IED separately.

Overall Comorbidity With Psychiatric Syndromal and Personality Disorders

NCR-S Survey Study (Table 1). In our reanalysis of the NCS-R survey data set, individuals with current or lifetime DSM-5 IED (American Psychiatric Association, 2013) had a higher rate of comorbidity with other psychiatric disorders compared with those with non-IED disorders (66.4% vs. 23.8% for current disorders; 79.3% vs. 40.8% for lifetime disorders). While this degree of comorbidity is high, it is in the same range of overall comorbidity displayed by those indexed as having mood, anxiety, substance use, or posttraumatic stress disorders. Accordingly, despite the fact that DSM-5 IED is highly comorbid with other psychiatric disorders, it is displays no more overall comorbidity compared with other psychiatric disorders examined in this survey.

Clinical Research Studies (Table 1). The same set of analyses were conducted with our clinical research data set of 1642 individuals (e.g., Coccaro, Shima, & Lee, 2018) containing 453 healthy, and 443 psychiatric, controls and 746 individuals with current or past DSM-5 IED; we also differentiated those with and without a history of personality disorders (i.e., formerly referred to as Axis I and Axis II disorders, respectively). As in the NCS-R reanalysis before, overall comorbidity was similar for IED and for those with mood, anxiety, and posttraumatic stress disorders for both current and lifetime comorbidity; substance use disorder was only examined for lifetime comorbidity because individuals with current substance use disorder were not included in these studies. The lower odds ratios observed in the clinical research data set were likely due

Table 1 General Comorbidity of IED Compared With That of Current Disorders

With Versus Without Disorder	NCS-R Reanalysis OR (95% CI) [% Dx vs. % Non-Dx]	Clinical Research Analysis OR (95% CI) [% Dx vs. % Non-Dx]
Current IED versus Non-IED	5.68 (4.31–7.52) [66.4% vs. 23.8%]	2.67 (2.11–3.37) [39.5% vs. 18.8%]
Current Mood Dx versus Nonmood Dx	7.94 (6.80–9.35) [66.6% vs. 18.5%]	4.03 (2.93–5.52) [73.6% vs. 39.3%]
Current Anxiety Dx versus Nonanxiety Dx	6.67 (5.58–7.58) [45.6% vs. 10.3%]	3.30 (2.43–4.48) [68.2% vs. 39.4%]
Current SUD versus Non-SUD	5.56 (4.59–6.76) [64.2% vs. 24.5%]	N/A
Current PTSD versus Non-PTSD	11.90 (8.85–15.87) [82.8% vs. 26.1%]	10.87 (5.15–22.73) [91.3% vs. 44.8%]
Lifetime IED versus Non-IED	5.32 (4.12–6.90) [79.3% vs. 40.8%]	7.46 (5.88–9.52) [80.8% vs. 35.4%]
Lifetime Mood Dx versus Nonmood Dx	7.81 (6.99–8.77) [75.2% vs. 27.3%]	8.77 (6.76–11.49) [85.7% vs. 40.1%]
Lifetime Anxiety Dx versus Nonanxiety Dx	7.14 (6.45–7.87) [64.7% vs. 20.1%]	9.52 (6.17–14.71) [91.7% vs. 55.0%]
Lifetime SUD versus Non-SUD	5.88 (5.13–6.76) [73.0% vs. 33.9%]	5.32 (4.02–7.04) [84.7% vs. 49.9%]
Lifetime PTSD versus Non-PTSD	16.67 (12.35–22.73) [91.9% vs. 39.2%]	90.91 (12.35–500) [99.3% vs. 59.7%]

to the fact that the clinical research, compared with that of the NCS-R data set (a large population-based sample) had a smaller number of participants overall (1642 vs. 9282), and a much smaller proportion of participants without psychopathology (27.5% vs. 74.3%). Including the presence of personality disorder in the analysis revealed that among those with current DSM-5 IED, nearly half (42.6%) had both a current syndromal psychiatric and personality disorder, or a personality disorder only (49.3%); 1.8% only had a current syndromal psychiatric disorder while 6.3% had no current comorbid disorder at all. For lifetime IED, however, far more individuals had both a lifetime syndromal psychiatric and a personality disorder compared with personality disorder only (68.7% vs. 23.3%); 3.7% had a lifetime syndromal psychiatric disorder only and 4.2% had no lifetime disorder at all.

Focusing on the comorbidity with personality disorders we found that the vast majority of individuals with DSM-5 IED met criteria for a personality disorder (91.9% for current, and 94.6% for past, IED). That said, the degree of comorbidity of personality disorder in those without current IED (e.g., depressive or anxiety) disorders was also substantial and not significantly different compared with those with current IED [IED: 91.7% vs. 43.7%, $P<.001$; OR: 14.08 (95% CI: 10.20–19.61); Depressive Disorder: 93.2% vs. 55.5%, $P<.001$; OR: 10.10 (6.21–17.54); Anxiety Disorder: 94.8% vs. 55.3%, $P<.001$; OR: 17.54 (95% CI: 9.52–31.25); Posttraumatic Stress Disorder: 95.7% vs. 58.8%, $P<.001$; OR: 14.93 (5.43–41.67)]. Thus the degree of comorbidity with general personality disorder may not meaningfully differ between those with current IED, depressive, anxiety, or posttraumatic stress disorders. That said, the finding that those with IED are highly comorbid with personality disorder is not unexpected given that several features displayed by those with IED apply toward meeting at least two, in not all, of the required General Criteria for DSM-5 Personality Disorder [i.e., issues with cognition (e.g., hostile attribution"), affectivity (e.g., intensity/appropriateness of emotional response), impulse control (e.g., impulsive aggression), and interpersonal dysfunction (distress and/or impairment associated with impulsive aggressive behavior)]. Finally, as will be discussed later, IED is more frequently observed in some personality disorders rather than others and is frequently observed in those with unspecified personality disorder (see Table 3 and later).

Comorbidity With Psychiatric (Table 2) **and Personality Disorders** (Table 3)

Overall Frequency of Comorbid Disorders. In the NCS-R data set, current DSM-5 IED was most frequently associated with current anxiety disorder (45.8%), followed by current substance use (23.9%), depressive (22.3%), posttraumatic stress (13.4%), and bipolar (8.4%) disorder. The pattern of results for lifetime comorbidity with IED was similar, but with higher frequency for each disorder: current anxiety disorder (58.7%), followed by any current substance use (41.0%), depressive (38.6%), bipolar (16.8%), and posttraumatic stress (16.5%) disorder. In the clinical research data set, current DSM-5 IED was most frequently associated with any current depressive disorder (21.1%), followed by anxiety (20.1%) and posttraumatic stress (11.7%) disorder; the remaining current disorders came in below 2.4%. The pattern of results for lifetime comorbidity with IED was similar except that lifetime

Table 2 Comorbidity of IED With Other Adult Psychiatric Syndromal Disorders

Adult Disorders	Current Comorbidity NCS-R Reanalysis OR (95% CI) [% IED vs. % Non-IED]	Lifetime Comorbidity NCS-R Reanalysis OR (95% CI) [% IED vs. % Non-IED]	Current Comorbidity Clinical Research Analysis OR (95% CI) [% IED vs. % Non-IED]	Lifetime Comorbidity Clinical Research Analysis OR (95% CI) [% IED vs. % Non-IED]
Bipolar Dx[1]	4.22 (2.99–5.99) [8.4% vs. 1.3%]	3.98 (2.95–5.41) [16.8% vs. 4.0%]	N/A	N/A
Depressive Dx[1,2,3]	3.04 (2.32–3.98) [22.3% vs. 7.5%]	2.83 (2.27–3.55) [38.6% vs. 19.3%]	2.07 (1.55–2.75) [21.1% vs. 10.5%]	4.98 (3.97–6.21) [59.7% vs. 22.7%]
Anxiety Dx[1,2,4]	4.17 (3.16–5.46) [45.8% vs. 16.4%]	3.89 (3.13–4.83) [58.7% vs. 27.5%]	2.70 (1.55–2.76) [20.1% vs. 10.9%]	2.92 (2.23–3.83) [27.2% vs. 11.7%]
Substance Use Dx[1,2]	3.98 (3.03–5.24) [23.9% vs. 5.1%]	3.79 (3.03–4.74) [41.0% vs. 12.9%]	N/A	4.13 (3.27–5.21) [46.7% vs. 17.1%]
Posttraumatic Stress Dx[1,2]	3.89 (2.74–5.52) [13.4% vs. 3.3%]	3.69 (2.73–4.98) [17.1% vs. 6.1%]	4.42 (2.75–7.14) 11.1% vs. 2.6%	6.63 (4.24–10.31) [16.4% vs. 3.0%]
Anorexia Nervosa[1,2]	N/A [0.0% vs. 0.0%]	1.20 (0.16–9.17) [0.3% vs. 0.2%]	0.52 (0.06–4.78) [0.2% vs. 0.4%]	2.04 (0.96–4.31) [2.5% vs. 1.4%]
Bulimia Nervosa[1,2]	8.33 (2.26–31.25) [1.3% vs. 0.1%]	4.13 (1.82–9.35) [1.9% vs. 0.5%]	3.98 (0.41–38.46) [0.5% vs. 0.1%]	1.20 (0.49–2.92) [1.6% vs. 1.1%]
Binge Eating Dx[1,2]	2.40 (0.73–7.87) [1.3% vs. 0.5%]	2.61 (1.33–5.12) [2.7% vs. 1.1%]	2.56 (1.07–6.10) [2.4% vs. 0.9%]	6.94 (2.82–16.95) [4.2% vs. 0.6%]
Obs-Comp Dx[2]	N/A	N/A	4.40 (1.36–14.29) [1.9% vs. 0.4%]	5.26 (2.35–11.76) [4.2% vs. 0.9%]
Non-IED Impulse Control Dx[2]	N/A	N/A	5.49 (1.45–20.83) [1.5% vs. 0.3%]	7.04 (2.64–18.52) [3.5% vs. 0.5%]

Notes: 1 = NCS-R Reanalysis; 2 = Coccaro (Data on File); 3 = Coccaro (2018) (Dep Dx submitted); 4 = Coccaro (2018) (Anx Dx submitted); 6 = Jennings, Wildes, and Coccaro (2017).

Table 3 Comorbidity of IED With Personality Disorders

Personality Disorder	Current Comorbidity (IED vs. Other) Clinical Research Analysis OR (95% CI) [% IED vs. % Non-IED]	Lifetime Comorbidity (IED vs. Other) Clinical Research Analysis OR (95% CI) [% IED vs. % Non-IED]
PD cluster group[1]		
Odd	3.26 (2.30–4.16) [18.2% vs. 5.6%]	4.41 (2.99–6.49) [18.0% vs. 4.4%]
Dramatic	3.92 (3.50–5.65) [46.9% vs. 14.7%]	8.00 (6.06–10.53) [48.2% vs. 10.2%]
Anxious	1.84 (1.42–2.39) [25.0% vs. 14.7%]	2.51 (1.92–3.29) [26.6% vs. 12.4%]
NOS	2.77 (2.18–3.52) [32.4% vs. 15.2%]	3.08 (2.40–3.94) [31.0% vs. 14.4%]
PDs associated with IED[1]		
Paranoid PD	4.10 (2.80–5.95) [17.3% vs. 4.2%]	6.02 (3.88–9.35) [16.9% vs. 3.1%]
Antisocial PD	5.81 (3.97–8.55) [31.8% vs. 9.0%]	17.86 (10.00–32.26) [33.0% vs. 5.6%]
Borderline PD	4.52 (3.39–6.06) [20.3% vs. 3.9%]	9.62 (6.76–13.89) [21.0% vs. 1.6%]
Narcissistic PD	2.69 (1.85–3.92) [13.5% vs. 4.9%]	4.33 (2.82–6.67) [14.3% vs. 3.3%]
Obsessive -Compulsive PD	2.28 (1.66–3.14) [17.6% vs. 8.0%]	3.17 (2.25–4.48) [18.6% vs. 6.5%]

Note: 1 =Includes data from Coccaro et al. (2018) with more recent (unpublished) data.

substance use disorder (46.7%) followed depressive disorder (59.7%), instead of any anxiety disorder (27.2%); frequency of the other lifetime disorders was similar as with current disorders (e.g., posttraumatic stress disorder: 16.4%). Thus the most frequent comorbid classes of syndromal adult psychiatric disorders appear to be depressive, anxiety, substance use, and post-traumatic stress disorders. We discuss IED comorbidity with syndromal psychiatric disorders in greater detail along with the odds ratios for each comparison. Exploration of odds ratios provides insight as to the level of risk that each disorder is associated with IED regardless of the frequency that that disorder has in those with IED.

Mood Disorders: Bipolar Disorder (Table 2). Given that agitated, aggressive, and impulsive behavior is often present in bipolar disorder some clinical investigators suggest a relationship between these two disorders (McElroy, Soutullo, Beckman, Taylor Jr., & Keck Jr., 1998). For example, the co-occurrence of the two was reported as greater than half in one clinical study in which some individuals with IED by DSM-IV criteria appeared to have "micro-manic episodes" with manic-like affective symptoms (e.g., irritability, increased energy, and racing thoughts) occurring prior to, and during, aggressive episodes in up to 62%–99% of cases (McElroy et al., 1998). For nearly all other published studies, the current co-occurrence of bipolar disorder (BP I and BP II) is treated as exclusionary for the diagnosis of IED. Despite this, the lifetime co-occurrence rate of IED and bipolar disorder is not zero. In at least two published clinical studies, where such data were available, the lifetime co-occurrence of these two disorders was about 10% (Coccaro, Posternak, & Zimmerman, 2005; Kessler et al., 2006). In our NCS-R reanalysis we found significant comorbidity for current bipolar disorder in those with DSM-5 IED with an elevated odds ratio of at least fourfold for current IED with current bipolar disorder and an elevated odds ratio of fourfold for lifetime IED with lifetime bipolar disorder. The frequency of IED comorbid with bipolar disorder was 8.4% for current comorbidity and 16.8% for lifetime morbidity. The presence of bipolar disorder did not rule out IED in these cases, however, because age of onset of IED was earlier than that of bipolar disorder in each case by a mean difference of about 7 years indicating a substantial period of time when IED was present in the absence of bipolar disorder. While this suggests delimitation of the two disorders, it is possible that the early presence of IED may be a harbinger of a later bipolar disorder that has not yet clinically emerged.

Mood Disorders: Depressive Disorder (Table 2). In early clinical studies, lifetime IED, diagnosed using either Research or DSM-IV criteria, has been reported to co-occur with depressive disorder three to four more often relative to depressive disorder among those with non-IED disorders (Coccaro, 2011; Coccaro et al., 1998, 2005). In our NCS-R reanalysis, the odds ratio for current IED was threefold higher in those with current depressive disorder (major depression and dysthymia) without difference as a function of the type of depressive disorder; the odds ratio was similarly high for lifetime IED with lifetime depressive disorder. The frequency of IED with depressive disorder was 22.3% for current comorbidity and nearly twice that for lifetime comorbidity (38.6%). In our clinical research data set, current

DSM-5 IED was also significantly associated with current depressive disorder (i.e., major depression, persistent depressive disorder, or other specified depressive disorder) without difference as a function of the type of depressive disorder. The odds ratio trended up to two- to five-fold for current and lifetime comorbidity, respectively, and the frequency ranged from about a fifth for current comorbidity to nearly three-fifths for lifetime comorbidity making depressive disorder a key comorbid disorder occurring with IED.

Mood Disorders: Disruptive Mood Dysregulation Disorder (DMDD). The DSM-5 criteria sets for IED and DMDD are very similar and have only two important differences. First, DMDD requires three, as opposed to two, impulsive aggressive outbursts per week and, second, DMDD requires that persistent anger and/or irritability be present (e.g., ≥50% of the time) in between impulsive aggressive outbursts. DMDD was developed to enable clinicians to utilize a nonbipolar diagnosis for children/adolescents who are persistently irritable, and who have frequent temper tantrums, but who do not otherwise meet criteria for pediatric bipolar disorder. Most importantly, empiric data demonstrates that DMDD is not related to bipolar disorder and that DMDD should be diagnosed instead of pediatric bipolar disorder when DMDD criteria are met (Fava & Leibenluft, 2018). In those with DMDD, the diagnosis of IED should not be made when the age of onset of the aggressive outbursts occurs prior to 10 years of age. Despite the similarities in the two disorders, we have found that DMDD criteria are, otherwise, not met in the vast majority of adults with DSM-5 IED since 92% of all DSM-5 individuals studied have short-lived periods of inter-outburst anger averaging less than 40% of the time between outbursts (Coccaro, 2018a). Further examination found that only 2% of the remaining individuals could have met DSM-5 criteria for DMDD. Thus it is unlikely that the presence of IED in adulthood is better explained by DMDD.

Anxiety Disorders (Table 2). Similar to depressive disorders, lifetime IED has also been associated with anxiety disorders in early clinical studies (Coccaro et al., 2005). In our NCS-R reanalysis, we found an elevated odds ratio of fourfold for current DSM-5 IED with any current DSM-5 anxiety disorder (Panic Disorder, Social Phobia, Simple Phobia, Generalized Anxiety Disorder, and Anxiety Disorder-Not Otherwise Specified); the same was true for lifetime comorbidity. The findings from our clinical research data set were similar except that the odds ratio for current anxiety disorder with IED was significantly lower.

Addictive Disorders: Substance Use Disorders (Table 2). Similar to depressive and anxiety disorders, IED has also been associated with several substance use disorders (SUD) such as alcohol and other drugs of abuse in early clinical studies (Coccaro et al., 2005). In our NCS-R reanalysis, the odds ratio for DSM-5 IED with SUD was about fourfold for current and lifetime comorbidity. Among the SUDs, significant comorbidity was observed for IED comorbidity with: alcohol use disorder [15.1% vs. 2.0%; OR = 5.26 (95% CI: 3.53–7.81)], cannabis use disorder [7.1% vs. 0.6%; OR = 6.45 (95% CI: 3.56–11.63)], and for nicotine use disorder [14.3% vs. 3.1%; OR = 4.24 (95% CI: 2.86–6.29)], Coccaro, Fanning, & Lee, 2017. In our clinical research data set, where current SUD was exclusionary for study entry, the odds ratio for lifetime IED with lifetime SUD was fourfold with a substantial frequency of nearly fifty percent (46.7%). Thus these three substance use disorders appear to account for the relationship between SUDs overall and IED.

Addictive Disorders: Behavioral Addictive Disorders. In its most recent edition, DSM-5 moved Pathological Gambling Disorder (PGD) from the Impulse Control Disorders section to the Addictions section. The NCS-R community survey including pathological gambling disorder (PGD) late in its study and such data was available in only a third of all NCS-R respondents. While an early paper (Kessler et al., 2008) suggested significant comorbidity between DSM-IV PGD and DSM-IV IED, our NCS-R reanalysis revealed no cases in which current DSM-5 IED was comorbid with current DSM-5 PGD. When examined as a function of lifetime comorbidity, no difference was seen between the rates of the two disorders [0.9% vs. 1.1%, OR = 0.82 (95% CI: 0.11–6.05), $P = .846$]. Analysis of our clinical research data, however, finds a statistically significant increase in comorbidity between IED and PDG [1.5% vs. 0.2%; OR = 6.65 (95% CI: 1.43–30.90), $P < .05$]. The number of comorbid cases was small but onset of IED preceded that of PGD in nearly all cases (88%) and the age of onset of IED preceded that of PGD by about 7 years (9.2 ± 3.4 years vs. 17.0 ± 8.6 years) PDG. Thus of the different potentially comorbid disorders studied, PDG seemed to have one of the weaker comorbidities with IED. To our knowledge there is no data on the comorbidity of IED with other behavioral addictive disorders.

Trauma and Stress Disorders: Posttraumatic Stress Disorder (Table 2). DSM-5 Posttraumatic Stress Disorder (PTSD) is the only trauma and stress disorder with a specific diagnostic criterion related to aggression. Accordingly, an excess of IED with PTSD should be expected. In our NCS-R reanalysis, the increase in odds ratio for DSM-5 IED with PTSD was fourfold for current comorbidity and fourfold for lifetime comorbidity. In our clinical research studies, the increase in odds ratio for DSM-5 IED with PTSD was similar, as was the frequency of comorbidity for both current and lifetime disorders.

Trauma and Stress Disorders: Adjustment Disorder. While adjustment disorder was not included in the NCS-R data set, analysis of our clinical research data set reveals a nonsignificant increase in current Adjustment Disorder in those with current IED [1.6% vs. 0.9%; OR=1.60 (95% CI: 0.76–4.63, P=.232)]. Thus this preliminary data suggests IED may not be associated with adjustment disorder, but further research in the area is needed.

Eating Disorders (Table 2). Epidemiologic studies suggest overlap among eating disorders, particularly bulimic spectrum disorders, and intermittent explosive disorder (IED). (Fernandez-Aranda et al., 2006; Hudson, Hiripi, Pope, & Kessler, 2007; Kessler et al., 2013). In our NCS-R reanalysis, an elevated odds ratio was observed for current DSM-5 and current bulimia only. Analysis of the clinical research data set (which did not include individuals younger than 18 years of age), however, found an elevated odds ratio for both IED and Bulimia Nervosa for both current and lifetime disorders and for lifetime IED and Binge Eating Disorder. That said our clinical research data set had far fewer individuals with eating disorders than the NCS-R data set. Thus the presence of IED appears to increase the risk of binge eating which occurs in both bulimia nervosa and binge eating disorder.

Obsessive-Compulsive and Related Disorders: Obsessive Compulsive Disorder (Table 2). While data on Obsessive Compulsive Disorder (OCD) is not available from the NCS-R study, analysis of our clinical research data set reveals a nearly 10-fold increase in current OCD in those with current DSM-5 IED. The increase in odds ratio for lifetime comorbidity, however, was much lower at nearly threefold. Given the small number of comorbid cases in both sets of analyses, however, these data must be viewed with caution until future studies are conducted.

Other Impulse Control Disorders (Table 2). In addition to IED, the current DSM-5 Impulse Control Disorders (ICD) include Pyromania, Kleptomania, and Conduct Disorder and Oppositional Defiant Disorder (formally in the DSM-IV section entitled, "Disorders First Appearing in Childhood"). While the latter two disorders have been included in recent community surveys (and will be discussed later), neither pyromania nor kleptomania has been included in any community survey. Analysis of our clinical research data set reveals only a small number of individuals with current or past DSM-5 IED and lifetime Pyromania ($n=7$), Kleptomania ($n=6$), or Impulse Control Disorder-Not Otherwise Specified ($n=4$) and so we chose to examine all impulse control disorders (ICD; $n=8$ for current, $n=18$ for lifetime). While the association of current DSM-5 IED in those with current ICD was small in proportion, the comorbidity was statistically significant [1.7% vs. 0.3%; Odds Ratio: 6.69 (95% CI: 1.34–33.31), $P<.05$]. The association of lifetime IED with lifetime ICD was larger in magnitude [3.5% vs. 0.4%; Odds Ratio: 9.03 (95% CI: 2.60–31.38), $P<.001$]. While the data are limited, IED appears to show evidence of increased comorbidity with other impulse control disorders.

Disruptive Behavior Disorders First Appearing in Childhood. The nature of the relationship between IED and Disruptive Behavior Disorders as conceptualized in the DSM-IV [DBDs: Conduct Disorder (CD), Oppositional Defiant Disorder (ODD) and Attention Deficit/Hyperactivity Disorder (ADHD)]. This grouping was changed in DSM-5 with CD and ODD reassigned to the Disruptive and Impulse Control Disorders section. Examining this group is important because both sets of disorders begin before adulthood and clinicians, often, do not make the diagnosis of IED in the presence of these DBDs.

Some degree of co-occurrence between IED and DBDs is expected because some form of aggression and/or impulsivity (which is related to aggression) is included in the diagnostic criteria set for each disorder. Examples of predatory/premeditated aggression (e.g., robbery, extortion, sexual abuse, physical cruelty) are described in the CD criteria; examples of impulsive aggression (e.g., arguing, temper tantrums) are described in the ODD criteria; and examples of impulsivity (e.g., blurts out answers, interrupts others), but not aggression, are described in the ADHD criteria.

For example, in our NCS-R reanalysis, the order of frequency of current IED with DBD was highest for ADHD (14.3%), followed by CD (5.9%), and ODD (5.0%), with elevated odds ratios five-fold, or greater, for each. Odds ratios for lifetime comorbidity were similarly high although the order of frequency was flipped for ADHD (18.5%) and CD (22.7%); the frequency for ODD was 21.8%. Interestingly, comorbidity of any DBD with IED was associated with an increase in aggression score suggesting a synergy with DBD and IED with respect to aggression. Thus, a history of a DBD may well place an adult at greater risk of IED and of greater aggressiveness than IED alone.

Personality Disorders (Table 3). Impulsive and/or aggressive behavior is frequently observed in those with DSM-5 Personality Disorders, especially in those belonging to "dramatic cluster" (i.e., antisocial, borderline, histrionic, and narcissistic) personality disorders even though features related to impulsivity and/or aggression are only formally included in the diagnostic criteria for antisocial and borderline personality disorders. IED is also comorbid with other personality disorders such as paranoid, narcissistic, and obsessive compulsive personality disorders, none of which include impulsivity or aggression as a diagnostic criterion. In fact, it is difficult to know the true extent of comorbidity between IED and personality disorder in general because individuals with DSM-5 IED are also highly likely to meet the general criteria for DSM-5 Personality Disorder simply by having affect (e.g., anger) dysregulation and by having dysfunction in interpersonal relationships due to frequent impulsive aggressive outbursts. Moreover, we have found that the most frequent (though not greatest risk) personality disorder seen in those with IED is Personality Disorder-Not Otherwise Specified (PD-NOS) suggesting that the two go hand in hand because of the fluid diagnostic boundaries for personality disorder.

Not surprisingly, we found the frequency of current DSM-5 IED with comorbid dramatic cluster personality disorder was highest at 46.9% compared with 34.2% for PD-NOS, 25.0% for anxious cluster, and 18.2% for odd cluster personality disorders. Among the 10 specific personality disorder diagnoses, only five were associated with current or lifetime DSM-5 IED. In order of frequency, these were as follows: Antisocial PD (AsPD: 31.8% current; 33.0% lifetime), Borderline PD (BPD: 20.3% current; 21.0% lifetime), Obsessive-Compulsive PD (OC-PD: 17.6% current; 18.6% lifetime), Paranoid PD (PARA-PD: 17.3% current; 16.9% lifetime), and Narcissistic PD (NARC-PD: 13.5% current; 14.3% lifetime). Examination of all personality disorder traits revealed a significant association with five traits with elevated, and two traits with reduced, odds ratios for IED. Odds ratios for the former traits were as follows: "Intense Anger" in BPD [OR=62.50 (95% CI: 37.04–111.11)], "Irritability/Aggressiveness" in ASPD [OR=8.06 (95% CI: 4.18–15.63)], "Rigidity/Stubbornness" in OCPD [OR=2.79 (95% CI; 1.71–4.55)], "Arrogant/Haughty" in NARC PD [OR=2.25 (95% CI: 1.10–4.78)], and "Bears Grudges" in PARA-PD [−OR=2.27 (95% CI: 1.29–3.98)]. The latter two traits were as follows: "Reluctance to Confide" in PARA-PD [−OR=0.52 (95% CI: 0.23–0.94)] and "Rapid Shifting/Shallow Expression of Emotions"

HIST-PD [−3; OR=0.47 (95% CI: 0.23–0.95)]. Thus while IED is comorbid with selective personality disorders, it is most related to personality traits related to anger and aggressiveness/irritability as well as traits that increase the likelihood of perceiving social threat in interactions with others (rigidity, stubbornness, arrogance, grudge bearing).

Age of Onset and Temporal Order of IED and Comorbid Disorders (Table 4A)

As shown before, IED has a rich pattern of comorbidity across several classes of psychiatric disorders. Examination of the relative age of onset, and temporal order, of IED and comorbid disorders provides insight into the nature of this comorbidity. Based on both the NCS-R and our own clinical research data sets, DSM-5 IED becomes apparent by childhood/early adolescence (Mean±SD: 13.4±6.8 years and 14.2±6.8 years from these respective data sets). Mean age of onset of IED typically precedes that of most comorbid disorders examined including mood, nonphobic anxiety (e.g., Panic Disorder, GAD, Anxiety Disorder-NOS), substance use, and trauma and stress disorders among others. The one exception for adult psychiatric disorders was for the age of onset of phobic anxiety disorders (e.g., Specific Phobia, Social Phobia), which have their onset about 4 years prior to the onset of IED, peaking during childhood. With the exception of phobic anxiety disorders, DSM-5 IED onsets about 4 to 7 years before the most frequent comorbid disorders in the NCS-R data set (see Table 4A). A similar result was observed in our clinical research data set ranging from nearly 2 to 10 years. Table 4B shows that the temporal order of onset for IED occurs before these disorders at a rate ranging from 58.7% to 82.2% for the NCS-R data set and from 50.9% to 81.2% for the clinical research data set, compared with the range of a comorbid disorder occurring before IED of 11.7% to 31.7% and 14.0% to 40.5% for the two data sets, respectively. The proportions for simultaneous onset of IED and comorbid disorder were lowest for both NCS-R and clinical research data sets. Thus for nearly all disorders examined, IED appears before the comorbid disorder indicating that the comorbid disorder in question does not lead to IED, though IED may increase the risk of the future comorbid disorder. It is also possible that IED and the comorbid disorders share an underlying propensity for both disorders in which IED appears first (see Table 4B).

Table 4A Mean Age of Onset (±SD) of IED in Individuals With Comorbid Adult Disorders

	NCS-R Reanalysis		Clinical Research Analysis	
Adult Disorder	**IED Age of Onset**	**Comorbid Dx Age of Onset**	**IED Age of Onset**	**Comorbid Dx Age of Onset**
Bipolar Disorder	14.6±7.1***	21.5±10.8	N/A	N/A
Depressive Disorder	14.8±7.2***	20.9±11.5	13.9±5.9***	23.6±10.4
Anxiety Disorder	13.6±7.1	10.6±8.3***	14.0±6.2*	16.1±10.4
Nonphobic Anxiety Disorder	16.2±8.3***	20.0±10.4	14.1±6.1***	21.4±10.6
Phobic Anxiety Disorder	13.8±7.3	8.1±5.1***	13.9±6.0	11.5±6.8**
Substance Use Disorder	12.3±5.5***	19.5±6.8	14.2±6.8***	20.2±6.2
Posttraumatic Stress Disorder	15.4±8.2*	20.2±12.9	13.5±5.9†	15.4±9.0

Notes: *$P<.05$, **$P<.01$, ***$P<.001$, †$P<.075$, by paired t-test.

Table 4B Temporal Association of Disorder Onset in Individuals With IED and Comorbid Diagnoses

	NCS-R Reanalysis			Clinical Research Analysis		
Adult Disorders	**IED First**	**IED Second**	**Same Age**	**IED First**	**IED Second**	**Same Age**
Any Bipolar Disorder	75.8%*	14.5%	9.7%	N/A	N/A	N/A
Any Depressive Disorder	64.8%*	27.6%	7.6%	81.2%*	14.0%	4.8%
Any Anxiety Disorder	27.3%	64.8%*	7.9%	45.3%	44.8%	9.9%
Any Nonphobic Anxiety Disorder	59.3%*	31.5%	9.3%	70.3%*	25.4%	4.3%
Any Phobic Anxiety Disorder	23.3%	68.8%*	7.9%	21.8%	66.4%*	11.8%
Any Substance Use Disorder	82.2%*	11.7%	6.1%	76.7%*	19.3%	4.0%
Posttraumatic Stress Disorder	58.7%*	31.7%	9.5%	50.9%	40.5%	8.6%

Notes: *$P<.05$ by Sign Test.

Magnitude of Aggression Scores as a Function of Comorbidity

An important consideration in understanding the nature of the comorbidity between IED and other disorders is how levels of aggression compare between those with IED alone, with the comorbid disorder alone, and those with both disorders (and compared with healthy and psychiatric controls). Table 5 shows that, for all relevant comorbid disorders, mean (± sem) scores of Life History of Aggression (LHA; after correcting for demographic variables) were higher for the comorbid disorder alone compared with both psychiatric and healthy controls. Notably, mean LHA scores for those with DSM-5 IED alone were substantially higher than those among those with the comorbid disorder alone (or any other non-IED group) and that the combination of DSM-5 IED with the comorbid disorder resulted in mean LHA scores of similar magnitude of those with IED alone. This strongly suggests that high aggression scores go with aggressive disorders (IED) regardless of the presence of the comorbid disorder since those with IED alone are as aggressive as those with IED and another comorbid disorder and, in turn, more aggressive than those with the comorbid disorder alone. Where data were available, we have also shown that scores relevant to the severity of depression, anxiety, and substance use display the complementary pattern in which, for example, high mean depression scores are observed in those with depressive disorder alone and in those with IED and depressive disorder.

Table 5 Life History of Aggression Score as a Function of Adult Disorder Comorbidity With IED: Clinical Research Analysis (ANCOVA Marginal Means ± SEM)

Adult Disorders[a]	HC	PC	Comorbid Disorder	IED	IED + Comorbid Disorder
Depressive Disorder	4.8 ± 0.2	7.3 ± 0.3	9.0 ± 0.3	18.0 ± 0.3	17.9 ± 0.2[b]
Anxiety Disorder	4.8 ± 0.2	7.8 ± 0.3	8.6 ± 0.5	18.0 ± 0.2	17.7 ± 0.4[b]
Substance Use Disorder	4.8 ± 0.2	7.3 ± 0.3	9.3 ± 0.4	17.6 ± 0.3	18.3 ± 0.3[b]
Posttraumatic Stress Disorder	4.8 ± 0.2	7.8 ± 0.2	10.5 ± 0.9	17.7 ± 0.2	19.1 ± 0.5[c]
"Aggressive" Personality Disorder	4.8 ± 0.2	7.3 ± 0.3	9.7 ± 0.4	17.2 ± 0.3	18.5 ± 0.5[c]

[a]AsPD, BPD, NARC-PD, PARA-PD, OC-PD.
[b]IED + Comorbid Dx = IED > Comorbid Dx > PC > HC.
[c]IED + Comorbid Dx > IED > Comorbid Dx > PC > HC.
Notes: *HC*, healthy controls; *PC*, psychiatric controls; *IED*, intermittenet explosive disorder.

Summary

From a cross-sectional viewpoint, IED, as with other DSM-5 disorders, frequently occurs with other psychiatric and personality disorders. In fact, analyses of extant data suggest that the extent of comorbidity of IED with other syndromal psychiatric disorders is about the same as is the extent of comorbidity of other syndromal psychiatric (e.g., mood, anxiety, substance use disorders) with other syndromal psychiatric disorders. The most common disorders include mood, anxiety, substance use, and posttraumatic stress disorders with the most common personality disorders including antisocial, borderline, obsessive compulsive, narcissistic, and obsessive-compulsive personality disorders. Among personality disorder traits, IED is most frequently associated with anger and aggression/irritability and with personality disordered traits that increase the likelihood of perceiving social threat in interactions with others (rigidity, stubbornness, arrogance, grudge bearing). Importantly, with the exception of phobic anxiety disorders (i.e., social and simple phobias), the mean age of onset of IED is lower than that of other syndromal psychiatric disorders and typically begins before the comorbid disorder in question. Further, aggression scores of those with IED and the comorbid disorder in question are similar to those who have IED but not the comorbid disorder in question and higher than that in those without IED but with the comorbid disorder in question. Where available, we have also found that behavioral scores relevant to other psychiatric disorders go with the presence of the comorbid disorder regardless of the presence of IED (Coccaro, 2012, 2018b, 2018c). For example, aggression scores are highest in those with IED and depressive disorder with IED while depression scores are highest in those with depressive disorder alone and in those with IED and depressive disorder. This strongly suggests a separation of aggression and other psychopathology in those with IED and other psychiatric disorders. Accordingly, these data support the idea that when recurrent, problematic, impulsive aggression is sufficient to make the diagnosis of IED, the diagnosis of IED should be made in the presence of other syndromal psychiatric/personality disorders unless there is evidence that impulsive aggressive behaviors only occur during the course of a comorbid disorder.

References

American Psychiatric Association (Ed.), (1980). *Diagnostic and statistical manual of mental disorders* (3rd ed.). Washington, DC: American Psychiatric Association.

American Psychiatric Association (Ed.), (1994). *Diagnostic and statistical manual of mental disorders* (4th ed.). Washington, DC: American Psychiatric Association.

American Psychiatric Association (Ed.), (2013). *Diagnostic and statistical manual of mental disorders* (5th ed.). Washington, DC: American Psychiatric Association.

Coccaro, E. F. (2011). Intermittent explosive disorder: Development of integrated research criteria for Diagnostic and Statistical Manual of Mental Disorders, Fifth Edition. *Comprehensive Psychiatry, 52*(2), 119–125.

Coccaro, E. F. (2012). Intermittent explosive disorder as a disorder of impulsive aggression for DSM-5. *The American Journal of Psychiatry, 169*, 577–588.

Coccaro, E. F. (2018a). DSM-5 intermittent explosive disorder: Relationship with disruptive mood dysregulation disorder. *Comprehensive Psychiatry, 84*, 118–121.

Coccaro, E. F. (2018b). Comorbidity between mood disorders and intermittent explosive disorder. *Journal of Affective Disorders*, [Under Review].

Coccaro, E. F. (2018c). Comorbidity between anxiety disorders and intermittent explosive disorder. *Journal of Anxiety Disorders*, [Under Review].

Coccaro, E. F., Fanning, J. R., & Lee, R. (2017). Intermittent explosive disorder and substance use disorder: Analysis of the National Comorbidity Survey Replication Sample. *The Journal of Clinical Psychiatry, 78*(6), 697–702.

Coccaro, E. F., Kavoussi, R. J., Berman, M. E., & Lish, J. D. (1998). Intermittent explosive disorder-revised: Development, reliability, and validity of research criteria. *Comprehensive Psychiatry, 39*(6), 368–376.

Coccaro, E. F., Posternak, M. A., & Zimmerman, M. (2005). Prevalence and features of intermittent explosive disorder in a clinical setting. *The Journal of Clinical Psychiatry, 66*(10), 1221–1227.

Coccaro, E. F., Shima, C. K., & Lee, R. J. (2018). Comorbidity of personality disorder with Intermittent Explosive Disorder. *Journal of Psychiatric Research, 106*, 15–21.

Fava, M., & Leibenluft, E. (2018). Aggression in unipolar mood disorders. In E. F. Coccaro & M. S. McCloskey (Eds.), *Aggression across the diagnostic spectrum*. Washington, DC: American Psychiatric Press, Inc.

Fernandez-Aranda, F., Jimenez-Murcia, S., Alvarez-Moya, E. M., Granero, R., Vallejo, J., & Bulik, C. M. (2006). Impulse control disorders in eating disorders: Clinical and therapeutic implications. *Comprehensive Psychiatry, 47*, 482–488.

Hudson, J. I., Hiripi, E., Pope, E. H., & Kessler, R. C. (2007). The prevalence and correlates of eating disorders in the national comorbidity survey replication. *Biological Psychiatry, 61*, 348–358.

Jennings, K. M., Wildes, J. E., & Coccaro, E. F. (2017). Intermittent explosive disorder and eating disorders: Analysis of national comorbidity and research samples. *Comprehensive Psychiatry, 75*, 62–67.

Kessler, R. C., Berglund, P., Chiu, W. T., Demler, O., Heeringa, S., Hiripi, E., et al. (2004). The US National Comorbidity Survey Replication (NCS-R): design and field procedures. *International Journal of Methods in Psychiatric Research, 13*, 69–92.

Kessler, R. C., Berglund, P. A., Chiu, W. T., Deitz, A. C., Hudson, J. I., Shahly, V., et al. (2013). The prevalence and correlates of binge eating disorder in the World Health Organization World mental health surveys. *Biological Psychiatry, 73*, 904–914.

Kessler, R. C., Coccaro, E. F., Fava, M., Jaeger, S., Jin, R., & Walters, E. (2006). The prevalence and correlates of DSM-IV intermittent explosive disorder in the National Comorbidity Survey Replication. *Archives of General Psychiatry, 63*(6), 669–678.

Kessler, R. C., Hwang, I., LaBrie, R., Petukhova, M., Sampson, N. A., & Shaffer, H. J. (2008). DSM-IV pathological gambling in the National Comorbidity Survey Replication. *Psychological Medicine*, *38*(9), 1351–1360.

McElroy, S. L., Soutullo, C. A., Beckman, D. A., Taylor, P., Jr., & Keck, P. E., Jr. (1998). DSM-IV intermittent explosive disorder: A report of 27 cases. *The Journal of Clinical Psychiatry*, *59*(4), 203–210.

Further Reading

Coccaro, E. F., Schmidt, C. S., Samuels, J., & Nestadt, G. (2004). Lifetime and one-month prevalence rates of Intermittent Explosive Disorder in a community sample. *The Journal of Clinical Psychiatry*, *65*, 820–824.

PART II

Etiology and Correlates

CHAPTER FIVE

Neurotransmitters and Intermittent Explosive Disorder

Royce J. Lee, Emil F. Coccaro
Clinical Neuroscience & Psychopharmacology Research Unit, Department of Psychiatry and Behavioral Neuroscience, Pritzker School of Medicine, University of Chicago, Chicago, IL, United States

Contents

Introduction

How does disturbed neural signaling lead to impulsive aggression and IED? The dominant theory remains the serotonergic hypothesis. Over the last 2 decades, an exponentially expanding literature from the clinical neurosciences has helped us to understand how variation in serotonin signaling triggers aggressive outbursts. At the same time, research has followed threads of connection from serotonin signaling in the synapse to a wide brain network and further out into the body's immune and metabolic systems. The issue of neurotransmission in IED, as with other neuropsychiatric disorders, is increasingly seen from a systems neuroscience perspective.

Intermittent Explosive Disorder
https://doi.org/10.1016/B978-0-12-813858-8.00005-X

This chapter will summarize what we know about neurotransmitters in IED within a coherent conceptual model of disturbed neural circuit function that incorporates neurotransmitters, neuromodulators, and other signaling molecules.

Relevance of Social-Emotional Information Processing and Predictive Encoding

The role of neurotransmission in IED is complex and not reducible to a "chemical imbalance." This is due, in part, to the fact that brain signaling molecules do not always have a specific relationship to single instances or even recurrent patterns of behavior. The computational functions of the brain are complex enough that often the same signaling molecule involved in one circuit may be present in another circuit with opposite action. An example of this may be the role of dopamine signaling in the direct and indirect pathways of the striatum or the role of GABAergic signaling in hidden layer networks. Whereas intuitive models can be simple to understand, they may lack the sophistication required when applied to complex systems. Given the relevance of serotonergic function to IED, an impactful model would need to include markers of serotonin function in conjunction with other biological and psychological factors. Here we would propose a *social-emotional information processing (SEIP)/predictive coding* theory in order to organize the existing knowledge on neurotransmitters in impulsive aggression in a biologically plausible framework. To explain the model next two paragraphs will define SEIP and predictive coding.

SEIP was developed to understand the cycle of cognitions and actions of aggression in children (Crick & Dodge, 1994; Dodge, 1993). In the SEIP model, there are six phases of the aggressive response: (1) social information encoding, (2) attribution of the intent of the behavior of the other participant in the social interaction, (3) clarification of goals, (4) response generation, (5) response evaluation, and (6) response enactment. Evidence supports the validity of the SEIP model in adults with impulsive aggression. Adults with IED have reduced encoding of social cues (Coccaro, Lee, & Kavoussi, 2009; Coccaro, Noblett, & McCloskey, 2009), heightened hostile attribution and intensified negative emotional response (Coccaro, Fanning, & Lee, 2016; Coccaro, Keedy, et al., 2016; Coccaro, Lee, et al., 2016; Coccaro, Lee, & Gozal, 2016), and a bias to choose directly, or relationally, aggressive responses to socially ambiguous cues. Although biological correlates of SEIP stages have been identified, how these stages are dynamically coded by the brain is difficult to study without modeling approaches. *Predictive coding* provides such a model.

Predictive encoding, first developed as a computational model of consciousness (Friston, Stephan, Montague, & Rolan, 2014), has been applied to the function of the NMDA receptor (Corlett, Honey, & Fletcher, 2016) and brain circuits in psychosis (Sterzer et al., 2018). In the predictive encoding model, cortical brain networks learn and develop through a form of Bayesian inference. Cortical brain network activity is dedicated to generating probabilistic predictions that are updated by new sensory data, informing the next prediction in a recurrent loop. What is being predicted? For humans, who are social mammals, reward and stressors are among the most powerful engines of behavior. Such processes are codified in the brain through the frontostriatal circuits computing temporal difference (TD) error (Wolpert, Doya, & Kawato, 2003).

In humans with impulsive aggression, dysfunction in three brain circuits has been identified. These three circuits are part of a *SEIP/predictive coding* brain network. These include: (1) Ventral prefrontal-amygdala circuits that include the insula and periaqueductal gray involved in fear learning (Coccaro, Fanning, et al., 2016; Coccaro, Keedy, et al., 2016; Coccaro, Lee, Breen, & Irwin, 2015; Coccaro, Lee, et al., 2016; Coccaro, Lee, & Gozal, 2016; Coccaro, Lee, McCloskey, Csernansky, & Wang, 2015; McCloskey et al., 2016), (2) frontostriatal circuits involved in reinforcement learning and cognitive control (Chen, Muggleton, & Chang, 2014; Endrass, Schuermann, Roepke, Kessler-Scheil, & Kathmann, 2016; Heritage & Benning, 2012), and (3) frontoparietal circuits involved in social cognition (Lee et al., 2016). Function of the ventral prefrontal-amygdala circuits corresponds with negative emotional response and encoding of social-emotional information. Function of frontostriatal circuits corresponds with clarification of goals, response generation, and response evaluation (Kogo & Trengove, 2015). Function of the frontoparietal circuits corresponds to attribution of intent in social interaction. Neurotransmitters and neuromodulators play both universal and context-specific roles in all three of these *SEIP/predictive coding* circuits.

The Role of Neuromodulators in Impulsive Aggression and IED

Having broadly reviewed the neural circuit topology implicated in impulsive aggression and IED, it is now possible to intelligently explore how neurotransmitter and neuromodulator function in these circuits plays its role. With respect to the monoamine neurotransmitters and acetylcholine, Kenji Doya has proposed the Metalearning hypothesis of neuromodulator function in learning (Doya, 2002). It proposes that (1) dopamine signals the temporal difference error, acting as a global learning signal; (2) serotonin controls delay discounting, weighing the balance between short- and long-term reward predictions and thus modifying the dopaminergic learning signal; (3) norepinephrine controls surprise, or arousal; and (4) acetylcholine controls the balance between memory encoding, or learning rate, and memory stability.

Serotonin and Impulsive Aggression

According to the Metalearning theory, serotonin signaling in the brain has a computational role in delay discounting. This involves suppression of reflex ive actions under stress and a way of weighing the future compared with today. Experimental data are supportive of the role of serotonin in delay discounting. In human, studies using tryptophan depletion have confirmed that serotonin increases delayed reward discounting in humans (Schweighofer et al., 2008), likely by modifying the dopaminergic temporal difference learning signal in the striatum (Tanaka et al., 2007). How does 5-HT accomplish this?

5-HT neurons in the cortex arise from the rostral 5-HT system, whose cell bodies reside in the midbrain and rostral pons (Piñeyro & Blier, 1999). Cortical neurons, even nonserotonergic neurons, contain 5-HT receptors. Serotonergic signaling is at its global low during REM sleep, is higher in deep sleep, and most active while awake and active. Stress results in marked increases in the release of brain 5-HT (Amat, Matus-Amat, Watkins, & Maier, 1998), and thus it would not be unreasonable to consider serotonin as part of the stress response. Two major subtypes, 5-HT_{1A} and 5-HT_{2A} receptors, are expressed in the majority of prefrontal pyramidal cell neurons and are frequently colocalized (Amargós-Bosch et al., 2004). Cortical excitatory activity is modulated by the predominantly inhibitory 5-HT_{1A} and mixed inhibitory/excitatory 5-HT_2 receptor (Amargós-Bosch et al., 2004). (Aghajanian & Marek, 1997; Jakab & Goldman-Rakic, 1998). 5-HT2a/c receptors are localized in nearly all glutamatergic neurons in the prefrontal cortex (Weber & Andrade, 2010), and are thus ideally distributed to modulate excitatory glutamatergic signaling in the brain. In animal models, disruptions of 5-HT impair delay discounting (Mobini, Chiang,

Ho, Bradshaw, & Szabadi, 2000) and reversal learning (Clarke et al., 2005; Clarke, Walker, Dalley, Robbings, & Roberts, 2007). 5-HT modulation of reward may also occur more directly, as striatal 5-HT2 receptors have been found to inhibit dopamine efflux (Ng, Lee, & Wong, 1999).

Initial human explorations of the serotonin system and aggression involved measurement of 5-hydroxyinoleacetic acid (5-HIAA), the metabolite of 5-HT. First related to suicidal behavior (Åsberg, 1997), low 5-HIAA levels in the cerebrospinal fluid levels were then associated with impulsive aggression (Brown, Goodwin, Ballenger, Goyer, & Major, 1979; Linnoila et al., 1983; Virkkunen, Nuutila, Goodwin, & Linnoila, 1987). Combined with the prescient clinical observation that impulsive aggression was encountered in the personality disordered population, the relationship of the serotonergic system was systematically tested with a series of 5-HT receptor subtype-specific drugs, using neuroendocrine measures as a biological readout of receptor sensitivity. The conclusion of this body of work was that 5-$HT_{2a/c}$ receptor sensitivity is blunted in impulsive aggression (Coccaro, Kavoussi, Cooper, & Hauger, 1997; Coccaro, Kavoussi, & Hauger, 1997; reviewed in Yanowitch & Coccaro, 2011). The findings from pharmacochallenge studies have been confirmed in a meta-analytic review of 171 studies of the serotonin-aggression relationship, with pharmacochallenge studies yielding the strongest ($r=-0.21$), and CSF 5-HIAA concentration studies yielding the smallest ($r=-0.06$) effect size (Duke, Bègue, Bell, & Eisenlohr-Moul, 2013).

These first findings highlighted an important paradox: CSF 5-HIAA level decreases would suggest decreased serotonin signaling in aggression. On the other hand, blunted postsynaptic receptor function likely reflects chronically enhanced serotonin signaling. Is serotonergic function increased or decreased in IED? We will review both sides of the argument.

The strongest evidence for low serotonin signaling in impulsive aggression comes from experimental work in humans manipulating serotonin availability. In humans, depletion of the molecular precursor to serotonin, tryptophan, affects brain function in frontoamygdala circuits. Tryptophan depletion enhances amygdala activation to fearful face stimuli in subjects (Cools et al., 2005), enhances recognition of fearful faces in healthy controls (Harmer, Rogers, Tunbridge, Cowen, & Goodwin, 2003), and causes more severe mood induction following a stressor (Richell, Deakin, & Anderson, 2005). Mixed results have been seen regarding the effects of serotonergic depletion on response inhibition, a subtype of impulsivity (Dougherty, Richard, James, & Mathias, 2010; Rubia et al., 2005). Instead, serotonergic depletion interferes with delay discounting (Dougherty et al., 2010). These alterations in emotion processing and behavioral inhibition explain how tryptophan depletion increases aggressive responding in simulated social provocations (Bjork, Dougherty, Moeller, & Swann, 2000; Bond, Wingrove, & Critchlow, 2001; Cleare & Bond, 1995; Marsh, Dougherty, Moeller, Swann, & Spiga, 2002).

Individuals with IED are particularly susceptible to the effects of tryptophan depletion on mood and affective reactivity, with increased anger and subjectively perceived intensity of angry emotional faces (Lee, Gill, Chen, McCloskey, & Coccaro, 2012). It thus seems that IED is associated with a vulnerability to the effects of low serotonergic tone on the regulation of anger and perception of angry faces. Given the evidence of compromised ventral prefrontal cortical-amygdala connectivity in IED (Coccaro, McCloskey, Fitzgerald, & Phan, 2007), the findings from the acute tryptophan depletion study suggest that serotonin alters social behavior by affecting ventral prefrontal-amygdala functional connectivity. Indeed, a recent tryptophan depletion study in impulsive aggressive individuals confirms this, finding that tryptophan depletion is associated with diminished connectivity between the ventral prefrontal cortex and amygdala (Passamonti et al., 2012). These findings are bolstered by research in borderline personality disorder subjects finding that uptake of a PET radioligand for the 5-HT precursor, tryptophan, is inversely correlated with measures of impulsivity (Leyton et al., 2001). Chronic administration of the serotonin precursor molecule tryptophan has been found to decrease aggressive behavior in healthy controls (Moskowitz, Pinard, Zuroff, Annable, & Young, 2003).

Another body of work finds evidence for enhanced serotonergic signaling in impulsive aggression. A genetic polymorphism of the monoamine oxidase A associated with low activity (thus predicting a decreased rate of serotonergic breakdown) has been associated with impulsive aggression (Chester et al., 2015). Interestingly, measurement of brain MAO activity with a radioactive pet ligand similarly finds that low MAO-A activity is associated with aggression (Alia-Klein et al., 2008). Metabolic PET brain imaging, when used in conjunction with pharmacochallenge with the 5-$HT_{2a/c}$ agonist fenfluramine, has revealed that impulsive aggressive personality disordered patients have a blunted metabolic response in the prefrontal cortex (Siever et al., 1999). These findings have been replicated in subsequent experiments using fenfluramine (Soloff, Meltzer, Greer, Constantine, & Kelly, 1999) and later with the 5-$HT_{2a/c}$ agonist meta-chlorophenylpiperizine (m-CPP; New et al., 2002). When probed directly with a radioligand for the 5-HT_{2a} receptor, [(11)C]MDL100907, impulsive aggression has been found to be associated with downregulation of brain 5-HT_{2a} receptor expression (Rosell et al., 2010). Such downregulation has also been found with the 5-HT_{1A} receptor using the radioligand [c-11] WAY-100635 (Parsey et al., 2002). A neuroendocrine study of postsynaptic 5-HT_{1a} sensitivity similarly found evidence of reduced sensitivity in impulsive aggression (Almeida, Lee, & Coccaro, 2010). Findings of blunted 5-$HT_{2a/c}$ receptor expression are generally interpreted as reflecting compensatory downregulation of postsynaptic receptors in response to increased synaptic 5-HT release (Jørgensen et al., 2016; Meyer et al., 2001).

Consistent with the hypothesis that increased serotonergic signaling is associated with aggression, atypical antipsychotic drugs have been found to reduce anger and aggression in borderline personality disorder (Black et al., 2014; Zanarini, Frankenburg, & Parachini, 2004). Because olanzapine and quetiapine have numerous other pharmacological actions outside of 5-HT_{2a} receptor antagonism, follow-up research with a specific 5-HT_{2a} receptor antagonist in impulsive aggression would be of interest to confirm the importance of this receptor subtype.

The basic science literature has generally confirmed the relevance of serotonin signaling to aggressive behavior, but has had difficulty with discerning the direction of effect of serotonin. Most evidence supports the view that the 5-HT_{1a} has an important role, but what remains unclear is the association is due to increased or decreased postsynaptic 5-HT_{1a} signaling (De Boer & Koolhaas, 2005).

We have reviewed two bodies of replicated but seeming paradoxical findings regarding serotonergic signaling in impulsive aggression. The most likely explanation for this is that 5-HT_{1a} and 5-$HT_{2a/c}$ signaling are separable signals with distinct roles in shaping brain activity and thus behavior. The evidence suggests that impulsive aggression is likely inhibited by 5-HT_{1a} and facilitated by 5-$HT_{2a/c}$ neuromodulation. Distinct roles for these two signaling pathways have been hypothesized for stress reactivity, with 5-HT_{1A} signaling proposed to mediate passive coping while 5-$HT_{2a/c}$ signaling proposed to mediate active coping (Carhart-Harris & Nutt, 2017).

The action of selective serotonin reuptake inhibitor (SSRI) medications illustrates the complexity of the serotonergic system through dual modulation of 5-HT_{1a} and 5-$HT_{2a/c}$ signaling. Chronic SSRI treatment reduces cortical 5-HT_{2a} binding, likely through postsynaptic receptor desensitization (Peremans et al., 2005). However, the antidepressant actions of SSRI treatment are thought to depend on increased 5-HT_{1a} signaling in the dentate gyrus of the hippocampus (Samuels et al., 2015). In humans, blocking the degradation of serotonin with serotonin reuptake inhibitors (SSRI) has been found to reduce impulsive aggression in IED. In a randomized, double-blind, placebo-controlled trial of the SSRI fluoxetine, fluoxetine was found to be superior to placebo in reducing verbal aggression in IED patients (Coccaro, Lee, et al., 2009; Coccaro, Noblett, et al., 2009). More severely aggressive subjects, who were also more likely to have blunted 5-HT receptor sensitivity to d-fenfluramine, were less likely to improve with fluoxetine treatment (Coccaro et al., 2007). Fluoxetine has similarly found to reduce aggressive behavior in depressed patients with anger attacks (Fava et al., 1993). The therapeutic effect of SSRI treatment of aggression may be by increasing OFC activity. PET brain imaging in conjunction with open-label fluoxetine treatment in 10 BPD-IED patients revealed that fluoxetine treatment was associated with an increase in OFC metabolism (New et al., 2004). Increased OFC activity may be due to 5-HT_{2a} desensitization, as preclinical research has found that chronic treatment with citalopram reduces cortical 5-HT_{2a} binding (Peremans et al., 2005), releasing the OFC from inhibitory modulation by 5-HT_{2A} (Bergqvist, Dong, & Blier, 1999). The effects of SSRI administration on aggression may not be restricted to the prefrontal cortex. A recent study of the effects of acute administration of the SSRI citalopram on the neural response to emotional face stimuli found that citalopram dosing was associated with increased activity in the left TPJ in IED compared with healthy control individuals (Cremers, Lee, Keedy, Phan, & Coccaro, 2015). Such effects could indicate that SSRI treatment may reduce aggression by increasing mentalizing ability and could be conceptualized as an extension of the Metalearning model of serotonin function into the sphere of social interaction. SSRIs may also reduce aggression by altering the time course of angry emotional responses to stimuli, consistent with the effects of tryptophan depletion on anger. A recent computational study modeled frustration in motor learning by adapting the Rescorla-Wagner learning rule (Grzyb, Boedecker, Asada, Pobil, & Smith, 2011). In this model, prediction error (P_e) at the current time ($P_e(t+1)$) is based on modification of prediction error at a previous time point $P_e(t)$ by the outcome of action (A_0) after the previous time point and a frustration factor E_f. This frustration factor is modeled as a leaky integrator ($df/dt = -L^*f + A_0$) with an onset and decay time, such that $P_e(t+1) = P_e(t) + (P_e(t) - A_0)^* E_f$. One can see that according to this model, frustration, or anger, can increase prediction error in a time-dependent fashion. This prediction error would drive motor action. In this section, we have posited that 5-HT tone affects the magnitude of the frustration (anger) function as well as the computation of past prediction error through delay discounting. In real-world terms, this translates to serotonin decreasing anger intensity and increasing future reward sensitivity in the context of social interaction.

Norepinephrine and Impulsive Aggression

As norepinephrine (NE) is released in acute stress (Berridge & Waterhouse, 2003), it is plausibly linked to aggressive behavior. Frustration causes norepinephrine release in the right amygdala (Young & Williams, 2010). Via release from cell groups A6 and A4 in the locus coeruleus, projections of noradrenergic neurons to the cortex increase cortical arousal through effects on alpha-1 and alpha-2 noradrenergic receptors. Behaviorally this results in vigilance and reaction speed. According to the Metalearning hypothesis, norepinephrine mediates the effect of surprise on decision-making and motor behavior, favoring the exploration of new motor responses over habitual and older motor responses (Doya, 2002). While alpha-2 receptor sensitivity is not altered in impulsive aggression (Coccaro & Kavoussi, 2010), CSF levels of the norepinephrine metabolite 3-methoxy-5-hydroxyphenylglycol (MHPG) have been positively correlated with aggression in adult males with personality disorders (Brown et al., 1979) and adults with depression (Placidi et al., 2001; Prochazka & Ågren, 2003). Aggressive individuals show higher plasma norepinephrine release during aggressive responding, albeit without baseline differences. This means that peripheral norepinephrine release may be triggered by frustration or anger, and is not necessarily the cause of aggressive behavior (Gerra et al., 1997). On the other hand, treatment with antidepressant medications that increase norepinephrine worsens aggression in personality disordered patients (Soloff, George, Nathan, Schulz, & Perel, 1986).

Dopamine and Impulsive Aggression

Given the central role of dopamine in temporal difference learning in the Metalearning model, it would be expected to play an important role in aggressive behavior. However, the role of dopamine in aggression is complex. Low levels of striatal dopamine release signal worse than expected outcomes, which would be predicted to cause frustration. Consistent with this, human studies of the homovanillic acid (HVA), the major metabolite of dopamine, has found decreased levels of CSF HVA in impulsive aggression

(Coccaro & Lee, 2010; Linnoila et al., 1983; Virkkunen et al., 1987) and decreased DA storage capacity in the striatum/midbrain (Schlüter et al., 2013). PET imaging has been utilized to measure dynamic and regional brain dopamine release. A study using 6-[18F]-fluoro-L-DOPA PET imaging during a modified Point Subtraction Aggression Paradigm (PSAP) session found to be decreased dopamine release to be associated with aggressive responding after provocation (Schlüter et al., 2013). Another PET study, also conducted during the PSAP, showed that male patients with comorbid BPD-IED showed lower striatal glucose metabolism as measured by (18)-flouro-deoxyglucose (FDG) PET imaging (Perez-Rodriguez et al., 2012).

The regulation of aggression behavior, beyond that of external stimulus evaluation, may involve striatal circuits involved in decision-making. Externalizing psychopathology (Hall, Bernat, & Patrick, 2007) and violent offending (Vila-Ballo, Hdez-Lafuente, Rostan, Cunillera, & Rodriguez-Fornells, 2014) have both been associated with decreased amplitude of the Error-Related Negativity, an ERP that is elicited by the commission of errors. Likewise, BPD has been associated with decreased feedback-related negativity (FRN), a stimulus-locked ERP, and to positive and negative outcomes (Endrass et al., 2016). These neurophysiological findings suggest that dopamine does not undergo the phasic dips that would signal error and could help to regulate aggression. Thus dopamine release may decrease sensitivity to frustration or anger, which would in turn reduce aggression. An fMRI study of the Point-Subtraction Paradigm (PSAP) in aggressive children with Attention Deficit Hyperactivity Disorder (ADHD) and control children found that aggressive children failed to show normative activation of the anterior cingulate region during aggressive responding (Bubenzer-Busch et al., 2016). A separate study in normal subjects found a similar normative result: aggressive responding, this time during the Taylor Aggression Paradigm, was associated with anterior cingulate activation (Beyer, Münte, Göttlich, & Krämer, 2014). The interaction of dopamine and serotonin would also be expected to be of importance given the potential role of delay discounting in social behavior, as has recently been reviewed (Seo, Patrick, & Kennealy, 2008). In summary, the role of dopamine signaling in impulsive aggression and IED is not clear. Some evidence associates aggressive behavior with decreased levels of brain dopamine. Other evidence suggests that phasic dips in dopamine that would be expected to regulate behavior are lacking in humans with impulsive aggression.

Glutamate

Activation of all three circuits implicated in impulsive aggression requires excitation of pyramidal cell neurons and release of glutamate. Furthermore, glutamatergic neurotransmission includes the machinery of neuroplasticity, the molecular process of Hebbian learning. It is thus safe to say that glutamatergic signaling is implicated in all behavior, including aggression (Vekovischeva et al., 2004). CSF glutamate concentrations correlate positively with measures of both aggression and impulsivity in personality disordered and healthy control study participants (Coccaro, Lee, & Vezina, 2013). Given the presence of a global signal of increased excitatory neurotransmitter signaling, this finding seems to support the multicircuit model of aggression posited in this chapter. Namely, the finding that multiple brain circuits are hyperactive in response to social cues in IED and impulsive aggression is the likely explanation of increased glutamate.

Gamma-Aminobutyric Acid

Gamma-aminobutyric acid (GABA) is the major inhibitory neurotransmitter in the brain. GABA is also important in shaping the oscillations of the local field potential that help to coordinate brain communication (Lozano-Soldevilla, 2018; Mann & Mody, 2010). Preclinical studies have shown that aggressive animals have reduced brain GABA levels and of glutamic acid decarboxylase (GAD), the enzyme that catalyzes glutamate into GABA. In humans, we have previously discovered an inverse relationship between impulsivity and CSF GABA levels, but no relationship specifically with aggression (Lee, Ferris, Van der Kar, & Coccaro, 2009). These results are largely consistent with a large body of work finding that benzodiazepine drugs, which are allosteric modulators of the GABA-A receptor, are associated with behavioral disinhibition (Cowdry & Gardner, 1988) and aggression (Albrecht et al., 2014). Work in animal models has linked benzodiazepine-facilitated aggression to alpha-2 GABA-A receptor expression, confirming the direct and expected pharmacodynamics effect of benzodiazepine drug on aggression (Newman et al., 2015). It is known that benzodiazepine drug administration in humans causes a global reduction in brain metabolic activity (Wang et al., 1998). These reductions were strongest in the thalamus and occipital cortex, but include brain regions in the proposed three circuit model of aggression, such as the frontal cortex, parietal cortex, and basal ganglia.

Neuropeptides and Impulsive Aggression

Neuropeptides are protein-like molecules released in the brain to play a neuromodulator role on neural signaling. Unlike the monoamine neuromodulators and neurotransmitters, neuropeptide expression and release have a relatively high specificity for regional circuit distribution and behavioral effect. However, like other neuromodulators, they act on metabotropic receptors to depolarize or hyperpolarize the postsynaptic neuron.

Oxytocin

Oxytocin acts on a single oxytocin receptor subtype, a metabotropic G-protein-linked receptor. In humans, oxytocin receptors have recently been confirmed to be expressed in the gyrus rectus of the orbitofrontal cortex and ventral and subgenual anterior cingulate cortex but not the insula or olfactory cortex (Rogers et al., 2018). Previous work localized oxytocin binding sites to the forebrain, lateral septal nucleus, hypothalamus, and globus pallidus (Loup, Tribollet, Dubois-Dauphin, & Dreifuss, 1991). The distribution is consistent with the known role of oxytocin in enhancing the salience of social information. Preclinical work with the social neuropeptides has linked the expression of oxytocin and vasopressin to prosocial behaviors (Caldwell & Albers, 2016). Although oxytocin has been purported to suppress anxiety, in preclinical models the effect of oxytocin on behavior is context dependent, as is seen with social modulation of oxytocin effects on fear conditioning (Guzmán et al., 2013). In humans, CSF oxytocin levels are inversely correlated with life history of aggression measures in adults with impulsive aggression (Lee et al., 2009). In the periphery, plasma levels of oxytocin have been found to be inversely related to aggression in individuals with BPD (Bertsch et al., 2013; Bertsch, Schmidinger, Neumann, & Herpetz, 2013). Intranasal oxytocin has also been found to reduce amygdala activation to threatening faces in females with BPD (Bertsch, Schmidinger, et al., 2013). Surprisingly, administration of intranasal oxytocin to humans increases, rather than decreases, aggressive responding in simulated social interaction (Ne'eman, Perach-Barzilay, Fischer-Shofty, Atias, & Shamay-Tsoory, 2016). In our laboratory, intranasal oxytocin failed to exhibit the expected antiaggressive effect on the Point Subtraction Paradigm (PSAP). However, an indirect "cybernetic" effect of oxytocin was found in decreasing computer confederate aggression, likely via a tendency of subjects when given oxytocin to increase defensive "C" button presses (Lee, 2014). Work in healthy humans has recently confirmed that intranasal oxytocin does not reduce behavioral aggression (Romney, Hahn-Holbrook, Norman, Moore, & Holt-Lunstad, 2018). In summary, oxytocin has a confirmed role in signaling the salience of social cues in the environment, and thus might be expected to predict social reward and thus facilitate predictive encoding of that reward. The weight of evidence suggests that in facilitating social behavior, oxytocin should reduce aggressive behavior. However, findings from the experimental literature reveal that the increased salience of social cues may not always translate to a reduction in aggressive behavior, perhaps due to frustration of predicted social reward.

Vasopressin

Vasopressin binds to three subtypes of G-protein-linked metabotropic receptors in the brain and periphery (Ring, 2005): the V1a, V1b, and V2 receptors. The V1a receptor is found in the limbic system and cortex, while the V1b is located in the limbic system and pituitary gland. The V2 receptor is localized in the kidney and is not thought to play a neuromodulator role in the brain. In humans, vasopressin receptors have been localized to the agranular insular cortex, the frontal operculum, primary olfactory cortex, and the subgenual cingulate gyrus (Rogers et al., 2018), as well as the amygdala, bed nucleus of the stria terminalis, thalamus, hippocampus, and medal septal nucleus (Loup et al., 1991). A large body of work has revealed a direct link between vasopressin signaling and both offensive and defensive aggressive behavior (Albers, 2012). In humans, genetic variation of the vasopressin V1a receptor has been found to predict differences in metabolic reactivity of the amygdala to emotional face stimuli (Meyer-Lindenberg et al., 2009). CSF levels of vasopressin are positively correlated with life history of aggression in adults with and without personality disorder (Coccaro, Kavoussi, Hauger, Cooper, & Ferris, 1998). A novel vasopressin V1a receptor antagonist has been found to reduce the brain response to repeated emotional face stimuli, suggesting the social behavior may be shaped by pharmacological blockade of vasopressin receptors (Lee et al., 2013). In summary, vasopressin has been found to signal the salience of social cues. This signaling would be expected to enhance encoding of social emotional information. Although work in animal models and some work in humans would predict that vasopressin promotes aggressive behavior, and blocking it with antagonists should reduce it, experimental evidence for this is so far lacking.

Substance P

The endogenous receptor for substance P is the Neurokinin-1 (NK1) receptor. NK-1 receptors are widely distributed in the CNS and include expression in the limbic system (Yip & Chahl, 2001). In animal models, substance P promotes aggression via activation of NK1 receptors in the hypothalamus and amygdala (Bhatt, TR, & Siegel, 2003; Han, Shaikh, & Siegel, 1996). Pharmacological blockade of the NK1 receptor reduces defensive aggression in cats (Shaikh & Siegel, 1994). In humans, CSF levels of substance P is correlated with life history of aggression (Coccaro, Lee, Owens, Kinkead, & Nemeroff, 2012).

Neuropeptide Y

Neuropeptide Y (NPY) is synthesized in GABA inhibitory neurons and acts on Y1, Y2, Y4, and Y5 G-protein-linked receptors as a neuromodulator. NPY is expressed in the amygdala, hypothalamus, hippocampus, basal ganglia, and brainstem (Robinson & Thiele, 2017). NYP has established roles in feeding, control of metabolism and fat deposition, stress reactivity, and anxiety. Its role in a multitude of behaviors has been conceptualized as promoter of stress resilience (Reichmann & Holzer, 2016). Somewhat counterintuitively, work in animal models has revealed that stimulation of Y1 receptors is associated with increased aggression (Karl et al., 2004; Kask & Harro, 2000; Rutkoski, Lerant, Nolte, Westberry, & Levenson, 2002). Consistent with this finding, in humans, CSF NPY concentration positively correlated with life history of aggression (Coccaro et al., 2012).

Neuroinflammation

Brain activity is tightly linked to immune system function. Why this is so is not completely understood. One possibility is that the process of neuroplasticity requires the immune systems for the clearance of synaptic proteins. Hebbian plasticity, a use-dependent shaping of neural function, utilizes multiple components of the immune system to target synapse and neurons (Mottahedin et al., 2017). Sleep, which takes up a large portion of mammalian life, may have in fact evolved to assist in the processing of this metabolic load. By taking brain inputs and outputs offline, sleep permits the immune system to enhance relevant synapses through long-term potentiation (LTP) and degrade irrelevant synapses through long-term depression (LTD) (Tononi & Cirelli, 2014). Crosstalk between the immune system and the brain involves multiple signaling pathways, including acetylcholine (Rosas-Ballina & Tracey, 2009) and serotonin (Pelletier & Siegel, 2009). It is also known that cytokines, proteins released by immune system B and T cells, have direct effects on behavior due to their neuromodulator function in the brain. Inflammatory cytokines such as Interleukin 1β (IL-1β; Hassanain, Zalcman, Bhatt, & Siegel, 2003) and Interleukin 2 (IL-2; Bhatt & Siegel, 2006) modulate aggressive behavior in animals (i.e., defensive-rage aggression model in cat)

In humans, impulsive aggression is associated with increased peripheral expression of IL-6 and both peripheral and central C reactive protein (Coccaro, Lee, Breen, et al., 2015; Coccaro, Lee, & Coussons-Read, 2014; Coccaro, Lee, McCloskey, et al., 2015). Impulsive aggression has also been associated with increased oxidative stress, as evidenced by elevated 8-hydroxy-2'-deoxyguanosine and 8-isoprostane in impulsive aggression (Coccaro, Fanning, et al., 2016; Coccaro, Keedy, et al., 2016; Coccaro, Lee, et al., 2016; Coccaro, Lee, & Gozal, 2016). Immune activation in impulsive aggression extends into the brain. Impulsive aggression is associated with elevations in CSF levels of CSF CRP (Coccaro, Lee, & Coussons-Read, 2015a) and soluble CSF sIL-1RII receptor protein (Coccaro, Lee, & Coussons-Read, 2015b). The presence of normal levels of the tryptophan metabolite kynurenine in the CSF of adults with IED suggests that neuroinflammation does not affect aggression by decreasing serotonin synthesis (Coccaro, Fanning, et al., 2016; Coccaro, Keedy, et al., 2016; Coccaro, Lee, et al., 2016; Coccaro, Lee, & Gozal, 2016).

The endocannabinoid system, whose signaling molecules can cross the blood-brain barrier, is a vast signaling network that is ideally situated to provide crosstalk between brain and immune signaling pathways. There is a rich animal literature linking endocannabinoid signaling and aggression (Kolla & Mishra, 2018). Cannabinoid receptors are expressed in microglial and glial cells involved in neuroinflammation (Walter & Stella, 2004). Cannabinoid CB1 receptors are the most widely expressed metabotropic receptor in the brain (Herkenham et al., 1990). Full CB1 agonists are associated with extreme aggression (Kolla & Mishra, 2018). One of the major endogenous endocannabinoids is anandamide, or *N*-arachidonoylethanolamine (AEA). AEA is synthesized from arachidonic acid and essential fatty acids and acts as a neuromodulator in the brain. AEA levels have been found to be inversely related to affective intensity in human with and without personality disorder (Coccaro, Hill, Robinson, & Lee, 2018) but were not related to aggression specifically.

According to the *SEIP/predictive coding* model, coordinated brain activity is shaped through neuroplastic processes to enhance the predictive ability of the social brain. This process appears to result in metabolic stress as reflected in immune system activation. More work needs to be done in this exciting area of neuroscience to more completely understand the clinical relevance of neuroinflammation in impulsive aggression. It is not yet clear how the scientific understanding of the complex signaling networks in neuroinflammation will lead to new therapeutic approaches. It appears that currently available medications, such as fluoxetine and valproate, do not reduce inflammation in impulsive aggressive subjects (Coccaro, Lee, Breen, et al., 2015; Coccaro, Lee, McCloskey, et al., 2015). If immune activation plays a causal role, then targeting neuroinflammation with antiinflammatory medications may be a promising approach. On the other hand, if immune activation is stress related, it is possible that attempts to halt inflammation may be too late in the causal pathway.

Summary

This review of neurotransmitter and neuromodulator abnormalities in impulsive aggression has placed the body of research in a model of brain function relevant to IED. According to this *SEIP/predictive coding* framework, neurotransmitters and neuromodulators have a role as signaling molecules in circuits that enable social interaction. These circuits both facilitate and restrain aggressive responding. Depending on the balance of stress demands on the system and its biological vulnerabilities, variability can be seen in the balance of facilitation versus restraining of aggression. Neurobiological research has pointed to disturbed serotonin signaling in impulsive aggression. Impulsive aggression is indeed caused by serotonin dysregulation but in distinct, receptor-specific pathways. Recent research has not provided evidence to the contrary, but has rather expanded the network of connections to serotonin to distributed brain circuits and even out into the body in immune and intracellular signaling cascades. In total, the resulting neurobiological portrait of IED is of a person with a lifelong history of angry outbursts, with evidence of disturbed, stress-related 5-HT signaling. This 5-HT dysfunction worsens the very system that can regulate stress reactivity, centered on hubs in the prefrontal cortex. Contributing to this positive feedback loop may be an overtaxed immune system, tasked with cleaning up the metabolically costly synaptic downsides of stress.

Despite progress in understanding the basic biological mechanism of IED, many unanswered questions remain regarding the role of neurotransmitters and neuromodulators. The task is daunting, because the brain is an enormously complicated system; its functions are not captured simply. System-based approaches have increasingly been called on in the treatment of other complex medical disorders and will likely be required to understand and treat IED. Neurotransmitter and neuromodulator signaling systems have a key role in how brain circuits learn about social interaction over time. This work can be considered as part of the larger effort to understand IED as a brain-based disorder of interpersonal reactivity.

References

Aghajanian, G. K., & Marek, G. J. (1997). Serotonin induces excitatory postsynaptic potentials in apical dendrites of neocortical pyramidal cells. *Neuropharmacology*, *36*(4–5), 589–599.

Albers, H. E. (2012). The regulation of social recognition, social communication and aggression: Vasopressin in the social behavior neural network. *Hormones and Behavior*, *61*(3), 283–292.

Albrecht, B., Staiger, P. K., Hall, K., Miller, P., Best, D., & Lubman, D. I. (2014). Benzodiazepine use and aggressive behaviour: A systematic review. *The Australian and New Zealand Journal of Psychiatry*, *48*, 1096–1114.

Alia-Klein, N., Goldstein, R. Z., Kriplani, A., Logan, J., Tomasi, D., Williams, B., et al. (2008). Brain monoamine oxidase A activity predicts trait aggression. *Journal of Neuroscience*, *28*(19), 5099–5104.

Almeida, M., Lee, R., & Coccaro, E. F. (2010). Cortisol responses to ipsapirone challenge correlate with aggression, while basal cortisol levels correlate with impulsivity, in personality disorder and healthy volunteer subjects. *Journal of Psychiatric Research*, *44*(14), 874–880.

Amargós-Bosch, M., Bortolozzi, A., Puig, M., Serrats, J., Adell, A., & Artigas, F. (2004). Co-expression and In vivo interaction of serotonin1A and serotonin2a receptors in pyramidal neurons of pre-frontal cortex. *Cerebral Cortex*, *14*(3), 281–299.

Amat, J., Matus-Amat, P., Watkins, L. R., & Maier, S. F. (1998). Escapable and inescapable stress differentially and selectively alter extracellular levels of 5-HT in the ventral hippocampus and dorsal periaqueductal gray of the rat. *Brain Research*, *797*(1), 12–22.

Åsberg, M. (1997). Neurotransmitters and suicidal behavior. The evidence from cerebrospinal fluid studies. *Annals of the New York Academy of Sciences*, *836*, 158–181.

Bergqvist, P. B., Dong, J., & Blier, P. (1999). Effect of atypical antipsychotic drugs on 5-HT2 receptors in the rat orbito-frontal cortex: An in vivo electrophysiological study. *Psychopharmacology*, *143*(1), 89–96.

Berridge, C. W., & Waterhouse, B. D. (2003). The locus coeruleus-noradrenergic system: Modulation of behavioral state and state-dependent cognitive processes. *Brain Research Reviews*, *42*(1), 33–84.

Bertsch, K., Gamer, M., Schmidt, B., Schmidinger, I., Walther, S., Kästel, T., et al. (2013). Oxytocin and reduction of social threat hypersensitivity in women with borderline personality disorder. *American Journal of Psychiatry*, *170*(10), 1169–1177.

Bertsch, K., Schmidinger, I., Neumann, I. D., & Herpetz, S. C. (2013). Reduced plasma oxytocin levels in female patients with borderline personality disorder. *Hormones and Behavior*, *63*(3), 424–429.

Beyer, F., Münte, T. F., Göttlich, M., & Krämer, U. M. (2014). Orbitofrontal cortex reactivity to angry facial expression in a social interaction correlates with aggressive behavior. *Cerebral Cortex*, 3057–3063.

Bhatt, S., & Siegel, A. (2006). Potentiating role of interleukin 2 (IL-2) receptors in the midbrain periaqueductal gray (PAG) upon defensive rage behavior in the cat: Role of neurokinin NK(1) receptors. *Behavioural Brain Research*, *167*, 251–260.

Bhatt, S., TR, G., & Siegel, A. (2003). NK1 receptors in the medial hypothalamus potentiate defensive rage behavior elicited from the midbrain periaqueductal gray of the cat. *Brain Research*, *966*, 54–64.

Bjork, J. M., Dougherty, D. M., Moeller, F. G., & Swann, A. C. (2000). Differential behavioral effects of plasma tryptophan depletion and loading in aggressive and nonaggressive men. *Neuropsychopharmacology*, *22*(4), 357–369.

Black, D. W., Zanarini, M. C., Romine, A., Shaw, M., Allen, J., & Schulz, S. C. (2014). Comparison of low and moderate dosages of extended-release quetiapine in borderline personality disorder: A randomized, double-blind, placebo-controlled trial. *The American Journal of Psychiatry*, *171*(11), 1174–1182.

Bond, A. J., Wingrove, J., & Critchlow, D. G. (2001). Tryptophan depletion increases aggression in women during the premenstrual phase. *Psychopharmacology*, *156*(4), 477–480.

Brown, G. L., Goodwin, F. K., Ballenger, J. C., Goyer, P. F., & Major, L. F. (1979). Aggression in humans correlates with cerebrospinal fluid amine metabolites. *Psychiatry Research*, *1*(2), 131–139.

Bubenzer-Busch, S., Herpertz-Dahlmann, B., Kuzmanovic, B., Gaber, T. J., Helmbold, K., Ullisch, M. G., et al. (2016). Neural correlates of reactive aggression in children with attention-deficit/hyperactivity disorder and comorbid disruptive behaviour disorders. *Acta Psychiatrica Scandinavica*, *133*(4), 310–323.

Caldwell, H. K., & Albers, H. E. (2016). Oxytocin, vasopressin, and the motivational forces that drive social behaviors. *Current Topics in Behavioral Neurosciences*, *27*, 51–103.

Carhart-Harris, R. L., & Nutt, D. J. (2017). Serotonin and brain function: A tale of two receptors. *Journal of Psychopharmacology*, *31*(9), 1091–1120.

Chen, C. Y., Muggleton, N. G., & Chang, J. R. (2014). Inefficiency of post-error adjustment in impulsive violent offenders. *NeuroReport*, *25*(13), 1024–1029.

Chester, D. S., DeWall, C. N., Derefinko, K. J., Estus, S., Peters, J. R., Lynam, D. R., et al. (2015). Monoamine oxidase A (MAOA) genotype predicts greater aggression through impulsive reactivity to negative affect. *Behavioural Brain Research*, *283*, 97–101.

Clarke, H. F., Walker, S. C., Crofts, H. S., Dalley, J. W., Robbins, T. W., & Roberts, A. C. (2005). Prefrontal serotonin depletion affects reversal learning but not attentional set shifting. *The Journal of Neuroscience*, *25*(2), 532–538.

Clarke, H. F., Walker, S. C., Dalley, J. W., Robbings, T. W., & Roberts, A. C. (2007). Cognitive inflexibility after prefrontal serotonin depletion is behaviorally and neurochemically specific. *Cerebral Cortex*, *17*(1), 18–27.

Cleare, A. J., & Bond, A. J. (1995). The effect of tryptophan depletion and enhancement on subjective and behavioural aggression in normal male subjects. *Psychopharmacology*, *118*(1), 72–81.

Coccaro, E. F., Fanning, J., & Lee, R. (2016). Development of a social emotional information processing assessment for adults (SEIP-Q). *Aggressive Behavior*.

Coccaro, E. F., Hill, M. N., Robinson, L., & Lee, R. J. (2018). Circulating endocannabinoids and affect regulation in human subjects. *Psychoneuroendocrinology*, *92*, 66–71.

Coccaro, E. F., & Kavoussi, R. J. (2010). GH response to intravenous clonidine challenge: Absence of relationship with behavioral irritability, aggression, or impulsivity in human subjects. *Psychiatry Research*, *178*(2), 443–445.

Coccaro, E. F., Kavoussi, R. J., Cooper, T. B., & Hauger, R. L. (1997). Central serotonin activity and aggression: Inverse relationship with prolactin response to d-fenfluramine, but not CSF 5-HIAA concentration, in human subjects. *American Journal of Psychiatry, 154*(10), 1430–1435.

Coccaro, E. F., Kavoussi, R. J., & Hauger, R. L. (1997). Serotonin function and antiaggressive responses to fluoxetine: A pilot study. *Biological Psychiatry, 42*, 546–552.

Coccaro, E. F., Kavoussi, R. J., Hauger, R. L., Cooper, T. B., & Ferris, C. F. (1998). Cerebrospinal fluid vasopressin levels: Correlates with aggression and serotonin function in personality-disordered subjects. *Archives of General Psychiatry, 55*(8), 708–714.

Coccaro, E. F., Keedy, S. K., Gorka, S. M., King, A. C., Fanning, J. R., Lee, R. J., et al. (2016). Differential fMRI BOLD responses in amygdala in intermittent explosive disorder as a function of past Alcohol Use Disorder. *Psychiatry Research: Neuroimaging, 257*, 5–10.

Coccaro, E. F., & Lee, R. (2010). Cerebrospinal fluid 5-hydroxyindolacetic acid and homovanillic acid: Reciprocal relationships with impulsive aggression in human subjects. *Journal of Neural Transmission (Vienna), 117*, 241–248.

Coccaro, E. F., Lee, R., Breen, E. C., & Irwin, M. R. (2015). Inflammatory markers and chronic exposure to fluoxetine, divalproex, and placebo in intermittent explosive disorder. *Psychiatry Research, 229*(3), 844–849.

Coccaro, E. F., Lee, R., & Coussons-Read, M. (2014). Elevated plasma inflammatory markers in individuals with intermittent explosive disorder and correlation with aggression in humans. *JAMA Psychiatry, 71*, 158–165.

Coccaro, E. F., Lee, R., & Coussons-Read, M. (2015a). Cerebrospinal fluid and plasma C-reactive protein and aggression in personality-disordered subjects: A pilot study. *Journal of Neural Transmission, 122*(2), 321–326.

Coccaro, E. F., Lee, R., & Coussons-Read, M. (2015b). Cerebrospinal fluid inflammatory cytokines and aggression in personality disordered subjects. *International Journal of Neuropsychopharmacology, 18*(7).

Coccaro, E. F., Lee, R., Fanning, J. R., Fuchs, D., Goiny, M., Erhardt, S., et al. (2016). Tryptophan, kynurenine, and kynurenine metabolites: Relationship to lifetime aggression and inflammatory markers in human subjects. *Psychoneuroendocrinology, 71*, 189–196.

Coccaro, E. F., Lee, R., & Gozal, D. (2016). Elevated plasma oxidative stress markers in individuals with intermittent explosive disorder and correlation with aggression in humans. *Biological Psychiatry, 79*(2), 127–135.

Coccaro, E. F., Lee, R., McCloskey, M., Csernansky, J. G., & Wang, L. (2015). Morphometric analysis of amygdla and hippocampus shape in impulsively aggressive and healthy control subjects. *Journal of Psychiatric Research, 69*, 80–86.

Coccaro, E. F., Lee, R., Owens, M. J., Kinkead, B., & Nemeroff, C. B. (2012). Cerebrospinal fluid substance P-like immunoreactivity correlates with aggression in personality disordered subjects. *Biological Psychiatry, 72*, 238–243.

Coccaro, E. F., Lee, R. J., & Kavoussi, R. J. (2009). A double-blind, randomized, placebo-controlled trial of fluoxetine in patients with intermittent explosive disorder. *Journal of Clinical Psychiatry, 70*(5), 653–662.

Coccaro, E. F., Lee, R., & Vezina, P. (2013). Cerebrospinal fluid glutamate concentration correlates with impulsive aggression in human subjects. *Journal of Psychiatric Research, 47*, 1247–1253.

Coccaro, E. F., McCloskey, M. S., Fitzgerald, D. A., & Phan, K. L. (2007). Amygdala and orbitofrontal reactivity to social threat in individuals with impulsive aggression. *Biological Psychiatry, 62*, 168–178.

Coccaro, E. F., Noblett, K. L., & McCloskey, M. S. (2009). Attributional and emotional responses to socially ambiguous cues: Validation of a new assessment of social/emotional information processing in healthy adults and impulsive aggressive patients. *Journal of Psychiatric Research, 43*(10), 915–925.

Cools, R., Calder, A. J., Lawrence, A. D., Clark, L., Bullmore, E., & Robinson, T. W. (2005). Individual differences in threat sensitivity predict serotonergic modulation of amygdala response to fearful faces. *Psychopharmacology*, *180*(4), 670–679.

Corlett, P. R., Honey, G. D., & Fletcher, P. C. (2016). Prediction error, ketamine and psychosis: An updated model. *Journal of Psychopharmacology*, *30*(11), 1145–1155.

Cowdry, R. W., & Gardner, D. L. (1988). Pharmacotherapy of borderline personality disorder. Alprazolam, carbamazepine, trifluoperazine, and tranylcypromine. *Archives of General Psychiatry*, *45*(2), 111–119.

Cremers, H., Lee, R., Keedy, S., Phan, K. L., & Coccaro, E. F. (2015). Effects of escitalopram administration on face processing in intermittent explosive disorder: An fMRI Study. *Neuropsychopharmacology*, *41*(2), 590–597.

Crick, N. R., & Dodge, K. A. (1994). A review and reformulation of social information-processing mechanisms in children's social adjustment. *Psychological Bulletin*, *115*(1), 74–101.

De Boer, S. F., & Koolhaas, J. M. (2005). 5-HT1A and 5-HT1B receptor agonists and aggression: A pharmacological challenge of the serotonin deficiency hypothesis. *European Journal of Pharmacology*, *526*(1), 125–139.

Dodge, K. A. (1993). Social-cognitive mechanisms in the development of conduct disorder and depression. *Annual Review of Psychology*, *44*, 559–584.

Dougherty, D. M., Richard, D. M., James, L. M., & Mathias, C. W. (2010). Effects of acute tryptophan depletion on three different types of behavioral impulsivity. *International Journal of Tryptophan Research*, *3*, 99–111.

Doya, K. (2002). Metalearning and neuromodulation. *Neural Networks*, *15*(4–6), 495–506.

Duke, A. A., Bègue, L., Bell, R., & Eisenlohr-Moul, T. (2013). Revisiting the serotonin-aggression relation in humans: A meta-analysis. *Psychological Bulletin*, *139*(5), 1148–1172.

Endrass, T., Schuermann, B., Roepke, S., Kessler-Scheil, S., & Kathmann, N. (2016). Reduced risk avoidance and altered neural correlates of feedback processing in patients with borderline personality disorder. *Psychiatry Research*, *243*, 14–22.

Fava, M., Rosenbaum, J. F., Pava, J. A., McCarthy, M. K., Steingard, R. J., & Bouffides, E. (1993). Anger attacks in unipolar depression, Part 1: Clinical correlates and response to fluoxetine treatment. *American Journal of Psychiatry*, *150*(8), 1158–1163.

Friston, K. J., Stephan, K. E., Montague, R., & Rolan, R. J. (2014). Computational psychiatry: The brain as a phantastic organ. *The Lancet Psychiatry*, *1*(2), 148–158.

Gerra, G., Zaimovic, A., Avanzini, P., Chittolini, B., Giucastro, G., Caccavari, R., et al. (1997). Neurotransmitter-neuroendocrine responses to experimentally induced aggression in humans: Influence of personality variable. *Psychiatry Research*, *66*(1), 33–43.

Grzyb, B., Boedecker, J., Asada, M., Pobil, A. P., & Smith, L. B. (2011). Between frustration and elation: Sense of control regulates the lntrinsic motivation for motor learning. In *Workshops at the twenty-fifth AAAI conference on artificial intelligence* (pp. 10–15): AAAI Publications.

Guzmán, Y. F., Tronson, N. C., Jovasevic, V., Sato, K., Guedea, A. L., Mizukami, H., et al. (2013). Fear-enhancing effects of septal oxytocin receptors. *Nature Neuroscience*, *16*(9), 1185–1187.

Hall, J. R., Bernat, E. M., & Patrick, C. J. (2007). Externalizing psychopathology and the error-related negativity. *Psychological Science*, *18*(4), 326–333.

Han, Y., Shaikh, M. B., & Siegel, A. (1996). Medial amygdaloid suppression of predatory attack behavior in the cat: II. Role of a GABAergic pathway from the medial to the lateral hypothalamus. *Brain Research*, *716*(1–2), 72–83.

Harmer, C. J., Rogers, R. D., Tunbridge, E., Cowen, P. J., & Goodwin, G. M. (2003). Tryptophan depletion decreases the recognition of fear in female volunteers. *Psychopharmacology*, *167*(4), 411–417.

Hassanain, M., Zalcman, S., Bhatt, S., & Siegel, A. (2003). Interleukin-1 beta in the hypothalamus potentiates feline defensive rage: role of serotonin-2 receptors. *Neuroscience*, *120*, 227–233.

Heritage, A. J., & Benning, S. D. (2012). Impulsivity and response modulation deficits in psychopathy: Evidence from the ERN and N1. *Journal of Abnormal Psychology*, *122*(1), 215–222.

Herkenham, M., Lynn, A. B., Little, M. D., Johnson, M. R., Melvin, L. S., de Costa, B. R., et al. (1990). Cannabinoid receptor localization in brain. *Neurobiology*, *87*(5), 1932–1936.

Jakab, R. L., & Goldman-Rakic, P. S. (1998). 5-Hydroxytryptamine2A serotonin receptors in the primate cerebral cortex: Possible site of action of hallucinogenic and antipsychotic drugs in pyramidal cell apical dendrites. *Proceedings of the National Academy of Sciences of the United States of America*, *95*(2), 735–740.

Jørgensen, L. M., Weikop, P., Villadsen, J., Visnapuu, T., Ettrup, A., Hansen, H. D., et al. (2016). Cerebral 5-HT release correlates with [11C]Cimbi36 PET measures of 5-HT2A receptor occupancy in the pig brain. *Journal of Cerebral Blood Flow & Metabolism*, *37*(2), 425–434.

Karl, T., Lin, S., Schwarzer, C., Sainsbury, A., Couzens, M., Wittmann, W., et al. (2004). Y1 receptors regulate aggressive behavior by modulating serotonin pathways. *Proceedings of the National Academy of Sciences of the United States of America*, *101*(34), 12742–12747.

Kask, A., & Harro, J. (2000). Inhibition of amphetamine- and apomorphine-induced behavioural effects by neuropeptide Y Y1 receptor antagonist BIBO 3304. *Neuropharmacology*, *39*(7), 1292–1302.

Kogo, N., & Trengove, C. (2015). Is predictive coding theory articulated enough to be testable? *Frontiers in Computational Neuroscience*, *9*, 111.

Kolla, N. J., & Mishra, A. (2018). The endocannabinoid system, aggression, and the violence of synthetic cannabinoid use, borderline personality disorder, antisocial personality disorder, and other psychiatric disorders. *Frontiers in Behavioral Neuroscience*, *12*, 41.

Lee, R. (2014). The psychopharmacology of criminality and oxytocin modulation of social behavior in aggressive individuals. In M. DeLisi & M. G. Vaughn (Eds.), *The Routledge International Handbook of Biosocial Criminology* (pp. 236–250). London and New York: Routledge/Taylor & Francis Group.

Lee, R., Arfanakis, K., Evia, A. M., Fanning, J., Keedy, S., & Coccaro, E. F. (2016). White matter integrity reductions in intermittent explosive disorder. *Neuropsychopharmacology*, *41*(11).

Lee, R., Ferris, C., Van der Kar, L. D., & Coccaro, E. F. (2009). Cerebrospinal fluid oxytocin, life history of aggression, and personality disorder. *Psychoneuroendocrinology*, *34*(10), 1567–1573.

Lee, R. J., Coccaro, E. F., Cremers, H., McCarron, R., Lu, S. F., Brownstein, M. J., et al. (2013). A novel V1a receptor antagonist blocks vasopressin-induced changes in the CNS response to emotional stimuli: An fMRI study. *Frontiers in Systems Neuroscience*, 7, 100.

Lee, R. J., Gill, A., Chen, B., McCloskey, M., & Coccaro, E. F. (2012). Modulation of central serotonin affects emotional information processing in impulsive aggressive personality disorder. *Journal of Clinical Psychopharmacology*, *32*(3), 329–335.

Leyton, M., Okazawa, H., Diksic, M., Paris, J., Rosa, P., Mzengeza, S., et al. (2001). Brain Regional alpha-[11C]methyl-L-tryptophan trapping in impulsive subjects with borderline personality disorder. *The American Journal of Psychiatry*, *158*(5), 775–782.

Linnoila, M., Virkkunen, M., Scheinin, M., Nuutila, A., Rimon, R., & Goodwin, F. K. (1983). Low cerebrospinal fluid 5-hydroxyindoleacetic acid concentration differentiates impulsive from nonimpulsive violent behavior. *Life Sciences*, *33*(26), 2609–2614.

Loup, F., Tribollet, E., Dubois-Dauphin, M., & Dreifuss, J. J. (1991). Localization of high-affinity binding sites for oxytocin and vasopressin in the human brain. An autoradiographic study. *Brain Research*, *555*(2), 220–232.

Lozano-Soldevilla, D. (2018). On the physiological modulation and potential mechanisms underlying parieto-occipital alpha oscillations. *Frontiers in Computational Neuroscience*, *12*(20), 1.

Mann, E. O., & Mody, I. (2010). Control of hippocampal gamma oscillation frequency by tonic inhibition and excitation of interneurons. *Nature Neuroscience*, *13*(2), 205–212.

Marsh, D. M., Dougherty, D. M., Moeller, F. G., Swann, A. C., & Spiga, R. (2002). Laboratory-measured aggressive behavior of women: Acute tryptophan depletion and augmentation. *Neuropsychopharmacology*, *26*(5), 660–671.

McCloskey, M. S., Phan, K. L., Angstadt, M., Fettich, K. C., Keedy, S., & Coccaro, E. F. (2016). Amygdala hyperactivation to angry faces in intermittent explosive disorder. *Journal of Psychiatric Research*, *79*, 34–41.

Meyer, J. H., Kapur, S., Eisfeld, B., Brown, G. M., Houle, S., DaSilva, J., et al. (2001). The effect of paroxetine on 5-HT2A receptors in depression: An [18F]setoperone PET imaging study. *American Journal of Psychiatry*, *158*(1), 78–85.

Meyer-Lindenberg, A., Kolachana, B., Gold, B., Olsh, A., Nicodemus, K. K., Mattay, V., et al. (2009). Genetic variants in AVPR1A linked to autism predict amygdala activation and personality traits in healthy humans. *Molecular Psychiatry*, *14*, 968–975.

Mobini, S., Chiang, T. J., Ho, M. Y., Bradshaw, C. M., & Szabadi, E. (2000). Effects of central 5-hydroxytryptamine depletion on sensitivity to delayed and probabilistic reinforcement. *Psychopharmacology*, *152*(4), 390–397.

Moskowitz, D. S., Pinard, G., Zuroff, D. C., Annable, L., & Young, S. N. (2003). Tryptophan, serotonin and human social behavior. *Advances in Experimental Medicine and Biology*, *527*, 215–224.

Mottahedin, A., Ardalan, M., Chumak, T., Riebe, I., Ek, J., & Mallard, C. (2017). Effect of neuroinflammation on synaptic organization and function in the developing brain: Implications for neurodevelopmental and neurodegenerative disorders. *Frontiers in Cellular Neuroscience*, *11*, 190.

Ne'eman, R., Perach-Barzilay, N., Fischer-Shofty, M., Atias, A., & Shamay-Tsoory, S. G. (2016). Intranasal administration of oxytocin increases human aggressive behavior. *Hormones and Behavior*, *80*, 125–131.

New, A. S., Buchsbaum, M. S., Hazlett, E. A., Goodman, M., Koenigsber, H. W., Lo, J., et al. (2004). Fluoxetine increases relative metabolic rate in prefrontal cortex in impulsive aggression. *Psychopharmacology*, *176*(3–4), 451–458.

New, A. S., Hazlett, E. A., Buchsbaum, M. S., Goodman, M., Reynolds, D., Mitropoulou, V., et al. (2002). Blunted prefrontal cortical 18Fluorodeoxyglucose positron emission tomography response to meta-chlorophenylpiperazine in impulsive aggression. *Archives of General Psychiatry*, *59*(7), 621–629.

Newman, E. L., Smith, K. S., Takahashi, A., Chu, A., Hwa, L. S., Chen, Y., et al. (2015). α2-containing GABA(A) receptors: A requirement for midazolam-escalated aggression and social approach in mice. *Psychopharmacology*.

Ng, N. -K., Lee, H. -S., & Wong, P. T. -H. (1999). Regulation of striatal dopamine release through 5-HT1 and 5-HT2 receptors. *Journal of Neuroscience Research*, *55*(5), 600–607.

Parsey, R. V., Oquendo, M. A., Simpson, N. R., Ogden, R. T., Van Heertum, R., Arango, V., et al. (2002). Effects of sex, age, and aggressive traits in man on brain serotonin 5-HT1A receptor binding potential measured by PET using [C-11]WAY-100635. *Brain Research*, *954*(2), 173–182.

Passamonti, L., Crockett, M. J., Apergis-Schoute, A. M., Clark, L., Rowe, J. B., Calder, A. J., et al. (2012). Effects of acute tryptophan depletion on prefrontal-amygdala connectivity while viewing facial signals of aggression. *Biological Psychiatry*, *71*(1), 36–43.

Pelletier, M., & Siegel, R. M. (2009). Wishing away inflammation? New links between serotonin and TNF signaling. *Molecular Interventions*, *9*(6), 299–301.

Peremans, K., Audenaert, K., Hoysbergs, Y., Otte, A., Goethals, I., Gielen, I., et al. (2005). The effect of citalopram hydrobromide on 5-HT2A receptors in the impulsive-aggressive dog, as measured with 123I-5-I-R91150 SPECT. *European Journal of Nuclear Medicine and Molecular Imaging, 32*, 708–716.

Perez-Rodriguez, M. M., Hazlett, E. A., Rich, E. L., Ripoll, L. H., Weiner, D. M., Spence, N., et al. (2012). Striatal activity in borderline personality disorder with comorbid intermittent explosive disorder: Sex differences. *Journal of Psychiatric Research, 46*(6), 797–804.

Piñeyro, G., & Blier, P. (1999). Autoregulation of serotonin neurons: Role in antidepressant drug action. *Pharmacological Reviews, 51*(3), 533–591.

Placidi, G. P., Oquendo, M. A., Malone, K. M., Huang, Y. Y., Ellis, S. P., & Mann, J. J. (2001). Aggressivity, suicide attempts, and depression: Relationship to cerebrospinal fluid monoamine metabolite levels. *Biological Psychiatry, 50*(10), 783–791.

Prochazka, H., & Ågren, H. (2003). Self-rated aggression and cerebral monoaminergic turnover: Sex differences in patients with persistent depressive disorder. *European Archives of Psychiatry and Clinical Neuroscience, 253*(4), 185–192.

Reichmann, F., & Holzer, P. (2016). Neuropeptide Y: A stressful review. *Neuropeptides, 55*, 99–109.

Richell, R. A., Deakin, J. F. W., & Anderson, I. M. (2005). Effect of acute tryptophan depletion on the response to controllable and uncontrollable noise stress. *Biological Psychiatry, 57*(3), 295–300.

Ring, R. (2005). The central vasopressinergic system: Examining the opportunities for psychiatric drug development. *Current Pharmaceutical Design, 11*(2), 205–225.

Robinson, S., & Thiele, T. (2017). Chapter seven—The role of neuropeptide Y (NPY) in alcohol and drug abuse disorders. *International Review of Neurobiology, 136*, 177–197.

Rogers, C. N., Ross, A. P., Sahu, S. P., Siegel, E. R., Dooyeman, J. M., Cree, M. A., et al. (2018). Oxytocin- and arginine vasopressin-containing fibers in the cortex of humans, chimpanzees, and rhesus macaques. *American Journal of Primatology, 80*, e22875.

Romney, C., Hahn-Holbrook, J., Norman, G. J., Moore, A., & Holt-Lunstad, J. (2018). Where is the love? A double-blind, randomized study of the effects of intranasal oxytocin on stress regulation and aggression. *International Journal of Psychophysiology*. epub ahead of print.

Rosas-Ballina, M., & Tracey, K. J. (2009). The neurology of the immune system: Neural reflexes regulate immunity. *Neuron, 64*(1), 28–32.

Rosell, D. R., Tjompson, J. L., Slifstein, M., Xu, X., Frankle, W. G., New, A. S., et al. (2010). Increased serotonin 2A receptor availability in the orbitofrontal cortex of physically aggressive personality disordered patients. *Biological Psychiatry, 67*(12), 1154–1162.

Rubia, K., Lee, F., Cleare, A. J., Tunstall, N., Fu, C. H., Brammer, M., et al. (2005). Tryptophan depletion reduces right inferior prefrontal activation during response inhibition in fast, event-related fMRI. *Psychopharmacology, 179*(4), 791–803.

Rutkoski, N. J., Lerant, A. A., Nolte, C. M., Westberry, J., & Levenson, C. W. (2002). Regulation of neuropeptide Y in the rat amygdala following unilateral olfactory bulbectomy. *Brain Research, 951*(1), 69–76.

Samuels, B. A., Anacker, C., Levinstein, M. R., Pickenhagen, A., Tsetsenis, T., Madronal, N., et al. (2015). 5-HT1A receptors on mature dentate gyrus granule cells are critical for the antidepressant response. *Nature Neuroscience, 18*(11), 1606–1616.

Schlüter, T., Winz, O., Henkel, K., Prinz, S., Rademacher, L., Schmaljohann, J., et al. (2013). The impact of dopamine on aggression: An [18F]-FDOPA PET Study in healthy males. *The Journal of Neuroscience, 33*(43), 16889–16896.

Schweighofer, N., Bertin, M., Shishida, K., Okamoto, Y., Tanaka, S. C., Yamawaki, S., et al. (2008). Low-serotonin levels increase delayed reward discounting in humans. *Journal of Neuroscience, 28*(17), 4528–4532.

Seo, D., Patrick, C. J., & Kennealy, P. J. (2008). Role of serotonin and dopamine system interactions in the neurobiology of impulsive aggression and its comorbidity with other clinical disorders. *Aggression and Violent Behavior, 13*(5), 383–395.

Shaikh, M. B., & Siegel, A. (1994). Neuroanatomical and neurochemical mechanisms underlying amygdaloid control of defensive rage behavior in the cat. *Brazilian Journal of Medical and Biological Research*, *27*(12), 2759–2779.

Siever, L. J., Buchsbaum, M., New, A. S., Spiegel-Cohen, J., Wei, T., Hazlett, E. A., et al. (1999). d,l-Fenfluramine response in impulsive personality disorder assessed with [18F] fluorodeoxyglucose positron emission tomography. *Neuropsychopharmacology*, *20*(5), 413–423.

Soloff, P. H., George, A., Nathan, R. S., Schulz, P. M., & Perel, J. M. (1986). Paradoxical effects of amitriptyline on borderline patients. *American Journal of Psychiatry*, *143*(12), 1603–1605.

Soloff, P. H., Meltzer, C. C., Greer, P. J., Constantine, D., & Kelly, T. M. (1999). A fenfluramine-activated FDG-PET study of borderline personality disorder. *Biological Psychiatry*, *47*(6), 540–547.

Sterzer, P., Adams, R. A., Fletcher, P., Frith, C., Lawrie, S. M., Muckli, L., et al. (2018). The predictive coding account of psychosis. *Biological Psychiatry*, *84*, 634–643.

Tanaka, S. C., Schweighofer, N., Asahi, S., Shishida, K., Okamoto, Y., Yamawaki, S., et al. (2007). Serotonin differentially regulates short- and long-term prediction of rewards in the ventral and dorsal striatum. *PLoS One*, *2*(12).

Tononi, G., & Cirelli, C. (2014). Sleep and the price of plasticity: From synaptic and cellular homeostasis to memory consolidation and integration. *Neuron*, *81*(1), 12–34.

Vekovischeva, O. Y., Aitta-Aho, T., Kankaanpaa, S., Seppala, T., Honkanen, A., Sprengel, R., et al. (2004). Reduced aggression in AMPA-type glutamate receptor GluR-A subunit-deficient mice. *Genes, Brain and Behavior*, *3*(5), 253–654.

Vila-Ballo, A., Hdez-Lafuente, P., Rostan, C., Cunillera, T., & Rodriguez-Fornells, A. (2014). Neurophysiological correlates of error monitoring and inhibitory processing in juvenile violent offenders. *Biological Psychology*, *102*(1), 141–152.

Virkkunen, M., Nuutila, A., Goodwin, F. K., & Linnoila, M. (1987). Cerebrospinal fluid monoamine metabolite levels in male arsonists. *Archives of General Psychiatry*, *44*(3), 241–247.

Walter, L., & Stella, N. (2004). Cannabinoids and neuroinflammation. *British Journal of Pharmacology*, *141*(5), 775–785.

Wang, G. J., Volkow, N. D., Fowler, J. S., Hitzemann, R. J., Pappas, N. R., & Netusil, N. (1998). Evaluation of gender difference in regional brain metabolic responses to lorazepam. *Psychiatry Research*, *82*(1), 37–46.

Weber, E. T., & Andrade, R. (2010). Htr2a gene and 5-HT2A receptor expression in the cerebral cortex studied using genetically modified mice. *Frontiers in Neuroscience*, *4*(36), 1.

Wolpert, D. M., Doya, K., & Kawato, M. (2003). A unifying computational framework for motor control and social interaction. *Philosophical Transactions of the Royal Society, B: Biological Sciences*, *358*(1431), 593–602.

Yanowitch, R., & Coccaro, E. F. (2011). The neurochemistry of human aggression. *Advances in Genetics*, *75*, 151–169.

Yip, J., & Chahl, L. (2001). Localization of NK1 and NK3 receptors in guinea-pig brain. *Regulatory Peptides*, *98*, 55–62.

Young, E. J., & Williams, C. L. (2010). Valence dependent asymmetric release of norepinephrine in the basolateral amygdala. *Behavioral Neuroscience*, *124*(5), 633–644.

Zanarini, M. C., Frankenburg, F. R., & Parachini, E. A. (2004). A preliminary, randomized trial of fluoxetine, olanzapine, and the olanzapine-fluoxetine combination in women with borderline personality disorder. *Journal of Clinical Psychiatry*, *65*(7), 903–907.

CHAPTER SIX

Neuroimaging in Aggression and IED

Sarah K. Keedy, Majd Alsayed, Emil F. Coccaro
Clinical Neuroscience & Psychopharmacology Research Unit, Department of Psychiatry and Behavioral Neuroscience, Pritzker School of Medicine, University of Chicago, Chicago, IL, United States

Contents

Over the past few decades, neuroimaging techniques have been developed to allow observation of both the structure and function of the living brain, shedding light on the neural substrates of behavior, including human aggression. Such work has informed our understanding of brain systems underlying both normal expressions of aggression and the problematic impulsive aggression seen in Intermittent Explosive Disorder (IED). In this chapter, we provide a brief overview of neuroimaging techniques, then highlight and review the contributions neuroimaging studies have made to understanding normal and problematic impulsive aggression.

Overview of Neuroimaging

In research applications of neuroimaging, brain images are acquired through various techniques and then submitted to different measurement and computational procedures, typically yielding quantitative information.

https://doi.org/10.1016/B978-0-12-813858-8.00006-1

This is in contrast to clinical applications of neuroimaging, which usually consist of visual review of images by an expert (e.g., a neuroradiologist) who describes any identified pathology and writes a clinically oriented report. The quantitative information from research neuroimaging goes beyond the qualitative identification of abnormality, as in clinical neuroimaging, and characterizes what are often more subtle relationships between a spectrum of normal to abnormal properties of the brain in relation to diagnosis, behavior, or traits. Neuroimaging clinical populations, such as IED, for research purposes is a heavily multidisciplinary endeavor, involving clinicians, statisticians, bioengineers, physicists, and more.

There are two types of research neuroimaging—structural and functional. Structural imaging characterizes tissues comprising the brain and can be used for volume, shape, or other studies of the brain's physical properties. Computerized tomography (CT) was the first neuroimaging technique, available in the 1970s, providing structural images. CT images allow identification of tissue types (blood, bone, cerebrospinal fluid, or gray and white matter), by the darkness of the grayscale images. Images from CT have played roles in lesion studies linking gross brain alterations to behavioral changes, including in studies relevant to aggression (Herzberg & Fenwick, 1988).

The most prolific neuroimaging technique for understanding human brain–behavior links is, by far, magnetic resonance imaging (MRI). In structural MRI studies, accessible since the 1980s, images can have high enough resolution to allow anatomical measurement at the millimeter scale, with good gray vs. white matter tissue differentiation. Gray and white matter differentiation is important because they serve different functions. Gray matter is mostly neuronal cell bodies. These cells conduct the functions of the brain, such as sensory processing, cognition, and emotional functions, so observations of relatively more or less gray matter, or altered shape of a gray matter structure within the brain, can have implications for how the neurons developed, organized, or are degenerating, and can impact their capacity to fulfill their functions. Studies that utilize cross sectional samples do not typically point directly to any of these interpretations of changes in amount of tissue but can support hypotheses regarding them. However, even longitudinal studies using MRI cannot usually resolve the nature of change at the cellular level. More microscopic methods, animal work, or postmortem tissue analyses are needed. Still, MRI-based observations are important as they document the human brain in vivo and changes can be correlated to behavioral changes, strengthening conclusions regarding the importance of the brain regions involved, especially in relation to a behavior measured (Johansen-Berg, 2012).

The white matter rendered in conventional MRI is that which comprises white matter tracts, which are cells wrapping around the connecting portions of the gray matter cells (axons of the neurons) reaching across distances to communicate. Thus white matter facilitates connectivity among the brain's subdivided parts, helping form cortico-cortical connections or cortical–subcortical connections. White matter volume can be measured in MRI in a similar fashion to gray matter volume. Relatively less white matter in one group compared to another may indicate poor quality of connections between brain regions, impacting efficiency of communication and function of the connected parts. There is an MRI technique called diffusion tensor imaging (DTI) that is used to study another property of white matter—how freely water is moving within its tracts. As water is generally expected to move within a more restricted longitudinal (oval) shape in accordance with the shape of the white matter cells wrapping around the axons, the metrics from DTI that describe this are taken as observations of the integrity of the white matter. Major white matter tracts traversing larger distances across the brain are easier to render with DTI, and smaller, thinner ones, or places where white matter fibers going different directions intersect, are more challenging to image, but computational approaches combined with more refined MRI acquisitions are improving our capacity to resolve these problems (Chanraud, Zahr, Sullivan, & Pfefferbaum, 2010).

Functional neuroimaging renders information about neural activity. Functional MRI (fMRI) is one such technique. First used in research starting in the 1990s, fMRI involves collecting an image of the brain about every 2 seconds for a period of several minutes, usually while the person performs some mental task. The images are acquired in a manner that is sensitive to the blood oxygen-level dependent (BOLD) signal. Through the use of signal processing principles, spatial transformations, and statistical techniques, this time series of images is used to localize brain regions where the BOLD signal is higher or lower, providing insight into which parts of the brain were more or less metabolically active. The BOLD signal is the key measurement from fMRI, as it reflects increased neuronal activity, though indirectly. The rationale is that greater neural activity must occur where there is greater demand for oxygen (Logothetis, 2003). Usually "activation" via a BOLD signal measurement is meant as "relatively active" compared to some control task. It is also considered relative to the background "noise" of the brain conducting its constant business of homeostatic and other regulatory processes, taking in external stimuli, blocking out irrelevant signals, and, of course, conscious thought (appreciation of this constant activity in the brain negates any serious consideration of the axiom "humans only use 10% of their brain" (Beyerstein, 2004)). Further, it would be a mistake to think of parts of the brain not identified as "active" during some task to be *non*-active for that task; they may simply not be differentially active in a key manner for the purposes of the study. For example, the primary visual cortex of the occipital lobe at the back of the brain becomes active when a person views emotional faces. However, the occipital lobe is not differentially active across emotional expressions and so is not reported as "active" in such studies. Usually the interest is in what may be uniquely active within the brain during viewing of, for example, threatening faces.

A great deal of methodological and technical creativity has gone into fMRI studies to capture brain activity during experimentally controlled cognition or behavior. Subjects may passively view stimuli, such as pictures, many of which have become standardized sets used by multiple research groups. Subjects may perform mental operations such as judging similarity of objects, silently repeating words, or imagining a scene in accordance with a script read to them. In addition to showing stimuli in the scanner to monitor the brain as it processes input or conducts a mental task, responses documenting answers or judgments can be recorded during scanning, serving as external indicators of thought. This recording is conducted via a number of MRI-compatible human–computer interface devices such as button boxes located at the fingertips, eye movements recorded via eye trackers, and more. All of this is implemented in a context of also requiring the participant to lie as still as possible while being scanned.

A final type of neuroimaging to mention is positron emission tomography (PET), which arguably can convey either functional or structural information about the brain. This technique relies on measuring properties of radioactive materials injected intravenously, so as a method, has practical limitations. However, it predated fMRI as a means for assessing how different brain areas become "active" under different behavioral conditions or between different groups. PET has therefore provided some of the evidence regarding key brain areas underlying aggression. "Activation" in PET is defined by relative increases in metabolic demand in different brain regions. Although fMRI has surpassed this type of PET imaging in terms of safety and in terms of spatial and temporal resolution, PET has a unique capacity to convey molecular information about the brain, and so is a form of structural imaging. Through the use of different radioactive ligands specifically designed to detect the presence or availability of neurotransmitters (chemical messengers facilitating communication from one neuron to the next) or their receptors, PET is able to measure these molecular features of the brain and to do so with regional specificity (Nasrallah & Dubroff, 2013).

The field of research neuroimaging is relatively young, but now mature enough to retrospectively recognize challenges in its past associated with its youth. Issues include small samples, poor statistical control, and other factors that limit scientific rigor (Poldrack et al., 2017). This understanding helps explain inconsistencies in the literature. There is increasing attention to the need for the field to develop and enforce standards for methods and reporting them (Carp, 2012). Awareness of such concerns will be critically applied wherever possible in the subsequent sections.

Neural Substrates of Human Aggression

A basic framework for understanding how human brains produce aggressive behavior draws from the principal observation that phylogenetically conserved motivational brain systems come under greater control as animals become more behaviorally complex. Aggressive behavior is observed across many species, including those with much simpler brains than mammals (let alone humans). Control and modulation of aggressive behavior in mammals comes by way of one of the distinguishing anatomical features of this group—the neocortex. Mammals possess this large outer layer of brain tissue in proportionally larger and more complex connectivity profiles as behavior becomes more complex, and in particular, more social (Barton, 1996; Hofman, 2012). The fact that there are complex control mechanisms in human brains regulating aggression fits with the dimensional nature of aggression as a human behavioral characteristic. Aggression is commonly observed but at varying frequency or intensity among individuals, and this range is related to the variety of factors impacting whether aggression occurs, including those internal to the person (traits, motivational state) or external (social or other environmental). From this array, a useful focus for this chapter is on key constructs known to contribute to the problematic impulsive aggression of IED. These are internal factors and include social–emotional information processing and relevant behavioral traits predisposing toward aggression (e.g., tending toward "approach" responses rather than "avoidance" responses across a variety of situations). These factors are mediated most clearly by three key brain regions: the amygdala, the orbitofrontal cortex, and the temporoparietal junction. We discuss each in turn as follows, highlighting structural and functional neuroimaging studies supporting their roles first in healthy individuals and then in IED.

Studies of Healthy Individuals

Amygdala

The amygdala shows significant responsivity to negative, especially threatening, stimuli. In this way, it plays a role in aggression by signaling emotional provocation. The amygdala is a group of nuclei located bilaterally in the anterior medial temporal lobe. It is "corticoid" rather than cortical, meaning it does not show the organized cellular layering characteristic of neocortex. As nonneocortex, the amygdala has identifiable analogs in submammalian groups like lizards (Medina, Bupesh, & Abellan, 2011), and for our purposes here, represents that part of evolutionarily conserved brain systems for motivated behaviors such as aggression. Each nucleus in the human amygdala has its own connectivity profile with other parts of the brain, but when taken together, the connections paint a picture of the amygdala's role. It integrates external sensory information (such as threatening facial expressions), aspects of the internal milieu (such as current arousal state), and memory (knowledge of what is threatening), and influences behavior accordingly (Price, 2003).

Some evidence supports a correlation between structural properties of the amygdala such as its volume and propensity toward aggression among healthy people, though this is not always found. One small study of 20 healthy women reported greater history of lifetime aggression associated with smaller amygdala volumes (Matthies et al., 2012). This study was conducted using manual tracing of the amygdala size from MRI images. As opposed to these positive findings associating amygdala and aggression, no association of amygdala volume was found with life history of aggression in a large population-based community sample (Coccaro et al., 2018). This latter study employed a "voxelwise" search for such associations across the whole brain, meaning the whole brain was divided into $2 \times 2 \times 2$ mm cubes, or voxels, with each voxel assigned a value representing estimated density of gray matter within it, calculated with automated methods as part of a technique called voxel-based morphometry (Ashburner & Friston, 2000).

Another study of amygdala size addressed the nature of the structure as a subdivided set of nuclei serving different roles in aggression (Gopal et al., 2013). In this study, hand-traced volumes of the whole amygdala were not associated with aggression or impulsivity. However, when amygdala traces were divided into a dorsal (top) half and a ventral (bottom) half, significant associations with variables of aggression were observed. Smaller left dorsal halves, thought to be influenced by the size of the central nucleus of the amygdala with outputs to the autonomic nervous system (internal milieu/stress), were associated with greater life history of aggression scores. The ventral half, presumably influenced largely by the size of basolateral nuclei of the amygdala where sensory input is received, associated bilaterally with motor impulsivity measures, displayed no relationship with aggression. This implies that the dorsal portion of the (left) amygdala may have more relevance to aggression through its impact on the autonomic nervous system, such that a smaller volume may lead to reduced regulation of stress responses induced by the autonomic nervous system. A key caveat for this study is that the sample contained 41 psychiatric patients with aggression scores in the problematic range; however, the diagnoses of the subjects were not those of usual interest to aggression research (i.e., many had psychotic and mood disorders rather than IED, psychopathy, or personality disorder).

Studies of the functioning of the amygdala in healthy groups have been far clearer than structural imaging in establishing the structure's role in aggression. Interestingly, straightforward studies in healthy populations have been more recent, following up on hypotheses about the role of the amygdala generated from animal, lesion, and clinical studies (including of IED, reviewed later in this chapter). These amygdala function studies have largely utilized fMRI, consistent with their recency, and the majority tend to employ tasks of viewing standardized faces making threatening facial expressions. Specifically, the faces are usually expressing anger or fear and are gazing at the camera. Angry faces are considered a less ambiguous social threat and therefore brain responses to them are of clearer interpretive value in understanding the role of a provocative threat in aggression. Fearful faces are more ambiguous, as they may indicate a variety of potential circumstances, yet are also informative for aggression research given the potential indication that fearful faces signal the need to prepare an aggressive response.

Carlson and colleagues conducted an fMRI study with 15 male and female healthy volunteers and found left amygdala response to very briefly presented fearful faces was stronger for those who reported more anger expression (Carlson, Greenberg, & Mujica-Parodi, 2010). This is consistent with one role of the amygdala as a rapid threat detector via its capacity to receive sensory input so brief that it may not be fully consciously processed. Such a rapid pathway for detection of threat is an important survival mechanism. These results are consistent with this aspect of the amygdala's role, such that those with more sensitive amygdala responsiveness to rapidly detected threat are experiencing more instances of registering threat and therefore responding aggressively. This amygdala activation did not correlate with reported levels of experienced anger. On the other hand, right amygdala response was reduced when viewing fearful faces that were presented for longer periods of time, and so were fully consciously processed. This right amygdala response did correlate with greater propensity to experience anger. This association of lower amygdala response to fully processed emotional information and higher trait anger levels is consistent with reports of hypo-responsiveness of the amygdala in association with premeditated (as opposed to impulsive) aggression (Marsh & Blair, 2008).

Beaver and colleagues imaged 22 healthy people with fMRI and assessed a trait called "behavioral approach," a general pattern of lifelong behavior, or trait, associated with greater likelihood for aggression. They also assessed the opposite trait, behavioral inhibition, associated with lower tendency toward aggression. Left amygdala response to angry, but not sad, faces correlated with higher propensity for behavioral approach (Beaver, Lawrence, Passamonti, & Calder, 2008). The left-sided finding is consistent with that of Carlson et al. (2010), though both are small studies.

Carre and colleagues assessed only dorsal and ventral amygdala responses to threatening faces in relation to trait anger, anxiety, and gender in a robustly sized group of healthy individuals ($n=103$) (Carre, Fisher, Manuck, & Hariri, 2012). They found that while the whole group showed the expected amygdala response (encompassing both dorsal and ventral portions) to angry or fearful faces, men ($n=46$) with higher trait anger and higher trait anxiety (which correlate with one another significantly) had greater bilateral dorsal amygdala responsiveness to just angry faces, with a slightly more robust result for left dorsal amygdala. This finding further specified the role of left amygdala activation in response to threatening faces for men more likely to be aggressive. No such clear relationship of anger and amygdala activation to threat was found for women. Interestingly, gender is often used as a "covariate of no interest" in neuroimaging (or other) analyses when the sample includes men and women. This methodological step means that any differences in the activation to the stimuli that may exist between men and women is not examined, but is instead "tossed out" and analyses then move on to the construct of interest. Whether sex-specific effects would be found in other studies using this common covarying approach to gender is therefore unknown. However, it does seem likely sex effects would be found routinely if explicitly sought. This is for at least two reasons: (a) behaviorally, men and women differ in propensity toward aggression (Archer, 2004) and (b) there is differential brain activity in accordance with sex hormone levels (Rubin et al., 2017) and menstrual cycle phase particularly impacting social cognition (Mareckova et al., 2014). If these factors were controlled for, clearer patterns may emerge for threat processing in women, but they are not commonly assessed.

Beyond threatening face processing, there is additional evidence from functional neuroimaging that supports the role of the amygdala in the normal range of aggression. One example is a social threat task conducted during fMRI scans in an all-female healthy sample ($n=36$) involving playing a game against an opponent (Buades-Rotger, Beyer, & Kramer, 2017). The subject could choose to fight or flee when the perceived opponent was either highly provocative (aggressive) toward them, or less so. Results were that amygdala activation was only noted when fleeing a highly provocative (threatening) opponent. Amygdala activation was not identified as uniquely involved in a choice to "fight" the opponent. This sheds some light on threat signaling rather than participation in aggression per se for the amygdala. As the sample was restricted to females, further study is needed to determine whether men would show a similar result.

Frontal Cortex

The frontal cortex plays an important role in key aspects of impulsive aggression. It regulates amygdala responsivity, and participates in social information processing in a variety of ways, such as holding representations of reward/punishment valuations and mediating impulsivity. Whereas the amygdala is identifiable across many species, neocortex is unique to mammals, and the frontal portion is particularly developed in primates (Kass, 2013). Frontal cortex is comprised of functional portions that do not necessarily respect the obvious physical, anatomical boundaries provided by the gyri and sulci. Instead, these functional zones, identified via early cytoarchitecture studies and recent neuroimaging studies (Petrider, Tomaiuolo, Yeterian, & Pandya, 2012) span adjacent portions of different frontal gyri and are usually referred to with directional labels such as "medial prefrontal" or "dorsolateral prefrontal" cortex. These functionally unified zones spanning across frontal gyri portend the complex connections of frontal cortex within itself and with the rest of the brain, working to regulate and integrate demands from the outside environment and internal goals and motivations, such as it does in mediating aggression.

There are several portions of frontal cortex key to determining normal aggression, but most focus has been on orbitofrontal cortex (OFC) due to its anatomic and functional connection to the amygdala (Ghashghaei, Hilgetag, & Barbas, 2007). OFC is located across the orbital surface of the frontal lobe, the portion at the base of the front of the brain located over the eyes (orbits). It can usually be usefully further divided into lateral and medial portions, both of which are involved in aggression. There is no clear evidence for structural characteristics of OFC, detectable with neuroimaging, relating to normal ranges of human aggression. For example, the population-based community sample study assessing gray matter volume correlates of life history of aggression scores found no relationship with OFC gray matter volume (Coccaro et al., 2018). Another study used DTI to address whether integrity of the white matter connecting OFC and amygdala related to levels of normal aggression by scanning 93 younger (age 18-30, mean 23) healthy males and administering psychometric and analog laboratory measures of aggression (Beyer, Munte, Wiechert, Heldmann, & Kramer, 2014). They found no relationship of the white matter between OFC and amygdala to aggression, nor did any white matter tract correlate with aggression in exploratory analyses. While this finding may seem counterintuitive given established anatomical connectivity of amygdala and OFC, the sensitivity of neuroimaging methods to detect properties that quantitatively relate to a normal range of behavior may be inadequate. Further, the functional connectivity of OFC and amygdala is not solely dependent on white matter, and DTI measures of white matter between gray matter structures have not been shown to have reliable association with fMRI-based measures of connectivity.

Functional neuroimaging has demonstrated the role of OFC in normal aggression. In contrast to amygdala studies, the literature on OFC's involvement with anger or aggression is older and includes PET imaging. This literature hones in on the experience of emotions, whereas in the amygdala literature, focus has been more on emotional information processing (e.g., processing facial expressions). One such study of emotional experience utilized an emotion induction technique during PET scanning, asking 18 healthy adults to think of events from their own past that evoked either anxiety, anger, or emotionally neutral memories (Kimbrell et al., 1999). Subjects also viewed pictures of faces depicting the desired emotion for each memory. Anger increased activity in left lateral OFC, as did anxiety, but anger also evoked relatively greater right lateral OFC activation compared to anxiety. Another study attempted anger induction during

PET scanning using personal narratives of the 8 male participants to induce the feelings (Dougherty et al., 1999). Increased left lateral OFC activation was found during anger-inducing memories. Yet another approach reported was to ask 15 healthy volunteers to imagine acting aggressively per a scene described to them by experimenters during PET imaging (Pietrini, Guazzelli, Basso, Jaffe, & Grafman, 2000). They also scanned the subjects while imagining a nonaggressive but similar scene, attempting to control for general mental imagery processes. Results showed medial OFC having lower activity under an imagined "unrestrained" aggression condition relative to the nonaggression condition.

These PET studies show contradictory outcomes in terms of lower vs. higher activation in OFC during anger/aggression. This is likely related to the different tasks used, where personal memory vs. nonexperienced imagining likely invoked the frontal cortex in fairly different manners. Further, the computations involved to analyze the data, including contrasting the anger conditions against different kinds of control conditions, can result in conclusions of greater or lesser activation and are not straightforward to compare. However, OFC as key to experienced anger and aggression is a reasonable conclusion to draw on the basis of these studies.

One PET study examined emotional face viewing and reported OFC activation for viewing angry, but not sad, faces in 13 healthy males (Blair, Morris, Frith, Perrett, & Dolan, 1999). However, there was no amygdala response to angry faces. This, along with the lack of amygdala response in the emotion induction studies previously discussed, raises some concern for whether PET is as sensitive to anger-related change in the amygdala as it is for OFC. To some extent the PET method (e.g., choice of radioactive substance, design of stimulus presentation) may play a role in differential sensitivity.

Other paradigms of experiencing and enacting aggression in a healthy sample have been conducted in fMRI studies and further characterize the role of OFC. Beyer and colleagues had 32 healthy males being scanned while viewing videos of someone looking angry or neutral while also enduring provocative, aggressive actions by the person in the videos (e.g., using an adapted Taylor Aggression Paradigm) (Beyer, Munte, Gottlich, & Kramer, 2015). Medial and lateral portions of OFC were activated in association with viewing the angry faces and experiencing behavioral aggression. However, the more reduced the medial OFC activation was while viewing angry faces, the more aggressive the subject was when given the opportunity. Curiously, the amygdala did not show any differential responsivity to any task condition. Another study of experiencing aggression by another person in an experimentally controlled manner with the chance to act aggressively back (Skibsted et al., 2017), conducted in twelve females and eight males, also found OFC activation when being provoked, as well as increased amygdala response. However, the task, smaller sample size, and/or analysis approach did not prove sensitive enough to reveal any brain regions associated with choosing to respond aggressively.

Functional connectivity, or correlated fluctuations in activity over time, is of interest for OFC and amygdala to better understand their roles in aggression. In one study, connectivity was assessed from fMRI scans acquired while healthy males ($n=13$) engaged in violent and nonviolent acts in a video game, a potential analog to engaging in aggressive behavior (Klasen et al., 2013). The amygdala-OFC connectivity was further compared while the participants took a placebo or quetiapine, a drug known to reduce aggressive behavior. The subjects reported lower feelings of anger and aggression while taking quetiapine compared to placebo, and OFC-amygdala connectivity was reduced during aggressive acts compared to nonviolent acts in the game while taking the quetiapine. This suggests that altered synchrony between the two regions may be a mechanism of this medication-induced reduction in anger and aggression.

Other Prefrontal Cortical Areas

We have noted the lack of amygdala and OFC brain volume correlates with aggression in a population-based community sample. Despite this negative finding, the investigators did report that gray matter volume in medial prefrontal and lateral prefrontal cortex correlated inversely with a greater life history of aggression (Coccaro et al., 2018). This suggests that the role of these cortices may be more important in the normal range of aggression than is appreciated in the literature that focuses on amygdala and OFC, which largely stems from clinical studies. Similarly, in a study of self-reported healthy young adults ($n=138$), which similar to Coccaro et al. (2018) searched the whole brain for correlation between aggression and gray matter density, lower gray matter in medial prefrontal cortex correlated only with the proneness for physical (but not verbal) aggression (Chester, Lynam, Milich, & Dewall, 2017). Finally, an fMRI study of healthy individuals (8 female, 10 male) reported reduced medial prefrontal gyrus activation during anger induction, but not during anxiety induction, offering some functional insight into the role of the more dorsal medial frontal region

(Kimbrell et al., 1999). Overall, further work is needed to clarify the role of these prefrontal regions in the normal range of aggression.

Temporoparietal Junction

A final key brain area for aggression may be the temporoparietal junction (TPJ), a portion of neocortex located, as the name implies, at the junction of two lobes, the temporal and the parietal. It is thought to support functions such as distinguishing self from other, and "mentalizing," or understanding the thoughts, feelings, or perspective of others (Carter & Huettel, 2013; Eddy, 2016). Impulsive aggression could be mitigated or exacerbated on the basis of such information since attribution of hostile intent versus a more innocent attribution of action taken by another increases the risk of aggressive behavior toward the "other." While structural neuroimaging studies have not found TPJ to be associated with aggression in healthy individuals, one functional neuroimaging study has reported an association. TPJ was active in an fMRI study of healthy women ($n=36$) engaging in a task where an opponent behaved more or less aggressively and the participants could fight back or flee (Buades-Rotger et al., 2017). Analyses indicated that the TPJ was activated when fleeing from high aggression, suggesting that such behavior is accompanied by heightened signaling regarding the understanding of the other person's intentions. Attention to this region is newer for human aggression research and further studies should continue to shed light on its role.

Intermittent Explosive Disorder

The behavioral nature of IED is extensively described elsewhere in this book. Briefly, it is a psychiatric condition diagnosed when aggression occurs at an abnormally high frequency and/or intensity, and is maladaptive. It is distinguished from other forms of problematic aggression, such as premediated aggression as may occur in psychopathy, by the reactive/impulsive nature of the aggressive acts. There have been neuroimaging studies of other psychiatric conditions where impulsive aggression is problematic, such as borderline personality disorder, known to have not only the aggressive behavior overlap, but also diagnostic overlap with IED. However, this overlap is not often formally assessed and reported in studies of borderline personality disorder, so it is not straightforward to apply the findings to IED. While such literature has been used to support hypotheses on neural alterations associated with IED, there is now a body of neuroimaging literature focused on IED that is directly informative and is the focus of the review below.

Amygdala

Alterations to structural properties of the amygdala have been found in IED. A straightforward study of gray matter volume across the entire brain in a sample of 57 people with IED found that, compared with 53 healthy people and 58 people with other psychiatric disorders, the right amygdala had reduced gray matter (Coccaro et al., 2016). Further, this study found a correlation showing less gray matter was associated with a more extensive history of aggressive behavior. The shape of the amygdala was also abnormal in roughly the same sample, with significantly more areas of inward deformation compared with healthy controls (Coccaro, Lee, McCloskey, Csernansky, & Wang, 2015), specifying further the nature of the altered amygdala structure in IED.

Neuroimaging studies addressing functional brain alterations in IED have focused on social threat processing. Viewing emotional faces expressing threat (anger and fear) has therefore been a centerpiece of these neuroimaging studies and reveals altered amygdala function. The first study directly observing subjects with IED ($n=10$) compared with controls used fMRI during emotional face viewing and found greater amygdala response to angry faces for those with IED (Coccaro, McCloskey, Fitzgerald, & Phan, 2007). Further, the more the amygdala showed this heightened reactivity to angry faces, the greater the extent of their prior aggressive behavior. Similar heightened response to angry faces in the amygdala was found in a larger ($n=20$) IED sample (McCloskey et al., 2016). The findings from these two studies are consistent despite their employing slightly different versions of the emotional faces tasks. The earlier study asked participants to identify gender of the emotional faces, rendering the emotional processing aspect implicit. The later study asked participants to label the emotions they were viewing as positive or negative, making emotional processing explicit. The observation of heightened amygdala response to angry faces in IED regardless of these task conditions suggests the heightened amygdala response is not impacted readily in IED by the higher order processes invoked by the different task instructions. Rather, the deficit appears to be a more bottom-up, sensory processing alteration.

One study reported on both structural and functional aspects of the amygdala in groups of men characterized as high on reactive aggression to a problematic degree (not formally a study of IED, but reasonably approximating it) (Bobes et al., 2013). Amygdala function was assessed with an emotional face processing task, using fearful or neutral expressions. The aggressive men had increased amygdala reactivity to neutral faces and less gray matter in left dorsal amygdala. These functional and structural findings overlapped in location. These abnormalities were also correlated with self-reported reactive aggression, such that greater abnormality in amygdala associated with greater aggression, and the amygdala abnormalities did not correlate with callous traits as seen in conditions associated with premeditated aggression. The heightened response to neutral faces is similar to prior reports of aggressive individuals perceiving neutral faces more negatively (Best, Williams, & Coccaro, 2002). Lack of heightened reactivity to fearful faces is consistent with the Coccaro et al. (2007) study, which used fearful faces but did not find significantly increased activity for them in IED.

Orbitofrontal Cortex

The only study addressing OFC size in IED was the Coccaro et al. (2016) study, which employed a whole brain search for gray matter differences between IED, healthy and psychiatric controls. Findings included reduced OFC volume in IED. OFC was also part of the composite measure, along with amygdala and other regions, which correlated negatively with severity of aggression (smaller volume associated with greater aggression).

The first study of IED subjects viewing emotional faces (Coccaro et al., 2007) found reduced OFC activation for angry expressions compared to controls. Further, healthy controls demonstrated a negative correlation between left amygdala and OFC activation during this task, whereas IEDs did not show any correlation between those regions. While the later study with a larger IED sample (McCloskey et al., 2016) did not report OFC activation differences between IEDs and controls for anger or any expression, assessment of right amygdala connectivity to OFC did show alteration. Controls displayed a negative correlation, as in the earlier study, but IED subjects displayed a positive correlation between the brain regions. While these smaller studies have inconsistencies, they both fit a hypothesis of a dysregulated circuit between the highly interconnected amygdala and OFC for processing and regulating responses to threat.

A PET study assessing receptors for the neurotransmitter serotonin sheds some light on how results of functional neuroimaging studies of IED may be inconsistent in OFC: they could be due to state-dependent effects. Specifically, the state-dependent effect could be how recently aggressive behavior occurred. The finding was that IED ($n=14$) subjects with at least three acts of physical aggression in the past year had lower serotonin levels in the OFC compared with IED subjects without such recent aggression and compared with healthy controls (Rosell et al., 2010). Hence, the recency of aggression in IED may be reflected in aspects of OFC physiology. When OFC function is normal in some studies, it may be due to a preponderance of subjects without such recent aggression history. On the other hand, serotonin receptor binding measured in PET has unclear association to the BOLD signal measured in fMRI studies, so these are tentative interpretations and further research is needed. However, other PET studies have found reduced serotonergic modulation in OFC in impulsive aggressive individuals (New et al., 2002; Siever et al., 1999).

Another study of potential, though indirect, evidence for reduced OFC function in IED involved nine individuals convicted of murder or attempted murder, and whose crimes were described as uncontrolled, emotionally charged, and who were described as individuals who could generally be triggered by physical or verbal aggression from others (Raine et al., 1998). These "affective murderers" were compared with murderers whose crimes were predatory/premeditated. The comparison was on brain metabolism as assessed with PET imaging while performing an attention task. Results showed lower lateral and medial prefrontal metabolism for the affective murderers. All murderers had increased subcortical metabolism (amygdala, midbrain, hippocampus, and thalamus). Hence, those with unplanned impulsive violence were characterized by lower function in frontal brain regions thought to normally inhibit and modulate limbic regions, including those subcortical areas showing increased metabolism.

Other Frontal Cortex

There are additional areas in the frontal cortex that appear to be structurally altered in IED that are relatively recent observations and require further study. In the population-based study of brain volume and aggression referred to earlier, about 10% of the subjects reported elevated life histories aggression, similar to the level observed in those with IED. This subgroup displayed a 10% reduction in both the medial prefrontal cortex and the left lateral prefrontal cortex (Coccaro et al., 2018). A study of white matter integrity, as assessed via DTI, was conducted in those with IED ($n=42$) compared with psychiatric (but nonaggressive) controls ($n=42$) and healthy controls ($n=40$) (Lee et al., 2016). Results were that IEDs had reduced white matter integrity in portions of a major white matter tract called the superior longitudinal fasciculus, connecting frontal and temporoparietal regions. The location of the alterations to this large tract was fairly central, potentially contributing to disruption in long-range communication from frontal to posterior and temporal regions. Further, these reductions in white matter integrity correlated with worse aggression. Such problems with communication across the brain's major regions may help explain altered functional activation and behavioral disturbance, as there could be less optimal regulation and information integration given a degraded communication conduit.

Temporoparietal Junction

No study, to date, has reported changes in TPJ volume or other structural aspects in IED, though the white matter alterations noted in the Lee et al. (2016) study could certainly impact connectivity of TPJ to other areas. One functional imaging study has implicated TPJ as a potential location of change associated with medication known to reduce aggression in IED (Cremers, Lee, Keedy, Phan, & Coccaro, 2016). The study used an emotional face processing task during fMRI. Subjects took either escitalopram, a selective serotonin reuptake inhibitor (SSRI), or placebo. A primary finding was that IEDs ($n=17$) had increased activity in TPJ while taking escitalopram and viewing a variety of emotional faces compared to controls ($n=14$) and to placebo. This was observed in the absence of change in the amygdala in IED. This location of enhanced neural function associated with the SSRI in IED could impact perspective taking or more accurate assessment of others' minds, though these constructs were not measured in the study. Overall, this enhancement to social cognitive processing is a potential therapeutic approach for IED.

Conclusion

Neuroimaging studies spanning structural and functional methods support a model specifying some key neural substrates underlying normal human aggression and problematic impulsive aggression as exemplified by those diagnosed with IED. These brain regions include the amygdala, with its rapid threat-detecting properties particularly tuned to social threat, and the OFC, which regulates the amygdala and appears to play a role in the experience of anger as well as social threat processing and responding. IED is associated with alterations in these brain regions. Additional portions of the frontal lobe and the TPJ are emerging as having key roles, as well, for aggression and its regulation, with TPJ of particular interest as a treatment target. Overall, this picture is consistent with the complex nature of neurocognitive determinants of human aggression, as well as with the relative newness of neuroimaging methods in research, yielding some converging evidence, but some that is in need of further, more rigorous study.

References

Archer, J. (2004). Sex differences in aggression in real-world settings: A meta-analytic review. *Review of General Psychology*, *8*, 291–322.

Ashburner, J., & Friston, K. J. (2000). Voxel-based morphometry—The methods. *NeuroImage*, *11*, 805–821.

Barton, R. A. (1996). Neocortex size and behavioural ecology in primates. *Proceedings of the Royal Society B: Biological Sciences*, *263*, 173–177.

Beaver, J. D., Lawrence, A. D., Passamonti, L., & Calder, A. J. (2008). Appetitive motivation predicts the neural response to facial signals of aggression. *Journal of Neuroscience*, *28*, 2719–2725.

Best, M., Williams, J. M., & Coccaro, E. F. (2002). Evidence for a dysfunctional prefrontal circuit in patients with an impulsive aggressive disorder. *Proceedings of the National Academy of Sciences of the United States of America*, *99*, 8448–8453.

Beyer, F., Munte, T. F., Gottlich, M., & Kramer, U. M. (2015). Orbitofrontal cortex reactivity to angry facial expression in a social interaction correlates with aggressive behavior. *Cerebral Cortex*, *25*, 3057–3063.

Beyer, F., Munte, T. F., Wiechert, J., Heldmann, M., & Kramer, U. M. (2014). Trait aggressiveness is not related to structural connectivity between orbitofrontal cortex and amygdala. *PLoS One*, *9*.

Beyerstein, B. L. (2004). Do we really use only 10 percent of our brains? *Scientific American*, *290*, 116.

Blair, R. J. R., Morris, J. S., Frith, C. D., Perrett, D. I., & Dolan, R. J. (1999). Dissociable neural responses to facial expressions of sadness and anger. *Brain: A Journal of Neurology*, *122*, 883–893.

Bobes, M. A., Ostrosky, F., Diaz, K., Romero, C., Borja, K., Santos, Y., et al. (2013). Linkage of functional and structural anomalies in the left amygdala of reactive-aggressive men. *Social Cognitive and Affective Neuroscience*, *8*, 928–936.

Buades-Rotger, M., Beyer, F., & Kramer, U. M. (2017). Avoidant responses to interpersonal provocation are associated with increased amygdala and decreased mentalizing network activity. *eNeuro*, *4*.

Carlson, J. M., Greenberg, T., & Mujica-Parodi, L. R. (2010). Blind rage? Heightened anger is associated with altered amygdala responses to masked and unmasked fearful faces. *Psychiatry Research: Neuroimaging*, *182*, 281–283.

Carp, J. (2012). The secret lives of experiments: Methods reporting in the fMRI literature. *NeuroImage*, *63*, 289–300.

Carre, J. M., Fisher, P. M., Manuck, S. B., & Hariri, A. R. (2012). Interaction between trait anxiety and trait anger predict amygdala reactivity to angry facial expressions in men but not women. *Social Cognitive and Affective Neuroscience*, 7, 213–221.

Carter, R. M., & Huettel, S. A. (2013). A nexus model of the temporal-parietal junction. *Trends in Cognitive Sciences*, *17*, 328–336.

Chanraud, S., Zahr, N., Sullivan, E. V., & Pfefferbaum, A. (2010). MR diffusion tensor imaging: A window into white matter integrity of the working brain. *Neuropsychology Review*, *20*, 209–225.

Chester, D. S., Lynam, D. R., Milich, R., & Dewall, C. N. (2017). Physical aggressiveness and gray matter deficits in ventromedial prefrontal cortex. *Cortex*, *97*, 17–22.

Coccaro, E. F., Cremers, H., Fanning, J., Nosal, E., Lee, R., Keedy, S., et al. (2018). Reduced frontal grey matter, life history of aggression, and underlying genetic influence. *Psychiatry Research: Neuroimaging*, *271*, 126–134.

Coccaro, E. F., Keedy, S. K., Gorka, S. M., King, A. C., Fanning, J. R., Lee, R. J., et al. (2016). Differential fMRI BOLD responses in amygdala in intermittent explosive disorder as a function of past Alcohol Use Disorder. *Psychiatry Research: Neuroimaging*, *257*, 5–10.

Coccaro, E. F., Lee, R., McCloskey, M., Csernansky, J. G., & Wang, L. (2015). Morphometric analysis of amygdala and hippocampus shape in impulsively aggressive and healthy control subjects. *Journal of Psychiatric Research*, *69*, 80–86.

Coccaro, E. F., McCloskey, M. S., Fitzgerald, D. A., & Phan, K. L. (2007). Amygdala and orbitofrontal reactivity to social threat in individuals with impulsive aggression. *Biological Psychiatry*, *62*, 168–178.

Cremers, H., Lee, R., Keedy, S., Phan, K. L., & Coccaro, E. (2016). Effects of escitalopram administration on face processing in intermittent explosive disorder: An fMRI study. *Neuropsychopharmacology*, *41*, 590–597.

Dougherty, D. D., Shin, L. M., Alpert, N. M., Pitman, R. K., Orr, S. P., Lasko, M., et al. (1999). Anger in healthy men: A PET study using script-driven imagery. *Biological Psychiatry*, *46*, 466–472.

Eddy, C. M. (2016). The junction between self and other? Temporo-parietal dysfunction in neuropsychiatry. *Neuropsychologia*, *89*, 465–477.

Ghashghaei, H., Hilgetag, C. C., & Barbas, H. (2007). Sequence of information processing for emotions based on the anatomic dialogue between prefrontal cortex and amygdala. *NeuroImage*, *34*, 905–923.

Gopal, A., Clark, E., Allgair, A., D'amato, C., Furman, M., Gansler, D. A., et al. (2013). Dorsal/ventral parcellation of the amygdala: Relevance to impulsivity and aggression. *Psychiatry Research: Neuroimaging*, *211*, 24–30.

Herzberg, J. L., & Fenwick, P. B. C. (1988). The etiology of aggression in temporal-lobe epilepsy. *British Journal of Psychiatry*, *153*, 50–55.

Hofman, M. A. (2012). Design principles of the human brain: An evolutionary perspective. *Progress in Brain Research*, *195*, 373–390.

Johansen-Berg, H. (2012). The future of functionally-related structural change assessment. *NeuroImage*, *62*, 1293–1298.

Kass, J. H. (2013). The evolution of brains from early mammals to humans. *Wiley Interdisciplinary Reviews: Cognitive Science*, *4*, 33–45.

Kimbrell, T. A., George, M. S., Parekh, P. I., Ketter, T. A., Podell, D. M., Danielson, A. L., et al. (1999). Regional brain activity during transient self-induced anxiety and anger in healthy adults. *Biological Psychiatry*, *46*, 454–465.

Klasen, M., Zvyaginstev, M., Schwenzer, M., Mathiak, K. A., Sarkheil, P., Weber, R., et al. (2013). Quetiapine modulates functional connectivity in brain aggression networks. *NeuroImage*, *75*, 20–26.

Lee, R., Arfanakis, K., Evia, A. M., Fanning, J., Keedy, S., & Coccaro, E. F. (2016). White matter integrity reductions in intermittent explosive disorder. *Neuropsychopharmacology*, *41*, 2697–2703.

Logothetis, N. K. (2003). The underpinnings of the BOLD functional magnetic resonance imaging signal. *Journal of Neuroscience*, *23*, 3963–3971.

Mareckova, K., Perrin, J. S., Khan, I. N., Lawrence, C., Dickie, E., McQuiggan, D. A., et al. (2014). Hormonal contraceptives, menstrual cycle and brain response to faces. *Social Cognitive and Affective Neuroscience*, *9*, 191–200.

Marsh, A. A., & Blair, R. J. R. (2008). Deficits in facial affect recognition among antisocial populations: A meta-analysis. *Neuroscience and Biobehavioral Reviews*, *32*, 454–465.

Matthies, S., Rusch, N., Weber, M., Lieb, K., Philipsen, A., Tuescher, O., et al. (2012). Small amygdala - high aggression? The role of the amygdala in modulating aggression in healthy subjects. *World Journal of Biological Psychiatry*, *13*, 75–81.

McCloskey, M. S., Phan, K. L., Angstadt, M., Fettich, K. C., Keedy, S., & Coccaro, E. E. (2016). Amygdala hyperactivation to angry faces in intermittent explosive disorder. *Journal of Psychiatric Research*, *79*, 34–41.

Medina, L., Bupesh, M., & Abellan, A. (2011). Contribution of genoarchitecture to understanding forebrain evolution and development, with particular emphasis on the amygdala. *Brain, Behavior and Evolution*, *78*, 216–236.

Nasrallah, I., & Dubroff, J. (2013). An overview of PET neuroimaging. *Seminars in Nuclear Medicine*, *43*, 449–461.

New, A. S., Hazlett, E. A., Buchsbaum, M. S., Goodman, M., Reynolds, D., Mitropoulou, V., et al. (2002). Blunted prefrontal cortical (18)fluorodeoxyglucose positron emission tomography response to meta-chlorophenylpiperazine in impulsive aggression. *Archives of General Psychiatry*, *59*, 621–629.

Petrider, M., Tomaiuolo, F., Yeterian, E. H., & Pandya, D. N. (2012). The prefrontal cortex: Comparative architectonic organization in the human and the macaque monkey brains. *Cortex*, *48*, 46–57.

Pietrini, P., Guazzelli, M., Basso, G., Jaffe, K., & Grafman, J. (2000). Neural correlates of imaginal aggressive behavior assessed by positron emission tomography in healthy subjects. *American Journal of Psychiatry*, *157*, 1772–1781.

Poldrack, R. A., Baker, C. I., Durnez, J., Gorgolewski, K. J., Matthews, P. M., Munafo, M. R., et al. (2017). Scanning the horizon: Towards transparent and reproducible neuroimaging research. *Nature Reviews Neuroscience*, *18*, 115–126.

Price, J. L. (2003). Comparative aspects of amygdala connectivity. *Annals of the New York Academy of Sciences*, *985*, 50–58.

Raine, A., Meloy, J. R., Bihrle, S., Stoddard, J., Lacasse, L., & Buchsbaum, M. S. (1998). Reduced prefrontal and increased subcortical brain functioning assessed using positron emission tomography in predatory and affective murderers. *Behavioral Sciences & the Law*, *16*, 319–332.

Rosell, D. R., Thompson, J. L., Slifstein, M., Xu, X. Y., Frankle, W. G., New, A. S., et al. (2010). Evidence increased 5-HT2A receptor availability in the orbitofrontal cortex is associated with impulsive physical aggression in a state dependent manner. *Biological Psychiatry*, *67*, 246s.

Rubin, L. H., Yao, L., Keedy, S. K., Reilly, J. L., Bishop, J. R., Carter, C. S., et al. (2017). Sex differences in associations of arginine vasopressin and oxytocin with resting-state functional brain connectivity. *Journal of Neuroscience Research*, *95*, 576–586.

Siever, L. J., Buchsbaum, M. S., New, A. S., Spiegel-Cohen, J., Wei, T., Hazlett, E. A., et al. (1999). d,l-fenfluramine response in impulsive personality disorder assessed with [F-18] fluorodeoxyglucose positron emission tomography. *Neuropsychopharmacology*, *20*, 413–423.

Skibsted, A. P., DA Cunha-Bang, S., Carre, J. M., Hansen, A. E., Beliveau, V., Knudsen, G. M., et al. (2017). Aggression-related brain function assessed with the point subtraction aggression paradigm in fMRI. *Aggressive Behavior*, *43*, 601–610.

CHAPTER SEVEN

Aggression and Intermittent Explosive Disorder: Medical and Lifestyle Correlates

Emil F. Coccaro*, Mitchell E. Berman†, Michael S. McCloskey‡
*Clinical Neuroscience & Psychopharmacology Research Unit, Department of Psychiatry and Behavioral Neuroscience, Pritzker School of Medicine, University of Chicago, Chicago, IL, United States
†Department of Psychology, Mississppi State University, Starkville, MS, United States
‡Mechanisms of Affect Dysregulation Laboratory (MAD LAB), Department of Psychology, Temple University, Philadelphia, PA, United States

Contents

Frequent outbursts of anger and impulsive aggression are problematic from more than a behavioral point of view. Numerous studies suggest that such behaviors are unhealthy from a physical and medical viewpoint as well. This chapter will review these issues in terms of medical comorbidity, including cardiovascular disease, traumatic brain injury, and the daily consumption of psychoactive substances and general behaviors related to health.

Intermittent Explosive Disorder
https://doi.org/10.1016/B978-0-12-813858-8.00007-3

Cardiovascular Disease

Persistent anger and displays of aggression have long been thought to affect cardiovascular health. Specifically, studies in the late 1950s first made the connection between anger and coronary disease in the context of certain personality types (Friedman & Rosenman, 1959). These investigators studied 83 males with an "intense, sustained drive for achievement and being continually involved in competition and deadlines" (i.e., the "A" personality group) and 83 males who had the opposite characteristics (i.e., the "B" personality group). Those with the "Type A" personality were found to have a sevenfold increased risk of having clinical coronary artery disease compared to those with the "Type B" personality. The group identified "Type A" personality was described as having free-floating hostility, triggered by minor incidents; time urgency and impatience (i.e., "short-fused"); and a competitive drive leading to "stress" and an "achievement-driven" mentality (see Friedman, 1996). A large longitudinal study followed 3154 healthy men (39–59 years of age) for eight and a half years (Rosenman, Brand, Sholtz, & Friedman, 1976) and found that the risk of coronary artery disease was twice as great for those with "Type A," compared with "Type B" personality. Another report, coming after following the same subjects for an additional thirteen and a half years (Ragland & Brand, 1988), however, concluded that while classic risk factors were associated with coronary heart disease (i.e., systolic hypertension, serum cholesterol, smoking, age), the presence of "Type A" personality was not. Later, it became clear that the key behavioral correlate for coronary heart disease was "hostility" (e.g., anger and aggression) as opposed to other features of the "Type A" behavioral pattern (Williams, 2001). This is consistent with data from a large community survey ($n=20{,}103$ from the Collaborative Psychiatric Epidemiologic Survey: CPES, Alegria, Jackson, Kessler, & Takeuchi, 2003) which reported that the presence of DSM-IV IED is associated with an increased odds ratio of 1.42 (95% CI: 1.01–1.99) for heart disease, 1.31 (95% CI: 1.08–1.59) for hypertension, and 2.10 (95% CI: 1.29–3.14) for stroke compared with those without IED (McCloskey, Kleabir, Berman, Chen, & Coccaro, 2010). Importantly, these data represent the results after accounting for differences in demographic features as well as presence of other behavioral risk factors for these conditions. This is also in line with observations that elevated levels of C-Reactive Protein (CRP), a marker of inflammation, are associated with coronary heart disease (Libby, Ridker, & Hansson, 2009) and that elevated levels of CPR are also associated with hostility (Suarez, 2004), aggression (Coccaro, 2006;

Marsland, Prather, Petersen, Cohen, & Manuck, 2008), and the presence of DSM-5 IED (Coccaro, Lee, & Coussons-Read, 2014). While it is not known if these elevations are causal to aggression in humans, animal studies suggest that inflammatory mediators can directly increase the expression of aggression in animal studies (Zalcman & Seigel, 2006).

Other Medical Conditions Including Pain and Infection

Other Medical Conditions and Pain

In addition to cardiovascular disease, the reanalysis of the CPES data (McCloskey et al., 2010) revealed elevated odds ratios for those with IED, compared to those without IED, for headache [1.64 (95% CI: 1.40–1.91)], neck/back pain [1.39 (95% CI: 1.19–1.62)], ulcer [1.36 (95% CI: 1.09–1.69)], arthritis [1.31 (95% CI: 1.09–1.58)], and chronic pain [1.27 [95% CI: 1.02–1.58)].

It is notable that each of these conditions is characterized by "chronic pain." Despite the relatively common prevalence (and chronic course) of IED, this association has received little attention in the literature even though those with IED are highly likely to get physically injured as a consequence of aggressive behaviors. For example, an investigation of DSM-III diagnoses in patients (*N*=283) presenting to a clinic for "...mixed chronic pain..." (p. 183) found that almost 17% of men received a DMS-III IED diagnosis (Fishbain, Goldberg, Meagher, Steele, & Rosomoff, 1986) which is remarkable given that DSM-III criteria identify a fraction of those who meet DSM-IV or DSM-5 criteria for IED. Curiously, an IED diagnosis in women was relatively rare (less than 2% of 127 women).

Possible mechanisms for an IED-Pain relationship include issues related to elevated levels of inflammatory proteins and that chronic pain could make one more irritable and less tolerant of stressors. In addition, a history of aggression could be associated with physical trauma that could lead to painful injuries or IED-associated alterations in biologic systems that regulate pain could be in play. However, experimental and longitudinal studies that could help identify the mechanisms responsible for the relationship between pain and IED aggression have yet to be conducted.

Diabetes

While the CPES study did not identify IED as a risk factor for diabetes, another very large (*n*=54,095) community study in 19 countries (de Jonge et al., 2014) reports an elevated odds ratio for Type II Diabetes for those with DSM-IV IED compared to those without IED [1.6 (95% CI: 1.1–2.1)].

Notably, the elevated odds ratio for IED and diabetes was similar, if not higher, than that for depression and diabetes [1.3 (95% CI: 1.1–1.5)].

Infection

The role of infectious agents in psychiatric disorders has been investigated in the etiology of a variety of behavioral disorders but not so in aggression. This is surprising in that inflammatory cytokines, typically released during infection, directly applied to selected brain areas can increase defensive aggressive responding in mammals (Bhatt & Siegel, 2006; Hassanain, Bhatt, Zalcman, & Siegel, 2005). In addition, treatment of chronic Hepatitis C infection with interferon is associated with an increase in anger (Kraus, Schafer, Faller, Csef, & Scheurlen, 2003; McHuthison, Gordon, & Schiff, 1998). In fact, acute increases of inflammatory cytokines in response to infectious agents, or to endotoxin (which produces a "sickness syndrome" without infection), is associated with irritability and to a sensitization of the amygdala to increase responding to social threat (Inagaki, Muscatell, Irwin, Cole, & Eisenberger, 2012) which increases the risk of an aggressive encounter (Coccaro, Fanning, Keedy, & Lee, 2016; Coccaro, Fitzgerald, Lee, McCloskey, & Phan, 2016). Finally, in vitro studies have shown that leukocytes from human subjects display a direct relationship between levels of aggression proneness and the magnitude of the inflammatory response (Suarez, Lewis, Krishnan, & Young, 2004; Suarez, Lewis, & Kuhn, 2002) which suggests that those with IED may display stronger, though perhaps impaired, responses to infection.

While little is known about bacterial infection we have found that individuals with IED are at risk for latent toxoplasmosis, a parasite that infects many worldwide. In a recent study in over 300 study participants (Coccaro et al., 2016), those with IED were more likely to be seropositive for IgG antibodies to *Toxoplasma gondii* compared with healthy and psychiatric controls; *T. gondii* seropositivity was also associated with higher aggression but not state depression or anxiety scores. Additional studies are needed to determine if there is a rationale to treat the low-grade inflammation, or latent toxoplasmosis, which may be present in individuals with IED. The medical and comorbid psychiatric problems associated with IED highlight the importance of examining antecedents and correlates of IED in order to identify potential mechanisms of prevention and intervention.

Traumatic Brain Injury

There is little question that serious brain injury can be associated with aggression, particularly when the injury compromises brain tissue in regions and circuits involved in emotional regulation and aggression. Since individuals with IED engage in frequently acts of aggression it is not surprising that those with IED engage in behavior that increases the risk of suffering a head injury in the context of fighting, playing competitive sports, or automobile accidents. That said, mild traumatic brain injury [mTBI; head injury resulting in alteration of consciousness, posttraumatic amnesia, and/or short-lived loss of consciousness (LOC)] is quite prevalent in the United States, with an estimated occurrence of over 1.3 million such injuries in the United States each year (CDC Grand Rounds, 2013). While a substantial number, this figure likely underestimates the problem because many people experiencing generally mild head injury do not seek medical treatment (Voss, Connolly, Schwab, & Scher, 2015). Data regarding aggression in the postconcussive mTBI phase have been reported in a number of studies (e.g., Dyer, Bell, McCann, & Rauch, 2006; Farrer, Frost, & Hedges, 2012, 2013; Rao et al., 2009; Rosellini et al., 2016; Slaughter, Fann, & Ehde, 2003) and suggest that many with mTBI (e.g., 10%–30%) experience lingering physical and behavioral disturbances, including aggression, well beyond the first few weeks after injury. The directional causality between mTBI and aggression remains in question, though several studies suggest that preexisting disturbances of mood, substance abuse or aggressive behavior, are more predictive of future post-TBI aggressive behavior than the presence of an mTBI itself (Elbogen et al., 2012; Gallaway et al., 2012; MacManus et al., 2012; Rosellini et al., 2016; Tateno, Jorge, & Robinson, 2003).

Our own work in this area finds that those with IED are significantly more likely to have a life history of at least one mTBI compared with healthy and psychiatric controls (Mosti & Coccaro, 2018); Fig. 1. When examined dimensionally, we found that while those with history of a single head injury (with or without LOC) had higher aggression scores than those without any history of head injury, individuals with two or more head injuries with LOC had strikingly higher aggression scores than those with only one head injury (with or without LOC). Accordingly, while individuals with one head injury are modestly more aggressive than those without any head injury, individuals with multiple head injuries with LOC display aggression scores three to four times higher than the former group. One limitation in our study was that we did not have data on the timing of head injury in relation to the onset of aggressive behavior. Thus we cannot, unequivocally, say that the head injuries in the individuals in this sample did not cause aggressive behavior. However, it is more likely that the trait of aggression increased the risk of head injury than the reverse because aggressive behavior begins very early in life (see Chapter on Development of Aggression in this volume) and individuals with this temperament are likely to place themselves in

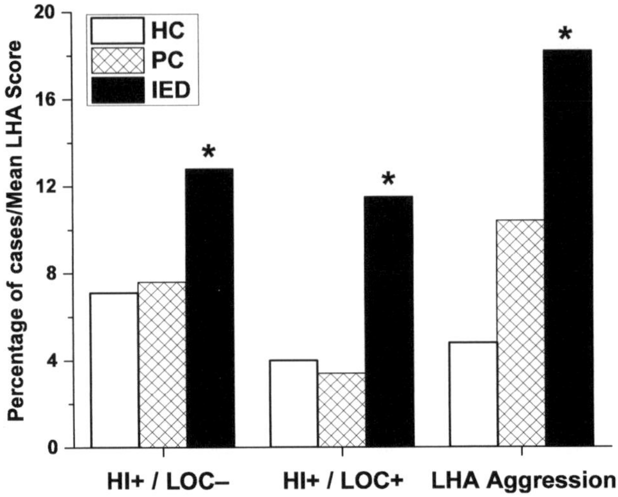

Fig. 1 Percentage of cases with and without history of Head Injury (HI) and/or Loss of Consciousness (LOC) and LHA Aggression Score in healthy (HC) and psychiatric (PC) controls and in those with IED.

circumstances associated with bodily injury. In addition, none of our study participants had head injuries serious enough to result in a loss of consciousness longer than 30 min (mean duration of LOC: 3.7 ± 6.4 min) making these mild, rather than more serious, head injuries in which we would expect grossly long-term altered behavior. Further, these findings are in general agreement with the results of studies examining individuals soon after mTBI which report that premorbid aggression better predicts the occurrence of post-TBI aggression than does recent history of mTBI itself (Dyer et al., 2006; Farrer et al., 2012, 2013; Rao et al., 2009; Rosellini et al., 2016; Slaughter et al., 2003). While more severe TBI can be associated with changes in brain structure and aggression (Epstein et al., 2016), we have found that the lower volumes of fronto-limbic gray matter in study participants with IED were not influenced by history of mTBI (Coccaro, Fanning, et al., 2016; Coccaro, Fitzgerald, et al., 2016). Thus we suggest that the presence of mTBI in these study participants was likely due to the dimensional presence of impulsive-aggressive behavior, across individuals, rather than to a primary effect of mTBI on measures of aggression.

Consumption of "Everyday" Psychotropic Agents

Based on the clear relationship between alcohol and aggression (Parrott & Eckhardt 2018), and on the previous reports of a relationship between prenatal smoking and antisocial behavior in offspring (Pratt, McGloin, & Fearn, 2006), we have looked more closely at the consumption of "everyday psychotropics" such as alcohol, nicotine (and caffeine) in our reanalysis of the NCS-R study data, our PENN Twins study data, and in our clinical research study participants.

Alcohol

In our reanalysis of the NCS-R data, we found that alcohol use disorder [5.78 (95% CI: 3.79–8.85)] was associated with a higher odds ratio for those with IED, compared to those without IED (Coccaro, Fanning, & Lee, 2017). Specifically, those with IED reported a greater degree of current and lifetime consumption at a trend level of statistical significance compared with healthy, but not psychiatric controls. Dimensional analysis, however, revealed similar relationships between levels of aggression and current ($\beta=0.10$, $P=.001$) and lifetime ($\beta=0.10$, $P=.002$) consumption of alcohol.

Nicotine

As with alcohol, we found that nicotine use disorder [4.06 (95% CI: 2.65–6.24)], in the NCS-R reanalysis, was associated with a higher odds ratio for IED, compared to those without IED (Coccaro et al., 2017). Current and lifetime consumption of nicotine was significantly greater among those with IED compared with both psychiatric and healthy controls. In addition, nicotine consumption revealed significant relationships between levels of aggression and current ($\beta=0.14$, $P<.001$) and lifetime ($\beta=0.12$, $P<.001$) consumption of nicotine.

Caffeine

While the NCS-R data set did not include information related to the consumption and/or abuse of caffeine, we found, in our clinical research program data set, that current and lifetime caffeine consumption was significantly greater among those with IED and other psychiatric disorders (i.e., psychiatric controls) compared with healthy controls. While levels of caffeine consumption were nonsignificantly higher for IED versus psychiatric control study participants, multiple regression analysis revealed a significant relationship between levels of aggression and current ($\beta=0.14$, $P<.001$) and lifetime ($\beta=0.14$, $P<.001$) consumption of caffeine.

Examination of Each Agent Together

When examining the relationship of each of these agents and IED/Aggression, simultaneously, we found that the quantity of current consumption of each correlated directly with levels of aggression for caffeine ($\beta=0.11$, $P=.001$) and nicotine ($\beta=0.10$, $P=.002$) consumption, but less so for alcohol ($\beta=0.05$, $P=.076$). For lifetime consumption, levels of aggression were significantly related to caffeine ($\beta=0.12$, $P=.001$) and alcohol ($\beta=0.07$, $P=.049$), but not nicotine ($\beta=0.05$, $P=.216$), consumption. These data suggest that consumption of these "everyday psychotropics" have a modest, but significant, relationship with aggression across study participants with a wide range of aggression scores.

While detailed neurobiological explanations for these associations are beyond the scope of this chapter, the relationship between aggression and nicotine may relate to observations that cigarette smokers have lower numbers of platelet 5-HT transporters (Patkar et al., 2003). This is quite relevant because lower numbers of platelet (Coccaro, Lee, & Kavoussi, 2009) and brain (Frankle et al., 2005) 5-HT transporters are inversely related with aggression. The relationship between caffeine and aggression, on the other hand, is not fully understood. However, laboratory studies have shown that caffeine administration reduces (Cherek, 1984), while the withdrawal of caffeine (i.e., substituting decaffeinated coffee) increases (Cherek, Bennett, Roache, & Gtrabowski, 1989), aggression in healthy volunteers.

Global Health Issues

Data regarding global health issues were not well represented in the NCS-R study. Thus we have looked at our population-based twin study data to shed light on the possibility of a relationship between general health, exercise, and obesity. These data come from our PENN Twins data set in which we randomly selected one member of a twin pair for examination of a number of behavioral variables (Coccaro & Jacobson, 2006). Since we included a psychiatry screener in that study we also have an estimate of those who self-identify as "angry" to serve as a proxy for IED. Confirming this status, "angry," compared with "nonangry," study participants had substantially higher scores on measures of aggression (BPA Aggression: 38.3 ± 9.8 *vs.* 29.3 ± 8.7, $P<.001$), trait anger (BPA Anger: 23.4 ± 6.0 *vs.* 15.8 ± 5.2, $P<.001$), and impulsiveness (BIS-11 Impulsivity: 71.2 ± 10.4 *vs.* 63.1 ± 9.9, $P<.001$).

General Health

Analysis of our PENN Twins data set reveals that those with self-identified as "angry" are more likely to report poorer general health than those who do not report being "angry" (Fig. 2A).

Exercise

In turn, "angry" study participants were less likely to engage in exercise than "nonangry" study participants (Fig. 2B; unpublished data). Regression analysis confirmed that the higher one's aggression, anger, and impulsivity scores, the less likely individuals engage in regular exercise. When aggression, anger, and impulsivity scores are examined simultaneously, we find that the variance is due to unique influence of trait anger, that is, after trait anger is entered into the statistical model, aggression and impulsivity scores do not add explanatory power to this relationship.

Obesity

Despite rating themselves as in "less" good health (and less likely to engage in regular exercise) as "nonangry" study participants, "angry" study participants did not differ in body mass index (BMI) or differ across BMI-Weight categories (underweight, normal, overweight, obese); Fig. 2C. In addition, aggression, anger, and impulsivity scores did not differ as a function of BMI or "obesity" status.

Summary

Aggression as a dimension and IED as a disorder, in addition to being problematic, may be unhealthy from a physical and medical viewpoint. Hostility has long been associated with cardiovascular problems, and this seems to be true of IED, which carries an increased risk of for hypertension, stroke, and heart disease. IED is also associated with other medical conditions including headaches, arthritis, and chronic pain. These relationships may be in part linked to elevated levels of inflammatory proteins found among individuals with IED. Individuals with IED also show an increased prevalence of mild traumatic brain injury such as concussion, which may be both an antecedent and consequence of aggressive behavior. Finally, those with IED are more likely to use legal drugs such as nicotine and alcohol. Overall, the data strongly supports a relationship between IED and negative health outcomes, though the exact nature of the relationship warrants further study.

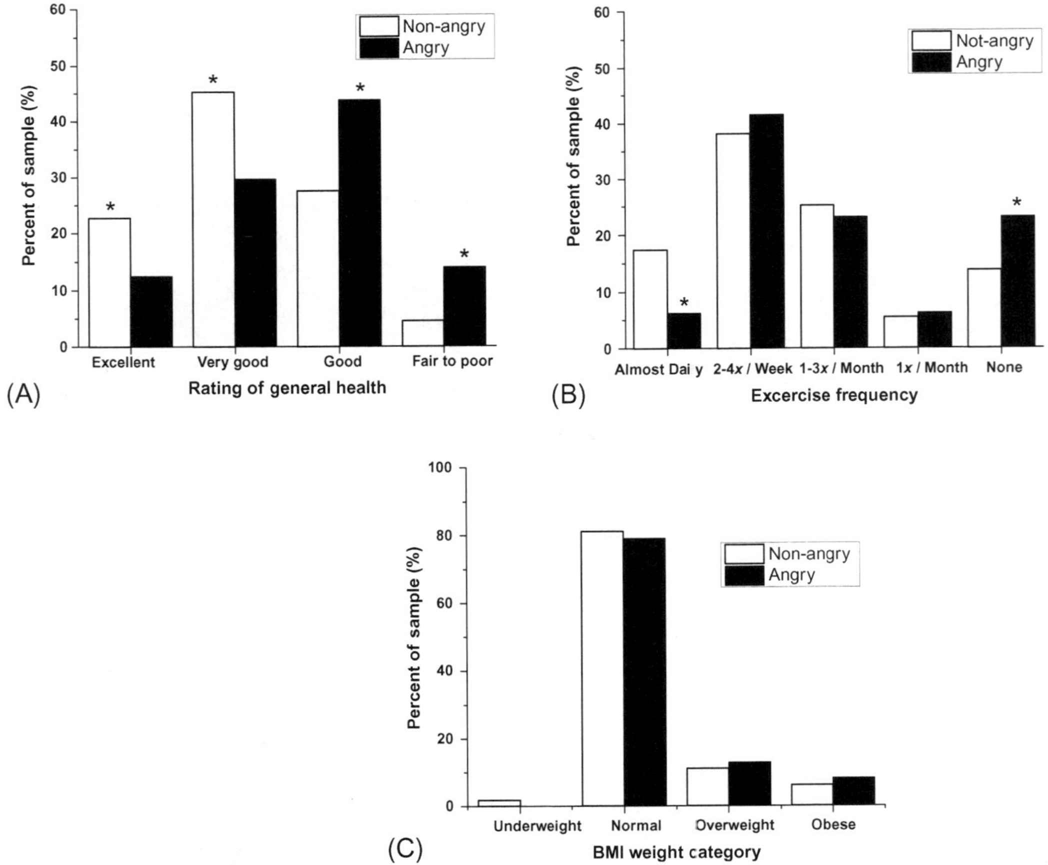

Fig. 2 A. Rating of general health as a function of identifying as having, and not having, "anger issues". B. Rating of exercise frequency as a function of identifying as having, or not having, "anger issues". C. BMI weight category as a function of having, or not having, "anger issues".

References

Alegria, M., Jackson, J. S., Kessler, R. C., & Takeuchi, D. (2003). *Collaborative Psychiatric Epidemiological Surveys (CPES), 2001–2003. ICPSR20240-v4.* Ann Arbor, MI: Institute for Social Research, Survey Research Center.

Bhatt, S., & Siegel, A. (2006). Potentiating role of interleukin 2 (IL-2) receptors in the midbrain periaqueductal gray (PAG) upon defensive rage behavior in the cat: Role of neurokinin NK(1) receptors. *Behavioral Brain Research, 167*(2), 251–260.

CDC Grand Rounds. (2013). Reducing severe traumatic brain injury in the United States. *MMWR Morbidity and Mortality Weekly Report, 62*(27), 549–552.

Cherek, D. R. (1984). Effects of cigarette smoking on human aggressive behavior. *Progress in Clinical and Biological Cesearch, 169*, 333–344.

Cherek, D. R., Bennett, R. H., Roache, J. D., & Gtrabowski, J. (1989). Human aggressive and non-aggressive responding during acute tobacco abstinence. *NIDA Research Monograph, 95*, 435–436.

Coccaro, E. F. (2006). Association of C-reactive protein elevation with trait aggression and hostility in personality disordered subjects: A pilot study. *Journal of Psychiatric Research, 40*(5), 460–465.

Coccaro, E. F., Fanning, J. R., Keedy, S. K., & Lee, R. J. (2016). Social cognition in intermittent explosive disorder and aggression. *Journal of Psychiatric Research, 83*, 140–150.

Coccaro, E. F., Fanning, J. R., & Lee, R. (2017). Intermittent explosive disorder and substance use disorder: Analysis of the national comorbidity study—Replication sample. *The Journal of Clinical Psychiatry, 78*, 697–702.

Coccaro, E. F., Fitzgerald, D. A., Lee, R., McCloskey, M. S., & Phan, K. L. (2016). Frontolimbic morphometric abnormalities in intermittent explosive disorder. *Biological Psychiatry: Clinical Neuroscience and Neuroimaging, 1*, 32–38.

Coccaro, E. F., & Jacobson, K. C. (2006). PennTwins: A population-based cohort for twin studies. *Twin Research and Human Genetics, 9*(6), 998–1005.

Coccaro, E. F., Lee, R., & Coussons-Read, M. (2014). Elevated plasma inflammatory markers in individuals with intermittent explosive disorder and correlation with aggression in humans. *JAMA Psychiatry, 71*(2), 158–165.

Coccaro, E. F., Lee, R., Groer, M. W., Can, A., Coussons-Read, M., & Postolache, T. T. (2016). Toxoplasma gondii infection: Relationship with aggression in psychiatric subjects. *The Journal of Clinical Psychiatry, 77*(3), 334–341.

Coccaro, E. F., Lee, R., & Kavoussi, R. J. (2009). Inverse relationship between numbers of 5-HT transporter binding sites and life history of aggression and intermittent explosive disorder. *Journal of Psychiatric Research, 44*, 137–142.

de Jonge, P., Alonso, J., Stein, D. J., Kiejna, A., Aguilar-Gaxiola, S., & Viana, M. C. (2014). Associations between DSM-IV mental disorders and diabetes mellitus: A role for impulse control disorders and depression. *Diabetologia, 57*, 699–709.

Dyer, K. F., Bell, R., McCann, J., & Rauch, R. (2006). Aggression after traumatic brain injury: Analysing socially desirable responses and the nature of aggressive traits. *Brain Injury, 20*, 1163–1173.

Elbogen, E. B., et al. (2012). Protective factors and risk modification of violence in Iraq and Afghanistan War veterans. *Journal of Clinical Psychiatry, 73*(6), e767–e773.

Epstein, D. J., Legarreta, M., Bueler, E., King, J., McGlade, E., & Yurgelun-Todd, D. (2016). Orbitofrontal cortical thinning and aggression in mild traumatic brain injury patients. *Brain and Behavior: A Cognitive Neuroscience Perspective, 6*, e00581.

Farrer, T. J., Frost, R. B., & Hedges, D. W. (2012). Prevalence of traumatic brain injury in intimate partner violence offenders compared to the general population: A meta-analysis. *Trauma Violence Abuse, 13*, 77–82.

Farrer, T. J., Frost, R. B., & Hedges, D. W. (2013). Prevalence of traumatic brain injury in juvenile offenders: A meta-analysis. *Child Neuropsychology*, *19*, 225–234.

Fishbain, D. A., Goldberg, M., Meagher, B. R., Steele, R., & Rosomoff, H. (1986). Male and female chronic pain patients categorized by DSM-III psychiatric diagnostic criteria. *Pain*, *26*(2), 181–197.

Frankle, W. G., Lombardo, I., New, A. S., Goodman, M., Talbot, P. S., Huang, Y., et al. (2005). Brain serotonin transporter distribution in subjects with impulsive aggressivity: A positron emission study with [11C]McN 5652. *The American Journal of Psychiatry*, *162*, 915–923.

Friedman, M. (1996). *Type A Behavior: Its Diagnosis and Treatment*. New York: Plenum Press (Kluwer Academic Press).

Friedman, M., & Rosenman, R. H. (1959). Association of specific overt behavior pattern with blood and cardiovascular findings: Blood cholesterol, blood clotting time, incidence of arcus senilis, and clinical coronary artery disease. *JAMA*, *169*(12), 1286–1296.

Gallaway, M. S., et al. (2012). Factors associated with physical aggression among US Army soldiers. *Aggressive Behavior*, *38*(5), 357–367.

Hassanain, M., Bhatt, S., Zalcman, S., & Siegel, A. (2005). Potentiating role of interleukin-1beta (IL-1beta) and IL-1beta type 1 receptors in the medial hypothalamus in defensive rage behavior in the cat. *Brian Research*, *1048*(1–2), 1–11.

Inagaki, T. K., Muscatell, K. A., Irwin, M. R., Cole, S. W., & Eisenberger, N. I. (2012). Inflammation selectively enhances amygdala activity to socially threatening images. *NeuroImage*, *59*, 3222–3226.

Kraus, M. R., Schafer, A., Faller, H., Csef, H., & Scheurlen, M. (2003). Psychiatric symptoms in patients with chronic hepatitis C receiving interferon alfa-2b therapy. *The Journal of Clinical Psychiatry*, *64*, 708–714.

Libby, P., Ridker, P. M., & Hansson, G. K. (2009). Inflammation in atherosclerosis: From pathophysiology to practice. *Journal of the American College of Cardiology*, *54*(23), 2129–2138.

MacManus, D., et al. (2012). Violent behaviour in U.K. military personnel returning home after deployment. *Psychological Medicine*, *42*(8), 1663–1673.

Marsland, A. L., Prather, A. A., Petersen, K. L., Cohen, S., & Manuck, S. B. (2008). Antagonistic characteristics are positively associated with inflammatory markers independently of trait negative emotionality. *Brain, Behavior, and Immunity*, *22*(5), 753–761.

McCloskey, M. S., Kleabir, K., Berman, M. E., Chen, E. Y., & Coccaro, E. F. (2010). Unhealthy aggression: Intermittent explosive disorder and adverse physical health outcomes. *Health Psychology*, *29*(3), 324–332.

McHuthison, J., Gordon, S., & Schiff, E. (1998). Interferon alpha-2b alone or in combination with ribavirin as initial treatment for chronic hepatitis C. *The New England Journal of Medicine*, *339*, 1485–1492.

Mosti, C., & Coccaro, E. F. (2018). Mild traumatic brain injury and aggression, impulsivity, and history of other- and self-directed aggression. *The Journal of Neuropsychiatry and Clinical Neurosciences*, *30*(3), 220–227.

Parrott, D. J., & Eckhardt, C. I. (2018). Effects of alcohol on human aggression. *Current Opinion in Psychology*, *19*, 1–5.

Patkar, A. A., Gopalakrishnan, R., Berrettini, W. H., Weinstein, S. P., Vergare, M. J., & Leone, F. T. (2003). Differences in platelet serotonin transporter sites between African-American tobacco smokers and non-smokers. *Psychopharmacology*, *166*(3), 221–227.

Pratt, T. C., McGloin, J. M., & Fearn, N. E. (2006). Maternal cigarette smoking during pregnancy and criminal/deviant behavior: a meta-analysis. *International Journal of Offender Therapy and Comparative Criminology*, *50*, 672–690.

Ragland, D. R., & Brand, R. J. (1988). Coronary heart disease mortality in the Western Collaborative Group Study. Follow-up experience of 22 years. *American Journal of Epidemiology, 127*(3), 462–475.

Rao, V., Rosenberg, P., Bertrand, M., Salehinia, S., Spiro, J., Vaishnavi, S., et al. (2009). Aggression after traumatic brain injury: Prevalance and correlates. *The Journal of Neuropsychiatry and Clinical Neurosciences, 21*, 240–249.

Rosellini, A. J., Monahan, J., Street, A. E., Heeringa, S. G., Hill, E. D., Petukhova, M., et al. (2016). Predicting non-familial major physical violent crime perpetration in the US Army from administrative data. *Psychological Medicine, 46*, 303–316.

Rosenman, R. H., Brand, R. J., Sholtz, R. I., & Friedman, M. (1976). Multivariate prediction of coronary heart disease during 8.5 year follow-up in the Western Collaborative Group Study. *The American Journal of Cardiology, 37*(6), 903–910.

Slaughter, B., Fann, J. R., & Ehde, D. (2003). Traumatic brain injury in a county jail population: Prevalence, neuropsychological functioning and psychiatric disorders. *Brain Injury, 17*, 731–741.

Suarez, E. C. (2004). C-reactive protein is associated with psychological risk factors of cardiovascular disease in apparently healthy adults. *Psychosomatic Medicine, 66*(5), 684–691.

Suarez, E. C., Lewis, J. G., Krishnan, R. R., & Young, K. H. (2004). Enhanced expression of cytokines and chemokines by blood monocytes to in vitro lipopolysaccharide stimulation are associated with hostility and severity of depressive symptoms in healthy women. *Psychoneuroendocrinology, 29*(9), 1119–1128.

Suarez, E. C., Lewis, J. G., & Kuhn, C. (2002). Relation of aggression, hostility, and anger to lipopolysaccharide-stimulated tumor necrosis factor (TNF)-alpha by blood monocytes from normal men. *Brain, Behavior, and Immunity, 16*(6), 675–684.

Tateno, A., Jorge, R. E., & Robinson, R. G. (2003). Clinical correlates of aggressive behavior after traumatic brain injury. *The Journal of Neuropsychiatry and Clinical Neurosciences, 15*(2), 155–160.

Voss, J. D., Connolly, J., Schwab, K. A., & Scher, A. I. (2015). Update on the epidemiology of concussion/mild traumatic brain injury. *Current Pain and Headache Reports, 19*, 32.

Williams, R. B. (2001). In A. Baum, T. A. Revenson, & J. E. Singer (Eds.), *Hostility: Effects on health and the potential for successful behavioral approaches to prevention and treatment*. Mahwah, NJ: Erlbaum. Handbook of Health Psychology.

Zalcman, S. S., & Seigel, A. (2006). The neurobiology of aggression and rage: Role of cytokines. *Brain, Behavior, and Immunity, 20*(6), 507–514.

Further Reading

Cherek, D. R., Steinberg, J. L., & Brauchi, J. T. (1994). Effects of regular and decaffeinated coffee on human aggressive behavior. *Psychiatry Research, 11*, 251–258.

Cherek, D. R., Steinberg, J. L., & Brauchi, J. T. (2003). Effects of caffeine on human aggressive behavior. *Psychiatry Research, 8*, 1137–1145.

CHAPTER EIGHT

Social Cognition in Intermittent Explosive Disorder

Emil F. Coccaro, Kristin A. Ridder
Clinical Neuroscience & Psychopharmacology Research Unit, Department of Psychiatry and Behavioral Neuroscience, Pritzker School of Medicine, University of Chicago, Chicago, IL, United States

Contents

Introduction

There is no question that human aggressive behavior is under both genetic and environmental influence. In fact, twin studies conducted by our group, as well as and other groups, have shown that no less than 50% of the variance in aggression scores are due to nongenetic, "environmental," factors (also see the chapter on Behavioral/Molecular Genetics, this volume). Such variance is due to shared (common to both twins) and nonshared (unique to each twin) environmental factors as well as measurement error. Shared and nonshared factors include parenting behavior/exposure to violence, exposure to physical and sexual trauma, as well as exposure to potentially addictive psychopharmacologic agents, among others. The relationship between aggression and some of these factors is discussed in greater detail in other chapters in this volume. In this chapter, we will discuss the influence of parenting behavior and exposure to violence as it relates to their impact on social-emotional information processing (SEIP) also referred to as social cognition.

Intermittent Explosive Disorder
https://doi.org/10.1016/B978-0-12-813858-8.00008-5

Social-Emotional Information Processing

Early work in developmental psychology by Bandura (1973) suggested that cognitive learning processes are important in the transmission of aggression from parent to child. The now famous Bobo doll experiment, in which children are shown how to be aggressive toward a proxy object by a parental figure, demonstrated that children learn behavior by imitating, or modeling, someone else's behavior so that children learn to be aggressive by observing aggression in their families and in the community (Bandura, 1973).

Later studies, also, demonstrated that maltreatment during childhood has negative effects on a number of cognitive functions (Irigara et al., 2013) including deficits in verbal and episodic memory, working memory, attention, and executive functions. Childhood maltreatment has also been shown to adversely impact social-emotional development in adolescence and adulthood and is associated with negative cognitive schemas regarding self and others, deficits in affect regulation, conditioned associations between abuse stimuli, emotional distress, and memories/cognitions of maltreatment triggered by environmental stimuli. In addition, childhood maltreatment has been associated with social information processing problems, including reductions in encoding relevant social cues, increased hostile attribution bias, as well as a general tendency to select, and value, aggressive responses to hypothetical socially ambiguous interactions (Weiss, Dodge, Bates, & Pettit, 1992).

Research regarding the development and maintenance of aggression highlights a variety of social cognitive processes and has shown that aggressive individuals are more likely than others to interpret both ambiguous and benign cues as hostile, and that hostile attribution biases are positively related to aggressive behavior (Dodge, 1980; Teisl & Cicchetti, 2008). Importantly, a meta-analysis of more than forty studies reports robust and significant associations between a hostile attribution of intent and aggressive behavior (de Castro, Veerman, Koops, Bosch, & Monshouwer, 2002). Based on this work, Dodge, Bates, and Pettit (1990) proposed a social information processing theory to explain 'the cycle of violence' described by previous investigators. This group suggested that abused children are more likely to develop deficient patterns of social information processing, which result in increased levels of aggression. This theory (Crick & Dodge, 1994; Dodge, 1986) described six steps of SIP: (1) encoding (i.e., selective attention to internal and environmental cues such as facial cues and verbalizations), (2) interpretation and mental representation of these cues (e.g. attributions of intent, a function of attention to particular cues), (3) clarification of goals (i.e., selecting desired goals and outcome of the situation), (4) response access or construction (i.e., generation of possible responses), (5) response evaluation and decision (i.e., determination of the quality of each alternative response and evaluation of the likelihood that each alternative will produce the desired outcomes), and (6) behavioral enactment (i.e., behavioral response; Crick & Dodge, 1994). Deficits in social information processing have been shown to partially mediate the effects of early life maltreatment on later aggressive behavior across the lifespan (e.g. Calvete & Orue, 2011; Dodge et al., 1990; Dodge, Pettit, Bates, & Valente, 1995; Taft, Schumm, Marshall, Panuzio, & Holtzworth-Munroe, 2008). In prospective studies, Weiss et al. (1992) have demonstrated that harsh discipline significantly predicted child aggression six months later, even after controlling for socioeconomic status, child temperament, and marital violence. The results showed that harsh parental discipline predicted later school aggression that was partially mediated by impairments in social information processing. In another longitudinal study, Dodge et al. (1995) reported that one-third of the variance (33%) in the relationship between aggression exposure in childhood and later behavioral problems was accounted for by attention to and encoding of relevant social cues, hostile interpretations of peers' intentions, accessing of aggressive behavioral responses to cues, and favorable evaluation of the consequences and desirability of aggressive responses

In addition to social cognitive factors, other work has pointed to the relevance of emotional regulation in the development of aggression especially in the context of the relationship between childhood maltreatment and later aggressive behavior. For example, Briere (2002) proposes that normal emotion regulation develops through the process of trial-and-error learning to manage uncomfortable internal states and that children progressively develop increasingly sophisticated strategies of internal coping as they encounter more challenging and stressful experiences. If so, it is extremely difficult for children exposed to violence at the hands of their caretakers to develop these adaptive skills because ongoing aggression toward the child disrupts their trial-and-error learning leading to affective instability, difficulty in inhibiting expression of strong negative affect, and difficulty in limiting their dysphoric state. Such individuals tend to be emotionally hyper-responsive and overreact to negative/stressful events due to their inability to effectively regulate their emotions and this results in aggression and related behaviors such as substance abuse, inappropriate sexual behavior, bingeing/purging, or self-injury (Briere & Gil, 1998). Supporting this view is data showing a positive relationship between a history of child abuse and emotion dysregulation (Cloitre, Stovall-McClough, Zorbas, & Charuvastra, 2008; Kim & Cicchetti, 2010).

While the literature tends to separate cognitive and emotional factors in this regard, it is likely that both are involved in the development and maintenance of aggression. Lemerise and Arsenio (2000) first proposed to include emotion processes in social information processing models in order to expand the explanatory power of these models to understand aggressive behavior. In their review of the interdependence of cognition and emotion, Storbeck and Clore (2007) posit that emotion processes modulate and mediate basic cognitive processes. Others (Teisl & Cicchetti, 2008) have demonstrated that maladaptive cognitive and emotional processes made unique contributions to the relationship between child physical abuse and peer nominations of aggression and disruptive behavior in a sample of children aged 6 to 12. In their study scores of social information processing accounted uniquely for 10% of the variance in the overall indirect effect, while scores of emotion regulation accounted uniquely for 55% of the variance in the indirect relationship between child abuse and aggression. Thus each factor contributed unique variance to the relationship between child abuse and aggression. Others suggest that social cognitive and emotional processes interact with one another (Lee & Hoaken, 2007). In fact, neural mechanisms that underlie social and emotional processes may be partly redundant and interactive and results of fMRI studies reveal interactions between regions of the brain thought to be involved in the processing of these types of information (Norris, Chen, Zhu, Small, & Cacioppo, 2004). The authors employed fMRI to examine brain activity while participants viewed pictures that included emotional or social content. They suggested that regions of the brain previously implicated in social and/or emotional processes showed evidence of an interaction in processing. Evidence for such an interaction in social and emotional processing was provided by patterns of brain activation in the superior temporal sulcus, the middle occipito-temporal cortex, and the thalamus. These regions of the brain that have been implicated in processing social information appeared especially active when the stimuli also conveyed emotional information (Fig. 2).

Social-Emotional Information Processing in IED

Similar studies in IED had to wait until SEIP research protocols were developed for use in adults as opposed to children and young adolescents.

We published our first work in this area, late in the last decade, with a six-item assessment of attribution and emotional response (Coccaro, Noblett, & McCloskey, 2009). This assessment began as a 10 vignette questionnaire that briefly described socially ambiguous interactions reflecting five physically aggressive and five relationally aggressive scenarios. Our assessment was developed in three phases in a group of population-based individuals. In the first phase we determined the optimal format of the assessment and settled on eight vignettes (four from each type) and reported on its psychometric properties. The second phase replicated these findings in separate, but similar, group of individuals while the third phase examined the assessment's properties in a third group of research participants with and without IED.

Among the six SEIP assessment questions following each vignette were four assessing attribution and two assessing negative emotional response. Two questions in the former set asked about hostile attribution (HA) and one each asked about instrumental attribution (IA) and benign attribution (BA). The two HA questions asked to what extent the intent of the "other's" action in the vignette was designed to hurt the person directly or hurt the person's status/reputation. The IA question asked to what extent the intent of the "other's" action in the vignette was designed to enable the "other" to reach his/her objective while the BA question asked to what extent the "other's" action was accidental in intent. The two negative emotional response (NER) questions asked the subject how angry, and how upset and/or embarrassed, they would be if the "other" in the vignette had acted that way with them. Analyses of these data confirmed that each form of attribution was a valid reliable variable and that the same was true for the negative emotional response variable. Across community subjects, HA but not IA, correlated directly with measures of aggression and hostile automatic thoughts while BA correlated inversely with these variables. In turn, HA displayed a strong positive relationship with NER while IA showed little correlation and BA showed an inverse correlation with NER confirming the idea that HA, but not IA, is associated with anger and that BA is associated with a dampening of anger. This supports the strategy of assisting angry individuals to reframe their social cognition so that they see aversive behavior as not personal to them (i.e., "instrumental" behavior on the part of the other, or accidental in nature). Analysis of the non-population-based study participants demonstrated that those with IED had significant higher HA and NER, and lower BA, scores compared with those of healthy controls confirming that elevated HA and NER scores are important features of IED.

Our second study (Coccaro, Fanning, Fisher, Couture, & Lee, 2017; Coccaro, Fanning, & Lee, 2017) extended this work by also including an assessment of response, evaluation, and decision (RED) making in the context of social threat (Coccaro, Fanning, Keedy, & Lee, 2016). In addition, this study replicated the nature of the psychometric properties of the attribution and negative emotional response variables and reported, further, that SEIP vignettes with relationally aggressive scenarios evoked higher HA and NER scores compared with vignettes with physically aggressive scenarios. The latter observation suggests that social threat directed at one's place in their social world is associated with a greater SEIP response than social threat limited to physical assault/injury.

RED variables were assessed in response to three different kinds of possible responses to the social threat described in the SEIP vignettes: socially appropriate responses, directly aggressive responses, and relationally aggressive responses. For each possible response, participants were asked how likely, or how favorably, they viewed each possible response in terms of: (a) how good is it to act this way ("response valuation"); (b) if you acted this way, how would you feel about yourself, how likely is it that you would get what you want, that others will like you, that others would respect you ("outcome expectation"); (c) how easy would it be to act this way ("response efficacy") and, how likely is it that you would act this way ("response enactment"). Each individual RED variable demonstrated good psychometric properties in terms of reliability and construct validity. In addition, each RED variable for socially appropriate, and for each aggressive, response interacted as expected. That is, RED variable scores for both socially appropriate responses (Mean $\pm$ SD: $r=0.61\pm0.14$), and for both aggressive responses (Mean $\pm$ SD: $r=0.73\pm0.06$) were highly intercorrelated but not with regard to contrasting types of responses (i.e., socially appropriate with aggressive responses; Mean $\pm$ SD: $r=-0.03\pm0.11$).

In addition, for socially acceptable responses Total RED scores displayed inverse, though nonsignificant, correlations with HA ($r=-0.21$) and NER (-0.02) scores, displaying positive and statistically significant correlations, instead, with IA ($r=0.41$) and BA ($r=0.30$) scores. In comparison, Total RED scores for aggressive responses revealed moderately strong positive correlations with HA ($r=0.50$); NER also correlated with Total RED scores ($r=0.40$) while BA was inversely, and statistically significantly, correlated with the Total RED scores ($r=-0.31$) and IA was uncorrelated ($r=-0.09$). These observations suggest that the more an individual's view of another person's agonistic behavior is instrumental or benign, the more likely they are to value a socially acceptable response to potential social threat. In contrast, the more likely an individual's view of the other's behavior is hostile the more likely they are to value an aggressive response to potential social threat.

In the clinical research sample reported in the study, Total RED scores for socially appropriate responses were significantly lower among IED compared with healthy control subjects but significantly higher among IED compared with those among healthy control subjects in keeping with the idea that impulsively aggressive individuals view aggressive responding to ambiguous social threat positively. That said, it is important to note that, even among those with IED, socially acceptable responses to social threat are viewed, overall, more favorably than aggressive responses (i.e., RED scores of 1.76 ± 0.03 for socially appropriate responses *vs.* 1.07 ± 0.04 for aggressive responses, $P < .001$) indicating that the key observation is that those with IED are more likely to favor aggressive responses than are healthy, or psychiatric, controls.

Our third study (Coccaro et al., 2016) included a larger, nonoverlapping, sample of individuals with IED ($n=100$) as well as healthy ($n=100$), and nonaggressive psychiatric ($n=100$), controls. Inclusion of the latter group allowed for a control of general psychopathology in the IED group. In this study, those with IED were found to have higher HA, NER, and Total RED scores compared with both healthy and psychiatric controls. Since inclusion of nonaggressive psychiatric subjects controls for the general psychopathology present in IED, and others with a nonaggressive psychiatric disorder, these findings show that aberrant SEIP is associated with impulsive aggression rather than to other aspects of psychopathology (Fig. 1).

Most importantly, this study included a detailed analysis of which aspects of SEIP correlated with history of actual aggressive events using the Life History of Aggression assessment. Placing all SEIP variables into the same statistical model revealed that the unique correlates of actual aggressive behavior were the NER ($\beta=0.31$, $P<.001$) and Total RED ($\beta=0.32$, $P<.001$), but not the HA ($\beta=-0.07$, $P=.342$), variable scores suggesting that negative emotional responses (NER) to ambiguous agonistic interactions and the positive view of behaving in an aggressive manner (RED) may be more critical to the display of aggressive behavior in social agonistic interactions than HA, which up until now has been thought to be the key variable in SEIP.

Our next effort was to put the SEIP stimuli into video form and to create a computer-based Video-SEIP assessment (V-SEIP; Coccaro et al., 2016) that enables the assessment of "encoding" which cannot be done with a

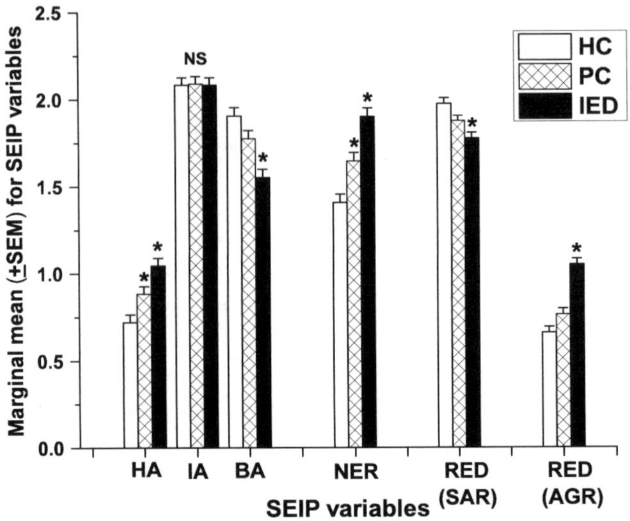

Fig. 1 Marginal means (±SEM) after ANCOVA for SEIP attributional, emotional, and response and evaluation variables in healthy (HC) and psychiatric (PC) controls and in those with IED.

paper-and-pencil assessment. For our V-SEIP assessment we produced short (e.g., 10 s) video clips of each vignette along with short video clips illustrating socially appropriate, directly aggressive, and relationally aggressive responses. After viewing the vignette video clip, study participants were asked to recall and record all the relevant elements shown in the video clip ("encoding"; ENC). These recalled elements were scored by behavioral raters as "relevant" or "irrelevant" to the main action in the video clip according to an *a priori* list of elements. IED study participants identified fewer relevant vignette elements compared with both healthy and psychiatric control study participants. This study also replicated the findings reported in the previous papers regarding HA, NER, and RED variables (Fig. 2). Most importantly, simultaneous analysis of all SEIP variables revealed that ENC, NER, and Total RED, but not HA, scores uniquely correlated with history of aggressive behavior. ENC scores correlated inversely, while NER and RED scores correlated positively with life history of aggression. The standardized beta coefficients were similar for ENC (-0.17, $P<.05$) and NER ($+0.18$, $P<.05$), but substantially greater for the Total RED ($+0.54$, $P<.001$), scores supporting the role of these three SEIP variables, especially RED, in aggression and IED. Given the NER results in the previous study ($\beta=0.31$, $P<.001$), it appears that the variance related to NER in this study may be split between NER and ENC.

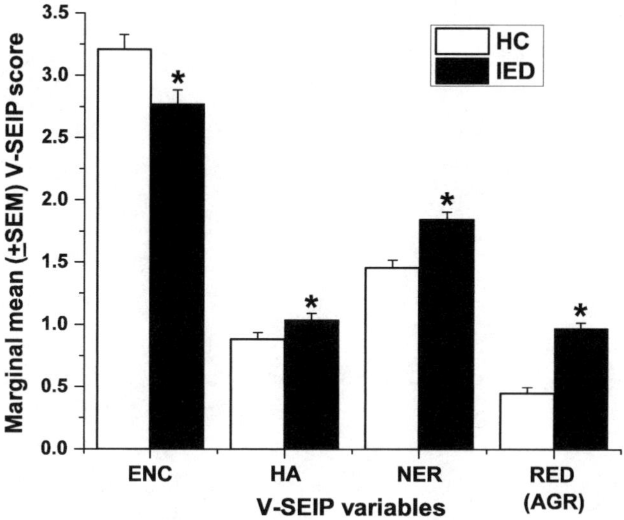

Fig. 2 Marginal means (±SEM) after ANCOVA for Video-SEIP scores for encoding, hostile attribution, negative emotional response, and response and evaluation variables in healthy controls (HC) and those with IED.

When we expose healthy human subjects to these SEIP videos (both aggressive and nonaggressive in nature) in the fMRI scanning environment we find that the stages of ENC, HA, and NER have differential activations in cortico-limbic circuits. As part of an ongoing study, we have found that individuals with IED have reduced activity, compared with healthy controls, when viewing both aggressive and neutral SEIP videos during these three SEIP phases: (a) reduced activation in the medial prefrontal cortex and anterior cingulate cortex during encoding, (b) reduced activation in the dorsolateral prefrontal cortex and temporoparietal junction during attribution, and (c) reduced activation in the superior prefrontal cortex and periaqueductal gray during negative emotional response. This strongly suggests that deficits in SEIP have relevant correlates in cortico-limbic circuit functioning and does not simply represent a psychological construct.

These findings are important for work designed to improve aberrant SEIP in impulsively aggressive individuals. If variables related to ENC, NER, and RED variables are critical to aggressive responding, then potential interventions should focus on strategies that can improve attention to relevant stimuli, reduce angry reactions to agonistic social threat, and reduce the favorable view of aggressive responses in those with impulsive aggression. Cognitive-behavioral interventions for IED (McCloskey, Noblett, Deffenbacher, Gollan, & Coccaro, 2008; also see Chapter on Psychological

Interventions) include cognitive restructuring which aims to reduce hostile automatic thoughts (and presumably HA) by assisting the patient to understand that what they experience as social threat is, in fact, something benign. In addition, cognitive-behavioral interventions also include coping skills training whereby the patient reexperiences situations that trigger their anger, under the therapist's supervision and guidance, so that they can employ different responses to threat and reduce reactive anger. While training to reduce the favorability of aggressive responses to social threat is not formally included in this type of intervention, it often comes up during the treatment.

At this time, there is no formal clinical treatment program that employs interventions designed to modify SEIP variables. However, recent work has been published that suggests that interventions that reduce HA can reduce aggressive behavior in children and adolescents. One set of studies developed a computer task that trains individuals to view mixed, morphed, angry-happy faces as more happy than angry (Penton-Voak et al., 2013). In this study of healthy volunteers the investigators reported a significant reduction in the amygdala response to angry faces after such training. In another study, such training was reported to reduce actual aggressive behavior in adolescents with conduct disorder as rated by both adolescent and staff (Stoddard et al., 2016). While these individuals were not diagnosed as IED, some would likely meet criteria IED. The observation that reducing hostile attribution can have an antiaggressive effect is not inconsistent with the data reported before which suggests that HA is not uniquely related to aggression. This is because HA is related to aggression, by itself, but that other facets of SEIP, when added, better account for the relationship between SEIP and aggression. This is especially true when one first adds NER to the model. This raises the possibility that designing interventions that focus on improving encoding, reduce anger proneness, and reduce the mind-set that aggressive responses to social threat are "appropriate" given the situation, maybe more effective than simply reducing hostile attribution bias.

Conclusion

SEIP represents a critical set of processes under the rubric of social cognition. It has been shown to be related to aggression, especially impulsive aggression, and undoubtedly places an important role in the proximal factors that lead to impulsive aggressive behavior. SEIP can be assessed in human subjects fairly easily from both a psychometric and neuropsychobiological point of view. It is likely that clinical/therapeutic strategies that work to reduce aberrant SEIP will be important in treating impulsive aggressive individuals with deficits in SEIP.

References

Bandura, A. (1973). *Aggression*. Englewood Cliffs, NJ: Prentice Hall.

Briere, J. (2002). Treating adult survivors of severe childhood abuse and neglect: Further development of an integrative model. In J. B. Myers, L. Berliner, J. Briere, C. T. Hendrix, C. Jenny, T. A. Reid, & T. A. Reid (Eds.), *The APSAC Handbook on Child Maltreatment* (2nd ed., pp. 175–203).Thousand Oaks, CA, USA: Sage Publications, Inc.

Briere, J., & Gil, E. (1998). Self-mutilation in clinical and general population samples: Prevalence, correlates, and functions. *American Journal of Orthopsychiatry, 68*, 609–620.

Calvete, E., & Orue, I. (2011). The impact of violence exposure on aggressive behavior through social information processing in adolescents. *The American Journal of Orthopsychiatry, 81*, 38–50.

Cloitre, M., Stovall-McClough, K. C., Zorbas, P., & Charuvastra, A. (2008). Attachment organization, emotion regulation, and expectations of support in a clinical sample of women with childhood abuse histories. *Journal of Traumatic Stress, 21*, 282–289.

Coccaro, E. F., Fanning, J. R., Fisher, E., Couture, L., & Lee, R. J. (2017). Social emotional information processing in adults: Development and psychometrics of a computerized video assessment in healthy controls and aggressive individuals. *Psychiatry Research, 248*, 40–47.

Coccaro, E. F., Fanning, J. R., Keedy, S., & Lee, R. (2016). Social cognition in intermittent explosive disorder and aggression. *Journal of Psychiatric Research, 83*, 140–150.

Coccaro, E. F., Fanning, J. R., & Lee, R. (2017). Social emotional information processing in adult subjects: Developing an assessment of response evaluation and decision processing. *Aggressive Behavior, 43*, 47–59.

Coccaro, E. F., Noblett, K. L., & McCloskey, M. S. (2009). Attributional and emotional responses to socially ambiguous cues: Validation of a new assessment of social/emotional information processing in healthy adults and impulsive aggressive patients. *Journal of Psychiatric Research, 43*, 915–925.

Crick, N. R., & Dodge, K. A. (1994). A review and reformulation of social information-processing mechanisms in children's social adjustment. *Psychological Bulletin, 115*, 74–101.

de Castro, B. O., Veerman, J. W., Koops, W., Bosch, J. D., & Monshouwer, H. J. (2002). Hostile attribution of intent and aggressive behavior: A meta-analysis. *Child Development, 73*, 916–934.

Dodge, K. A. (1980). Social cognition and children's aggressive behavior. *Child Development, 51*, 162–170.

Dodge, K. A. (1986). A social information processing model of social competence in children. In M. Perlmutter (Ed.), vol. 18. *The Minnesota Symposium of Child Psychology 1986* (pp. 77–125). Hillsdale, NJ: Erlbaum.

Dodge, K. A., Bates, J. E., & Pettit, G. S. (1990). Mechanisms in the cycle of violence. *Science, 250*, 1678–1683.

Dodge, K. A., Pettit, G. S., Bates, J. E., & Valente, E. (1995). Social information-processing patterns partially mediate the effect of early physical abuse on later conduct problems. *Journal of Abnormal Psychology, 104*, 632–643.

Irigara, T. Q., Pachecol, J. B., Grassi-Oliveira, R., Fonseca, R. P., de Carvalho Leite, J. C., & Kristensen, C. H. (2013). Child maltreatment and later cognitive functioning: A systematic review. *Psicologia: Reflexão E Crítica, 26*(2), 376–387.

Kim, J., & Cicchetti, D. (2010). Longitudinal pathways linking child maltreatment, emotion regulation, peer relations, and psychopathology. *Journal of Child Psychology and Psychiatry, 51*(6), 706–716.

Lee, V., & Hoaken, P. S. (2007). Cognition, emotion, and neurobiological development: Mediating the relation between maltreatment and aggression. *Child Maltreatment, 12*(3), 281–298.

Lemerise, E. A., & Arsenio, W. F. (2000). An integrated model of emotion processes and cognition in social information processing. *Child Development, 71*, 107–118.

McCloskey, M. S., Noblett, K. L., Deffenbacher, J. L., Gollan, J. K., & Coccaro, E. F. (2008). Cognitive-behavioral therapy for intermittent explosive disorder: A pilot randomized clinical trial. *Journal of Consulting and Clinical Psychology, 76*(5), 876–886.

Norris, C. J., Chen, E. E., Zhu, D. C., Small, S. L., & Cacioppo, J. T. (2004). The interaction of social and emotional processes in the brain. *Journal of Cognitive Neuroscience, 16*, 1818–1829.

Penton-Voak, I. S., Thomas, J., Gage, S. H., McMurran, M., McDonald, S., & Munafò, M. R. (2013). Increasing recognition of happiness in ambiguous facial expressions reduces anger and aggressive behavior. *Psychological Science, 24*(5), 688–697.

Stoddard, J., Sharif-Askary, B., Harkins, E. A., Frank, H. R., Brotman, M. A., Penton-Voak, I. S., et al. (2016). An open pilot study of training hostile interpretation bias to treat disruptive mood dysregulation disorder. *Journal of Child and Adolescent Psychopharmacology, 26*(1), 49–57.

Storbeck, J., & Clore, G. L. (2007). On the interdependence of cognition and emotion. *Cognition & Emotion, 21*(6), 1212–1237.

Taft, C. T., Schumm, J. A., Marshall, A. D., Panuzio, J., & Holtzworth-Munroe, A. (2008). Family-of-origin maltreatment, posttraumatic stress disorder symptoms, social information processing deficits, and relationship abuse perpetration. *Journal of Abnormal Psychology, 117*(3), 637–646.

Teisl, M., & Cicchetti, D. (2008). Physical abuse, cognitive and emotional processes, and aggressive/disruptive behavior problems. *Social Development, 17*(1), 1–23.

Weiss, B., Dodge, K. A., Bates, J. E., & Pettit, G. S. (1992). Some consequences of early harsh discipline: Child aggression and a maladaptive social information processing style. *Child Development, 63*(6), 1321–1335.

Further Reading

Crick, N. R., & Dodge, K. A. (1996). Social information-processing mechanisms in reactive and proactive aggression. *Child Development, 67*(3), 993–1002.

CHAPTER NINE

Psychological Trauma and Intermittent Explosive Disorder

Jennifer R. Fanning*, Lauren Pasetes†
*Center for Depression, Anxiety and Stress Research, McLean Hospital, Belmont, MA, United States
†Clinical Neuroscience and Research Psychopharmacology Unit, Department of Psychiatry & Behavioral Neuroscience, Pritzker School of Medicine, University of Chicago, Chicago, IL, United States

Contents

Introduction

Human needs for safety, affiliation, respect, and autonomy are near universal, and when met, support striving, fulfillment, and subjective well-being (Maslow, 1943; Tay & Diener, 2001). Traumatic experiences thwart these needs and challenge beliefs about safety, justice, and self-worth. Traumatic events involve situations that are life threatening or overwhelm one's capacity for coping. During a life-threatening event, behaviors are mobilized to support survival in the form of freezing, fighting back, fleeing, or sheltering in place (Bracha, 2004; Cannon, 1932; Taylor et al., 2000). In the days and weeks following a traumatic event, sequelae such as disturbed sleep, heightened arousal, emotional lability, and intrusive recollections of the event are the norm (Shalev, 2002). Over time, these negative effects may dissipate and the individual may return to their pretrauma level of

Intermittent Explosive Disorder
https://doi.org/10.1016/B978-0-12-813858-8.00009-7

functioning, thus recovering from the trauma. For some individuals, however, a traumatic experience sets into motion pervasive and lasting effects on identity, interpersonal relationships, and emotional and physiological functioning. A common long-term effect of trauma is increased anger and aggressive behavior—problems that have their roots in the cognitive, emotional, interpersonal, and physiological effects of the trauma. When the aggressive behavior is disproportionate, recurrent, and impairing, it may be diagnosed as intermittent explosive disorder (IED), a psychological disorder characterized by recurring and inappropriate aggressive outbursts. This chapter describes the relationship between trauma, aggression, and intermittent explosive disorder, and reviews phenomenology, cross-cultural studies of trauma and aggression, and theoretical perspectives.

Psychological Trauma

Trauma has been described as a stressful experience that overwhelms one's capacity for coping (van der Kolk, 2000). When first defined in the Diagnostic and Statistical Manual of Mental Disorders-3rd Edition (DSM-III), trauma was considered to be an event that was psychologically distressing and "outside the range of usual human experience" (APA, 1980). Far from being rare, however, systematic investigations reveal trauma exposure to be quite prevalent in the general population. In fact most people (around 90%; Kilpatrick et al., 2013) experience a traumatic event in their lifetime, and exposure to multiple potentially traumatic experiences is also prevalent. The current DSM-5 defines trauma as an event that involves actual or threatened death, serious injury, or sexual assault, which can be experienced firsthand, witnessed, or learned about happening to a loved one (APA, 2013). This definition distinguishes trauma from other life stressors, such as job loss or divorce. An alternative classification system, the International Statistical Classification of Diseases (10th Edition; ICD-10; WHO, 1992) defines trauma more broadly as "a stressful event or situation...of an exceptionally threatening or catastrophic nature, which is likely to cause pervasive distress in almost anyone." Commonly experienced traumatic events include experiencing physical or sexual assault (53% lifetime prevalence), witnessing assault (33%), violent or accidental death of a loved one (52%), accident or fire (48%), and disaster (51%), based on national data weighted to estimate prevalence in the U.S. general population (Kilpatrick et al., 2013). Traumatic events can occur at any age; however, rates of exposure peak in late adolescence and early adulthood (Breslau, 2009). Risk factors for exposure to trauma include lower education, low socioeconomic status, early conduct problems, and family history of psychopathology (Breslau et al., 1998; Breslau, Davis, & Andreski, 1995; Breslau, Davis, Andreski, & Peterson, 1991; Perkonigg, Kessler, Storz, & Wittchen, 2000).

Posttraumatic Stress Disorder

Experiencing psychological trauma is associated with increased rates of psychiatric disorders, including depression, anxiety, substance use disorders, and most notably, posttraumatic stress disorder (PTSD), which occurs in 6%–8% in the general population (Breslau, 2009; Frans, Rimmo, Aberg, & Fredrikson, 2005; Kessler, Sonnega, Bromet, Hughes, & Nelson, 1995; Kilpatrick et al., 2013). PTSD was formally recognized as a psychiatric diagnosis in the DSM-III in 1980, following lobbying by military veterans' groups and other stakeholders (Scott, 1990). Before that time, the constellation of symptoms comprising what we now recognize as PTSD was described in literature and historical accounts as "war neuroses," "shell shock," and "soldier's heart," among other terms. In the DSM-III, PTSD was characterized by three symptom "clusters": *reexperiencing* symptoms, characterized by intrusive memories of the traumatic experience, nightmares, and traumatic flashbacks; *numbing*, reflected in diminished interest in activities and relationships and constricted affect; and *hypervigilance*, characterized by exaggerated startle response to surprising stimuli, irritability, poor sleep, survivor's guilt, and traumatic amnesia. In DSM-5, the criteria include four symptom clusters that begin or worsen following a traumatic event: *intrusion* symptoms (e.g., intrusive memories, nightmares), *avoidance* (of thoughts and feelings, people and places associated with the traumatic event), *arousal* (sleep disturbance, irritability, hypervigilance), and *negative alterations in mood and cognition* (e.g., exaggerated negative beliefs about one's self or the world). The latter cluster includes persistent negative beliefs about oneself, others, and the world, and distorted cognitions about the causes and consequences of the traumatic event. From its earliest inclusion in the DSM, the diagnosis of PTSD has required that the symptoms develop following a DSM qualifying trauma. Of course, stressful events falling outside of this definition also negatively impact health and behavior. Studies show that a variety of adverse experiences in childhood (ACEs) are associated with physical and mental health problems, violence risk, and aggression (Duke, Pettingell, McMorris, & Borowsky, 2010; Felitti et al., 1998; Matsuura, Hashimoto, & Toichi, 2013). Compared to earlier editions, the current DSM-5 criteria for

PTSD more explicitly recognize externalizing behavior problems associated with PTSD, specifically noting that angry outbursts, verbal and physical aggression, and other forms of risky and self-destructive behavior are common sequelae of trauma (APA, 2013).

Relationship Between Trauma, PTSD, and Aggression

One of the first large-scale studies of PTSD was initiated in 1983 when the United States Congress commissioned a systematic study of Vietnam veterans. The purpose of the study, called the National Vietnam Veterans Readjustment Survey (NVVRS; Kulka et al., 1988), was to estimate the prevalence of PTSD, comorbid conditions, and readjustment concerns, and to assess the healthcare needs of veterans, particularly those with PTSD, through the Veterans Health Administration system. The study revealed that the vast majority of veterans who developed chronic PTSD during the war experienced significant readjustment problems after leaving the military. Male veterans with the greatest exposure to war stress had higher rates of hostility and physical aggression than did civilian control subjects and the less trauma-exposed Vietnam era veterans. Forty percent of veterans with PTSD scored in the highest range on a measure of hostility and 25% had committed 13 or more physically aggressive acts in the prior year. Women veterans showed a different pattern: those with the greatest war exposure showed less physical aggression than their less exposed female veteran counterparts. In addition to problems with anger, veterans with PTSD reported lower overall life satisfaction, higher isolation, a higher rate of homelessness, and more arrests and incarcerations than veterans without PTSD. Men with PTSD reported more marital problems. Additionally, the spouses/partners of male veterans with PTSD self-reported more physical aggression compared to partners of those without PTSD. In summary, the NVVRS revealed significant morbidity and functional impairment among veterans with PTSD, including significant difficulties managing aggressive behavior.

Since the NVVRS, a robust body of research has both reaffirmed the links between trauma, PTSD, and aggression, and also further elaborated these relationships. Across numerous studies, veterans with PTSD evidence more anger, hostility, and aggression than veterans without PTSD (Beckham, Feldman, & Kirby, 1997; Chemtob, Hamada, Roitblat, & Muraoka, 1994; Frueh, Henning, Pellegrin, & Chobot, 1997; Lasko, Gurvits, Kuhne, Orr, & Pitman, 1994; Novaco & Chemtob, 2002). Furthermore, the relationship between PTSD and aggression is robust even when excluding the irritability criteria from the PTSD diagnosis (Jakupcak, Hollie, & Felker, 2007; Novaco & Chemtob, 2002). Increased aggression is even observed in veterans with subthreshold PTSD symptoms (Jakupcak et al., 2007). PTSD is associated with both general aggression and intimate partner violence (IPV), which is aggression directed toward a current or former partner or spouse. Taft and colleagues examined general aggression and IPV by treatment-seeking combat veterans with and without partners. They found that partnered and nonpartnered combat veterans reported similar rates of general physical aggression (32% and 39%) in the past year and similar rates of general psychological aggression (81% and 87%). Among partnered combat veterans, 33% engaged in physical aggression toward their partner in the previous year, while 91% engaged in psychological aggression (Taft et al., 2009). Thus treatment-seeking combat veterans show similar rates of general aggression regardless of relationship status, and partnered veterans in this group show high rates of physical and psychological aggression. PTSD is also associated with aggression in civilians who have experienced trauma (including natural disaster, motor vehicle accident, violent crime, and sexual assault); among refugees and civilian survivors of war conflict; and among first responders (e.g., police and firefighters), who are exposed to traumatic events through their occupations (Andrews, Brewin, Rose, & Kirk, 2000; Ehlers, Mayou, & Bryant, 1998; Feeny, Zoellner, & Foa, 2000; Fincham, 2011; Hinton, Rasmussen, Nou, Pollack, & Good, 2009; Jayasinghe, Giosan, Evans, Spielman, & Difede, 2008; Meffert et al., 2008; Rees et al., 2013; Riggs, Dancu, Gershuny, Greenberg, & Foa, 1992; Silove et al., 2009). The robustness of the association between PTSD symptoms and aggression across both military and nonmilitary samples is supported by a meta-analysis of 39 studies, which showed an average correlation of 0.48 between PTSD symptoms and anger and 0.29 between PTSD symptoms and aggression (Orth & Wieland, 2006).

Clinical Features of Anger and Aggression in PTSD

The development of PTSD symptoms following trauma exposure plays an important role in predicting problems with aggressive behavior. An important question in understanding trauma-related aggression in combat-exposed samples is whether participating in combat, which is a socially sanctioned form of violence, increases the risk of anger and aggression through socalization or normalization of aggressive behavior (Beckham et al., 1997; Hiley-Young, Blake, Abueg, Rozynko, & Gusman, 1995). Studies that have controlled for combat exposure find little or no direct impact of combat exposure on anger and aggression (Chemtob et al., 1994; Elbogen, Fuller, et al., 2010; Lasko et al., 1994). Instead, the effects of combat exposure on aggression appear to be related to increased severity of posttraumatic stress symptoms (Taft, Kaloupek, et al., 2007; Taft, Vogt, Marshall, Panuzio, & Niles, 2007). Anger and aggression are most associated with arousal/reactivity PTSD symptoms (Elbogen, Fuller, et al., 2010; King & King, 2004; Taft et al., 2009). This symptom cluster is characterized by autonomic and behavioral dysregulation and hyperreactivity to stimuli. The relationship of hyperarousal to PTSD is consistent with the role of arousal in aggressive behavior more generally (Zillmann, Katcher, & Milavsky, 1972).

Other factors that may impact aggression among trauma-exposed individuals are substance use, comorbid depression, and traumatic brain injury. Individuals diagnosed with PTSD have increased rates of substance use disorders (SUDs; Kessler et al., 1995; Kramer, Polusny, Arbisi, & Krueger, 2014). SUDs are independently associated with aggressive behavior and have been found to exacerbate aggression in individuals with PTSD (King & King, 2004). Some research by Elbogen et al. (2014) has attributed violence in PTSD to substance use, but other studies have found that PTSD symptoms (particularly hyperarousal) impact aggressive behavior both directly (independently) and indirectly via effects on substance use (Savarese, Suvak, King, & King, 2001; Taft, Kaloupek, et al., 2007). Likewise, a significant percentage of individuals with PTSD also meet criteria for major depressive disorder and have experienced traumatic brain injury (TBI; Breslau, 2009; Stein & McAllister, 2009), and evidence suggests that both depression (Sherman, Sautter, Jackson, Lyons, & Han, 2006; Taft et al., 2005) and TBI (Grafman et al., 1996) are risk factors for aggressive behavior. Taft et al. (2005) found that veterans with PTSD (PTSD+) who engaged in intimate partner violence (IPV) reported significantly more depression than PTSD+ veterans who did not engage in IPV, and also had greater trauma exposure. O'Donnell, Cook, Thompson, Riley, and Neria (2008) modeled the associations between trauma, PTSD, depression, and aggression, and found that PTSD symptoms mediated the relationship between trauma (wartime captivity) and physical and verbal aggression, and that depression severity moderated (i.e., strengthened) the relationship between PTSD symptoms and aggression (O'Donnell et al., 2008). Likewise, although TBI is associated with aggressive behavior and is common among individuals who have experienced trauma, multivariate analyses suggest that neither TBI nor loss of consciousness due to head injury significantly impacts aggression (i.e., aggressive impulses, difficulty managing anger, or problems controlling aggressive behavior) above the effects of PTSD, based on research conducted on post-9/11 U.S. military veterans (Elbogen, Fuller, et al., 2010). Based on the research, PTSD symptoms are a key factor mediating the relationship between trauma exposure and aggression. While comorbidities such as alcohol use, depression, and TBI may exacerbate aggressive tendencies, they do not account for the relationship between trauma and aggression.

PTSD and Intermittent Explosive Disorder

Epidemiological studies and studies of large community samples that assess IED provide evidence of comorbidity between PTSD and clinically significant aggressive behavior. In the National Comorbidity Study Replication (NCS-R), approximately 15% of adults with IED by DSM-IV criteria also had lifetime PTSD (see Chapter 4 on "Comorbidity" for data regarding PTSD and IED by DSM-5 criteria). Having a diagnosis of PTSD was associated with a threefold increase in the odds of also having a lifetime diagnosis of IED. In fact, this figure may underestimate the association between DSM-IV PTSD and IED in the general population because the criteria used to identify IED are narrower than the DSM criteria for IED, in that the NCS-R criteria focus on physically aggressive, and not verbally aggressive, behavior (Kessler et al., 2006). The National Comorbidity Study Replication-Adolescent Supplement (NCR-R-SA) estimated the lifetime prevalence of IED (narrowly defined as meeting criteria in a one-year period) among U.S. adolescents aged 13–17 to be 5.3%. PTSD did not show significant comorbidity with IED among adolescents, based on odds ratios. Approximately 6% of adolescents with narrowly defined lifetime DSM-IV IED also evidenced lifetime PTSD. Approximately 7% of adolescents with lifetime PTSD evidenced lifetime IED (McLaughlin et al., 2012). One reason for the lack of association at this age may be the relatively later average age of onset of PTSD relative to IED. Median age of onset for PTSD is around 23 years; for IED it is 15 years. By age 15, only about 25% of lifetime PTSD cases have developed. By age 20, 75% of IED cases have developed (Kessler et al., 2005). Still, McLaughlin et al. (2012) observed that among comorbid IED and PTSD cases, the first onset was of PTSD in about half of cases, higher than would be predicted based on age of onset data alone. Accordingly, there is evidence both that IED is a risk factor for later PTSD, and that PTSD is a risk factor for IED. A large study of adults with IED recruited from the community showed significant comorbidity between IED and PTSD, with fourteen percent of subjects with IED also having PTSD during the lifespan (Fanning, Lee, & Coccaro, 2016). Individuals with IED often have extensive and diverse histories of trauma, including natural disasters, life-threatening traumas, and multiple trauma exposures. Exposure to multiple traumatic events is associated with greater odds of IED diagnosis (Fincham, 2011; Nickerson, Aderka, Bryant, & Hofmann, 2012; Silove et al., 2009).

IED in the Aftermath of Political Violence

Research from across the globe supports the notion that anger is a central component of the response to trauma. Silove and colleagues (2009) have studied the impact of war conflict and its aftermath on the population of Timor-Leste (East Timor) in Southeast Asia. The history of the now independent state in the 20th century was characterized by extreme violent conflict as it transitioned to independence. The period of occupation by Indonesia from 1975 to 1999, in particular, was marked by human rights violations including mass killings, torture, systematic rape, arbitrary detention, forced displacement, starvation, and preventable disease (Silove et al., 2009). Since Timor-Leste became established as an independent nation in 2002, the country has been marked by alternating periods of peace and internal conflict and has experienced persistent socioeconomic and developmental challenges (Liddell et al., 2013). Silove and colleagues' research has documented the prevalence and phenomenology of postconflict IED in the Timor-Leste population.

The East Timor Mental Health Epidemiological Needs Survey (ETMHENS) studied men and women aged 18 and older in urban and rural areas of East Timor and assessed trauma exposure and psychological distress, including depression and PTSD. The survey also assessed the presence and frequency of "anger attacks," using indigenous language terms for sudden, explosive attacks of anger. Anger attacks, as described by Fava et al. (1991), represent episodes of intense anger that are excessive reactions to provoking events, often accompanied by physiological hyperarousal (Fava et al., 1991). Anger attacks are analogous to anger outbursts that are the basis for the IED diagnosis. Silove et al. (2009) examined data from five census tracts (1554 respondents, response rate 80%), all of which had been affected by the military conflict, to assess the prevalence and correlates of explosive anger in the population. The study respondents were highly trauma exposed, reporting a mean number of 4.2 traumatic exposures and endorsing exposure to war-related traumas at high rates: house burnt down (scorched earth tactic; 59%), family members disappeared (36%), combat (33%), physically attacked (18%), saw loved ones murdered (18%), torture (11%), and unjust imprisonment (7%). Thirty-eight percent of the sample reported at least monthly explosive anger episodes. Among this group, the average number of anger attacks was thirteen per month. Episodes of explosive anger were described as sudden and extreme attacks of anger in response to minimal provocation. The anger was invariably accompanied by either verbal or physical aggression that was directed toward family members or others in the person's proximity. Respondents reported that they were significantly distressed by their anger episodes and experienced negative social consequences as a result. When asked, respondents attributed the anger to past injustices, desire for revenge, or social and economic stressors (Silove et al., 2009). These reports of recurrent impulsive, anger-driven aggression, that is out of proportion to the provocation, and that results in distress and impairment, map closely to the DSM criteria for IED. The concordance between the culturally specific assessment of explosive anger and IED as assessed by the Structured Clinical Interview for DSM-IV (SCID) IED module was confirmed in a follow-up study which showed a correct classification rate of IED of 91% (Liddell et al., 2013).

The rate of clinically significant explosive anger identified by Silove and colleagues was considerably higher than the estimated prevalence of post-traumatic stress (PTS; 5%) or clinically significant psychological distress (3%). However, most subjects with PTS (81%) and clinically significant distress (69%) also reported recurrent anger episodes. There was a "dose effect" of trauma exposure on anger attacks, and experiencing six or more traumas was particularly associated with recurrent anger attacks.

In a subsequent study by the same group, Rees et al. (2013) examined the prevalence and predictors of IED diagnosis among women living in Timor-Leste. The authors conducted an epidemiological survey of 2,964 urban and rural-living men and women and qualitative interviews with 77 women. They assessed psychiatric disorders (including IED, major depression, and PTSD); sociodemographic factors; and exposure to a range of stressors and traumas both gender specific and nonspecific. To assess trauma due to sexual violence researchers asked women whether they had experienced "trauma suffered specifically because you are a woman." The rate of IED among women was 12.2%, double the rate of the men surveyed (6.6%). Among women, meeting criteria for IED was associated with comorbid

PTSD diagnosis (tetrachoric correlation; $r_{tet}=0.35$) and severe psychological distress ($r_{tet}=0.41$). Fifty-nine percent of women with IED had psychiatric comorbidity. The authors examined the impact of various demographic factors, traumas, and stressors, on IED diagnosis in women using multiple logistic regression, controlling for PTSD and depression. Urban residency (OR=2.0), illness ("feeling sick"; OR=1.7), gender-based violence (incorporating sexual assault, rape or death threats related to respondents' political behavior, and domestic violence; OR=2.3), severe poverty (OR=1.2), and preoccupation with past injustices (OR=1.7) were associated with IED in the multivariate analysis. The results are notable for the high estimated prevalence of IED overall and the relatively higher prevalence in women, which is opposite of prevalence estimates in the United States (Kessler et al., 2006; Nickerson et al., 2012). Worldwide, men are disproportionately likely to experience combat through military service. However, women experience unique stressors during wartime because of gender specific violence and stressors associated with women's roles in society, including the disproportionate impact of extreme poverty. Silove and colleagues (Silove et al., 2009) propose a model for understanding the postconflict anger and aggression observed in Timor-Leste (see Theoretical Perspectives).

Researchers have also studied how conflict, interpersonal violence, and violations of human rights have impacted the development of PTSD and IED in postapartheid South Africa in the 2000s. Apartheid, a period of institutionalized racial segregation that ended in 1994, was characterized by state-perpetrated human rights violations (including politically motivated violence) that were met with both violent and nonviolent resistance. Additionally, postapartheid South Africa in the late 20th and 21st centuries has been characterized by very high rates of interpersonal violent crime, including high rates of homicide and sexual assault. A report by the European Institute for Crime Prevention and Control (Harrendorf, Heiskanen, & Malby, 2010) found that South Africa had the second highest homicide rate of 144 countries providing data, based on data collected in 2007 (Harrendorf et al., 2010).

The South African Stress and Health Study, a nationally representative study of adult men and women in South Africa (SASH; $N=4351$; 2002–2004), was conducted to assess mental health in the general population. The study used the World Mental Health Composite International Diagnostic Interview (WMH-CIDI) PTSD module to assess lifetime exposure to trauma events, including to various forms of interpersonal violence. In addition, items assessing lifetime exposure to detention, torture, and politically motivated assaults were added to assess exposure to politically motivated violence. Using data from the SASH study, Fincham et al. (2009) examined how sociodemographic factors and trauma exposure relate to IED in South Africa. The authors estimated the prevalence of broadly and narrowly defined IED (using the same measures and criteria as the NCS-R (Kessler et al., 2006) as 9.5% and 2.0%, respectively. Sixty-eight percent of respondents with narrow IED and 61% of those with broad IED met criteria for another DSM-IV disorder. In multivariate analysis, predictors of narrow IED included white race and mixed race, psychiatric comorbidity, and exposure to multiple (i.e., 6 or more) lifetime traumatic events. Exposure to one or more traumatic events was associated with increased odds of broad IED (i.e., three lifetime aggressive events, including 1 past-year event); however, only exposure to 6 or more traumatic events was associated with the more acute, recurrent aggressive behavior captured by narrow IED criteria. Data from this study showed similar prevalence rates for IED and PTSD. The study by Fincham and colleagues showed a dose effect of trauma on likelihood of aggressive behavior (i.e., broad IED); however, only repeated exposure to trauma (6 or more events) was associated with the persistent difficulty managing aggressive behavior that is characterized by IED. Although the authors did not assess whether PTSD or other mechanisms account for the link between trauma and IED, it is reasonable to predict, given the dose effect of trauma on PTSD symptom severity and the high rate of psychiatric comorbidity among those with IED, that these factors play a role in the relationship.

Studies focusing on civilian survivors of military conflict and political violence underscore the broad range of traumas that have been associated with aggression and IED and the diverse regions of the world in which this association has been observed. The high rate of clinically significant anger (38% in Timor-Leste) points to anger as a common posttraumatic reaction, even in the absence of diagnosed PTSD. Indeed, Silove et al. (2009) consider whether anger is a normative response to the type of extreme injustices widely experienced in Timor-Leste. East Timorese respondents themselves described posttraumatic anger as normal, but also as distressing and impairing (Silove et al., 2009). In fact, the extent to which posttraumatic reactions are normative reactions to extreme life events versus a failure to recover from a stressful event has historically been a central question about the PTSD diagnosis (Yehuda & McFarlane, 1995). Although diagnosing IED carries a risk of generating stigma and medicalizing a normative response to trauma, benefits of utilizing the diagnosis include identifying needs within the population for mental health and other support resources and facilitating individual referrals for treatment. Given that IED requires *recurring* aggressive behavior, the diagnosis identifies individuals with persistent problems with aggression that are highly likely to recur in the future.

Early Life Trauma and IED

Research in children and adolescents points to the impact of early experiences on development, health, behavior, and psychopathology across the lifespan. ACEs are stressful or traumatic experiences in childhood that may include abuse or neglect or types of household dysfunction, such as substance use, loss, or criminality within the family (SAMHSA, 2018). Children who experience ACEs are at greater risk for negative health and mental health outcomes later in life (Felitti et al., 1998). One category of ACE, childhood maltreatment, includes childhood experiences of physical, emotional, and sexual abuse, and emotional and physical neglect. Experiencing childhood maltreatment (CM) is associated with increased risk of psychopathology (Briere and Elliott, 2003; Green et al., 2010; Lobbestael, Arntz, & Bernstein, 2010; Scott, McLaughlin, Smith, & Ellis, 2012), aggression (Briere and Runtz, 1990; Dodge, Bates, & Peitit, 1990; Singer, Miller, Guo, Flannery, & Frierson, 1999; Song, Singer, & Anglin, 1998), and suicidal behavior (Miller, Esposito-Smythers, Weismoore, & Renshaw, 2013; Silverman, Reinherz, & Giaconia, 1996). In the NCS-R U.S. epidemiological study, approximately 53.4% of respondents reported at least one childhood adversity (such events included maltreatment, parental maladjustment, interpersonal losses, childhood physical illness, and economic adversity; McLaughlin et al., 2012). The most commonly reported childhood adversities were parental divorce (17.5% of respondents), family violence (14%), and family economic adversity (10.3%). The prevalence of self-reported maltreatment in childhood was as follows: physical abuse (8%), sexual abuse (6%), and neglect (6%). Exposure to multiple forms of adversity was relatively common. Among respondents who reported any childhood adversity, the mean number of adversities was 3.2. McLaughlin et al. (2012) observed, using data from the NCS-R, that indices of childhood maltreatment, family violence, parental impairment (mental illness, substance use, and criminality), parental loss, and childhood physical illness, were significantly associated with the first onset of disruptive behavior disorders, including IED, in multivariate analyses (odds ratios: 1.5 to 2.0). Another large-scale study, this one in adolescents, mirrored these findings. The 2007 Minnesota Student Survey, an anonymous survey of 136,549 6th, 9th, and 12th grade students asked students about adverse experiences and about their involvement in several types of aggressive and self-aggressive behaviors. The results showed that both CM-related childhood adversities and family dysfunction-related adversities (family alcohol- and drug-use and family violence) uniquely predicted self-reported aggressive behaviors (bullying, physical fighting, dating violence, and weapon-carrying) in both boys and girls (Duke et al., 2010). Furthermore, the number of types of adverse events students experienced had a cumulative effect on violent risk. Among girls, each reported type of adverse event increased the risk of violence by 38%–88%; among boys each adverse event type increased risk 35%–144%.

Traumatic events that are experienced early in life may have a particularly strong impact on the development of IED. Nickerson et al. (2012) analyzed data from the NCS-R study related to types of trauma exposure and age at first exposure. Data on trauma exposure were assessed using the World Health Organization (WHO) Composite International Diagnostic Interview (CIDI), which assessed 26 unique types of traumatic exposures, including exposure to war-related traumas, accident-related traumas, disaster-related traumas, and interpersonal traumas, among others. In a multivariate analysis, lifetime diagnosis of IED was associated with male gender, number of reported lifetime traumas, lifetime diagnoses of PTSD and generalized anxiety disorder (GAD), and exposure to a first traumatic event during childhood but not adulthood. These results extend other research on comorbidity between PTSD and IED, and suggest that early exposure to trauma is a particularly robust predictor of IED. Nickerson et al. further found that, when considering the impact of different trauma types simultaneously, only interpersonal trauma predicted IED diagnosis, and it did so both when the exposure occurred in childhood and when it occurred in adulthood. The odds of developing IED, however, were significantly higher (OR=3.55) when the exposure occurred in childhood versus adulthood (OR=1.78). These results on interpersonal trauma are also somewhat at odds with other studies linking diverse trauma exposures and diverse adverse experiences to aggressive behavior. The results highlight, however, the strength of the relationship between early traumatic experiences and interpersonal traumatic experiences, and the type of persistent, recurring, and impairing aggressive behavior that is characterized by IED.

A study conducted by our own research group investigated the relationship between childhood maltreatment, aggression, and self-directed aggression in a large sample of adults that included healthy individuals with no psychopathology, adults with IED, and psychiatric control subjects (Fanning, Meyerhoff, Lee, & Coccaro, 2014). Psychiatric control subjects met criteria for one or more lifetime Axis I or II psychiatric diagnoses.

CM was assessed using the revised Childhood Trauma Questionnaire (Bernstein et al., 2003), which scores exposure to CM along five dimensions, including physical abuse and neglect, emotional abuse and neglect, and sexual abuse. Compared to healthy subjects (HC) and psychiatric controls (PC), IED subjects reported more extensive histories of physical abuse and neglect and emotional abuse and neglect. IED subjects reported more sexual abuse than HCs and marginally more sexual abuse than PCs. Psychiatric control subjects reported more extensive abuse and neglect across all categories than healthy subjects. Lifetime aggression scores and trait impulsivity scores were significantly correlated with all aspects of CM, with effect sizes ranging from $r=0.18$ to 0.44 (small to moderate). Overall, maltreatment in childhood explained about 15% of the variance in both lifetime aggression and trait impulsivity. Multivariate logistic regression analyses assessed the unique relationships between aspects of CM and IED diagnosis, controlling for demographic differences. Among the five categories of CM, only physical abuse (as well as, marginally, emotional abuse) uniquely predicted IED diagnosis. Physical abuse remained a significant predictor of IED even after controlling for comorbid antisocial personality disorder (ASPD; Fanning et al., 2014). Previous research has associated physical abuse with a diagnosis of ASPD (Cohen et al., 2013; Lobbestael et al., 2010); however, not all individuals with ASPD display aggressive behavior. This study demonstrates that childhood physical abuse is a specific risk factor for persistent, impairing aggressive behavior (IED), over and above effects on antisocial or delinquent behavior.

Taken together, these studies suggest that a variety of adverse experiences in childhood are predictive of aggressive behavior, self-directed aggression, and disruptive behavior disorders. This includes both experiences that are considered traumatic by the DSM-definition (i.e., experiences that involve threat of death or serious injury) and other events that are considered adverse stressors that might not meet the DSM definition of a traumatic event. Although there is evidence that ACEs are related to aggressive and disruptive behavior, psychopathology, and poor health outcomes, there is a relative paucity of research on the relationship between ACEs and IED diagnosis.

Theoretical Perspectives

Theoretical models address the link between trauma and aggression from several perspectives including neurobiological, genetic, cognitive-behavioral, and sociological. In seeking to account for the prevalence of IED among the East Timor population, Silove and colleagues have considered how socioecological factors contribute to individual experiences of posttraumatic anger. Silove and Steel (2006) note that societies vary in their capacity to respond to disasters or conflicts. Conflicts are frequently followed by periods of chaos and disorder, and in many cases the community-level socioeconomic vulnerability predates the event. According to their model ADAPT (Adaptation and Development After Persecution and Trauma), conflicts and disasters disrupt key social domains including safety, social networks, justice, identities and roles, and institutions (political, religious, cultural, and social). Disruption of these domains compounds the trauma of the initial event and contributes to the development of posttrauma psychopathology (Silove & Steel, 2006). In the case of IED in Timor-Leste, Silove and colleagues propose that traumatic experiences of violence and persecution are compounded by frustrations related to the socioeconomic environment (such as high unemployment, poverty, and lack of access to health care), which serve to maintain the anger attacks even after the conflict has ended (Silove et al., 2009). Indeed, research by this group has found that postconflict distress mediates the relationship between trauma exposure and socioeconomic disadvantage and anger (Brooks, Silove, Steel, Steel, & Rees, 2011).

Focusing at the level of the individual, Miller and colleagues have observed that trauma-exposed individuals often develop psychopathology along internalizing or externalizing behavioral dimensions (Miller, Greif, & Smith, 2003; Miller, Kaloupek, Dillon, & Keane, 2004; Miller & Resick, 2007). The internalizing dimension is characterized by high negative emotionality and low positive emotionality, while the externalizing dimension is characterized by high negative emotionality and low behavioral control. Aggressive behavior among trauma-exposed individuals is often comorbid with other disinhibited behaviors such as substance abuse, impulsivity, and antisocial behavior. The symptom profile of trauma survivors, they propose, is explained by broad personality predispositions as well as genetic and environmental factors (Wolf et al., 2010). Indeed, there is evidence that certain specific genetic variations (e.g., MAO-A, FKBP5, ankyrin-3) interact with trauma exposure to increase aggression and other impulsive behaviors (Bevilacqua et al., 2012; Caspi et al., 2005; Logue et al., 2013; Waltes, Chiocchetti, & Freitag, 2016; Zannas & Binder, 2014).

Chemtob and colleagues have proposed a cognitive-behavioral "survival mode" theory of PTSD-related anger and aggression. The authors posit that individuals with PTSD continue to function in "survival mode" for an extended period after the traumatic event has ended (Chemtob et al., 1994; Chemtob, Roitblat, Hamada, Carlson, & Twentyman, 1988;

Novaco & Chemtob, 2002). This mode of functioning is adaptive for short time periods of actual acute threat; however, persistence of this mode of operating after the threat has passed is detrimental to adaptive functioning and results in the dysregulated emotions, physiology, and behaviors that are characteristic of PTSD. According to this hypothesis, perceived threats trigger "survival-mode" behavior; once engaged this behavioral response precludes more extensive cognitive processing of new events. Instead, cognitions are biased toward perceiving threats, and the result is increased vigilance and reduced self-monitoring. These response tendencies become entrenched through a positive feedback loop (Chemtob et al., 1988).

Like Chemtob's survival-mode model, social information processing (SIP) theories posit that biased cognitive and emotional responses to social stimuli support maladaptive social behavior including aggression and IED (Arsenio, 2000; Coccaro, Fanning, Keedy, & Lee, 2016; Crick & Dodge, 1994; Dodge et al., 1990; Taft, Schumm, & Marshall, 2008). In early work on SIP, Dodge et al. (1990) found that deficits, such as poor encoding of social cues, limited accessing of prosocial response options, facilitated access to aggressive response options, and hostile bias in interpreting social cues accounted for much of the relationship between physical abuse and aggressive behavior in children (Dodge et al., 1990). Aggressive adults with IED exhibit hostile attribution bias, more negative emotionality, and report less efficacy for engaging in prosocial responses than nonaggressive adults. They also anticipate more favorable outcomes for aggressive behavior than nonaggressive adults (Coccaro et al., 2016). Now there is evidence of cognitive biases supporting aggression in populations with PTSD and trauma exposure. Taft et al. (2008) observed that SIP deficits were associated with both physical and psychological intimate partner violence by military veterans, and SIP biases appeared to mediate the relationship between childhood maltreatment, PTSD symptoms, and IPV perpetration (Taft et al., 2008). Other cognitive-behavioral theories focus on the role of distorted cognitions and beliefs in the maintenance of PTSD. Specifically, following a traumatic event, many individuals who develop PTSD acquire overgeneralized negative beliefs about trust, self-esteem, esteem for others, power and control, and intimacy (Herman, 1997; Monson et al., 2006; Resick & Schnicke, 1993). These beliefs function to insulate the individual from further trauma, but they are maladaptive when they are extreme (unrealistic or overly rigid) and when they interfere with affective expression that is needed to reconsolidate the traumatic memories (Resick, Monson, & Chard, 2008). In cognitive processing therapy these maladaptive schemas are called "stuck points" and resolving these stuck points is a key focus of treatment. In prolonged exposure therapy for PTSD, developed by Foa and colleagues, anger is regarded as an avoidance strategy that facilitates emotional disengagement from traumatic memories. Although reinforcing in the short term, this coping strategy is maladaptive in the long term, as it contributes to the development and maintenance of PTSD (Feeny et al., 2000; Foa, Steketee, & Rothbaum, 1989; Jaycox & Foa, 1996; Riggs et al., 1992).

Research into the neurobiology of PTSD and IED has led to the development of neural circuit models of these disorders. Specifically, PTSD and IED are associated with characteristic variations in brain structure and function in common neural circuits, offering a potential explanation for the co-occurrence of PTSD and aggression. Specifically, individuals with PTSD show abnormal neural activity in brain regions associated with *emotional reactivity* to stimuli (amygdala and insula) and brain regions mediating *emotion regulation* (regions of prefrontal cortex [PFC] including the orbitofrontal cortex [OFC]; dorsolateral prefrontal cortex [DLPFC]; dorsomedial prefrontal cortex [DMPFC]; and ventrolateral prefrontal cortex [VLPFC]). Specifically, individuals with PTSD show *increased* blood oxygen-level dependent (BOLD) activity and regional cerebral blood flow (rCBF) in the amygdala (Liberzon et al., 1999; Rauch et al., 1996; Rauch et al., 2000; Shin et al., 2004; Shin et al., 2005) and insula (Rauch et al., 1996) and *decreased* response in OFC (Britton, Phan, Taylor, Fig, & Liberzon, 2005), medial PFC (Bremner, Narayan, et al., 1999; Bremner, Staib, et al., 1999; Shin et al., 2004; Shin et al., 2005), medial frontal gyrus (Shin et al., 2004), anterior cingulate cortex (ACC) (Bremner, Narayan, et al., 1999; Bremner, Staib, et al., 1999; Britton et al., 2005; Lanius et al., 2001; Lanius et al., 2003; Shin et al., 2004), and thalamus (Lanius et al., 2001; Lanius et al., 2003) to trauma-related stimuli and non-trauma-related threat stimuli (e.g., emotional faces). Studies find positive associations between symptom intensity and regional brain activation in the insula (flashbacks; Osuch et al., 2001), amygdala (total PTSD severity; Shin et al., 2004), PFC (inversely; Osuch et al., 2001; Shin et al., 2005), and medial frontal gyrus (inversely with total PTSD severity; Shin et al., 2004) during symptom provocation and emotion processing. Aggressive individuals, including those with IED, show impaired emotion regulation (Fettich, McCloskey, Look, & Coccaro, 2015) as well as abnormal brain structure and function in brain regions that support emotion regulation (Yang & Raine, 2009). Neuroimaging studies show that aggressive individuals have: (1) impaired frontal lobe functioning; (2) hyperactive amygdala activity in response to threat; and (3) abnormal connectivity between prefrontal regions and amygdala, disrupting emotion regulation (Anderson, Bechara, Damasio,

Tranel, & Damasio, 1999; Coccaro, Sripada, Yanowitch, & Phan, 2011; Davidson, 2000; Grafman et al., 1996; Yang & Raine, 2009). Accordingly, both PTSD and aggression are associated with abnormal brain functioning, including hyperreactivity in brain regions that support threat response and negative emotionality (e.g., amygdala and insula) and hypoactivity in regions that support emotion regulation (e.g., prefrontal cortex; Coccaro, McCloskey, Fitzgerald, & Phan, 2007; Etkin & Wager, 2007; McCloskey et al., 2016).

Summary

Exposure to trauma affects individuals in all countries whether highly developed or socioeconomically vulnerable. Research shows that anger is a central feature of the response to trauma. Empirical evidence provides robust support for the relationship between trauma exposure, anger, and hostility generally, and also evidence that trauma contributes to the persistent, recurring, distressing, and disabling aggression that is characterized by the diagnosis of IED. Adversity and trauma influence aggression through multiple pathways, including family disruption, individual and community-wide socioeconomic vulnerability, and mental health. Risk factors for posttraumatic aggression include exposure to multiple traumas, PTSD symptoms, depression, substance use, and TBI. Persistent, recurrent aggression as defined by IED appears to be robustly influenced by exposure to multiple traumatic events, childhood physical abuse, and PTSD. Research conducted across cultures (primarily the United States, Timor-Leste, and South Africa) points to the universality of the relationship between trauma, anger, and aggression but also to cross-cultural differences in manifestations of posttrauma psychopathology. Although anger is a normative response to extreme trauma and injustice, identifying cases of IED has the potential to support recovery by identifying postdisaster community needs, identifying individuals at high risk for future aggressive behavior, and facilitating referrals to treatment, and, by so doing, interrupting the cycle of violence.

References

American Psychiatric Association. (1980). *Diagnostic and statistical manual of mental disorders-3rd edition (DSM-III)*. Washington, DC: American Psychiatric Association.

American Psychiatric Association. (2013). *Diagnostic and statistical manual of mental disorders-5th edition (DSM-5)*. Washington, DC: American Psychiatric Association.

Anderson, S. W., Bechara, A., Damasio, H., Tranel, D., & Damasio, R. (1999). Impairment of social and moral behavior related to early damage in human prefrontal cortex. *Nature Neuroscience*, *2*(11), 1032–1037.

Andrews, B., Brewin, C. R., Rose, S., & Kirk, M. (2000). Predicting PTSD symptoms in victims of violent crime: The role of shame, anger, and childhood abuse. *Journal of Abnormal Psychology*, *109*(1), 69–73.

Arsenio, W. F. (2000). An integrated model of emotion processes and cognition in social information processing. *Child Development*, *71*(1), 107–118.

Beckham, J. C., Feldman, M. E., & Kirby, A. C. (1997). Interpersonal violence and its correlates in Vietnam veterans with chronic posttraumatic stress disorder. *Journal of Clinical Psychology*, *53*, 859–869.

Bernstein, D. P., Stein, J. A., Newcomb, M. D., Walker, E., Pogge, D., Ahluvalia, T., et al. (2003). Development and validation of a brief screening version of the childhood trauma questionnaire. Child Abuse and *Neglect*, *27*, 169–190.

Bevilacqua, L. C., Carli, V., Sarchiapone, M., George, D. K., Goldman, D., Roy, A., et al. (2012). Interaction between FKBP5 and childhood trauma and risk of aggressive behavior. *Archives of General Psychiatry*, *69*, 62–70.

Bracha, S. H. (2004). Freeze, flight, fight, faint: Adaptionist perspectives on the acute stress response spectrum. *CNS Spectrums*, *9*(9), 679–685.

Bremner, J. D., Narayan, M., Staib, L. H., Southwick, S. M., McGlashan, T., & Charney, D. S. (1999). Neural correlates of memories of childhood sexual abuse in women with and without posttraumatic stress disorder. *The American Journal of Psychiatry*, *156*(11), 1787–1795.

Bremner, J. D., Staib, L. H., Kaloupek, D., Southwick, S. M., Soufer, R., & Charney, D. S. (1999). Neural correlates of exposure to traumatic pictures and sound in combat veterans with and without posttraumatic stress disorder: A positron emission tomography study. *Biological Psychiatry*, *45*(7), 806–816.

Breslau, N. (2009). The epidemiology of trauma, PTSD, and other posttrauma disorders. *Trauma, Violence & Abuse*, *10*(3), 198–210.

Breslau, N., Davis, G. C., & Andreski, P. (1995). Risk factors for PTSD-related traumatic events: A prospective analysis. *American Journal of Psychiatry*, *152*(4), 529–535.

Breslau, N., Davis, G. C., Andreski, P., & Peterson, E. (1991). Traumatic events and posttraumatic stress disorder in an urban population of young adults. *Archives of General Psychiatry*, *48*(3), 216–222.

Breslau, N., Kessler, R. C., Chilcoat, H. D., Schultz, L. R., Davis, G. C., & Andreski, P. (1998). Trauma and posttraumatic stress disorder in the community. *Archives of General Psychiatry*, *55*(7), 626–632.

Briere, J., & Elliott, D. M. (2003). Prevalence and psychological sequelae of self-reported childhood physical and sexual abuse in a general population sample of men and women. *Child Abuse & Neglect*, *27*(10), 1205–1222.

Briere, J., & Runtz, M. (1990). Differential adult symptomatology associated with three types of child abuse histories. *Child Abuse & Neglect*, *14*(3), 357–364.

Britton, J. C., Phan, K. L., Taylor, S. F., Fig, L. M., & Liberzon, I. (2005). Corticolimbic blood flow in posttraumatic stress disorder during script-driven imagery. *Biological Psychiatry*, *57*(8), 832–840.

Brooks, R., Silove, D., Steel, Z., Steel, C. B., & Rees, S. (2011). Explosive anger in post-conflict Timor Leste: Interaction of socio-economic disadvantage and past human rights-related trauma. *Journal of Affective Disorders*, *131*(1-3), 268–276.

Cannon, W. B. (1932). *The Wisdom of the Body*. New York, NY: Norton.

Caspi, A., McClay, J., Moffitt, T. E., Mill, J., Martin, J., Craig, I. W., et al. (2005). Role of genotype in the cycle of violence in maltreated children: Fears of the future in children and young people. *Journal of Sociology Education Socialization*, *25*(2), 133–145.

Chemtob, C., Roitblat, H. L., Hamada, R. S., Carlson, J. G., & Twentyman, C. T. (1988). A cognitive action theory of post-traumatic stress disorder. *Journal of Anxiety Disorders, 2* (3), 253–275.

Chemtob, C. M., Hamada, R. S., Roitblat, H. L., & Muraoka, M. Y. (1994). Anger, impulsivity, and anger control in combat-related posttraumatic stress disorder. *Journal of Consulting and Clinical Psychology, 62*(4), 827–832.

Coccaro, E. F., Fanning, J. R., Keedy, S. K., & Lee, R. (2016). Social cognition in intermittent explosive disorder and aggression. *Journal of Psychiatric Research, 83*, 140–150.

Coccaro, E. F., McCloskey, M. S., Fitzgerald, D., & Phan, K. L. (2007). Amygdala and orbitofrontal reactivity to social threat in individuals with impulsive aggression. *Biological Psychiatry, 62*(2), 168–178.

Coccaro, E. F., Sripada, C. S., Yanowitch, R. N., & Phan, K. L. (2011). Corticolimbic function in impulsive aggressive behavior. *Biological Psychiatry, 69*(12), 1153–1159.

Cohen, L. J., Tanis, T., Bhattacharjee, R., Nesci, C., Halmi, W., & Galynker, I. (2013). Are there differential relationships between different types of childhood maltreatment and different types of adult personality pathology? *Psychiatry Research*, 1–10.

Crick, N. R., & Dodge, K. A. (1994). A review and reformulation of social information-processing mechanisms in children's social adjustment. *Psychological Bulletin, 115*(1), 74–101.

Davidson, R. J. (2000). Dysfunction in the neural circuitry of emotion regulation—A possible prelude to violence. *Science, 289*(5479), 591–594.

Dodge, K. A., Bates, J. E., & Peitit, G. S. (1990). Mechanisms in the cycle of violence. *Science, 250*, 1678–1683.

Duke, N. N., Pettingell, S. L., McMorris, B. J., & Borowsky, I. W. (2010). Adolescent violence perpetration: Associations with multiple types of adverse childhood experiences. *Pediatrics, 125*(4), e778–e786.

Ehlers, A., Mayou, R. A., & Bryant, B. (1998). Psychological predictors of chronic posttraumatic stress disorder after motor vehicle accidents. *Journal of Abnormal Psychology, 107*(3), 508–519.

Elbogen, E. B., Fuller, S., Johnson, S. C., Brooks, S., Kinneer, P., Calhoun, P. S., et al. (2010). Improving risk assessment of violence among military veterans: An evidence-based approach for clinical decision-making. *Clinical Psychology Review, 30* (6), 595–607.

Elbogen, E. B., Johnson, S. C., Wagner, H. R., Sullivan, C., Taft, C. T., & Beckham, J. C. (2014). Violent behaviour and post-traumatic stress disorder in US Iraq and Afghanistan veterans. *British Journal of Psychiatry, 204*(5), 368–375.

Etkin, A., & Wager, T. D. (2007). Functional neuroimaging of anxiety: A meta-analysis of emotional processing in PTSD, social anxiety disorder, and specific phobia. *American Journal of Psychiatry, 164*(10), 1476–1488.

Fanning, J. R., Lee, R., & Coccaro, E. F. (2016). Comorbid intermittent explosive disorder and posttraumatic stress disorder: Clinical correlates and relationship to suicidal behavior. *Comprehensive Psychiatry, 70*, 125–133.

Fanning, J. R., Meyerhoff, J. J., Lee, R., & Coccaro, E. F. (2014). History of childhood maltreatment in intermittent explosive disorder and suicidal behavior. *Journal of Psychiatric Research, 56*, 10–17.

Fava, M., Rosenbaum, J. F., McCarthy, M., Pava, J., Steingard, R., & Bless, E. (1991). Anger attacks in depressed outpatients and their response to flouxetine. *Psychopharmacology Bulletin, 27*, 275–279.

Feeny, N. C., Zoellner, L. A., & Foa, E. B. (2000). Anger, dissociation, and posttraumatic stress disorder among female assault victims. *Journal of Traumatic Stress, 13*(1), 89–100.

Felitti, V. J., Anda, R. F., Nordenberg, D., Williamson, D. F., Spitz, A. M., Edwards, V., et al. (1998). Relationship of childhood abuse and household dysfunction to many of the leading causes of death in adults. The Adverse Childhood Experiences (ACE) Study. *American Journal of Preventive Medicine, 14*(4), 245–258.

Fettich, K. C., McCloskey, M. S., Look, A. E., & Coccaro, E. F. (2015). Emotion regulation deficits in intermittent explosive disorder. *Aggressive Behavior, 41*(1), 25–33.

Fincham, D. (2011). Intermittent explosive disorder in South Africa: Prevalence, correlates, and role of traumatic exposures. *Psychopathology, 42*(2), 92–98.

Foa, E. B., Steketee, G., & Rothbaum, B. O. (1989). Behavioral/cognitive conceptualizations of post-traumatic stress disorder. *Behavior Therapy, 20*(2), 155–176.

Frans, O., Rimmo, P-A., Aberg, L., & Fredrikson, M. (2005). Trauma exposure and post-traumatic stress disorder in the general population. *Acta Psychiatrica Scandinavica, 111*(4), 291–299.

Frueh, B. C., Henning, K. R., Pellegrin, K. L., & Chobot, K. (1997). Relationship between scores on anger measures and PTSD symptomatology, employment, and compensation-seeking status in combat veterans. *Journal of Clinical Psychology, 53*(8), 871–878.

Grafman, J., Schwab, K., Warden, D., Pridgen, A., Brown, H. R., & Salazar, M. (1996). Frontal lobe injuries, violence, and aggression: A report of the Vietnam Head Injury Study. *Neurology, 46*(5), 1231–1238.

Green, J. G., Mclaughlin, K. A., Berglund, P. A., Gruber, M. J., Sampson, N. A., Zaslavsky, A. M., et al. (2010). Childhood adversities and adult psychiatric disorders in the National Comorbidity Survey Replication I. *Archives of General Psychiatry, 67* (2), 113–123.

Harrendorf, M., Heiskanen, M., & Malby, S. (2010). *International statistics on crime and justice.* Helsinki, Finland: European Institute for Crime Prevention and Control, Affiliated with the United Nations.

Herman, J. (1997). *Trauma and recovery.* New York, NY: Perseus Books Group, New York, NY.

Hiley-Young, B., Blake, D. D., Abueg, F. R., Rozynko, V., & Gusman, F. D. (1995). War-zone violence in Vietnam: An examination of premilitary, military, and postmilitary factors in PTSD in-patients. *Journal of Traumatic Stress, 8*(1), 125–141.

Hinton, D. E., Rasmussen, A., Nou, L., Pollack, M. H., & Good, M. J. (2009). Anger, PTSD, and the nuclear family: A study of Cambodian refugees. *Social Science and Medicine, 69*(9), 1387–1394.

Jakupcak, M. H., Hollie, A., & Felker, B. (2007). Anger, hostility, and aggression among Iraq and Afghanistan war veterans reporting PTSD and subthreshold PTSD. *Journal of Traumatic Stress, 20*(6), 945–954.

Jayasinghe, N., Giosan, C., Evans, S., Spielman, L., & Difede, J. (2008). Anger and post-traumatic stress disorder in disaster relief workers exposed to the September 11, 2001 World Trade Center disaster: One-year follow-up study. *The Journal of Nervous and Mental Disease, 196*(11), 844–846.

Jaycox, L. H., & Foa, E. B. (1996). Obstacles in implementing exposure therapy for PTSD: Case discussions and practical solutions. *Clinical Psychology & Psychotherapy, 3*, 176–184.

Kessler, R. C., Berglund, P., Demler, O., Jin, R., Merikangas, K. R., & Walters, E. E. (2005). Lifetime prevalence and age-of-onset distributions of DSM-IV disorders in the National Comorbidity Survey Replication. *Archives of General Psychiatry, 62*, 593–602.

Kessler, R. C., Coccaro, E. F., Fava, M., Jaeger, S., Jin, R., & Walters, E. (2006). The prevalence and correlates of DSM-IV intermittent explosive disorder in the National Comorbidity Survey Replication. *Archives of General Psychiatry, 63*, 669–678.

Kessler, R. C., Sonnega, A., Bromet, E., Hughes, M., & Nelson, C. B. (1995). Posttraumatic stress disorder in the National Comorbidity Survey. *Archives of General Psychiatry, 52*, 1048–1060.

Kilpatrick, D. G., Resnick, H. S., Milanak, M. E., Miller, M. W., Keyes, K. M., & Friedman, M. J. (2013). National estimates of exposure to traumatic events and PTSD prevalence using DSM-IV and DSM-5 criteria. *Journal of Traumatic Stress, 26*(5), 537–547.

King, L. A., & King, D. W. (2004). *Male-perpetrated domestic violence: Testing a series of multifactorial family models*. National Institute of Justice.

Kramer, M. D., Polusny, M. A., Arbisi, P. A., & Krueger, R. F. (2014). Comorbidity of PTSD and SUDs: Toward an etiologic understanding. In *Trauma and substance abuse: Causes, consequences, and treatment of comorbid disorders*. (2nd ed., pp. 53–75).

Kulka, R. A., Schlenger, W. E., Fairbank, J. A., Hough, R. L., Jordan, B. K., Marmar, C. R., et al. (1988). *Contractual report of findings from the National Vietnam Veterans Readjustment Study Volume I: Executive summary, description of findings, and technical appendices*. (vol. 27709).

Lanius, R. A., Williamson, P. C., Densmore, M., Boksman, K., Gupta, M. A., Neufeld, R. W., et al. (2001). Neural correlates of traumatic memories in posttraumatic stress disorder: A functional MRI investigation. *American Journal of Psychiatry*, *158*(11), 1920–1922.

Lanius, R. A., Williamson, P. C., Hopper, J., Densmore, M., Boksman, K., Gupta, M. A., et al. (2003). Recall of emotional states in posttraumatic stress disorder: An fMRI investigation. *Biological Psychiatry*, *53*(3), 204–210.

Lasko, N. B., Gurvits, T. V., Kuhne, A. A., Orr, S. P., & Pitman, R. K. (1994). Aggression and its correlates in Vietnam veterans with and without chronic posttraumatic stress disorder. *Comprehensive Psychiatry*, *35*(5), 373–381.

Liberzon, I., Taylor, S. F., Amdur, R., Jung, T. D., Chamberlain, K. R., Minoshima, S., et al. (1999). Brain activation in PTSD in response to trauma-related stimuli. *Biological Psychiatry*, *45*(7), 817–826.

Liddell, B. J., Silove, D., Tay, K., Tam, N., Nickerson, A., Brooks, R., et al. (2013). Achieving convergence between a community-based measure of explosive anger and a clinical interview for intermittent explosive disorder in Timor-Leste. *Journal of Affective Disorders*, *150*(3), 1242–1246.

Lobbestael, J., Arntz, A., & Bernstein, D. P. (2010). Disentangling the relationship between different types of childhood maltreatment and personality disorders. *Journal of Personality Disorders*, *24*(3), 285–295.

Logue, M. W., Solovieff, N., Leussis, M. P., Wolf, E. J., Melista, E., Baldwin, C., et al. (2013). The ankyrin-3 gene is associated with posttraumatic stress disorder and externalizing comorbidity. *Psychoneuroendocrinology*, *38*(10), 2249–2257.

Maslow, A. H. (1943). A theory of human motivation. *Psychological Review*, *50*(4), 370–396.

Matsuura, N., Hashimoto, T., & Toichi, M. (2013). Associations among adverse childhood experiences, aggression, depression, and self-esteem in serious female juvenile offenders in Japan. *The Journal of Forensic Psychiatry & Psychology*, *24*(1), 111–127.

McCloskey, M. S., Phan, K. L., Angstadt, M., Fettich, K. C., Keedy, S., & Coccaro, E. F. (2016). Amygdala hyperactivation to angry faces in intermittent explosive disorder. *Journal of Psychiatric Research*, *79*, 34–41.

McLaughlin, K. A., Green, J. G., Hwang, I., Sampson, N. A., Zaslavsky, A. M., & Kessler, R. C. (2012). Intermittent explosive disorder in the national comorbidity survey replication adolescent supplement. *Archives of General Psychiatry*, *69*(11), 1131–1139.

Meffert, M., Metzler, T. J., Henn-Haase, C., McCaslin, S., Inslicht, S., Chemtob, C., et al. (2008). A prospective study of trait anger and PTSD symptoms in police. *Journal of Traumatic Stress*, *21*(1), 410–416.

Miller, A. B., Esposito-Smythers, C., Weismoore, J. T., & Renshaw, K. D. (2013). The relation between child maltreatment and adolescent suicidal behavior: A systematic review and critical examination of the literature. *Clinical Child and Family Psychology Review*, *16* (2), 146–172.

Miller, M. W., Greif, J. L., & Smith, A. A. (2003). Multidimensional personality questionnaire profiles of veterans with traumatic combat exposure: Externalizing and internalizing subtypes. Psychological Assess*ment*, *15*(2), 205–215.

Miller, M. W., Kaloupek, D. G., Dillon, A. L., & Keane, T. M. (2004). Externalizing and internalizing subtypes of combat-related PTSD: A replication and extension using the PSY-5 scales. *Journal of Abnormal Psychology, 113*(4), 636–645.

Miller, M. W., & Resick, P. A. (2007). Internalizing and externalizing subtypes in female sexual assault survivors: Implications for the understanding of complex PTSD. *Behavior Therapy, 38*(1), 58–71.

Monson, C. M., Schnurr, P. P., Resick, P. A., Friedman, M. J., Young-Xu, Y., & Stevens, S. P. (2006). Cognitive processing therapy for veterans with military-related posttraumatic stress disorder. *Journal of Consulting and Clinical Psychology, 74*(5), 898–907.

Nickerson, A., Aderka, I. M., Bryant, R. A., & Hofmann, S. G. (2012). The relationship between childhood exposure to trauma and intermittent explosive disorder. *Psychiatry Research, 197*(1–2), 128–134.

Novaco, R. W., & Chemtob, C. M. (2002). Anger and combat-related posttraumatic stress disorder. *Journal of Traumatic Stress, 15*(2), 123–132.

O'Donnell, C. O., Cook, J. M., Thompson, R., Riley, K., & Neria, Y. (2008). Verbal and physical aggression in World War II former prisoners of war: Role of posttraumatic stress disorder and depression. *Journal of Traumatic Stress, 21*(1), 75–82.

Orth, U., & Wieland, E. (2006). Anger, hostility, and posttraumatic stress disorder in trauma-exposed adults: A meta-analysis. *Journal of Consulting and Clinical Psychology, 74*(4), 698–706.

Osuch, E. A., Benson, B., Geraci, M., Podell, D., Herscovitch, P., McCann, U. D., et al. (2001). Regional cerebral blood flow correlated with flashback intensity in patients with posttraumatic stress disorder. *Biological Psychiatry, 50*(4), 246–253.

Perkonigg, A., Kessler, R. C., Storz, S., & Wittchen, H. U. (2000). Traumatic events and post-traumatic stress disorder in the community: Prevalence, risk factors and comorbidity. *Acta Psychiatrica Scandinavica, 101*(1), 46–59.

Rauch, S. L., vad der Kolk, B. A., Fisler, R. E., Alpert, N. M., Fischman, A. J., Jenike, M. A., et al. (1996). Symptom Using Tomography. *Archives of General Psychiatry, 53*, 380–387.

Rauch, S. L., Whalen, P. J., Shin, L. M., McInerney, S. C., MacKlin, M. L., Lasko, N. B., et al. (2000). Exaggerated amygdala response to masked facial stimuli in posttraumatic stress disorder: A functional MRI study. *Biological Psychiatry, 47*(9), 769–776.

Rees, S., Silove, D., Verdial, T., Tam, N., Savio, E., Fonseca, Z., et al. (2013). Intermittent Explosive disorder amongst women in conflict affected Timor-Leste: Associations with human rights trauma, ongoing violence, poverty, and injustice. *PLoS One, 8*(8).

Resick, P. A., & Schnicke, M. (1993). *Cognitive processing therapy for rape victims*. Newbury Park, CA: Sage Publications, Inc.

Resick, P. A., Monson, C. M., & Chard, K. M. (2008). *Cognitive Processing Therapy: Veteran/military manual*. Washington, DC: Veterans Administration.

Riggs, D. S., Dancu, C. V., Gershuny, B. S., Greenberg, D., & Foa, E. B. (1992). Anger and post-traumatic stress disorder in female crime victims. *Journal of Traumatic Stress, 5*(4), 613–625.

Shalev, A. Y. (2002). Acute stress reactions in adults. *Biological Psychiatry, 51*(7), 532–543.

Savarese, V. W., Suvak, M. K., King, L. A., & King, D. W. (2001). Relationships among alcohol use, hyperarousal, and marital abuse and violence in Vietnam veterans. *Journal of Traumatic Stress, 14*(4), 717–732.

Scott, W. J. (1990). PTSD in DSM-III: A case in the politics of diagnosis and disease. *Social Problems, 37*(3), 294–310.

Scott, K. M., McLaughlin, K. A., Smith, D. A. R., & Ellis, P. M. (2012). Childhood maltreatment and DSM-IV adult mental disorders: Comparison of prospective and retrospective findings. *The British Journal of Psychiatry, 200*(6), 469–475.

Sherman, M. D., Sautter, F., Jackson, M. H., Lyons, J. A., & Han, X. (2006). Domestic violence in veterans with posttraumatic stress disorder who seek couples therapy. *Journal of Marital and Family Therapy, 32*(4), 479–490.

Shin, L. M., Orr, S. P., Carson, M. A., Rauch, S. L., Macklin, M. L., Lasko, N. B., et al. (2004). Regional cerebral blood flow in the amygdala and medial prefrontal cortex during traumatic imagery in male and female Vietnam veterans with PTSD. *Archives of General Psychiatry*, *61*(2), 168–176.

Shin, L. M., Wright, C. I., Cannistraro, P. A., Wedig, M. M., McMullin, K., Martis, B., et al. (2005). A functional magnetic resonance imaging study of amygdala and medial prefrontal cortex responses to overtly presented fearful faces in posttraumatic stress disorder. *Archives of General Psychiatry*, *62*(3), 273–281.

Silove, D., Brooks, R., Bateman Steel, C. R., Steel, Z., Hewage, K., Rodger, J., et al. (2009). Explosive anger as a response to human rights violations in post-conflict Timor-Leste. *Social Science and Medicine*, *69*(5), 670–677.

Silove, D., & Steel, Z. (2006). Understanding community psychosocial needs after disasters: Implications for mental health services. *Journal of Postgraduate Medicine*, *52*(2), 121–125.

Silverman, A. B., Reinherz, H. Z., & Giaconia, R. M. (1996). The long-term sequelae of child and adolescent abuse: A longitudinal community study. *Child Abuse & Neglect*, *20*(8), 709–723.

Singer, M. I., Miller, D. B., Guo, S., Flannery, D. J., & Frierson, T. (1999). Contributors to violent behavior among elementary and middle school children. *Pediatrics*, *104*, 878–884.

Song, L. Y., Singer, M. I., & Anglin, T. M. (1998). Violence exposure and emotional trauma as contributors to adolescents' violent behaviors. *Archives of Pediatrics & Adolescent Medicine*, *152*(6), 531–536.

Stein, M. B., & McAllister, T. W. (2009). Exploring the convergence of posttraumatic stress disorder and mild traumatic brain injury. *American Journal of Psychiatry*, *166*(7), 768–776.

Substance Abuse and Mental Health Services and Administration, & Mental Health Services, Administration (2018). *Adverse childhood experiences*. Retrieved January 13, 2019, from https://www.samhsa.gov/capt/practicing-effective-prevention/prevention-behavioral-health/adverse-childhood-experiences.

Taft, C. T., Kaloupek, D. G., Schumm, J. A., Marshall, A. D., Panuzio, J., King, D. W., et al. (2007). Posttraumatic stress disorder symptoms, physiological reactivity, alcohol problems, and aggression among military veterans. *Journal of Abnormal Psychology*, *116*(3), 498–507.

Taft, C. T., Pless, A. P., Stalans, L. J., Koenen, K. C., King, L. A., & King, D. W. (2005). Risk factors for partner violence among a national sample of combat veterans. *Journal of Consulting and Clinical Psychology*, *73*(1), 151–159.

Taft, C. T., Schumm, J. A., & Marshall, A. D. (2008). Family-of-origin maltreatment, posttraumatic stress disorder symptoms, social information processing deficits, and relationship abuse perpetration. *Journal of Abnormal Psychology*, *117*(3), 637–646.

Taft, C. T., Vogt, D. S., Marshall, A. D., Panuzio, J., & Niles, B. L. (2007). Aggression among combat veterans: Relationships with combat exposure and symptoms of posttraumatic stress disorder, dysphoria, and anxiety. *Journal of Traumatic Stress*, *20*(2), 135–145.

Taft, C. T., Weatherill, R. P., Woodward, H. E., Pinto, L. A., Watkins, L. E., Miller, M. W., et al. (2009). Intimate partner and general aggression perpetration among combat veterans presenting to a posttraumatic stress disorder clinic. *American Journal of Orthopsychiatry*, *79*(4), 461–468.

Tay, L., & Diener, E. (2001). Needs and subjective well-being around the world. *Journal of Personality and Social Psychology*, *101*(2), 354–365.

Taylor, S. E., Klein, L. C., Lewis, B. P., Gruenewald, T. L., Gurung, R. A., & Updegraff, J. A. (2000). Biobehavioral responses to stress in females: Tend and befriend, not fight or flight. *Psychological Review*, *107*(3), 411–429.

van der Kolk, B. (2000). Posttraumatic stress disorder and the nature of trauma. *Dialogues in Clinical Neuroscience*, *2*(1), 7–22.

Waltes, R., Chiocchetti, A. G., & Freitag, C. M. (2016). The neurobiological basis of human aggression: A review on genetic and epigenetic mechanisms. *American Journal of Medical Genetics Part B: Neuropsychiatric Genetics*, *171*(5), 650–675.

WHO (1992). *ICD-10 classifications of mental and behavioural disorder: Clinical descriptions and diagnostic guidelines*. Geneva: World Health Organization.

Wolf, E. J., Miller, M. W., Krueger, R. F., Lyons, M. J., Tsuang, M. T., & Koenen, K. C. (2010). Posttraumatic stress disorder and the genetic structure of comorbidity. *Journal of Abnormal Psychology*, *119*(2), 320–330.

Yang, Y., & Raine, A. (2009). Prefrontal structural and functional brain imaging findings in antisocial, violent, and psychopathic individuals: A meta-analysis. *Psychiatry Research*, *174*(2), 81–88.

Yehuda, R., & McFarlane, A. (1995). Conflict between current knowledge about pottraumatic stress disorder and its original conceptual basis. *American Journal of Psychiatry*, *152*, 1705–1713.

Zannas, A. S., & Binder, E. B. (2014). Gene-environment interactions at the FKBP5 locus: Sensitive periods, mechanisms and pleiotropism. *Genes, Brain, and Behavior*, *13*(1), 25–37.

Zillmann, D., Katcher, A. H., & Milavsky, B. (1972). Excitation transfer from physical exercise to subsequent aggressive behavior. *Journal of Experimental Social Psychology*, *8*, 247–259.

Further Reading

Arntz, A., Tiesema, M., & Kindt, M. (2007). Treatment of PTSD: A comparison of imaginal exposure with and without imagery rescripting. *Journal of Behavior Therapy and Experimental Psychiatry*, *38*(4), 345–370.

Beck, R., & Fernandez, E. (1998). Cognitive-behavioral therapy in the treatment of anger: A meta-analysis. *Cognitive Therapy and Research*, *22*(1), 63–74.

Chemtob, C. M., Novaco, R. W., Hamada, R. S., & Gross, D. M. (1997). Cognitive-behavioral treatment for severe anger in posttraumatic stress disorder. *Journal of Consulting and Clinical Psychology*, *65*(1), 184–189.

Deffenbacher, J., & McKay, M. (2000). *Overcoming situational and general anger*. Oakland, CA: New Harbinger Publications.

Digiuseppe, R., & Tafrate, R. C. (2003). Anger treatment for adults: A meta-analytic review. *Clinical Psychology: Science and Practice*, *10*(1), 70–84.

Foa, E. B., Riggs, D. S., Massie, E. D., & Yarczower, M. (1995). The impact of fear activation and anger on the efficacy of exposure treatment for post-traumatic stress disorder. *Behavior Therapy*, *26*, 487–499.

Forbes, D., Creamer, M., Hawthorne, G., Allen, N., & McHugh, T. (2003). Comorbidity as a predictor of symptom change after treatment in combat-related posttraumatic stress disorder. *Journal of Nervous and Mental Disease*, *191*(2), 93–99.

Galovski, T. E., Elwood, L. S., Blain, L. M., & Resick, P. A. (2014). Changes in anger relationships to responsivity to PTSD treatment. *Psychological Trauma*, *6*(1), 56–64.

Gerlock, A. A. (1994). Veterans' responses to anger management intervention. *Issues in Mental Health Nursing*, *15*(4), 393–408.

Grace, M., Niles, B. L., & Quinn, S. (2015). *Managing anger: A treatment for those with PTSD*. Boston, MA: National Center for PTSD.

Guina, J., Rossetter, S. R., DeRhodes, B. J., Nahhas, R. W., & Wlston, R. S. (2015). Benzodiazapines for PTSD: A systematic review and meta-analysis. *Journal of Psychiatric Practice*, *21*(4), 281–303.

Howell, K., & Day, A. (2003). Readiness for anger management: Clinical and theoretical issues. *Clinical Psychology Review*, *23*(2), 319–337.

Johnson, D. R., & Lubin, H. (2015). *Principles and techniques of trauma-centered psychotherapy*. Washington, DC: American Psychiatric Publishing.

Mackintosh, M. A., Morland, L. A., Frueh, B. C., Greene, C. J., & Rosen, C. S. (2014). Peeking into the black box: Mechanisms of action for anger management treatment. *Journal of Anxiety Disorder*, *28*(7), 687–695.

Monnelly, E. P., Ciraulo, D. A., Knapp, C., & Keane, T. (2003). Low-dose risperidone as adjunctive therapy for irritable aggression in posttraumatic stress disorder. *Journal of Clinical Psychopharmacology*, *23*(2), 193–196.

Morland, L. A., Greene, C. J., Rosen, C. S., Foy, D., Reilly, P., Shore, J., et al. (2010). Telemedicine for anger management therapy in a rural population of combat veterans with posttraumatic stress disorder: A randomized noninferiority trial. *The* Journal of Clinical Psychiatry, *71*(7), 855–863.

Reilly, P. M., & Shopshire, M. S. (2000). Anger management group treatment for cocaine dependence: Preliminary outcomes. *The* American Journal of Drug and Alcohol Abuse, *26*(2), 161–177.

Reilly, P.M, & Shopshire, M.S. (2002). Anger management for substance abuse and mental health clients: A cognitive behavioral therapy manual. Retrieved from https://store.samhsa.gov/shin/content/SMA12-4210/SMA12-4210.pdf.

Rosen, C., Adler, E., & Tiet, Q. (2013). Presenting concerns of veterans entering treatment for posttraumatic stress disorder. *Journal of Traumatic Stress*, *26*(1), 640–643.

Stapleton, J. A., & Taylor, S. (2006). Effects of three PTSD treatments on anger and guilt: Exposure therapy, eye movement desensitization and reprocessing, and relaxation training. *Journal of Traumatic Stress*, *19*(1), 19–28.

Taft, C. T., Creech, S. K., Gallagher, M. W., Macdonald, A., Murphy, C. M., & Monson, C. M. (2016). Strength at home couples program to prevent military partner violence: A randomized controlled trial. *Journal of Consulting and Clinical Psychology*, *84* (11), 935–945.

Taft, C. T., Howard, J., Monson, C. M., & Murphy, C. M. (2014). "Strength at home" intervention to prevent conflict and violence in military couples: Pilot findings. *Partner Abuse*, *5*(1), 41–57.

Taft, C. T., Macdonald, A. M., Candice, M., Walling, S. M., Resick, P. A., & Murphy, C. M. (2013). "Strength at home" group intervention for military populations engaging in intimate partner violence: Pilot findings. *Journal of Family Violence*, *28*(3), 225–231.

Taft, C. T., Murphy, C. M., & Creech, S. K. (2016). *Trauma-informed treatment and prevention of intimate partner violence*. Washington, DC: American Psychological Association.

Taft, C. T., Murphy, C. M., Creech, S. K., Monson, C. M., & Murphy, C. M. (2016). A randomized controlled clinical trial of the Strength at Home Men's Program for Partner Violence in military veterans. *Journal of Clinical Psychiatry*, 77(9), 168–1175.

Taylor, S., Thordarson, D. S., Maxfield, L., Fedoroff, I. C., Lovell, K., & Orgrodniczuk, J. (2003). Comparative efficacy, speed, and adverse effects of three PTSD treatments: Exposure therapy, EMDR, and relaxation training. *Journal of Consulting and Clinical Psychology*, *71*(2), 330–338.

Williams, D. R., Herman, A., Stein, D. J., Heeringa, S. G., Jackson, P. B., Moomal, H., et al. (2008). Twelve-month mental disorders in South Africa: Prevalence, service use and demographic correlates in the population-based South African Stress and Health Study. *Psychological Medicine*, *38*(2), 211–220.

Zohar, J., Amital, D., Miodownik, C., Kotler, M., Bleich, A., & Lane, R. M. (2002). Austin C: Double-blind placebo-controlled pilot study of sertraline in military veterans with posttraumatic stress disorder. *Journal of Clinical Psychopharmacology*, *22*(2), 190–195.

PART III

Evaluation and Treatment

CHAPTER TEN

Clinical Approach and Assessment of Intermittent Explosive Disorder

Emil F. Coccaro*, Royce J. Lee*, Michael S. McCloskey†
*Clinical Neuroscience & Psychopharmacology Research Unit, Department of Psychiatry and Behavioral Neuroscience, Pritzker School of Medicine, University of Chicago, Chicago, IL, United States
†Mechanisms of Affect Dysregulation Laboratory (MAD LAB), Department of Psychology, Temple University, Philadelphia, PA, United States

Contents

Aggression has always been, and continues to be, one of the major problems faced by human society. An estimated 43.7% of the US population is the victim of at least one physical assault in their lifetime (Kilpatrick et al., 2013). Therefore, addressing potentially reversible causes of aggression and its consequences remains an important public health and scientific goal. This volume has described what we understand about a major subtype of aggression, impulsive aggression and its medical diagnostic category, intermittent explosive disorder (IED).

While IED is more common than previously thought, only about one in three individuals with IED actually seek treatment (Kessler et al., 2006). Reasons for this are multiple but include the stigma associated with aggression, as well as a low public awareness of impulsive aggression as a brain-based and treatable behavior, both among the population at large and among clinicians. Other psychiatric disorders have also been hampered by these issues but advocates for serious disorders such as schizophrenia, mania, depression, and others, have made great strides in this regard and the degree of stigma with these disorders have greatly lessened over the past few decades. A good deal of that work involved the coming forward

Intermittent Explosive Disorder
https://doi.org/10.1016/B978-0-12-813858-8.00010-3

of well-known individuals speaking out about their own experiences with these disorders either as a patient or as a family member. In addition, organizations such as the National Alliance for the Mentally Ill (NAMI) and the Brain Behavior Research Foundation (formally known as NARSAD) have performed admirably in spreading the word that psychiatric disorders are both brain-based and treatable. Advocacy for individuals with IED is needed but as of yet, no advocacy organization has formed for IED, and so individuals with IED face two sources of stigma: one for a socially undesirable behavior (aggression) and another for mental illness. Thus there is clearly a need for advocacy for this important and common mental disorder.

A critical source of support for the development of therapeutic approaches to IED is the National Institutes of Mental Health (NIMH). While the NIMH supported projects directly relevant to IED in the 1990s and early 2000s, it has also declined to fund several clinical neuroscience and treatment projects even when peer-review rated such projects as outstanding. These projects, including one comparing the efficacy of pharmaceutical and/or cognitive-behavioral treatment of impulsive aggression, were deemed "low program priority" and were never funded. Notably, the percent of NIMH-funded projects with any relevance to aggression has dropped steadily from 3.6% in 2000 to 2.2% in 2018 despite the fact that about 7-8% of the US population report having at least three criteria A IED outbursts in any given year and that the lifetime prevalence of DSM-5 IED is about 3.8%. Further, there is a strong negative correlation between the proportion of NIMH-funded projects with any relevance to aggression, and time, between 2000 and 2018 ($r=-0.88$, $P<.001$). This is in stark contrast to NIMH-funded research in suicide where the proportion of funded projects rose steadily from 3.1% in 2000 to 9.0% in 2018 ($r=0.88$, $P<.001$) while the lifetime prevalence of suicidal behavior is about 0.4%. A similar trend is also present for Autism where the proportion of NIMH-funded projects in Autism, and Autism spectrum disorders, rose steadily by an order of magnitude, from 2.3% in 2000 to 22.3% in 2018 ($r=0.98$, $P<.001$) and where the lifetime prevalence for these disorders is about 1.7%. Accordingly, it is clear that NIMH support of other related behaviors/disorders, occurring in less than 2% of the US population, is far greater than that of impulsive aggression or disorders of impulsive aggression (IED) despite the greater prevalence of these disruptive behaviors. As of this writing, only about 0.2% of the proportion of currently funded NIMH projects are directly relevant to IED despite a lifetime prevalence rate of DSM-5 IED of about 3.8%. An additional 0.2% of NIMH-funded projects include nonhuman, basic science, projects directly relevant to aggression, while the remaining 1.8% of NIMH-funded projects are only broadly relevant to aggression and/or are related to other disorders in which aggression may appear.

Another issue is that IED is frequently comorbid with other psychiatric disorders. Clinicians may sometimes attribute the impulsive aggression in IED to a comorbid disorder. However, data from the chapter on comorbidity in this volume reaffirm the relevance of the IED diagnosis in accounting for aggressive behavior even in the context of comorbid Cluster B personality disorders. Thus we would argue, in the case of personality disorder comorbidity, that IED should remain a target for treatment. Less is known about prioritizing the treatment of IED in the setting of other comorbid conditions, such as PTSD, but this is a topic for future research.

IED and Treatment Seeking

Given this, how does one approach the evaluation of IED? Where do these individuals come from and do we engage them in treatment?

The number of individuals who meet DSM-5 criteria for IED who either speak with a medical/mental health professional, or who receive treatment for IED, is relatively low. Reanalysis of the NCS-R data set finds that only about 32% of those with DSM-5 IED discuss their "anger attacks" with their doctor, and only about 21% receive treatment for their aggressive behavior (see Chapter 3 in this volume). Thus IED appears to be an under-treated behavioral disorder. In the absence of outreach efforts to inform those in the community that IED is treatable and that treatment is available, this is not likely to change. In our clinical research program we inform the community of the availability of clinical research programs for IED via "public service announcements." While some of our "study participants" see us because someone has urged them to explore treatment, the vast majority come to us because, upon seeing our announcement, they recognize, typically for the first time, that they have a problem controlling their anger and aggression and that there may be help for it. For these individuals (like most with IED), the impulsive aggression they engage in is ego-dystonic and distressing. In contrast, the minority of individuals with IED who are referred to us by the courts tend not to follow through on appointments and are more likely to drop out of our program quickly. In most cases this is because these individuals are not convinced they have an anger problem and, thus, are not interested in changing their behavior. For these individuals impulsive aggression is seen as "ego-syntonic" or at least adaptive and/or warranted, though this response may (at least in some) reflect defensiveness and/or underreporting on the part of the individual. While this group is difficult to study, let alone treat, we have found that those with IED who come to us on their own recognize their need for evaluation and treatment and are reliable informants about their behavior even though this behavior is socially undesirable (Steakley-Freeman et al., 2018).

Diagnostic Assessment of IED

Once in the office, the initial diagnosis of IED is relatively easy to make because it focuses, primarily, on reports of actual behavior. When first evaluating for the presence of IED it is helpful to define for the patient what is meant by an impulsive aggressive outburst. For example, while "snapping" at someone is captured on measures of overt aggressive behavior (e.g., the Overt Aggression Scale—Modified for Outpatient Use: OAS-M; Coccaro, Harvey, Kupsaw-Lawrence, Herbert, & Bernstein, 1991), the lower threshold for an IED outburst requires a more significant temper outburst and/or a verbal argument, not simply an expression of irritation that can be conveyed by a "snap" (e.g., "What do you want? Damn it!").

As aggression is commonly seen as a negative and unwanted behavior, which may engender feelings of guilt and/or shame, it is also helpful to normalize aggression. This can be done by explaining that almost all people act of aggressively at some point in their lives and that aggression can even be a healthy protective response in some cases. Further, that for people who do have problems with aggression, once detected this can often be successfully treated.

After setting the stage, one can ask the patient to complete a self-assessment questionnaire of IED (e.g., Coccaro, Berman, & McCloskey, 2017) to get a quick read on whether frequent, problematic, impulsive aggressive behavior is present. If the assessment suggests possible IED, one can then begin a more detailed assessment by asking about how many times in the past week (or month) the patient has had an impulsive, angry, aggressive outburst characterized by having temper tantrums (A_1), verbal arguments (A_1), breaking objects (A_2), and/or physically assaulting (A_2) other people. In evaluating these DSM "A" IED criterion items, it is important to note that the display of impulsive aggressive behavior is a product of one's disposition to anger/aggression and what the individual actually experiences in their day-to-day life. For example, when someone is away from their day-to-day life (i.e., while on vacation) it is likely that they will experience fewer than usual social threats and appear less aggressive. Thus one does not need to have exactly two (2) impulsive aggressive outbursts every week in the previous three months, they only need an average of two aggressive outbursts per week, even if the weekly number of IED outbursts is quite variable depending on what is going on in the person's life.

If the individual does meet the aggression ("A") criteria for IED, the next step is to determine if the aggression is leading to distress and/or life problems. If it is not, then there is no need for further assessment of aggression. If the aggressive behavior does seem to be leading to problems in the individual's life then an assessment of the context of the aggression and any comorbid psychopathology will help in determining the appropriate course of action. For example, aggression (or "anger attacks") can be an associated symptom of depression, which will typically resolve with a cessation of the depressive episode. For those whom the problematic aggression is not associated with another disorder and is not severe enough to be considered an aggressive disorder, anger management may be an effective treatment (DiGuiseppe & Tafrate, 2003, Lee & DiGuiseppe, 2018).

For those who do meet the aggression criteria for IED, additional IED criteria should be assessed. The B criterion (aggression is grossly out of proportion to the provocation or stressor) is often fairly straightforward because in the review of one's aggressive outbursts it is very common for most outbursts to be clearly out of proportion to the situation. However, in other cases the extent to which the aggressive behavior is disproportionate to the provocation can be more complex and/or equivocal. Examples of this might include lashing out at a person who is berating them or physically assaulting someone who has assaulted them in the past. In these situations, if the aggressive behavior is initiated by the individual, or if the individual increases the aggression level in response to a lesser aggressive act (i.e., punching a person for teasing or insulting them), this would be considered clearly out of proportion. The caveat to this is if the person has been abused/assaulted by another previously. In that case, responding with physical aggression to the threat of being assaulted again *by that person*, even in the absence of an actual additional assault, would not be considered disproportionate, and thus would not count toward a diagnosis of IED.

The C criterion assesses whether most IED outbursts are unplanned, anger-based, and impulsive in nature. Here, the critical issue is that the aggressive outbursts meeting the A criteria be described as impulsive/anger-based, even if other outbursts are not. It is not unusual for aggressive acts to have both an anger-based and a more instrumental (means to an end) motivation. For example, fighting someone because they made you angry (anger-based) and because you are hoping that this will stop them from engaging in the behavior you don't like (instrumental). In these situations, anger tends to be the primary reason for aggressing. However, if this is initially unclear, one should assess the primary function of the aggressive behavior (e.g., "Do you think you would have fought them even if you knew it wouldn't change their behavior," "Do you think you would have fought them if you were not angry?," "What was your main reason for fighting, to get back at the person, or to try to get them to do what you wanted?")

The D criterion assesses the presence of significant distress and impairment associated with the impulsive aggressive behavior. Those with IED report at least a moderate degree of distress/impairment due to the social, occupational, or legal consequences of their aggressive behavior. This criterion is extremely important because a diagnosis of IED should not be made if there is not sufficient evidence of distress *or* psychosocial impairment. When assessing for this criterion, occasionally the individual being assessed will deny distress or impairment, despite clear evidence to the contrary (e.g., denying impairment despite being arrested for being in a fight or being fired for aggressive behavior at work). In this case, you can gently point out what appear to be the consequences of their aggression. This will typically lead to acknowledgment of negative impact of their aggressive behavior. In the rare case that the person continues to deny adverse consequences, you should use your clinical judgment to determine if impairment does exist.

The E criterion is not important when dealing with adults because it only requires the onset of recurrent, problematic, impulsive aggressive behavior after the age of six years. The F criterion, in contrast, is extremely important because it assess whether the impulsive aggressive behavior is better explained by another condition or disorder. To make the DSM-5 diagnosis of IED, individuals with impulsive aggressive outbursts cannot have these outbursts only when they are in an episode of some other comorbid condition. If so, a diagnosis of IED cannot be made because it is assumed that the impulsive aggressive behavior is driven by the psychopathology of the other condition. This differential diagnosis can be relatively straightforward when the potential comorbid condition is episodic and/or occurs later in life. However, for conditions that are more chronic, especially if they begin early in life (e.g., chronic posttraumatic stress disorder beginning in childhood) this distinction can be extremely difficult to make.

To aid in the diagnosis of IED, one may want to use a structured clinical interview, as these interviews are considered the most reliable means of diagnostic assessment (Ventura, Liberman, Green, et al., 1998). Two structured clinical interviews diagnose IED, the Structured Clinical Interview for the DSM-5 [SCID] and the IED-Module [IED-M]. The SCID, updated for the DSM-5, is one of the most frequently used omnibus diagnostic interviews in clinical and research settings (First, Williams, Karg, & Spitzer, 2015). The SCID-5 includes an optional module on the diagnosis of IED, which is located within the SCID Externalizing Disorder Module (First et al., 2015). There is also an unpublished stand-alone IED diagnostic interview, IED-M (see McCloskey & Coccaro, 2003 for a review of the IED-M). The IED-M was initially developed by Coccaro (1998) prior to the SCID-5 (but has since been revised to reflect DSM-5 IED criteria) to diagnose IED in conjunction with a full diagnostic interview (to assess for comorbid disorders that may better account for the patient's aggressive behavior). As it was developed to assess aspects of IED beyond the criteria for a diagnosis, the IED-M is a longer, more involved interview than the SCID-5 IED module. Though not required to diagnose IED, these interviews can be a useful diagnostic tool.

Assessing Severity of IED

Severity of IED can be assessed both from a lifetime and a present-time perspective. The Life History of Aggression (LHA; Coccaro, Berman, & Kavoussi, 1997) is a simple five-item assessment of aggression that quantifies the relative number of impulsive aggressive events over the person's lifetime. It can be done as an interview or as a questionnaire (Coccaro, Berman, & McCloskey, 2017). Scores range from 0 to 25 and scores of 12 and higher are typical of those with DSM-5 IED. In our studies, the average individual with IED has an LHA score of about 18 compared with about 5 for healthy controls and about 8 for nonaggressive psychiatric controls (see Table 1 in Chapter 3). The dispositional trait to engage in aggressive behavior can be assessed using the "verbal" aggression and "physical" aggression scales of the Buss Perry Aggression Questionnaire (BPAQ; Buss & Perry, 1992); typically, we combine these two scores into one "aggression" score. Trait anger can be assessed by the BPAQ "anger" score. State anger can be assessed with the state anger scale of the State-Trait and Expression of Anger Inventory (STAXI), though we have found that it correlates highly with trait anger among those with IED. History of actual impulsive behavior can be assessed with the Life History of Impulsive Behavior (LHIB; Coccaro & Schmidt-Kaplan, 2012) which is similar to the LHA but is given as a questionnaire as opposed to a clinical interview like the LHA. The dispositional trait of impulsivity can be assessed using the Barratt Impulsiveness Scale (Version 11; Patton, Stanford, & Barratt, 1995) though a more recent assessment, the Urgency, Premeditation, Perseverance, and Sensation Seeking scale (UPPS) may be better suited for the assessment of those with IED (Puhalla, Ammerman, Uyeji, Berman, & McCloskey, 2016) because it assesses negative urgency rather than simply general impulsivity.

Informed Consent and Psychoeducation

A renewed emphasis on person-centered care asks care providers to empower patients to participate in their health care by becoming informed partners in medical decision making. The first step in this process is sharing the diagnosis with the patient. In our experience, most patients receiving the IED diagnosis will likely be hearing about it for the first time. Therefore, psychoeducation is needed to teach the patients about what IED is. Such a conversation would include discussion about the diagnostic criteria and why the person's symptoms fulfill diagnostic criteria. This can be accomplished by literally reading the diagnostic criteria to the patient in the office. The conversation needs to also include information about risk factors (trauma, genetics, and biological risk factors such as altered serotonergic signaling) prognosis (currently not well understood), and what is understood about response to treatment (partial response to SSRI medications and CBT).

It is also important for the conversation to emphasize the patient's accountability for their own behavior. The IED diagnosis makes a probabilistic prediction of future aggression, but does not impair the ability to understand the law or the difference between right and wrong. Patients should know that their medical diagnosis would not provide a legal defense against any potential consequences of their aggressive behavior (also, see chapter on "Forensics," this volume). Finally, the clinician should be aware of the ethical context of the treatment of persons with aggression, which may include a duty to warn potential victims of death or serious harm when it is imminent. This can be accomplished by encouraging family involvement in the treatment. In cases where domestic violence is a risk, this may be an essential component of treatment contract. It is strongly encouraged that patients allow family members permission to discuss instances of anger and/or aggression with the clinician. Such collateral information can prove to be essential when assessing for symptomatic worsening or improvement with treatment. Finally, patients need to be reminded that health care providers are mandated reporters for child and/or elder abuse, depending on the state of residence. Although these conversations sound difficult, in our experience the patients with IED who bring themselves into treatment have already proven that they are strongly motivated to change. Usually, their awareness of the high cost of aggression to themselves and their family is what motivates them.

Assessing Interest in Treatment and Readiness to Change in IED

In order to get a sense of how prepared someone is to engage in treatment for IED, we use the Readiness to Change (RTC; Prochaska & DiClemente, 1992) scale adapted for "anger problems." The RTC is a 32-item questionnaire that assesses an individual's readiness to address their impulsive aggressive behaviors (e.g., "I have an anger problem and I really think I should work on it") on a five-point Likert scale (1="Rarely or Never" to 5="Almost Always or Always"). The RTC has four (4) subscores for precontemplation (i.e., if aware of an anger problem, places too much emphasis on the disadvantages of changing behavior), contemplation (i.e., recognize their anger problem, but ambivalent about changing behavior), action (i.e., recognize their anger problem and are changing their behavior), and maintenance (i.e., sustained behavior change), phases with higher scores reflecting a person's awareness that their frequent anger is as a problem and that they are ready and interested in addressing the problem. In our recent study on this topic (Steakley-Freeman, Lee, McCloskey, & Coccaro, 2018), we found clear separation of those with IED compared with healthy and nonaggressive psychiatric controls. More importantly, the proportion of IED study participants that had RTC scores significantly greater (two standard deviations) than the average of healthy volunteers was 25% for the precontemplation phase and more than 80% for the contemplation (95%), action (86%), and maintenance (82%) phases scores indicating that individuals with IED that come on their own to an "anger program" are clearly ready to acknowledge their anger problem and to work on it. Among those with IED, LHA scores did not correlate significantly with any RTC phase, suggesting that the level of aggressive behavior is not related to readiness to change, and therefore may not be relevant as to who is likely ready for treatment. Unfortunately, we have no data on those with IED that come to treatment because a third party wants them to, but we would expect that they would be higher in the precontemplation phase and much lower in the remaining RTC phases.

Assessing Aggression Change in IED

Change in aggression frequency and/or intensity in response to an intervention cannot be adequately assessed with the measures used to assess baseline aggression and/or impulsivity. This is because these baseline measures assess trait, not state, aggression, and thus are not designed to be sensitive to change. For assessment of IED treatment, one requires measures that assess aggressive behavior over relatively short periods of time (e.g., today, past week, past two weeks). To date, this has been done with variants of the Overt Aggression Scale first proposed in the late 1980s.

The Overt Aggression Scale (OAS; Yudofsky, Silver, Jackson, Endicott, & Williams, 1986) was first developed to assess aggressive behavior in inpatient or institutional settings. The OAS assesses four (4) subcomponents of aggressive acts for each aggressive act that occurred on an inpatient psychiatric unit. The subcomponents are verbal assault, assault against objects, assault against others, and assault against self with each scored according to severity on a 0–5 scale. While the OAS was appropriate for clinical trials in an inpatient setting, the OAS required modification for use in an outpatient setting, which is where the vast majority of potential subjects with recurrent, problematic, impulsive aggressive behaviors are. In preparation for a clinical trial to test the efficacy of fluoxetine compared with placebo, we developed the OAS Modified for Use in Outpatients (OAS-M, Coccaro et al., 1991). At the same time, another version of the OAS (Modified OAS: MOAS) was developed by another group (Kay, Wolkenfeld, & Murrill, 1988). The MOAS was developed primarily to study the phenomena of aggression, particularly in severe mental illness and institutional settings. It has also been used in clinical trials, though not clinical trials of a primary disorder of impulsive aggression (i.e., IED). The OAS-M and MOAS are similar in many ways (including in the weights of aggressive items) but the MOAS does not include a global irritability or anger score and does not include an assessment of the specific nature of impulsive aggressive outbursts as does the OAS-M. To date, the OAS-M has been used in several clinical trials of impulsive aggression and/or IED including five (5) trials with SSRIs (Coccaro, Lee, & Kavoussi, 2009; George et al., 2011; Lee, Kavoussi, & Coccaro, 2008; Silva et al., 2010), three (3) trials with anticonvulsants (Hollander et al., 2003, Mattes, 2005; Coccaro, 1998 unpublished data), and at least one trial with Cognitive Behavioral Therapy (McCloskey, Noblett, Deffenbacher, Gollan, &

Coccaro, 2008). In addition, the OAS-M has been used in at least three pharmaceutical industry trials.

The OAS-M has good psychometric properties (Coccaro et al., 1991; Coccaro, under review) but, because the frequency of aggressive behavior is positively skewed (i.e., very frequent aggression is less common), OAS-M scores are typically log-transformed. Most importantly, aggressive behavior is highly variable within individuals because aggression is a product of aggressive disposition and perceived social threats. Thus those performing clinical trials in IED should take care to enroll only those individuals with IED who demonstrate stable OAS-M scores on three weekly assessments over a two-week period (e.g., Aggression scores $\geq$15 and Global Anger and Aggression scores $\geq$6) prior to randomization (Coccaro, Lee, Breen, & Irwin, 2015).

While the OAS-M Aggression score constitutes a good assessment of acute aggressive behavior in research settings, we recommend that clinicians use the Global Anger and Aggression (formerly labeled as OAS-M Irritability) score, in conjunction with a review of all IED outbursts in the previous week (or two weeks maximum), in order to assess impulsive aggressive behavior during treatment.

Additional assessments could be used, though most available assessments of anger and/or aggression are trait related in nature. One can change the stem question for anger inventories, such as the State Trait Anger and Expression of Anger Inventory (STAXI; Spielberger, 1999) so that the Trait Anger items are completed with reference to the "past week" rather than "in general." Some ongoing clinical trials are doing this but the results are not in as of yet.

Summary

Despite being among the more common and problematic disorders, IED is not well understood among mental health providers and is far less familiar with the public. This facilitates the general perception of aggression problems seen in IED as evidence of immutable character flaws rather than addressable problems for which treatment is available. Even those with IED often fail to seek treatment for this reason. However, as IED becomes better recognized among treatment providers, the importance of accurate assessment of IED is key. Diagnostic assessment will focus on the form, function, and frequency of the aggressive behavior, as well as the role of any comorbidities. A nonjudgmental, normalizing approach will help reduce any patient hesitancy and anxiety about reporting their aggressive behavior, though in most cases this is minimal. Diagnosis can be aided by the use of structured clinical interviews. This can be augmented by trait measures of anger and aggression to provide additional information about IED severity. Once a patient shows a readiness to engage in treatment, progress can be monitored using weekly or biweekly measures of anger and aggression interviews such as the OAS-M, which are designed to be sensitive to change over time. Finally, accurate assessment of behavior referable to IED is integral to effective treatment.

References

Buss, A. H., & Perry, M. (1992). The aggression questionnaire. *Journal of Personality and Social Psychology*, *63*(3), 452–459.

Coccaro, E. F., (1998). Research Diagnostic Module for Intermittent Explosive Disorder (IED-M; unpublished instrument).

Coccaro, E. F., Berman, M. E., & Kavoussi, R. J. (1997). Assessment of life history of aggression: Development and psychometric characteristics. *Psychiatry Research*, *73*, 147–157.

Coccaro, E. F., Berman, M. E., & McCloskey, M. S. (2017). Development of a screening questionnaire for DSM-5 intermittent explosive disorder (IED-SQ). *Comprehensive Psychiatry*, *74*, 21–26.

Coccaro, E. F., Harvey, P. D., Kupsaw-Lawrence, E., Herbert, J. L., & Bernstein, D. P. (1991). Development of Neuropharmacologically based behavioral assessments of impulsive aggressive behavior. *The Journal of Neuropsychiatry and Clinical Neurosciences*, *3*, S44–S51.

Coccaro, E. F., Lee, R., Breen, E., & Irwin, M. R. (2015). Inflammatory markers and chronic exposure to fluoxetine, divalproex, and placebo in intermittent explosive disorder. *Psychiatry Research*, *229*, 844–849.

Coccaro, E. F., Lee, R. J., & Kavoussi, R. J. (2009). A double-blind, randomized, placebo-controlled trial of fluoxetine in patients with intermittent explosive disorder. *The Journal of Clinical Psychiatry*, *70*, 653–662.

Coccaro, E. F., & Schmidt-Kaplan, C. A. (2012). Life history of impulsive behavior: Development and validity of a new questionnaire. *Journal of Psychiatric Research*, *46*, 346–352.

DiGuiseppe, R., & Tafrate, R. C. (2003). Anger treatment for adults: A meta-analytic review. *Clinical Psychology: Science and Practice*, *10*(1), 70–84.

First, M. B., Williams, J. B. W., Karg, R. S., & Spitzer, R. L. (2015). *Structured clinical interview for DSM-5 research version*. Arlington, VA: American Psychiatric Association.

George, D. T., Phillips, M. J., Lifshitz, M., Lionetti, T. A., Spero, D. E., Ghassemzedeh, N., et al. (2011). Fluoxetine treatment of alcoholic perpetrators of domestic violence: A 12-week, double-blind, randomized, placebo-controlled intervention study. *The Journal of Clinical Psychiatry*, *72*(1), 60–65.

Hollander, E., Tracy, K. A., Swann, A. C., Coccaro, E. F., McElroy, S. L., Wozniak, P., et al. (2003). Divalproex in the treatment of impulsive aggression: Efficacy in cluster B personality disorders. *Neuropsychopharmacology*, *28*(6), 1186–1197.

Kay, S. R., Wolkenfeld, F., & Murrill, L. M. (1988). Profiles of aggression among psychiatric patients: I. Nature and prevalence. *The Journal of Nervous and Mental Disease*, *176*(9), 539–546.

Kessler, R. C., Coccaro, E. F., Fava, M., Jaeger, S., Jin, R., & Walters, E. (2006). The prevalence and correlates of DSM-IV intermittent explosive disorder in the National Comorbidity Survey Replication. *Archives of General Psychiatry*, *63*(6), 669–678.

Kilpatrick, D. G., Resnick, H. S., Milanak, M. E., Miller, M. W., Keyes, K. M., & Friedman, M. J. (2013). National estimates of exposure to traumatic events and PTSD prevalence using DSM-IV and DSM-5 criteria. *Journal of Traumatic Stress*, *26*(5), 537–547.

Lee, A. H., & DiGuiseppe, R. (2018). Anger and aggression treatments: A review of meta-analyses. *Current Opinion in Psychology*, *19*, 65–74.

Lee, R., Kavoussi, R. J., & Coccaro, E. F. (2008). Placebo-controlled, randomized trial of fluoxetine in the treatment of aggression in male intimate partner abusers. *International Clinical Psychopharmacology*, *23*(6), 337–341.

Mattes, J. A. (2005). Oxcarbazepine in patients with impulsive aggression: A double-blind, placebo-controlled trial. *Journal of Clinical Psychopharmacology*, *25*(6), 575–579.

McCloskey, M. S., & Coccaro, E. F. (2003). Questionnaire and interview measures of aggression in adults. In E. F. Coccaro (Ed.), *Aggression: Psychiatric Assessment and Treatment*. New York: Marcel Dekker.

McCloskey, M. S., Noblett, K. L., Deffenbacher, J. L., Gollan, J. K., & Coccaro, E. F. (2008). Cognitive-behavioral therapy for intermittent explosive disorder: A pilot randomized clinical trial. *Journal of Consulting and Clinical Psychology*, *76*(5), 876–886.

Patton, J. H., Stanford, M. S., & Barratt, E. S. (1995). Factor structure of the Barratt impulsiveness scale. *Journal of Clinical Psychology*, *51*(6), 768–774.

Prochaska, J. O., & DiClemente, C. C. (1992). Stages of change in the modification of problem behaviors. In M. Hersen, R. Eisler, & P. M. Miller (Eds.), *vol. 28. Progress in behavior modification*. New York: Academic Press.

Puhalla, A. A., Ammerman, B. A., Uyeji, L. L., Berman, M. E., & McCloskey, M. S. (2016). Negative urgency and reward/punishment sensitivity in intermittent explosive disorder. *Journal of Affective Disorders*, *201*, 8–14.

Silva, H., Iturra, P., Solari, A., Villarroel, J., Jerez, S., Jiménez, M., et al. (2010). Fluoxetine response in impulsive-aggressive behavior and serotonin transporter polymorphism in personality disorder. *Psychiatric Genetics*, *20*(1), 25–30.

Spielberger, C. D. (1999). *STAXI-2 state-trait anger expression inventory-2, professional manual*. Lutz, FL: Psychological Assessment Resources, Inc.

Steakley-Freeman, D., Lee, R., McCloskey, M. S., & Coccaro, E. F. (2018). Social desirability, deceptive reporting, and awareness of problematic aggression in intermittent explosive disorder compared with non-aggressive healthy and psychiatric controls. *Psychiatry Research*, *270*, 20–25.

Ventura, J., Liberman, R. P., Green, M. F., et al. (1998). Training and quality assurance with the Structured Clinical Interview for DSM-IV (SCID-I/P). *Psychiatry Research*, *79*, 163–173.

Yudofsky, S. C., Silver, J. M., Jackson, W., Endicott, J., & Williams, D. (1986). The overt aggression scale for the objective rating of verbal and physical aggression. *The American Journal of Psychiatry*, *143*(1), 35–39.

CHAPTER ELEVEN

The Clinician's Legal Responsibilities to Protect Others in the Safe Treatment and Management of Patients With IED

Alan R. Felthous*, Jacqueline Landess*, Maureen Hanlon†
*Forensic Psychiatry Division, Department of Psychiatry and Behavioral Neuroscience, Saint Louis University School of Medicine, Saint Louis, MO, United States
†Supreme Court of Missouri, Jefferson City, MO, United States

Contents

Intermittent Explosive Disorder
https://doi.org/10.1016/B978-0-12-813858-8.00011-5

With some level of severity and frequency, patients with IED have by their very diagnostic criteria of IED demonstrated their potential for directing aggressive behavior externally (American Psychiatric Association, 2013a, 2013b). By definition this aggression is impulsive, not premeditated. Considerable literature has been developed and has improved our scientific understanding of primary impulsive aggression (Barratt, Stanford, Kent, & Felthous, 1997; Barratt & Slaughter, 1998; Felthous & Stanford, 2015) as well as IED (Coccaro, 2003; Coccaro, Kavoussi, Berman, & Lish, 1998; Felthous, Bryant, Wingerter, & Barratt, 1991), the essence of which is impulsive aggression. A diagnosis of IED itself raises the question as to whether the person could physically harm or assault another, based on the symptoms and characterization of the disorder alone. This no doubt presents a challenge to the clinician in ensuring the safety of the patient with IED and the safety of others who routinely interact with the patient.

The clinician's duty to protect others who may be subjected to an IED patient's physical outbursts varies by jurisdiction and by state. Most states recognize a relationship between clinician and patient that not only requires the clinician to exercise due care in the treatment of his or her patient, but extends a duty to protect nonpatients from the patient's potential violence. In order for the duty to protect to extend to nonpatients, the patient's potential for violence with resulting harm to another must be *foreseeable*. Whether such a duty exists and how foreseeability is to be determined depends upon jurisdictional law, that is, statutes and the applicable rules from common law.

Courts have addressed cases wherein the violence resulting in harm to another person could be considered as impulsive in two basic ways based on the foreseeability of violence that could be impulsive. From the review by Beck in 1998, courts typically held that impulsive violence was not foreseeable. In these cases, the violence seemed to have occurred "out of the blue," without a threat or warning in advance that would have allowed the clinician to take protective action. Another consideration, however, is that IED is characterized by recurrent, impulsive aggression; one of the best predictors of future violence is a history of past, recurrent violence. Of course, most externalized aggression does not result in actionable physical harm, but recurrent impulsive aggression, especially if assaultive, can arguably render future acts of violence much more foreseeable than verbal threats. Without identifying such acts as impulsive or symptomatic of IED, courts have recognized prior aggressive and violent conduct as a factor in determining foreseeability and thus, may bolster a plaintiff's claim of negligence and/or failure to protect (e.g., *Jablonski by Pahls v. United States*, 1983).

The Duty to Hospitalize

Outpatients in treatment for IED typically do not require hospitalization and may not meet the requirements for emergency detention (ED) or civil commitment (CC). Nonetheless, in considering safe management and prevention of the most extreme forms of violence including homicide, we must consider the traditional and most effective method of preventing catastrophic violence available to clinicians, which is hospitalization. Failure to hospitalize or a wrongful discharge could be considered medical malpractice or it could be considered negligence without the need to establish deviation from standard medical care (Felthous, 1985). This type of protective duty and liability is based upon the fact that hospitalization allows the clinician to *control* the patient in order to prevent serious harm. The controlling nature of the relationship creates an exception to the general common law rule that one person (a clinician) is not responsible if a second person (a patient) harms a third person (the injured would be plaintiff).

Whether IED alone qualifies as a condition for which involuntary ED or CC applies is a matter for discussion (see Felthous, 1999, regarding protective dichotomous decisions such as whether to voluntarily or involuntarily hospitalize). Emergency hospitalization should be considered if extreme violence is determined to be imminent (and therefore foreseeable). Since IED is treatable, hospitalization not only serves the legitimate purpose of incapacitation and protection, but of adjusting pharmacotherapy and making other interventions more effectively. IED does not always occur as a single disorder; the patient may have co-occurring disorder(s) that further justify hospital admission. Thus hospitalization at least voluntarily, and sometimes involuntarily, can be an important and justified, even morally imperative, intervention in the safe treatment and management of a patient with IED.

This nonetheless begs the question of whether the law *requires* hospitalization. In many mental health codes the operational auxiliary verb is "may," not "shall," seemingly making hospitalization an optional intervention for the clinician, not a legal duty. Leading up to California's *Tarasoff* decision, to be discussed later, the California state legislature enacted law that provided immunity for a clinician's alleged failure to hospitalize or wrongfully discharge (Lanterman-Petris-Short Act, 1967). This was in support of the dehospitalization and community mental health public policies at the time. Other state courts found decisions not to hospitalize or to discharge followed by the patient harming another person, were also protected from liability by sovereign immunity where the clinicians were employed by the state, and by the honest error in professional judgment rule (Felthous, 1987). The latter depended upon such decisions being discretionary. "Discretion implies the right to be wrong" (*Canon v. Thumudo*, 1988) or the possibility of miscalculation.

But jurisdiction can make all the difference. Although statutory immunity in California precluded claims of failure to hospitalize or of wrongful discharge, the *Tarasoff* decision has been used to support wrongful discharge claims in other states wherein the individual victims themselves could not have been foreseeable, such as where the plaintiffs were injured or killed in motor vehicular crashes caused by the discharged patient (Felthous, 1989a).

An important feature of hospitalization is that the petition and testimony for involuntary civil commitment, although requiring the disclosure of otherwise confidential medical or mental health information, does not create a legal dilemma for the clinician. This is because civil commitment is uniformly recognized as an exception to privileged communication between patients and their physicians. Another important aspect of involuntary hospitalization is that it requires the clinician to make a judgment about the patient's risk (e.g., "imminent" or "substantial" danger to self or others). The basis of the determination of risk (e.g., "serious threat") should also be stated, but just weighing protective and risk factors is insufficient to initiate involuntary hospitalization. Some clinical determination of risk is essential.

The Duty to Warn or Protect

The watershed decision creating protective duties for clinicians beyond the traditional hospitalization option was the California Supreme Court's *Tarasoff* decision in 1976. Without recounting the facts and legal history of this case available elsewhere (e.g., Felthous, 1989b), we should attempt to unpack the Tarasoff principle itself, which is often misunderstood:

> *When a psychotherapist determines, or pursuant to the standards of his profession should determine, that his patient presents a serious danger of violence to another, he incurs an obligation to use reasonable care to protect the intended victim against such danger. The discharge of this duty may require the therapist to take one or more of various steps, depending on the nature of the case. Thus, it may call for him to warn the intended victim or others likely to apprise the victim of the danger, to notify the police, or to take whatever other steps are reasonably necessary under the circumstances (*Tarasoff v. Regents of the University of California*, 1976, p. 431).*

With *Tarasoff* the control through hospitalization is not the only method of protecting others; hospitalization is not even mentioned. As mentioned before, failure to hospitalize was protected by statutory immunity in California. So how did the Court find an exception to the general rule of nonresponsibility? With the help of a then recent law review article (Fleming & Maximov, 1974), the court interpreted the "Special Relation" exception of the Restatement (Second) of Torts, requiring "control" (American Law Institute, 1965), to mean that even in outpatient treatment, the therapist has enough control or influence over the patient so as to have a duty to protect other persons from the potential violent acts of the patient.

The Tarasoff Principle is a duty to protect, that is, to take any reasonable steps to protect. This is not simply a duty to warn, although protective disclosures are the only measures explicitly specified in this principle. The principle does not require that the patient must have expressed a threat to trigger the duty to take protective action: the psychotherapist could have identified a serious danger by any conceivable means, perhaps even a "gut feeling." Or the therapist could have come to this determination by following the standards of his profession, standards that the American Psychiatric Association asserted were nonexistent, in their amicus brief to the Court (American Psychiatric Association, 1974). In fact, this most unclear "foreseeability" determination could be left to the fact-finder without the testimony and cross-examination of a professional peer or expert witness, that would typically be required in malpractice lawsuits.

The jurisprudence of the mental health clinician's duty to warn or protect potential victims of a patient's serious danger has become diverse and inconsistent. Clinicians must familiarize themselves with the relevant jurisdictional laws. Texas, for example, has no clinical duty to warn, to control or protect (*Thapar v. Zezulka*, 1999) whereas the Washington Supreme Court has formulated a duty so broad that clinician's duties go beyond protective disclosures and measures to control the potentially violent patient (*Volk v. DeMeerleer*, 2016).

Unlike protection through hospitalizing the patient, protective disclosures do create a confidentiality versus protective disclosure dilemma. The disclosure could be to anyone who is thought to be at risk. Depending on the circumstances, protective disclosure can have adverse consequences for the patient, for example, job dismissal after an employer is warned or divorce after a spouse is warned. Relational or financial harm to the patient can mean legal liability for the clinician; and even without harm to anyone, disciplinary action from one's professional ethical board. In advancing protective disclosures as methods of protection under the new Tarasoff duty to protect, the California Supreme Court declared, "The protective privilege ends where the public peril begins" (*Tarasoff v. Regents of the University of California*, 1976, p. 347). Although a mellifluous and memorable alliteration, Justice Tobriner's statement was misleading in that protective disclosures are not in violation of privileged communication but of patient-physician/therapist confidentiality.

Impulsive aggression often occurs together with and may be considered as symptomatic and even diagnostic of antisocial and borderline personality disorders. If the aggression can be explained by one of these personality disorders, then the clinician should not diagnose the patient with IED. However, studies demonstrating pharmacotherapeutic efficacy in treating IED or impulsive aggression were conducted on subjects with antisocial or border line personality disorder (See Felthous & Stanford, 2015). A Federal Court in Kansas upheld a claim of failure to warn where the patient's only diagnosis was antisocial personality disorder (*Durflinger v. Artiles*, 1981). In *Doyle v. United States* (1982), a patient with an antisocial personality disorder shot and killed a college police officer. The Federal Court did not consider the act foreseeable because the patient had not threatened that particular police officer but the diagnosis was not a factor. In *Jablonski*, the Ninth Circuit upheld a claim of failure to warn where a patient diagnosed first with schizophrenic reaction, and then personality disorder with explosive features, killed the woman with whom he was living (*Jablonski by Pahls v. United States*, 1983).

Today's APA ethics code, in comparison with earlier editions, is more permissive of protective disclosures where the psychiatrist has concluded that such disclosure is necessary to prevent serious harm (American Psychiatric Association, 2013a, 2013b). Clinicians must nonetheless attend to jurisdictional law concerning both confidentiality and protective duties, as one can err in either direction, with resulting liability or other consequences.

The Duty of "Due Care"

From the inception of the Tarasoff Principle in 1976 to today, there have been several attempts to summarize this ever changing law

(Felthous, 1989a, 1989b; Felthous & Kachigian, 2001; Felthous & Kachigian, 2017; Walcott, Cerundolo, & Beck, 2001). After a period of remarkable diversification of this jurisprudence in the 1980s, courts at the end of the century appeared to be backing away from, limiting or rejecting Tarasoff-like duties (Felthous & Kachigian, 2001).

In the more recent publication of The Restatement (Third) of Torts, the American Law Institute inserted a new section, § 41, with a subsection directly addressing the diverse rules that have developed since the California Supreme Court rendered its more expansive interpretation of the Special Relation exception with its duty to control. The Third Restatement describes a duty of "due care" which was not limited to protective disclosures or hospitalization, but included various aspects of treating, managing, and caring for the patient, which if deficient, could, in the court's view, result in the patient harming others (American Law Institute, 2012). Thus according to the Third Restatement, the due care that the clinician owes to his patient now extends to anyone who could be harmed by the patient. Thus far, courts have not rushed to embrace Section 41 as applied to clinicians.

However, the Washington Supreme Court stands as one court that recently adopted Section 41 (*Volk v. DeMeerleer*, 2016). Previously, the Washington Supreme Court's earlier Section 315 Petersen rule had applied the Tarasoff duty to protect to find a clinician at fault in a case wherein the patient was discharged and then crashed his car into that of another driver, even though the driver's identity was not known in advance (*Petersen v. State*, 1988). In one sense the *Volk* "due care" rule makes sense. Where violence is due to a mental disorder, adequate treatment and safe management, including hospitalization of a potentially dangerous patient, may be more efficacious than protective disclosures alone. In principle, this approach expands the protective options for the clinician, as suggested in the last sentence of the Tarasoff Principle itself ("or to take whatever other steps are reasonably necessary under the circumstances" (p. 431)). At the same time, however, the due care rule also provides the trier of fact greater flexibility in speculating with hindsight what might have been done differently. Unrestrained Monday morning quarterbacking can be especially pernicious when not informed by the relevant standard of practice, as medical negligence, unlike medical malpractice, does not necessarily require expert testimony with opportunity for cross-examination. That a claim of medical negligence can be upheld without courtroom medical testimony is illustrated by the *Volk* case.

Current Directions in the Duty to Protect

As noted before, several courts began to retreat from Tarasoff in the last decade of the 20th century. Commentators agreed that courts were beginning to reject the Tarasoff Principle (Felthous & Kachigian, 2001; Walcott et al., 2001). But what then are the current directions since the turn of the century? We identified appellate "duty to protect" cases since the turn of the century. Following are highlighted cases both before and after the 2012 publication of the Third Restatement, with close attention to courts that have adopted or referenced Section 41, which expands third-party liability.

Twenty-First Century Cases Prior to the Third Restatement

Kentucky

The Commonwealth of Kentucky has a protective disclosure statute (KR § 202A.400 (1986)). Although state courts do not always acknowledge their state's Tarasoff statute (Kachigian & Felthous, 2004), the Sixth Circuit Court of Appeals has found that the facts of cases in Kentucky comported with Kentucky's statute which abrogates a common law duty (*Evans v. Morehead Clinic*, 1988; *Riley v. United Health Care of Hardin*, 1998). In *DeVasier v. James* (2009), the Supreme Court of Kentucky also recognized the duty and its limitations as established by the Kentucky statute. When Rene Cissell was evaluated in a hospital emergency room after having held a knife to his girlfriend's throat and inflicting a small cut, he told the intake nurse of this violent incident and she charted that he had "homicidal ideation," but no such threat was expressed to the attending psychiatrist who decided against hospitalization and released the patient. Cissell had told the clinical social worker that he did not want to harm his girlfriend but did not know if he could control himself. The following day, Cissell stabbed and killed his girlfriend.

Based upon the wording of the Tarasoff statute, the Supreme Court of Kentucky found in favor of the defendant psychiatrist because Cissell had not communicated a threat directly to Dr. James, as required by the statute, thus Dr. James had no duty to warn Cissell's girlfriend. Although the doctor knew of Cissell's recent violence toward his girlfriend, simply "being a threat" is insufficient to require warning, the only protective measure specified by statute. (For a concise summary, see Martin & Thomas, 2010.)

Arizona

Graham v. Value Options, Inc. (2010)[1] stands *per* se as an example of expansion of the liability application of foreseeability. According to the Arizona Court of Appeals, foreseeability was not necessary to establish a duty, but to establish causation, hence an issue for the jury, not the judge, and a determination of fact, not admissibility. In *Graham* patient Liu shot and killed two individuals he did not know. Previously, he was in treatment with the Regional Behavioral Health Authorities for Maricopa County, and followed primarily by Nurse Practitioner Sherry Young. He eventually showed "relapse indicators" but was assessed to not be a threat to himself or others. Because of his delusions, hallucinations, and difficulty functioning, Young recommended increasing evaluations from quarterly to monthly, home visits, and monthly psychiatric assessments to address dangerousness. Liu cancelled appointments and became difficult to contact. Eventually, Liu shot his victims. One of the victims' families filed suit, a claim against Value Options-AZ, alleging neglectful monitoring of Liu and failure in their duty to seek a court order for confinement and involuntary treatment. This claim asserted negligence, medical negligence, and independent negligence by the state. The jury trial awarded the Grahams $11 million as compensatory damages and $25 million in punitive damages.

The Arizona Court of Appeals upheld the compensatory but not the punitive award. This case appears to recognize potential liability for failing to hospitalize a psychotic patient who is not making violent threats and a duty to protect the general public including unidentified victims not limited by Arizona's earlier zone of danger rule (*Hamman v. County of Maricopa*, 1989). Arizona had enacted a Tarasoff statute in 1989 (Ariz. Rev. Stat. § 36-517.02 (2015)). In an earlier duty to protect case the Court of Appeals failed to reference the statute (*Tamsen v. Weber*, 1990). In a subsequent case the court found the state's Tarasoff statute to be unconstitutional (*Little v. All Phoenix South Community Mental Health Center*, 1995). Not surprisingly, the Court of Appeals made no mention of the state's Tarasoff statute in *Graham*.

[1] *Graham* was not published and created neither legal precedent nor persuasive application under Arizona Supreme Court rules (Ariz. R. Sup. Ct. 111(c)).

Colorado

Similar to Kentucky but dissimilar from Arizona, Colorado's courts have analyzed duty to protect cases based upon its Tarasoff statute (Colo. Rev. Stat. 13-21-117 (2016)). The Court of Appeals used the statute in analyzing the case and found that it created a duty. In *Fredericks v. Jonsson* (2010) the Colorado Probation Department asked for a mental health evaluation to assess, among other items, Wellington's risk for reoffending, victimizing, and violent and aggressive behavior. Psychologist Dr. Jonsson conducted the evaluation. The court opinion does not mention whether she made a judgment about his risk, but according to her evaluation and Wellington's deposition testimony, "Wellington told Dr. Jonsson that he used to have frequent violent fantasies involving family members of the Fredericks family but that he no longer had violent thoughts directed at them" (p. 1098). Two weeks after Dr. Jonsson submitted her report, Wellington became intoxicated, stole a car, drove to the Fredericks' home, and apparently attempted to enter the home by breaking a window. The Fredericks filed a complaint against Dr. Jonsson "claiming that she negligently failed to warn them or the probation department of the dangers" (p. 1098) Wellington posed to them. The Tenth Circuit interpreted Colorado's Tarasoff Statute to mean, "... the mental health provider has a duty to warn only when the patient himself predicts his violent behavior (by communicating—that is, expressing—his threat to the mental-health provider)" (p. 1105). Because Wellington did not tell Dr. Jonsson that he was dangerous, the Tenth Circuit found that Dr. Jonsson was not liable under Colorado's Tarasoff statute and supported the summary judgment granted by the district court.

In general, the literature and jurisprudence are divided on whether it is the risk of violence or the expressed threat that can trigger a duty to issue a protective warning (Felthous, 2006). From the Tenth Circuit's interpretation of Colorado's Tarasoff statute, it is the expressed threat, specifically: "[a] serious threat of imminent physical violence against a specific person or persons" (Col. Rev. Stat. § 13-21-117 (2016)) (for further analysis of *Fredericks* see Maxey, Wortzel, & Martinez, 2011).

Massachusetts

In *Shea v. Cartinas Hospital, Inc.* (2011), the Appeals Court of Massachusetts gave careful attention to the Commonwealth's Tarasoff statute (Mass. Gen. Law Ch. 123 § 36B(1)(b) (2018)). Potter was brought to the emergency room where he manifested evidence of mental instability. He was paranoid, disorganized, confused, and depressed and had a history of violent behavior, but he was thought to be in good self-control. He denied hallucinations and thoughts of suicide and homicide. He was admitted voluntarily and assessed to be "impulsive and a noncompliance risk but not a danger to himself or others" (p. 530). He was admitted voluntarily but requested to be discharged the next day. He had made no homicidal statements during his brief stay. He was discharged against medical advice whereupon the following day he met with a mental health services provider and stated he would not harm his girlfriend or anyone else. In a follow-up assessment by another provider, Potter again denied having thoughts of homicide or suicide. Following this assessment, Potter returned to the home of his mother and stepfather and stabbed them to death.

The Appeals Court of Massachusetts compared the facts of this case with the Commonwealth's Tarasoff Statute. Potter's history of physical violence was known to the clinicians. However, they had no "reasonable basis to believe there [was] a clear and present danger" and there was no "reasonably identified victim" (p. 530) as required by statute. Therefore the Appeals Court affirmed the summary judgment of the trial court.

Twenty-First Century Cases Since the Third Restatement

Louisiana

The Third Restatement was published in 2012, but it was not cited in *Brice v. Braggs* (2017) wherein the Court supported the trial court's summary judgment in favor of the psychiatrist, because the conditions of Louisiana's Tarasoff statute for triggering the duty to warn or protect were not met. In *Brice*, the psychiatrist stated that he did not have knowledge that the patient, who attacked a nurse during a home visit, had a history of violence or being violent.

This is consistent with prior Court of Appeals decisions in Louisiana. In *Grady v. Riley* (2002) and *Clark v. Baird* (1998) the Court found that the case did not meet the statutory conditions and in *Barbarin v. Dudley* (2000), *Durapau v. Jenkins* (1995), and *Hines v. Bick* (1990) the cases also did not meet the statutory conditions, but the Fourth Circuit Court of Appeals indicated that Louisiana may still have a common law duty (Kachigian & Felthous, 2004).

Montana

In Montana the clinician's duty to warn or protect is governed by its Tarasoff statute (Mont. Code. Ann. § 27-1-1102 (1987)). A district court issued summary judgment for the defendant, finding that the following three requirements of the statute were not present: (1) An actual threat of physical violence, (2) by specific means, (3) against a clearly identified or reasonably identifiable victim (*Gudmundsen v. State*, 2009), citing the *DeVasier* decision of Kentucky requiring a verbal threat over "being a threat" as critical to the statutory duty in that state. In a 2010 case, the Supreme Court of Montana found that the statutory duty was met, that is, "we considered a man's statement that he would kill his wife with his bare hands if she ever called the police to constitute an actual threat of physical violence by specific means against an identified victim" (*In re Mental Health of M.C.D.*, 2010).

Finally, in 2015, the Montana Supreme Court restated its position, in this case supporting a district court's summary judgment granted to the defendant, because there was no evidence of an actual, specific communicated threat (*Woods v. State*, 2015). Schiller had a history of becoming aggressive with his girlfriend when drinking and evaluators acknowledged that interruptions in his relationship with Catherine could result in "high-risk behavior" (p. 1255). Less than one month after his release from Montana State Hospital, Schiller purchased a handgun, his relationship with Catherine ended, and he saw her with a male acquaintance in a bar where Schiller was drinking. After Catherine and her companion left the bar, Schiller assaulted her companion and shot and killed Catherine. In supporting the district court's summary judgment, the Montana Supreme Court explained, "In this state there is no common law in any case where the law is declared by statute" (p. 1258), citing the Montana statute that so states (Section 1-1-108, MCA).

Vermont

Vermont does not have a Tarasoff statute. The Supreme Court of Vermont is one of only two courts to have cited Section 41 in a Tarasoff-like case, which it considered an evolution of Section 315 of the Second Restatement. In a previous decision, the court adopted the Tarasoff Principle in a case wherein the court expanded the duty and liability to include property damage (arson) but limited the duty and liability to identifiable victims (*Peck v. Counselling Services of Addision County*, 1985). In *Peck*, the Court relied on the Special Relation exception, Section 315 of the Second Restatement, as had the California Supreme Court in *Tarasoff*.

In *Kuligoski v. Brattleboro Retreat* (2016), E.R., a patient at Brattleboro Retreat, a mental health treatment facility, was diagnosed with schizophrenia and transferred to a state hospital. His violent behavior required restraints and he threatened to kill staff members. Despite having stopped his medication and threatening to kill himself, he was discharged. Although outpatient follow-up had been arranged and his mother was instructed to administer his medication, he did not attend his outpatient appointments and did not take medication. About three months later he assaulted a random victim, Michael Kuligoski.

Members of the Kuligoski family filed suit against Brattleboro Retreat and Northeast Kingdom Human Services (NKHS) claiming failure to warn of E.R.'s danger to others, failure to train his parents in how to manage him, failure to treat him, improper release, and negligent undertaking. The superior court found that the defendants owed no duty to the plaintiffs "because Michael Kuligoski was not an identifiable victim and the defendants were under no duty to control" (p. 436).

Despite discussing Section 41, the Vermont Supreme Court did not adopt it. However, in relying on Section 315 of the Second Restatement, the court did not find a duty to the general public. However, in finding that E.R.'s parents had the role as his caretakers, the Court found that the Retreat had a duty to warn E.R.'s parents of his propensity toward violence (*Kuligoski v. Brattleboro Retreat*, 2016).

Washington

To our knowledge, Section 41 of the Third Restatement has been explicitly integrated into Tarasoff jurisprudence only in the State of Washington. In *Volk v. DeMeerleer* (2016), the Washington State Supreme Court extended the clinician's duty to protect third persons from a patient who was undergoing outpatient psychiatric treatment. The patient James DeMeerleer had not been hospitalized and had not expressed a threat to harm his victims. Years before, he expressed thoughts of suicide and homicide upon learning his wife was having an affair and was going to divorce him but he assured his psychiatrist he would not act on such thoughts. In the course of treatment, DeMeerleer showed evidence of aggressive behavior, emotional distress and mental instability, and poor medication compliance but neither psychotic nor threatening behavior. He subsequently began dating a woman, Schiering. At some point, their relationship also ended. In his last visit with Dr. Ashby, DeMeerleer's condition had shown some improvement.

Around four months following DeMeerleer's last appointment with Dr. Ashby, he entered the house of Schiering, his ex-girlfriend, and shot and killed her and her son. He attempted to slash the throat of another son who managed to flee. Sometime after DeMeerleer's last visit with Dr. Ashby, he and Schiering mended their relationship but then ended it.

Schiering's mother, Beverly Volk, and Winkler (Schiering's older son) filed medical negligence and medical malpractice claims against Dr. Ashby and the Clinic. Defendants argued that the actual act of violence was not foreseeable, so the only protective recourse would have been civil commitment but that Washington's Tarasoff statute (Wash. Rev. Code § 71.05.120(2) (2016)) would have provided immunity because DeMeerleer never communicated to Dr. Ashby "an actual threat of physical violence against a reasonably identifiable victim or victims" (Wash. Rev. Code § 71.05.120 (2) (2016)).

The Washington Supreme Court heard the case on appeal and decided that medical malpractice claims pertain only to the duty of care the physician owes to her/his patient, not to nonpatient third persons. The Washington Supreme Court sustained the claim of medical negligence which in contrast to medical malpractice can extend the protective duty of due care to nonpatients. Unlike medical malpractice, medical negligence does not require expert courtroom testimony with the opportunity of cross-examination. The instant case referred to an affidavit completed by an expert witness, but there was no courtroom testimony regarding the medical standard, duty, or breach of duty.

Summary of Appellate Decisions in the 21st Century

The most recent cases in Tarasoff jurisprudence continued to show the diversity of opinions observed in the 1980s but with third-party liability constrained in several states (Colorado, Kentucky, Louisiana, Massachusetts, and Montana) by the state's Tarasoff statute. In general, courts respected the legislature's intent of defining and limiting the duty, more than was evident from an earlier survey of court responses to Tarasoff statutes (Kachigian & Felthous, 2004). Other courts expanded Tarasoff liability without requiring a threat of violence or an identifiable victim (Arizona, Vermont, and Washington), the Washington Supreme Court by adopting Section 41 of the Third Restatement; the Vermont Supreme Court without adopting Section 41.

Measures That May Protect the Clinician and Other Persons

Any measure that protects other persons from the patient's violent acts may also protect the clinician from third-party liability simply by preventing the damage that is essential for tort claims. This is not to conclude that all legal requirements actually reduce the risk of violence. According to one study, states with Tarasoff statutes requiring protective disclosures are associated with higher rates of homicide (Edwards, 2013). Although the study does not prove that warning the victim and police increases the risk of physical harm, it suggests the need for further examination as to whether and how disclosures are protective (Felthous & Kachigian, 2017). The California legislature amended its Tarasoff statute and changed the duty from one of warning to one of protection because of concern that in certain circumstances warnings themselves can be potentially counterproductive (Weinstock, Bonnici, Seroussi, & Leong, 2014).

Know the Law

The uncertain effectiveness of legally required protective measures notwithstanding, legal practice is ethical practice. The ethics code of the American Psychiatric Association essentially states that it is unethical to practice psychiatry in violation of legal requirements (American Psychiatric Association, 2013a, 2013b). Thus it behooves clinicians to become familiar with the third-party jurisprudence by which their practice is regulated. In doing so, the clinician must turn to both statutory law (e.g., Tarasoff statutes and legal regulations of confidentiality and disclosure of health care information) and common law (Felthous & Kachigian, 2017). In some states, clinicians will find that separate jurisdictional laws may be complementary and consistent. Or they can be contrary to one another (Kachigian & Felthous, 2004). Moreover, the legal requirements can change over time. All five district courts in Texas referenced a duty to warn and protect prompting Felthous and Scarano to anticipate that Texas courts would likely accept a qualified Justice Tobriner's dictum in *Tarasoff*, "Privileged communication (or for that matter confidentiality) ends where the public peril begins" (1999, p. 78). The state supreme court subsequently ruled that there is no duty to warn or protect through hospitalization in Texas and clinicians who issue protective disclosures do so "at their own peril" (*Thapar v. Zezulka*, 1999).

Risk Assessment

We hesitate to suggest a standard for assessing the risk that a patient will inflict substantial harm on another person. Appelbaum stated early in the evaluation of Tarasoff-like jurisprudence that psychiatrists ought to at least be able to ask the right questions (Appelbaum, 1985); however, even decades later there seems to be little consensus on what those questions might be and the APA has consistently denied through multiple amici briefs with other health professional organizations (APA, 1974; Washington State Medical Association et al., 2017) that psychiatrists possess the ability to accurately predict future violence against others.

Most remarkable is that some authorities, including the California Supreme Court in its Tarasoff Principle and the APA itself in its amicus brief response to *Tarasoff I* (*Tarasoff v. Regents of the University of California*, 1976), would assign clinicians a responsibility to issue protective disclosures or take other measures, if the clinician predicts the violent act, regardless of how the clinician came to that prediction (APA, 1974). For such a duty, there is no professional standard.

Most published cases in this type of third-party jurisprudence do not show that the clinician defendant did or did not conduct a risk assessment to determine whether the patient posed a threat of violence against others. Case factual histories do not typically state whether a risk assessment was performed and documented, an assessment that might have reduced the risk. Perhaps a risk assessment, even abbreviated, could have reduced the likelihood of the incident violent act and resultant professional liability. In *Littleton v. Good Samaritan Hospital* (1988), the Ohio State Supreme Court recognized the common law defense of clinical judgment. Clinicians should not be held liable for honest errors in clinical judgment, but there must be evidence that clinical judgment was in fact exercised. This would include an attempt to assess the risk of violence.

It would exceed the scope of our discussion here to address all acute and long-term risk factors for externally directed violence, still a highly inexact and uncertain science. We can suggest a reasoned, fact-based approach to risk assessment. Appelbaum recommended a three-step approach to managing a potentially violent patient: (1) Assess the patient's dangerousness, (2) select a course of action, and (3) implement this plan (Appelbaum, 1985).

Realizing that a protective plan may require dichotomous protective decisions such as whether to issue warnings or to initiate hospitalization, Felthous proposed an algorithm of critical questions to be addressed in guiding one's protective strategy: (1) Is the patient dangerous to others?; (2) If yes, is his or her dangerousness due to serious mental illness?; (3) If not due to serious mental illness, is the dangerousness imminent?; (4) Are potential victims of the patient's violence reasonably identifiable? (Felthous, 1999). Simon's comments about suicide risk assessment could be applied to risk assessment for homicide which is also "fundamentally a reasoned clinical judgment call" (Simon, 2011, p. 2) for which a determination of high, moderate, or low is preferred to simply documenting whether suicidal or homicidal ideation is present (p. 3). Risk and protective factors must be analyzed and synthesized such that the logic and basis for the determination of risk are transparent.

While a professional standard of care remains elusive, we would recommend that where a patient shows evidence of physically aggressive behavior or threats of violence against others, the clinician should attempt to assess the risk. If the concern arises over a threat against an identifiable potential victim, an attempt should be made to assess the seriousness of the threat, using, for example, the Borum criteria (Borum & Reddy, 2001). Even without a threat, if externalized aggression appears to be an issue, such as when a patient presents with IED, some attempt to assess the risk of serious violence against others should be made, with a conclusion and reasoned response to the conclusion. For example, "This patient presents some elevated risk of violence against others because of his Type 1 IED, but based upon his expressed desire not to physically harm others and his history of not having seriously harmed anyone in the past, he is deemed to be at low risk for such serious harm and safe for continued outpatient treatment and management. I expect that with treatment and monitoring, this risk will be rendered lower yet." Of course, if the patient later acts in a more aggressive and dangerous manner than previously anticipated, the risk will have to be reassessed. Only after clinicians have begun to perform and document risk assessments routinely and this is reflected in another generation of third-party lawsuits, can one comment on the effectiveness of these assessments in preventing violence among psychiatric outpatients. The protective value of risk assessments before discharging NGRI acquittees from hospital care is supported by research. Other measures, such as graduated step-down in security measures and conditional release, certainly contribute to the safe management and favorable outcome in terms of risk of violence of such cases.

Neutralization of Firearms

When a patient in treatment kills another person, it is often by means of a firearm (Felthous, 1989a, 1989b). Swanson et al. (2015) found that impulsively aggressive individuals tend to possess firearms or have easy access to them. Federal law requires background checks for firearm purchases and prohibits sales to individuals who have been committed or adjudicated as mentally ill or defective and state laws can be more restrictive (Swanson & Felthous, 2015). Whether impulsively aggressive individuals or those diagnosed with IED actually have a higher rate of homicide when they have access to firearms is an empirical question that remains to be investigated. Meanwhile, it is prudent to inquire about firearm access when treating a patient with IED or a patient who has threatened personal violence and to gain the patient's cooperation in having firearms removed from his access at least while his impulsive aggression is poorly controlled (Felthous & Kachigian, 2017).

Appropriate Treatment

Not explicitly included within the Tarasoff Principle, or most derivative rules extending a protective duty to nonpatients, is the possibility of reducing the risk of violence by providing effective treatment including pharmacotherapy. Treatment is more explicitly included in the due care rule of § 41 and in Washington Supreme Court's *Volk* decision. As applied to IED, efficacious pharmacotherapy of the patient may be protective and reduce the need for protective disclosures or hospitalization. Although evidence supports the efficacy and propriety of pharmacotherapy with an antiimpulsive aggression agent (AIAA) (Felthous, 2013; Felthous, Lake, Rundle, & Stanford, 2013; Felthous & Stanford, 2015; Coccaro & Kavoussi, 1997; Coccaro, Lee, & Kavoussi, 2009; Stanford et al., 2001), the use of an AIAA alone may not mitigate liability in a case involving impulsive aggression, in that no AIAA has been approved by the FDA for treatment of IED. Many physicians and psychiatrists may be unfamiliar and unpracticed in the pharmacotherapy of IED, creating doubt as to the actual "standard of practice." And ultimately, efficacious pharmacotherapy may involve art and skill as much as reliable science.

Personality disorder alone, and particularly antisocial personality or psychopathy, are not typically strong justifications for involuntary mental health services, even when coupled with dangerousness (Winick, LoPiccolo, Anand, & Hartswick, 2007). Nonetheless, when the duty is expanded from one of controlling a potentially dangerous patient through hospitalization to the broader duty of warning and/or protecting other, nonpatients, diagnosis matters less (Felthous, O'Shaughnessy, Kuten, François-Pursell, & Medrano, 2007), except for the association between antisocial and psychopathic disorders and aggressive behaviors (e.g., *Durflinger v. Artiles*, 1981).

Conclusions

The diagnosis of IED or of impulsive aggression is not made in the majority of published cases concerning the clinician's duty to warn or protect others of his or her patient's potential for violence. The Tarasoff type of professional liability varies from state to state, thus clinicians must become familiar with their relevant jurisdictional law. Whether a violent act was considered foreseeable and therefore supportive of actionable negligence depends on the specific circumstances, nature of the impulsive aggression, and jurisdictional law. If the impulsive act is seen as one as having occurred "out of the blue" and without any warning or indication of aggression, courts would be less likely to decide in favor of the plaintiff. But like suicide (e.g., Busch, Fawcett, & Jacobs, 2003), violent and homicidal acts can occur without threats or warnings. Some courts have found other evidence of foreseeability. It therefore behooves the prudent physician to conduct and document an assessment of risk, however imprecise such assessment may be, and to monitor and manage the risk by whatever means are clinically indicated, not limited to hospitalization and warning potential victims, such as by providing psychoeducation to the family and patient, pharmacotherapy, increasing outpatient visits, and/or implementing evidence-based therapies.

References

American Law Institute. (1965). *Restatement (second) of torts*. American Law Institute.

American Law Institute. (2012). *Restatement (third) of torts*. St. Paul, MN: American Law Institute.

American Psychiatric Association et al. Brief of Amicus Curiae in support of petition for rehearing of Tarasoff v. Regents of the University of California to the Supreme Court of the State of California, 1974.

American Psychiatric Association. (2013a). *Diagnostic and Statistical manual of mental disorders, DSM-5* (5th ed.). Washington, DC: American Psychiatric Publishing.

American Psychiatric Association (Ed.), (2013b). *The principles of medical ethics: With annotations especially applicable to psychiatry*. (3rd ed.). Arlington, VA: American Psychiatric Association.

Appelbaum, P. (1985). Rethinking the duty to protect. In J. Beck (Ed.), *The potentially violent patient and the Tarasoff decision in psychiatric practice* (pp. 110–130). Washington, DC: American Psychiatric Press.

Barbarin v. Dudley, (2000). 775 So. 2d 657 (La. Ct. App. 4th Cir. 2000).

Barratt, E. S., & Slaughter, L. (1998). Defining, measuring and predicting impulsive aggression: A heuristic model. *Behavioral Sciences & the Law, 16*, 285–302.

Barratt, E. S., Stanford, M. S., Kent, T. A., & Felthous, A. R. (1997). Neuropsychological and cognitive psychophysiological substrates of impulsive aggression. *Biological Psychiatry, 41*, 1045–1061.

Beck, J. C. (1998). Legal and ethical duties of the clinician treating a patient who is liable to be impulsively violent. *Behavioral Sciences & the Law, 16*, 375–389.

Borum, R., & Reddy, M. (2001). Assessing violence risk in *Tarasoff* situations: A fact-based model of inquiry. *Behavioral Sciences & the Law, 19*, 375–385.

Brice v. Braggs, (2017) No. 2017 CA 0382 (La. Ct. App. 1st Cir. 2017).

Busch, K. A., Fawcett, J., & Jacobs, D. G. (2003). Clinical correlates of inpatient suicide. *Journal of Clinical Psychiatry, 64*(1), 14–19.

Canon v. Thumudo (1988). 422 N.W. 2d 688 (Mich. 1988).

Clark v. Baird (1998). 714 So. 2d 840 (La. Ct. App. 4th Cir. 1998).

Coccaro, E. F. (2003). Intermittent explosive disorder. In E. F. Coccaro (Ed.), *Aggression: Psychiatric assessment and treatment* (pp. 149–166). New York, NY: Marcel, Dekker, Inc.

Coccaro, E. F., & Kavoussi, R. J. (1997). Fluoxetine and impulsive aggressive behavior in personality-disordered subjects. *Archives of General Psychiatry, 54*, 1081–1088.

Coccaro, E. F., Kavoussi, R. J., Berman, M. E., & Lish, J. D. (1998). Intermittent explosive disorder-revised: Development, reliability, and validity of research criteria. *Comprehensive Psychiatry, 39*(6), 368–376.

Coccaro, E. F., Lee, R. J., & Kavoussi, R. J. (2009). A double-blind, randomized placebo-controlled trial of fluoxetine in patients with intermittent explosive disorder. *The Journal of Clinical Psychiatry, 70*, 653–662.

DeVasier v. James (2009) 278 S.W. 3d 625 (Ky. 2009).

Doyle v. United States Dept. of Justice (1982). United States District Court, District of Columbia. 494 F. Supp. 842.

Durapau v. Jenkins (1995) 656 So. 2d 1067 (La. Ct. App. 5th Cir. 1995).

Durflinger v. Artiles (1981) 563 F. Supp. 322 (D. Kan. 1981).

Edwards, G.S. (2013) Doing their duty: An empirical analysis of the unintended effect of Tarasoff v. Regents on homicide activity, Social Science Network. http://ssrn.com/abstract=1544574 (Accessed 13 August 2013).

Evans v. Morehead Clinic (1988) 749 S.W.2d 696 (Ky. Ct. App. 1988).

Felthous, A. F. (1987). Liability of treaters for injuries to others: Erosion of three immunities. *Bulletin of the American Academy of Psychiatry and the Law, 15*(2), 115–125.

Felthous, A. R. (1985). Negligence without malpractice: Broadening liability for psychiatrists who release dangerous mental patients. *Medicine and Law, 4*, 453–462.

Felthous, A.R. (1989a) The duty to warn or protect to prevent automobile accidents. In R.I. Simon (ed.) American Psychiatric Annual Review of Clinical Psychiatry and the Law, Volume 1, Washington, DC: American Psychiatric Press, Inc., pp. 221 to 238.

Felthous, A. R. (1989b). *The psychotherapist's duty to warn or protect*. Springfield, IL: Charles C. Thomas.

Felthous, A. R. (1999). The clinician's duty to protect third parties. *The Psychiatric Clinics of North America, 22*(1), 49–60. Edited by P. Resnick.

Felthous, A. R. (2006). Warning a potential victim of a person's dangerousness: Clinician's duty or victim's right? *The Journal of the American Academy of Psychiatry and the Law, 34*, 338–348.

Felthous, A.R. (2013) 'The treatment of clinical aggression in prison' in Piaseki M. and Thienhaus O.J. (eds.) Kingston, NJ: Correctional Psychiatry Civic Research Press, pp. 4-1 to 4-54.

Felthous, A. R., Bryant, S. G., Wingerter, C. B., & Barratt, E. S. (1991). The diagnosis of intermittent explosive disorder in violent men. *Bulletin of the American Academy of Psychiatry and the Law, 19*(1), 71–79.

Felthous, A. R., & Kachigian, C. (2001). The *Fin de Millénaire* duty to warn or protect. *The Journal of Forensic Sciences, 46*(5), 1103–1112.

Felthous, A. R., & Kachigian, C. (2017). The duty to protect. In R. Rosner & C. L. Scott (Eds.), *Principles and practice of forensic psychiatry* (3rd ed., pp. 175–184). Boca Raton: CRC Press, Taylor & Francis Group.

Felthous, A. R., Lake, S. L., Rundle, B. K., & Stanford, M. S. (2013). Pharmacotherapy of Impulsive Aggression: A quality comparison of controlled studies. *International Journal of Law and Psychiatry, 36*, 258–263.

Felthous, A. R., O'Shaughnessy, R., Kuten, J., François-Pursell, I., & Medrano, J. (2007). The clinician's duty to warn or protect: In the United States, England, Canada, New Zealand, France, and Spain. In A. R. Felthous & H. Saß (Eds.), *The international handbook of psychopathic disorders and the law, vol. II, Laws and policies* (pp. 75–94). Chichester, England: John Wiley & Sons, Ltd.

Felthous, A. R., & Stanford, M. S. (2015). A proposed algorithm for the pharmacotherapy of impulsive aggression. *The Journal of the American Academy of Psychiatry and the Law, 43*(4), 456–467.

Felthous, A. R., & Scarano, V. R. (1999). *Tarasoff* in Texas. *Texas Medicine, 95*(3), 72–78.

Fleming, J. G., & Maximov, B. (1974). The patient or his victim: The therapist's dilemma. *California Law Review, 62*, 1025–1068.

Fredericks v. Jonsson (2010) 609 F. 3d 1096 (10th Cir. 2010).

Grady v. Riley (2002) 809 So. 2d 567 (La. Ct. App. 5th Cir. 2002).

Graham v. Value Options, Inc. (2010) 2010 WL 5054442 (Ariz. Ct. App., Oct. 28, 2010).

Gudmundsen v. State (2009) 203 P. 3d 813 (Mont. 2009).

Hamman v. County of Maricopa (1989) 775 P. 2d 1122 (Ariz. 1989).

Hines v. Bick (1990) 566 So. 2d 455 (La. Ct. App. 4th Cir. 1990).

In re Mental Health of M.C.D (2010) 225 P. 3d 124 (Mont. 2010).

Jablonski by Pahls v. United States (1983) 712 F. 2d 931 (9th Cir. 1983).

Kachigian, C., & Felthous, A. R. (2004). Court responses to "Tarasoff" statutes. *The Journal of the American Academy of Psychiatry and the Law, 32*(3), 263–273.

Kuligoski v. Brattleboro Retreat (2016) 156 A. 3d 436 (Vt. 2016).

Lanterman-Petris-Short Act (1967) Welf. & Inst. Code, Section 5000ff (1967).

Little v. All Phoenix South Community Mental Health Center (1995) 919 P. 2d 1368 (Ariz. 1995).

Littleton v. Good Samaritan Hospital and Health Center (1988) 529 N.E. 2d 449 (Ohio 1988).

Martin, C. M., & Thomas, P. F. (2010). Duty to warn clarified. *The Journal of the American Academy of Psychiatry and the Law, 38*(1), 137–139.

Maxey, J. J., Wortzel, H. S., & Martinez, R. (2011). Duty to warn or protect. *The Journal of the American Academy of Psychiatry and the Law, 39*(3), 430–432.

Peck (1985) 146 Vt. 61, 499 A 2d 422 (Vt. 1985).

Petersen v. State (1988) 424 N.W. 2d 159 (Wis. 1988).

Riley v. United Health Care of Hardin (1998) 165 F. 3d 28 (6th Cir. 1998).

Shea v. Carritas (2011) 79 Mass. App. Ct. 530 (2011).

Simon, R. I. (2011). Improving suicide risk assessment. *Psychiatric Times, 28*(11). Accessible at http://www.psychiatrictimes.com/print/article/10168/2000387?printable=true.

Stanford, M. S., Houston, R. J., Mathias, C. W., Greve, K. W., Villemarette-Pittman, N. R., & Adams, D. (2001). A double-blind placebo-controlled crossover study of phenytoin in individuals with impulsive aggression. *Psychiatry Research, 103*, 193–203.

Swanson, J. W., & Felthous, A. R. (2015). Guns, mental illness and the law: Introduction to this issue. *Behavioral Sciences & the Law, 33*(2), 167–177.

Swanson, J. W., Sampson, N. A., Petukhova, M. V., Zaslavsky, A. M., Appelbaum, P. S., Swartz, M. S., et al. (2015). Guns, impulsive angry behavior, and mental disorders: Results from the National Comorbidity Survey Replication (NCS-R). *Behavioral Sciences & the Law, 33*, 199–212.

Tamsen v. Weber (1990) 802 P. 2d 1063 (Ariz. Ct. App. 1990).

Tarasoff v. Regents of the University of California (1976) 551 P.2d 334 (Cal. 1976).

Thapar v. Zezulka (1999) 994 S.W. 2d 635 (Tex. 1999).

Volk v. DeMeerleer (2016) 386 P. 3d 254 (Wash. 2016).

Walcott, D. M., Cerundolo, P., & Beck, J. C. (2001). Current analysis of the *Tarasoff* duty: An revolution towards the limitation of the duty to protect. *Behavioral Sciences & the Law, 19*(3), 325–343.

Washington State Medical Association et al. (2017) Brief of *amici curiae* in support of reconsideration of *Volk v. DeMeerleer* to the Supreme Court of Washington.

Weinstock, R., Bonnici, D., Seroussi, A., & Leong, G. B. (2014). No duty to warn in California: Now unambiguously soley a duty to protect. *The Journal of the American Academy of Psychiatry and the Law, 42*, 101–108.

Winick, B. J., LoPiccolo, C., Anand, W., & Hartswick, L. (2007). Should psychopathy qualify for preventive outpatient commitment. In A. R. Felthous & H. Saß (Eds.), *The* international handbook of psychopathic disorders and the law: Vol. II, Laws and policies (pp. 61–73). Chichester, England: John Wiley and Sons, Ltd.

Woods v. State (2015) ex rel. Montana State Hosp., 340 P. 3d 1254 (Mont. 2015).

CHAPTER TWELVE

Pharmacologic Treatment of Intermittent Explosive Disorder

Royce J. Lee, Jennifer Wang, Emil F. Coccaro
Clinical Neuroscience & Psychopharmacology Research Unit, Department of Psychiatry and Behavioral Neuroscience, Pritzker School of Medicine, University of Chicago, Chicago, IL, United States

Contents

This chapter will cover the pharmacological treatment of Intermittent Explosive Disorder (IED) and impulsive aggression. It will primarily focus on the treatment of impulsive aggression in adults. The first section will review the theoretical and clinical framework of pharmacological treatment. The second section will review data from randomized, placebo-controlled trials of pharmacological approaches. The third and final section will review ethical, regulatory, and safety issues.

Theoretical Considerations in the Pharmacological Treatment of IED and Impulsive Aggression

A useful heuristic for classifying aggression in the clinic is to divide aggression into three main types: premeditated or "cold" aggression, frustration-based aggression, and impulsive aggression. This heuristic is useful even in cases where the IED diagnosis has been established. Premediated aggression, when part of a recurrent pattern, is most closely associated with antisocial personality disorder and psychopathy. Its goal often is monetary gain or social dominance. Anger may be expressed as part of the aggressive

Intermittent Explosive Disorder
https://doi.org/10.1016/B978-0-12-813858-8.00012-7

act, especially when the aggressive act has components of reactive, or impulsive aggression, such as those acts of aggression associated with revenge. Rarely, premediated aggression may be motivated by the pleasure experienced by causing suffering, as was once captured in DSM-III by sadistic personality disorder (Myers, Burket, & Husted, 2006) and Sexual Sadism Disorder. Generally, premeditated aggression is more difficult to treat and guidance from the empirical literature is scant. Additionally, the treatment frame is more likely to be forensic or compulsory; this is because in the absence of such a framework, treatment recommendations will not be followed. Because of a tendency toward deception, collateral sources of information are needed to corroborate self-reported symptoms. These are frequently the potential victims or legal entities entrusted with their protection. Thus the clinician in these cases is usually working as part of a team, with administrative or forensic components. Frustration-based aggression is most closely associated with developmental disorders, dementia, and neurological syndromes. It is by nature impulsive, but its triggers are rarely social. Its treatment frequently involves management of contingencies, but may also require psychopharmacological approaches when severe. The clinician in these cases is usually working with a family system or other custodial caregiver. Frequently, the patient with frustration-based aggression is unable to give consent for treatment, lacking the mental capacity for consent.

In contrast, the clinical treatment of IED is typically motivated by the patients themselves. Impulsive aggression is largely a social behavior, typically provoked by a social interaction. Because humans are social creatures, whose social identities are defined by their social context, disruptions of this social context by outbursts of anger and aggression incur a heavy cost over time. Naturally, this cost is shared by the patient as well as the "victims" of aggression: family members, friends, coworkers, and sometimes strangers. However, it is not unusual for the patient to be most aware of the cumulative cost of a lifetime of unnecessary outbursts of anger in the form of wrecked relationships, serious problems at work, or the legal ramifications of impulsive acts. In our experience, it is this self-awareness that facilitates and makes possible the treatment of IED (Steakley-Freeman, Lee, McCloskey, & Coccaro, 2018). In simple terms, many patients with IED willingly come in to the clinic and look for help. There are important caveats to this optimistic perspective. IED and impulsive aggression may coexist with predatory, premediated forms of aggression in certain contexts, such as domestic or child abuse. These can be considered special cases that have more in common with the treatment of premeditated aggression, discussed in the section on antidepressants. Because of the negative consequences of impulsive aggression, persons with IED may feel shame about their behavior. In the absence of a therapeutic relationship, minimization and denial are likely to be encountered. However, when a sufficient degree of trust exists, the clinician can assess impulsive aggression using a clinical interview. Impulsive aggressive individuals are by definition *probabilistically* inclined to aggressive behavior, its treatment usually voluntary, thus requiring informed consent. Fortunately, IED usually occurs in individuals who are able to give informed consent. We highlight this fact because no pharmacological approaches for impulsive aggression have FDA approval. Thus an important initial step in the consent process is informing the patient that any proposed treatment is off label, even when based on evidence from gold-standard randomized clinical trials. Failure to do risks ethical violation and legal liability.

Diagnosis of IED is done by clinical interview. Establishing whether the aggression is disproportionate to the provocation can be done by assessing if the aggression was initiated by the patient or if the patient increased the level of aggression. In DSM-5, IED can be staged by A_1 or A_2 criteria. Criterion A_1 describes recurrent verbal aggression or mild, noninjurious assault. Criterion A_2 describes recurrent physical assault (Coccaro, Lee, & McCloskey, 2014). Clinical interview should also rule out boundary conditions but include frequently comorbid conditions, such as personality disorder. A subtle but important issue in the diagnosis of IED is the question of comorbidity between IED and Borderline/Antisocial Personality Disorder (BPD/ASPD). Although DSM-5 suggests that BPD/ASPD can be considered an exclusionary condition (Criterion F), empirical data reveal that when the diagnostic criteria for both conditions are met, the IED diagnosis remains an important predictor of aggressive behavior (Coccaro, 2012). In fact, approximately 43% of individuals with IED may have comorbid BPD and/or ASPD (Coccaro, Shima, & Lee, 2018). Data from clinical trials suggest that interview measures of aggressive behavior may be more sensitive than self-report-based questionnaire measures to change, possibly due to the time lag before individuals recognize a change in their actual behavior (Coccaro, Berman, & Kavoussi, 1997). Tracking of aggression can be done using the Overt Aggression Scale-Modified (OAS-M; Coccaro, Harvey, Kupsaw-Lawrence, Herbert, & Bernstein, 1991). Another option is for the patient and/or family member to journal the frequency and severity of their aggressive behavior on a weekly basis. Use of such systematic measures can enhance the ability of the clinician to make informed decisions about treatment.

Psychopharmacological Approaches

After establishing the treatment framework and deciding to use medication, the choice of which medication to use can be guided by the available evidence. Treatment guidelines for impulsive aggression specifically are scarce. One recent review proposed a two-step treatment algorithm (Felthous & Stanford, 2015) that relies on clinical staging. Less severe aggression (corresponding broadly to DSM-5 IED A_1 Criterion), they argue, should first be treated with selective-serotonin reuptake inhibitor (SSRI) fluoxetine. If fluoxetine does not work, the next step would be a trial of an anticonvulsant or lithium. More severe aggression, corresponding to DSM5 IED A_2 Criterion, should be treated with an anticonvulsant or lithium, skipping fluoxetine. An exception to this may be severe aggression seen in the context of Cluster B personality disorder, in whom fluoxetine may remain the first choice. These recommendations are based on a reasonable interpretation of the literature and are useful. However, it is important to point out that the comparative trials between these agents are lacking. In their absence, it is impossible to know which approaches will be most effective for a given patient. Therefore we would argue that treatment decisions at this point should be informed by weighing the potential benefits of treatment versus the potential side effects in a given patient, rather than by a priori assumptions of differential efficacy. Operationalization of this decision making will be provided at the conclusion of this chapter. This next section will review the evidence for each drug class: SSRIs, mood stabilizers and anticonvulsants, benzodiazepines, and neuroleptics. For the sake of brevity, only the results of randomized controlled trials are discussed (Table 1).

SSRI Treatment of IED

The now replicated association of IED with serotonergic dysfunction (Yanowitch and Coccaro, 2011) establishes the biological plausibility of using SSRIs in the treatment of aggression. Of the SSRIs, the most evidence for efficacy has accumulated for fluoxetine. The first randomized, double-blinded, placebo-controlled trial (RCT) in IED was conducted in 40 adults with personality disorder (Coccaro & Kavoussi, 1997). In it, fluoxetine was superior to placebo as early as the end of the first month and continued to be superior to placebo in reducing aggression in the second and third months of treatment. Twenty to forty milligrams of fluoxetine reduced verbal and indirect aggression; no effect was seen on direct physical aggression, but such

Table 1 Randomized Clinical Trials IED and Impulsive Aggression

SSRI	Patient Type	N	Trial Type	Drugs	Results
Salzman et al., 1995	BPD	23	RCT	Fluoxetine vs. Placebo	Fluoxetine reduced OAS anger
Coccaro, Kavoussi, & Hauger, 1997	Personality disordered male and female adults with IED	40	RCT	Fluoxetine vs. Placebo	Fluoxetine reduced OAS-M Aggression and OAS-M Irritability
Coccaro et al., 2009	Personality disordered male and female adults with IED	100	RCT	Fluoxetine vs. Placebo	Fluoxetine reduced OAS-M Aggression and OAS-M Irritability
Silva et al., 2010	Borderline Personality Disordered	59	Open-Label	Fluoxetine Alone	Fluoxetine reduced OAS-M Aggression and OAS-M Irritability from Baseline to End of Study; Response observed only in those with the 5-HTT *ll* Genotype
George et al., 2011	Alcoholics with Intimate Partner Violence	24	RCT	Fluoxetine vs. Placebo	Fluoxetine reduced OAS-M Irritability
Coccaro et al., 2015	Personality disordered adults with IED	90	RCT	Fluoxetine vs. Divalproex vs. Placebo	Null results
Lithium					
Sheard et al., 1976	Prisoners with impulsive aggression	66	RCT	Lithium vs. Placebo	Decreased disciplinary sanctions
Anticonvulsants					
Barratt et al., 1997	Inmates with aggression	$N=60$	Double-Blind Randomized Controlled Trial (RCT)	Phenytoin vs Placebo	Phenytoin reduced impulsive aggression

Continued

Table 1 Randomized Clinical Trials IED and Impulsive Aggression—cont'd

SSRI	Patient Type	N	Trial Type	Drugs	Results
Stanford et al., 2001	Men with impulsive aggression	46	RCT	Phenytoin vs Placebo	Phenytoin reduced OAS aggression
Stanford et al., 2005	Men with impulsive aggression	28	RCT	Phenytoin vs Carbamazepine vs Valproate	Valproate and phenytoin > Carbamazepine > Placebo
Hollander et al., 2003	Cluster B IED PTSD	246	RCT	Divalproex 500–3000 mg vs. Placebo	No significant effect on OAS-M score
Mattes, 1990	Adults with IED and aggression	51	Single-blind, randomized trial	Carbamazepine vs. Propranolol	Carbamazepine but no propranolol reduced aggression in IED
Mattes, 2005	Outpatients with impulsive aggression	48	RCT	Oxcarbazepine vs Placebo	Oxcarbazepine reduced OAS aggression
Mattes, 2008	Outpatients with impulsive aggression	40	RCT	Levetiracetam vs. Placebo	Null results

events were rare and the statistical power to detect an effect was lacking. The beneficial effect of fluoxetine was restricted to interview measures of aggression but not a questionnaire measure (Anger, Irritability, and Assault Questionnaire; AIAQ). This may because the AIAQ asks for aggressive tendencies, the change in perception of which may lag in IED subjects. Notably, the antiaggressive effects were not due to reduced depression or anxiety.

In a larger sample of 100 adults with IED and personality disorder, fluoxetine was again found to be superior to placebo for aggression and irritability, and once again were not due to changed depression or anxiety (Coccaro, Lee, & Kavoussi, 2009). By the end of the study, 46% of fluoxetine-treated subjects were remitted from IED. Effects were seen as early as 2 weeks. The results of these two studies back up positive results on anger in an earlier RCT of fluoxetine in the treatment of 23 adults with BPD (Salzman et al., 1995) and also predated two other studies (George et al., 2011; Silva et al., 2010) that reported the antiaggressive effect of fluoxetine in adult individuals with history of impulsive aggression.

Not all trials have been positive. A double-blind, randomized comparison of fluoxetine, valproate, and placebo found that neither fluoxetine nor divalproex was superior to placebo in treating aggression. A secondary analysis revealed that beneficial effects of fluoxetine relative to placebo were seen only in highly impulsive aggressive subjects (OAS-M Aggression $\geq$15; OAS-M Irritability $\geq$6; Coccaro, Lee, Breen, & Irwin, 2015).

The clinical finding that fluoxetine reduces aggression in IED, particularly in highly aggressive individuals, has been supported by experimental research. In animal models, fluoxetine has been found to reduce aggression (Fuller, 1996). In humans, SSRIs have been associated with reduction of aggressive behavior in laboratory paradigms both when administered chronically (Cherek, Lane, Pietras, & Steinberg, 2002) and acutely (Berman, McCloskey, Fanning, Schumacher, & Coccaro, 2009) for those with a history of aggressive behavior.

Unfortunately, no other SSRIs have been tested in IED with rigorous RCTs though negative results on anger have been found for the effects of fluvoxamine relative to placebo in the treatment of BPD (Rinne, van den Brink, Wouters, & van Dyck, 2002).

Predictors of Response

There are no confirmed predictors of SSRI response. Preliminary information, as reviewed before, points to greater severity of aggression and irritability (Coccaro et al., 2015), higher pretreatment neuroticism and lower harm avoidance (Phan, Lee, & Coccaro, 2011), and greater pretreatment 5-HT function (Coccaro & Kavoussi, 1997). Additionally, preliminary data suggests that treatment-related suppression of amygdala activation to anger faces is linearly related to a more favorable antiaggressive response to either fluoxetine or divalproex (Coccaro et al., 2015). Pharmacogenomics holds great promise in predicting treatment response, but very little is known about this. Preliminary results from a pharmacogenetic study in 59 adults with borderline personality disorder suggest that individuals with long arm of the serotonin transporter are more likely to respond to fluoxetine in the treatment of aggression (Silva et al., 2010). Developmental stage may also determine the effect of SSRI medications on aggression, with adolescent patients, but not adult patients, more likely to suffer from increased aggression after the initiation of SSRI treatment (Halperin et al., 1997; Sharma, Guski, Freund, & Gøtzsche, 2016).

Anticonvulsants and Mood Stabilizers

Given the role of intense affective states in aggression, anticonvulsants and mood stabilizers have been studied as potential pharmacological treatments. The first, and often cited, research examining this question was a double-blind, crossover study of lithium vs. placebo in 66 incarcerated adolescent and young adults with history of impulsive aggression (Sheard, Marini, Bridges, & Wagner, 1976). Lithium was found to reduce the number of aggression-related infractions in this severe, forensic population.

Phenytoin has also demonstrated some efficacy at improving impulsive aggression specifically. In a study involving 60 incarcerated participants, phenytoin reduced impulsive, but not premedicated aggression (Barratt, Stanford, Felthous, & Kent, 1997). Supporting the potential utility of phenytoin for IED specifically, a double-blind placebo-controlled study was conducted in 46 men who met DSM-IV A and B criteria for IED (i.e., several episodes of discrete aggression disproportionate to the precipitating stressor) (Stanford et al., 2001). Individuals treated with daily phenytoin significantly decreased the number of weekly aggressive outbursts when compared to placebo and reported subjectively reduced anger and hostility. In aggregative, meta-analysis reveals that across studies, phenytoin reduces impulsive aggression with large effect size SMD = 1.34 (72.16–70.52; Johnson et al., 2014).

A case series has been reported of the positive effects of adjunctive carbamazepine in highly aggressive and treatment refractory psychotic adults with severe aggression (Young & Hillbrand, 1994). A randomized, single-blind comparison of carbamazepine and propranolol in adults with impulsive aggression and IED found carbamazepine to be superior in reducing rage outbursts (Mattes, 1990). Both drugs were safe. Interestingly, an IED diagnosis predicted better outcome with carbamazepine. These results are consistent with positive effects of carbamazepine on behavioral outbursts in BPD (Cowdry & Gardner, 1988).

Oxcarbazepine was developed as a modification of carbamazepine to eliminate hepatic and immune-related serious side effects. Oxcarbazepine is derived from carbamazepine by substitution of a carbon-carbon double bond on the dibenzazepine ring. In an RCT in adults with IED, oxcarbazepine reduced OAS aggression and was associated with higher patient-rated improvement compared to placebo (Mattes, 2005).

Further, although the anticonvulsant divalproex has decreased aggression and irritability in individuals with a personality disorder, it was no better than placebo at reducing aggression in IED (Hollander et al., 2003) in a study that was largely negative. These results, when combined with results from a previous RCT in BPD, suggest that divalproex has positive effects in BPD, but perhaps not in IED that is not comorbid with it. Negative results have also been reported for levetiracetam (Mattes, 2008).

Some preliminary statements can be made on predictors of individual differences in response to mood stabilizers and anticonvulsants. In terms of serious toxicity, the FDA has warned about the relationship between HLA-B*1502 and Stevens-Johnson syndrome with carbamazepine. It has also warned against using phenytoin as a substitute. While divalproex may be of use in BPD, in IED outside of this, it may not work. Phenytoin has been found to reduce aggression in severe cases of IED and is a potential choice in difficult cases. Carbamazepine has been found to reduce aggression in IED but not in ADHD.

Benzodiazepines

Benzodiazepines have been found to increase laboratory-measured aggression acutely in aggressive individuals (Berman & Stuart, 1995). Controlled data in BPD have found that alprazolam increased behavioral outbursts (Cowdry & Gardner, 1988). Somewhat counterintuitively, the scant literature that exists is not supportive of the use of benzodiazepines in IED.

This, combined with their potential for abuse, and the threat of death in overdose with narcotics, means that benzodiazepines are not likely to be effective in IED.

Antipsychotics

Somewhat surprisingly, there is no direct evidence of the efficacy of antipsychotic medications in IED. This is contrast to the FDA indication for irritability in children and adolescents with autism. In BPD, metaanalytic research reveals that antipsychotics worsen global severity (SMD = 0.3, 95% CI −0.22 to 0.82). However, pooled results from two studies ($n = 114$) reveal it does reduce anger intensity (SMD = −0.46, 95% CI −0.84 to −0.09(Lieb et al., 2010). Like haloperidol, olanzapine too reduces anger with a small effect size, when data from 631 patients and 3 trials are pooled (mean change SD −0.27, 95% CI −0.43 to −0.12). (Stoffers et al., 2010). In an RCT with 96 BPD outpatients, low dose of quetiapine reduced OAS-M aggression score compared to placebo (Black et al., 2014). In the context of psychotic disorders, evidence suggests that clozapine is the most effective antipsychotic medication approach to aggression (Citrome et al., 2001). Its antiaggressive effect was not immediate, but was independent of its effect on psychotic symptoms (Volavka et al., 2004). Evidence to support the use of atypical antipsychotics in the treatment of IED is scant. In boundary conditions, such as BPD and psychosis, the evidence indicates that antipsychotics reduce aggression but may not treat other aspects of the disorder, with serious side effects to consider.

Safety Considerations and Rational Approaches to Psychopharmacology

Managing a population of patients, it becomes plainly apparent that IED usually exists in a health/medical context. Medication interactions, risk of pregnancy, and toxicity require a careful approach when assessing the risks in relation to benefits of "off-label" medication prescribing.

Cytochrome P450 interactions with concomitant medications are not uncommon, especially in the aging population. Such interactions can alter the dose-response relationship with respect to side effects and toxicity. For fluoxetine, CYP2D6 inhibition makes coprescribing with antihistamines, muscle relaxers, tricyclic antidepressants, antipsychotics, and beta-blockers more technically difficult. Some of the potential CYP2D6 interactions could lead to prolongation of the cardiac QT interval, and thus would require serial EKG monitoring. Fluoxetine can trigger mania or hypomania in patients with bipolar disorder, or those who are susceptible to it. Discriminating the outbursts of IED from manic-related behaviors of bipolar disorder can be difficult, especially in retrospect.

For carbamazepine and divalproex, both CYP3A4 induction and inhibition can be problematic. Complex, system-level interactions make using carbamazepine and divalproex in women of childbearing age difficult to manage, as the oral contraceptive is metabolized more quickly due to protein binding issues. The relevance of pharmacogenomic testing of genetic variation in the CYP isoenzyme polymorphisms remains uncertain but will likely turn out to be of importance. A promising harbinger of this future is the availability of testing for HLA-B*1502 to reduce the risk of toxic epidermal necrosis (TENS) with carbamazepine and phenytoin.

Should treatment approaches be guided by risk profiles? If so, then a few possibilities come to mind. Firstly, females of childbearing age with IED may be easier to manage on an SSRI such as fluoxetine, rather than an anticonvulsant or atypical antipsychotic. Secondly, patients with a history of bipolar disorder or where it is strongly suspected should probably not receive an SSRI in the absence of a mood-stabilizing drug. If genetic testing reveals HLA-B*1502, an SSRI would be preferable.

This returns us to the issue of psychopharmacological treatment algorithms for IED. We previously discussed using clinical staging to guide the first line treatment of aggression in IED, in which IED cases meeting A1 criteria receive fluoxetine, and those meeting A2 criteria receive either carbamazepine or phenytoin. The clinical principles of the Felthous & Stanford two-step treatment algorithm (Felthous & Stanford, 2015) are sound and applicable to the population clinicians will treat. Integrating these with a rational approach to risk profiling may be the most practical approach. In such a scenario, females of childbearing age should probably receive a trial of fluoxetine before an anticonvulsant, regardless of IED criterion.

References

Barratt, E. S., Stanford, M. S., Felthous, A. R., & Kent, T. A. (1997). The effects of phenytoin on impulsive and premeditated aggression: a controlled study. *Journal of Clinical Psychopharmacology*, *17*(5), 341–349.

Berman, M. E., McCloskey, M. S., Fanning, J. R., Schumacher, J. A., & Coccaro, E. F. (2009). Serotonin augmentation reduces response to attack in aggressive individuals. *Psychological Science*, *20*(6), 714–720.

Berman, M., & Stuart, T. (1995). The effects of triazolam on aggression in men. *Experimental and Clinical Psychopharmacology*, *3*(4), 411–416.

Black, D. W., Zanarini, M. C., Romine, A., Shaw, M., Allen, J., & Schulz, S. C. (2014). Comparison of low and moderate dosages of extended-release quetiapine in borderline personality disorder: a randomized, double-blind, placebo-controlled trial. *American Journal of Psychiatry, 171*(11), 1174–1182.

Cherek, D. R., Lane, S. D., Pietras, C. J., & Steinberg, J. L. (2002). Effects of chronic paroxetine administration on measures of aggressive and impulsive responses of adult males with a history of conduct disorder. *Psychopharmacology (Berl), 159*, 266–274.

Citrome, L., Volavka, J., Czobor, P., Sheitman, B., Lindenmayer, J. P., McEvoy, J., et al. (2001). Effects of clozapine, olanzapine, risperidone, and haloperidol on hostility among patients with schizophrenia. *Psychiatric Services (Washington, DC) 52*(11), 1510–1514.

Coccaro, E. F. (2012). Intermittent explosive disorder as a disorder of impulsive aggression for DSM-5. *American Journal of Psychiatry, 169*(6), 577–588.

Coccaro, E. F., Berman, M. E., & Kavoussi, R. J. (1997). Assessment of life history of aggression: development and psychometric characteristics. *Psychiatry Research, 73*(3), 147–157.

Coccaro, E. F., Harvey, P. D., Kupsaw-Lawrence, E., Herbert, J. L., & Bernstein, D. P. (1991). Development of neuropharmacologically based behavioral assessments of impulsive aggressive behavior. *Journal of Neuropsychiatry and Clinical Neurosciences, 3*(2), S44–S51.

Coccaro, E. F., & Kavoussi, R. J. (1997). Fluoxetine and impulsive aggressive behavior in personality-disordered subjects. *Archives of General Psychiatry, 54*, 1081–1088.

Coccaro, E. F., Kavoussi, R. J., & Hauger, R. L. (1997). Serotonin function and antiaggressive responses to fluoxetine: a pilot study. *Biological Psychiatry, 42*, 546–552.

Coccaro, E. F., Lee, R., Breen, E. C., & Irwin, M. R. (2015). Inflammatory markers and chronic exposure to fluoxetine, divalproex, and placebo in intermittent explosive disorder. *Psychiatry Research, 229*(3), 844–849.

Coccaro, E. F., Lee, R. J., & Kavoussi, R. J. (2009). A double-blind, randomized, placebo-controlled trial of fluoxetine in patients with intermittent explosive disorder. *Journal of Clinical Psychiatry, 70*(5), 653–662.

Coccaro, E. F., Lee, R., & McCloskey, M. S. (2014). Validity of the new A1 and A2 criteria for DSM-5 intermittent explosive disorder. *Comprehensive Psychiatry, 55*(2), 260–267.

Coccaro, E. F., Shima, C. K., & Lee, R. J. (2018). Comorbidity of personality disorder with intermittent explosive disorder. *Journal of Psychiatric Research, 106*, 15–21.

Cowdry, R. W., & Gardner, D. L. (1988). Pharmacotherapy of borderline personality disorder. Alprazolam, carbamazepine, trifluoperazine, and tranylcypromine. *Archives of General Psychiatry, 45*(2), 111–119.

Felthous, A. R., & Stanford, M. S. (2015). A proposed algorithm for the pharmacotherapy of impulsive aggression. *The Journal of the American Academy of Psychiatry and the Law 43*(4), 456–467.

Fuller, R. W. (1996). The influence of fluoxetine on aggressive behavior. *Neuropsychopharmacology, 14*(2), 77–81.

George, D. T., Phillips, M. J., Lifshitz, M., Lionetti, T. A., Spero, D. E., Ghassemzedeh, N., et al. (2011). *The Journal of Clinical Psychiatry, 72*(1), 60–65.

Halperin, J. M., Newcorn, J. H., Schwartz, S. T., Sharma, V., Siever, L. J., Koda, V. H., et al. (1997). Age-related changes in the association between serotonergic function and aggression in boys with ADHD. *Biological Psychiatry, 41*(6), 682–689.

Hollander, E., Tracy, K. A., Swann, A. C., Coccaro, E. F., McElroy, S. L., Wozniak, P., et al. (2003). Divalproex in the treatment of impulsive aggression: efficacy in cluster B personality disorders. *Neuropsychopharmacology, 28*(6), 1186–1197.

Johnson, J., Jones, C., Lin, A., Wood, S., Heinze, K., & Jackson, C. (2014). Shame amplifies the association between stressful life events and paranoia amongst young adults using mental health services: implications for understanding risk and psychological resilience. *Psychiatry Research, 220*(1–2), 217–225.

Lieb, K., Völlm, B., Rücker, G., Timmer, A., Stoffers, J. M., Vo, B., et al. (2010). Pharmacotherapy for borderline personality disorder: cochrane systematic review of randomised trials. *British Journal of Psychiatry, 196*(1), 4–12.

Mattes, J. (1990). Comparative effectiveness of carbamazepine and propranolol for rage outbursts. *The Journal of Neuropsychiatry and Clinical Neurosciences, 2*(2), 159–164.

Mattes, J. (2005). Oxcarbazepine in patients with impulsive aggression: a double-blind, placebo-controlled trial. *Journal of Clinical Psychopharmacology, 25*(6), 575–579.

Mattes, J. A. (2008). Levetiracetam in patients with impulsive aggression: A double-blind, placebo-controlled trial. *The Journal of Clinical Psychiatry, 69*(2), 310–315.

Myers, W. C., Burket, R. C., & Husted, D. S. (2006). Sadistic personality disorder and comorbid mental illness in adolescent psychiatric inpatients. *The Journal of the American Academy of Psychiatry and the Law, 34*(1), 61–71.

Phan, K. L., Lee, R., & Coccaro, E. F. (2011). Personality predictors of anti-aggressive response to fluoxetine: inverse association with neuroticism and harm avoidance. *International Clinical Psychopharmacology, 26*, 278–283.

Rinne, T., van den Brink, W., Wouters, L., & van Dyck, R. (2002). SSRI treatment of borderline personality disorder: a randomized, placebo-controlled clinical trial for female patients with borderline personality disorder. *American Journal of Psychiatry, 159*(12), 2048–2054.

Salzman, C., Wolfson, A. N., Schatzberg, A., Looper, J., Henke, R., Albanese, M., et al. (1995). Effect of fluoxetine on anger in symptomatic volunteers with borderline personality disorder. *Journal of Clinical Psychopharmacology, 15*(1), 23–29.

Sharma, T., Guski, L. S., Freund, N., & Gøtzsche, P. C. (2016). Suicidality and aggression during antidepressant treatment: systematic review and meta-analyses based on clinical study reports. *BMJ, 352*, 65.

Sheard, M. H., Marini, J. L., Bridges, C. I., & Wagner, E. (1976). The effect of lithium on impulsive aggressive behavior in man. *American Journal of Psychiatry, 133*(12), 1409–1413.

Silva, H., Iturra, P., Solari, A., Villarroel, J., Jerez, S., Jiménez, M., et al. (2010). Fluoxetine response in impulsive-aggressive behavior and serotonin transporter polymorphism in personality disorder. *Psychiatric Genetics, 20*(1), 25–30.

Stanford, M. S., Houston, R. J., Mathias, C. W., Greve, K. W., Villemarette-Pittman, N. R., & Adams, D. (2001). A double-blind placebo-controlled crossover study of phenytoin in individuals with impulsive aggression. *Psychiatry Research, 103*(2–3), 193–203.

Stanford, M. S., Helfritz, L. E., Conklin, S. M., Villemarette-Pittman, N. R., Greve, K. W., Adams, D., et al. (2005). A comparison of anticonvulsants in the treatment of impulsive aggression. *Experimental and Clinical Psychopharmacology, 13*, 72–77.

Steakley-Freeman, D. M., Lee, R., McCloskey, M. S., & Coccaro, E. F. (2018). Social desirability, deceptive reporting, and awareness of problematic aggression in intermittent explosive disorder compared with non-aggressive healthy and psychiatric controls. *Psychiatry Research, 270*, 20–25.

Stoffers, J., Völlm, B. A., Rücker, G., Timmer, A., Huband, N., & Lieb, K. (2010). Pharmacological interventions for borderline personality disorder. In *Cochrane Database of Systematic Reviews* (p. CD005653).

Volavka, J., Czobor, P., Nolan, K., Sheitman, B., Lindenmayer, J. P., Citrome, L., et al. (2004). Overt aggression and psychotic symptoms in patients with schizophrenia treated with clozapine, olanzapine, Risperidone, or haloperidol. *Journal of Clinical Psychopharmacology, 24*(2), 225–228.

Yanowitch, R., Coccaro, E., & F. (2011). The neurochemistry of human aggression. *Advances in Genetics, 75*, 151–169.

Young, J., & Hillbrand, M. (1994). Carbamazepine lowers aggression: a review. *The Bulletin of the American Academy of Psychiatry and the Law, 22*(1), 53–61.

CHAPTER THIRTEEN

Psychosocial Interventions for Treatment of Intermittent Explosive Disorder

Michael S. McCloskey
Mechanisms of Affect Dysregulation Laboratory (MAD LAB), Department of Psychology, Temple University, Philadelphia, PA, United States

Contents

Introduction

Dysregulated anger and aggression is a feature of several psychological disorders including posttraumatic stress disorder (PTSD), antisocial and borderline personality disorders, and conduct disorder to name just a few (American Psychiatric Association, 2013). Problematic aggression is also seen in transdiagnostic public health problems such as intimate partner violence and child abuse. Thus anger and aggression have long been targets of interventions efforts. Studies support the efficacy of psychosocial interventions overall and cognitive-behavioral therapies (CBT) in particular for anger and interpersonal aggression, with multiple metaanalytic studies suggesting moderate to large effect of cognitive-behavioral interventions in reducing anger and aggression (Beck & Fernandez, 1998; Bowman-Edmondson & Cohen-Conger, 1996; Del Vecchio & O'Leary, 2004; DiGuiseppe & Tafrate, 2003; Lee & DiGuiseppe, 2018). Furthermore, though no specific form of CBT appeared clearly superior, multicomponent

Intermittent Explosive Disorder
https://doi.org/10.1016/B978-0-12-813858-8.00013-9

CBT containing both cognitive and behavioral components tend to have the greatest empirical support, with the likelihood that this type of intervention will be particularly useful when treating aggressive behavior (Del Vecchio & O'Leary, 2004).

At this time, there is growing support that psychosocial interventions can reduce aggression even in historically treatment-resistant populations. A metaanalysis of treatments for intimate partner violence using either CBT or advocacy-based intervention found significant reductions in physical violence for both treatments, albeit larger for CBT (standardized mean difference (SMD) = 0.79) than for advocacy programs (SMD = 0.13). A second metaanalysis also found that couples interventions, most of which were behavioral or cognitive-behavioral, significantly reduced partner violence (Karakurt, Whiting, van Esch, Bolen, & Calabrese, 2016). One notable exception, however, is antisocial personality disorder, where the few well-controlled trials do not show CBT, or other psychosocial, interventions effective in reducing anger and aggression (Davidson et al., 2009; National Collaborating Centre for Mental Health, 2010).

That said, one disorder not considered in any of the aforementioned studies and metaanalyses is Intermittent Explosive Disorder (IED). IED is unique from all other psychological disorders in that excessive affective aggression is pathognomonic for the disorder. Accordingly, individuals with IED have greater deficits in anger control and emotion regulation (Fettich, McCloskey, Look, & Coccaro, 2014) and report more distress and impairment related to their aggression, even relative to those with other psychiatric disorders (Kulper, Kleiman, McCloskey, Berman, & Coccaro, 2015; see also Chapter 3). The primacy and severity of anger, aggressiveness and associated deficits, can make treatment more challenging relative to those in other angry populations. In this chapter, we will look in depth at the limited research on psychosocial interventions for IED including a brief session by session description of a specific CBT intervention for IED.

Initial Trial of Angry Drivers With and Without IED

The first known study to examine the efficacy of psychosocial interventions for IED was an evaluation of a brief (four 90-minute sessions) cognitive-behavioral program for aggressive drivers (Galovski & Blanchard, 2002). The primary goal of the study was to determine if the CBT intervention reduced aggressive and angry driving as well as general anger and distress in a sample of 28 aggressive drivers (20 court-referred,

8 self-referred) relative to a self-monitoring control condition. Results showed that CBT reduced aggressive driving and general anger more than self-monitoring and that these changes remained at follow-up 2 months later. More central to this chapter, secondary analyses included a comparison of aggressive drivers who did ($n=9$) vs. who did not ($n=18$) meet criteria for IED. These results found that individuals with IED displayed only about half the reduction in aggressive driving that Non-IED drivers displayed, approaching statistical significance ($P=.06$). From this, the authors inferred that drivers with IED "may require a more intensive and prolonged treatment."

CRCST for IED

Research Findings

Cognitive restructuring, relaxation, and coping skills training (CRCST) is multicomponent CBT intervention developed by Deffenbacher and McKay to treat situational and general anger (Deffenbacher & McKay, 2000). This eight-session (plus assessment session) treatment, which included two sessions focusing on relaxation training, a third devoted to cognitive restructuring, and the remaining five teaching coping skills training (i.e., hierarchical imaginal exposure) to increasingly angering situations, was shown to be effective reducing anger and aggression in predominately nonclinical samples (e.g., Deffenbacher, Filetti, Lynch, Dahlen, & Oetting, 2001; Hazaleus & Deffenbacher, 1986). However, it had not been used to aggressive disorders such as IED until the early 2000s. McCloskey, Deffenbacher, and Coccaro modified CRCST for use with individuals with IED. This included extending the treatment to 12 sessions (plus a presession), increasing the time spent on cognitive restructuring to 2.5 sessions, inclusion of a time-out intervention to resist aggressive impulses, more time devoted to coping skills training (6 sessions), and a greater emphasis on relapse prevention during the latter sessions. These changes were based on the extant data on IED. For example, the decision to increase the time spent on cognitive restructuring was informed by studies showing that individuals with IED have both severe hostile attribution biases (Coccaro, Noblett, & McCloskey, 2009; Coccaro, Fanning, Keedy, & Lee, 2016; see also Chapter 8) and well as deficits in executive functioning (Best, Williams, & Coccaro, 2002). Likewise, the decision to include a time-out procedure early in the intervention was informed by both patient report and research showing that anger and aggressive outbursts for those with

IED feel more "out of control" (Kulper et al., 2015). Accordingly, we posited that time-out procedures can provide a straightforward behavioral strategy for responding to aggressive impulses while the person with IED is still in the process of learning other techniques.

A preliminary study on the efficacy of CRCST for IED compared group and individual formats of CRCST for IED (henceforth called CRCST) to a self-monitoring wait-list control (McCloskey, Noblett, Deffenbacher, Gollan, & Coccaro, 2008). Individual CRCST consisted of 12 weekly 50-minute sessions. Group CRCST consisted of 12 weekly 75-minute sessions led by two cotherapists. Group CRCST also differed from individual CRCST in that feedback and suggestions for participants were elicited from their fellow members. Finally, the self-monitoring group was an enhanced wait-list condition in which participants were asked to monitor and record all situations in which they became angry and/or aggressive. Participants in the self-motioning condition were informed that monitoring problematic behavior can reduce engagement in that behavior (Michie et al., 2012). Fifteen participants were evenly randomized into each of the three conditions. Primary outcome measures included past week aggression (Overt Aggression Scale-Modified (OAS-M); Coccaro, Harvey, Kupsaw-Lawrence, Herbert, & Bernstein, 1991)), as well as measures of cognitive hostility (Hostile Automatic Thoughts (Snyder, Crowson, Houston, Kurylo, & Poirier, 1997)), and anger (State-Trait Anger Expression Inventory-2 (Spielberger, 1999)). Secondary measures included symptoms of depression and anxiety as well as quality of life. All measures were given at pretreatment, posttreatment, and (for those in the CRCST conditions) 3-month follow-up.

Only four participants dropped out prior to posttreatment (two in each of the self-monitoring and group CRCST conditions) and, critically, history of aggression and other demographic/clinical characteristics did not differ between the groups. Intent-to-treat analyses showed that CRCST, in either format, produced significant decreases in aggressive behavior that were greater than the nonsignificant change from pre to post for the self-monitoring group. Combining the two CRCST conditions and comparing it to self-monitoring at posttest (controlling for pretest scores) yielded a large effect (Cohen's $d=0.98$) of CRCST on aggressive behavior (Fig. 1).

Similar results were found for trait anger with both CRSCT conditions showing a significant pre-post decrease in STAXI trait anger score that well exceeded the marginally significant pre-post reduction in anger among those in the self-monitoring group. This same pattern of both CRCST conditions

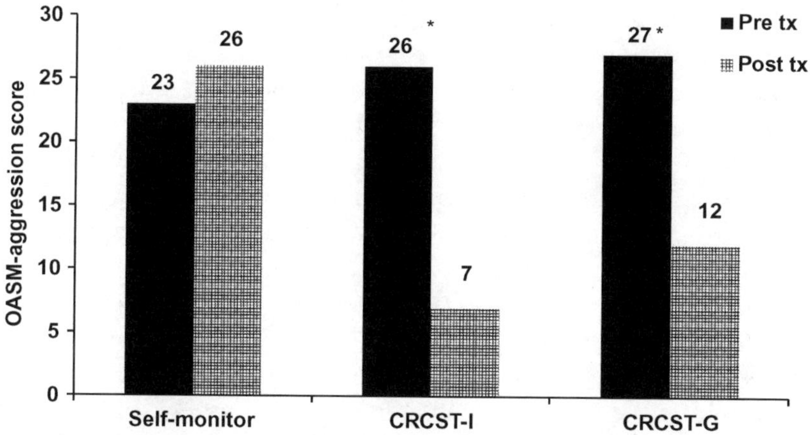

Fig. 1 Aggression as a function of time × treatment condition (McCloskey et al., 2008). Note: *CRCST-G*, group CRCST; *CRCST-I*, individual CRCST; *OASM*, overt aggression scale-modified; *Self-monitor*, self-monitoring control; *tx*, treatment; posttreatment OASM aggression scores (controlling for pretreatment) CRCST-I, CRCST-G < Self-monitor ($P < .01$). * = within group pre-post tx difference $P < .005$.

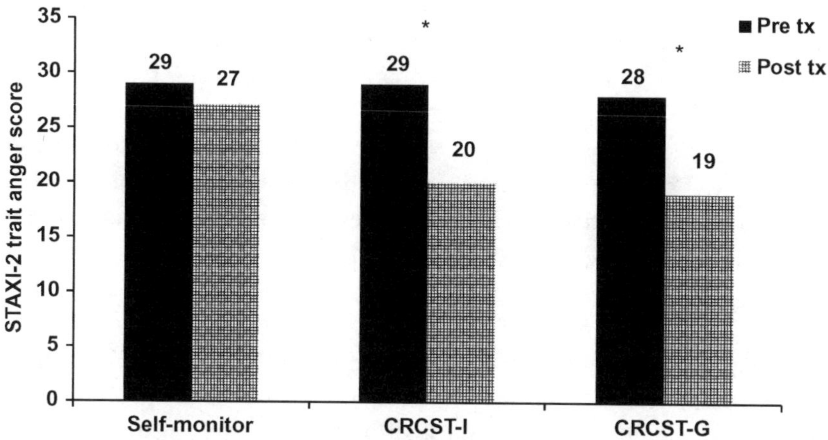

Fig. 2 Trait anger as a function of time × treatment condition (McCloskey et al., 2008). Note: *CRCST-G*, group CRCST; *CRCST-I*, individual CRCST; *Self-monitor*, self-monitoring control; *STAXI-2*, state trait anger expression inventory-2; *tx*, treatment; posttreatment STAXI-2 trait anger scores (controlling for pretreatment) CRCST-I, CRCST-G < Self-monitor ($P < .01$). * = within group pre-post tx difference $P < .001$.

being comparable and outperforming self-monitoring was also shown for pre-post deceases in depressive symptoms. Furthermore, these treatment gains (and the others listed as follows) for CRCST remained at 3-month follow-up (Fig. 2).

For some measures, there was a suggestion that individual CRCST may be preferable to group CRCST. For example, only individual CRCST displayed a greater decrease in hostile automatic thoughts from pre- to post-treatment relative to self-monitoring, with group CRCST not significantly different from either other condition. Likewise, only individual CRCST displayed a significantly greater improvement in quality of life from pre- to posttreatment relative to self-monitoring, with group CRCST, again, not significantly different from either other condition. That said, when examining only participants who completed the active phase of the study, group CRCST outperformed self-monitoring in improving quality of life. This was the only study finding that differed when examining the "intent to treat" sample vs. the "completer" sample. The strongest evidence that individual CRCST may be superior to group CRCST was that 47% of participants in the individual CRCST condition were "remitted" (i.e., no verbal or physical aggression reported on their posttreatment OAS-M) compared to 13% in the group CRCST condition and 7% in the self-monitoring condition. However, the difference between individual and group CRCST only represented a nonsignificant trend ($P = .10$) and, in the absence of an overall difference between conditions in reducing aggressive behavior, one must be cautious in interpreting this finding regarding remission.

Three of the four participants who refused to be randomized stated they were not willing to be a part of group therapy; the remaining participant was not willing to be in the self-monitoring condition. Thus individual CRCST seemed to be more initially desirable. However, this preference did not persist once treatment began as individual and group CRCST did not differ on measures of working alliance goals, task, or bond at either session 4 or the end of treatment (session 12).

Limitations include that this pilot study had a relatively small sample and that the therapists were licensed clinical psychologists with considerable experience working with those with IED, which may limit the generalizability to other treatment providers. Finally, treatment competence was not assessed. Despite these limitations, this study provides the first randomized clinical trial supporting the efficacy of CBT in treating IED.

After the 2008 study, additional minor modifications were made to the CRCST intervention (e.g., reducing jargon in description of cognitive distortions and reducing the number of strategies to challenge cognitive distortions). This slightly modified version of individual CRCST was compared to a supportive psychotherapy control. Data from that trial showed that CRCST, again, produced large pre-post decreases in anger, aggression, and associated symptoms that exceeded the more modest gains made by supportive psychotherapy. Furthermore, examination of predictors of CRCST across studies showed that the effects of CBT in treating IED are not impacted by most demographic variables or psychiatric comorbidities. A brief session by description of CBT for IED is provided as follows.

CRCST for IED Intervention

Pretreatment Session: During this brief (~30 minute) session, the rules for confidentiality are provided and the client is given the rationale for CRCST. The client's aggressive behavior is reviewed and their goals for treatment are discussed. The client and therapist then work on developing an anger scale that will be used throughout the treatment. The anger scale identifies cognitive, emotional, physiological, and behavioral anchors for varying levels of anger at 20-point increments from 0 (completely relaxed) through 100 (their angriest and most aggressive ever), with 40 set as the point at which the client's anger begins to cause mild aggressive behavior (e.g., "snapping at others"). At the end of the session the client is introduced to an anger and aggression log in which they record all angering events and their behavioral response. This log is used throughout the treatment with additional columns to record thoughts and coping responses as the client progresses through the treatment.

Session 1: After reviewing the previous week's anger log, a rationale for the utility of relaxation training is provided. Clients are then asked to develop a relaxation image, with the therapist eliciting emotional and sensory details of the scene. The client practices the scene in session after which the therapist gets feedback on how effective the scene was (i.e., how vivid, how relaxing) and either keeps or modifies the scene accordingly. Then progressive muscle relaxation is taught using the method outlined by Deffenbacher and McKay (2000). As with all sessions, the client is tasked with practicing the newly learned skills between sessions.

Session 2: Visual imagery and progressive muscle relaxation techniques from session 1 are reviewed with the client taking more of a lead in the exercise. The additional relaxation technique of deep (diaphragmatic) breathing is introduced. The client and therapist also work to help the client develop three to four general coping thoughts that can be used to help (the client) stay calm in angering situations. The client is asked to keep the coping thoughts close by (either in paper version or electronically) and refer to them when angry until they are memorized.

Session 3: Previously learned relaxation techniques are reviewed and the client is asked to provide their general coping thoughts from memory. Relaxation without tension is then presented, followed by combined relaxation skills in which deep breathing, relaxation without tension, and visual imagery are integrated. The use of time-out is then introduced with an emphasis on the utility of the technique and the importance of both taking the time-out prior to engaging in aggression and using relaxation skills and coping thoughts (versus perseveration) during the time-out.

Session 4: The client is introduced to the CBT model of anger and aggression in which thoughts moderate the relationship between events and emotional and behavioral responses. Several examples are provided by both the therapist and the client. The concept of "anger distortions" is then introduced with a focus on catastrophizing, overgeneralizing, mind-reading, blaming, name-calling, and "shoulds." Clients begin tracking their anger thoughts on their anger and aggression log.

Session 5: The CBT model and anger and aggression, and anger distortions are reviewed. Clients are then introduced to the use of strategies to challenge anger distortions. After the rationale is provided, clients are presented two strategies to "talk back" to each of the six of the anger distortions. For example, clients are taught the strategies of "being realistically negative" and "looking at the whole picture" to address problems with catastrophizing. For each strategy, the therapist provides an example and then has the client provide an example to demonstrate understanding.

Session 6: Anger distortions and strategies to talk back to the distortions are reviewed. Then coping skills training is introduced. The client provides details for a moderate (~40–50 on the anger scale) anger scene. Key anger thoughts and the underlying distortions are identified and new coping thoughts using the strategies learned in session 5 are developed. The client is then asked to imagine the anger scene in as much detail as possible, while the therapist emphasizes anger evoking imagery and thoughts. Once the client is feeling the anger from the scene (which they indicate by briefly raising their hand), the client is asked to wipe the scene and use their relaxation skills and new coping thoughts until they are no longer angry. The therapist and client process the scene and modify the angering and/or coping thoughts as needed and repeat the scene one to two times.

Session 7: Progress to date is reviewed including changes in anger and aggression frequency and intensity on the anger and aggression log. The effect of any changes in anger and aggressive behavior is assessed. Clients are asked which skills they find most helpful, and which ones are they still having trouble with. The clients then work on one to two moderate-high anger scenes (50–70 on the anger scale) using the methods outlined in session 6.

Session 8: Clients complete coping skills training for the anger scenes in session 7. The therapist then introduces the concept of coping skills training while remaining in the anger scene. Coping skills training is repeated with the client continuing to imagine the anger scene (rather than erase it) while engaging in relaxation skills and using their new coping thoughts. For the remainder of the CRCST sessions, coping skills training will be conducted in this way.

Session 9: Two high (70–90) anger scenes are developed, with the clients taking more of the lead in challenging anger distortions and developing new coping thoughts. The clients then practice coping skills training for these scenes.

Session 10: The therapist introduces the concept of overlap between anger, anxiety, and sadness/depression, highlighting the overlap in physiological (for anxiety) and cognitive (for both anxiety and depression) symptoms. General examples are provided by the therapist and then examples from the clients' life where feelings of anxiety or sadness led to anger/aggression (or vice versa) are elicited. The use of techniques learned to respond to high levels of anxiety and sadness is then addressed. Coping skills training on the two high anger scenes from session 9 is then practiced.

Session 11: Treatment gains to date and their current and future impact on the client's life are discussed. Treatment termination is addressed and a plan to address posttreatment provocation is developed. Coping skill training for highest (90–100) anger scenes is conducted.

Session 12: The concept of relapse prevention is introduced with the distinction between a "slip" and "relapse" being largely dependent on how the slip is addressed (i.e., explore why the slip occurred and develop a plan to more effectively address it next time *vs.* giving up). A relapse prevention plan is then developed with the client (e.g., continue to use cognitive restructuring, relaxation, and other coping skills in stressful situations; review how they are handling their anger each week). Coping skills for the worst highest anger scene is practiced. Finally, the therapist provides feedback on the positive changes noted and reinforces that continued improvement requires ongoing commitment (an analogy is often made to getting in good physical condition *vs.* staying in good physical condition). Prior to concluding treatment the therapist checks in on how the client is feeling and answers any questions the client has.

Other Cognitive-Behavioral Interventions for IED

Only two other published studies have examined psychosocial interventions for IED. Both are very recent and employ variants of cognitive-behavioral therapy (CBT). The first study (Costa et al., 2018) tested the efficacy of CBT group therapy among a group of 84 treatment-seeking individuals with IED from an Impulse Control Disorders Outpatient Unit in São Paulo, Brazil. Treatment consisted of 15 weekly 90-minute group sessions followed by three maintenance sessions every 2 weeks. All treatment sessions were conducted by two psychologists. CBT content included psychoeducation on the neurophysiology of anger, relaxation training, automatic thoughts and core beliefs, assertiveness training and problem solving, and relapse prevention. Participants completed the STAXI validated for use in Brazilian Portuguese (Biaggio, 2003) at pretreatment and at posttreatment.

Of the 84 participants, 25 (30%) dropped out prior to end of treatment. For the remaining 59 participants, highly significant decreases in trait anger, anger expression-in, and anger expression-out, along with a highly significant increase in anger control (all $P < .001$), were reported. The only nonsignificant finding was for state anger (which assesses anger "at this moment" and, thus, is not a strong estimate of general anger). These effects were large and tended to be slightly larger than the group CBT condition and slightly lower than individual CBT found by McCloskey et al. (2008).

It is important to note that this publication represents a preliminary analysis of a group CBT intervention and that it was not a randomized control trial, both of which limits the interpretability of the results, despite the fact that other randomized control trials of IED using a wait-list/self-monitoring tend to find little to no improvement in the control condition (Costa et al., 2018; McCloskey et al., 2008). In addition, aggression frequency and severity was not directly assessed. Finally, the trial only included participants who completed the trial and did not take into account the sizable dropout rate, which may have inflated the study effects. Despite these limitations, this study does provide evidence that individuals who complete a CBT intervention experience reductions in anger and anger expression, and increased their anger control.

A second study (Hewage et al., 2018) examined the efficacy of a trauma-focused CBT (TF-CBT) modified to be culturally appropriate for the individuals in postconflict Timor-Leste. Seventy-eight participants with

DSM-IV IED and a history of trauma were evenly randomized to TF-CBT or to a wait-list control condition. TF-CBT consisted of seven 120-minute individual sessions conducted with a highly experienced (20 years) clinician over 4 weeks. Drawing from the Adaptation and Development after Persecution and Trauma (ADAPT) model (Silove, 2013), the therapy content included aspects of narrative exposure therapy (Onyut et al., 2005), including creation of a personal narrative (Timor Lifeline) that integrated traumatic events the participant experienced and their patterns of explosive anger, as well as imaginal exposure to past traumatic events. Psychoeducation and core cognitive-behavioral techniques such as cognitive restructuring, as well as mindfulness-based relaxation, were integrated into TF-CBT, with modifications to increase the cultural sensitivity of the treatment (e.g., the use of traditional Timorese dolls to serve as proxies for the participant and other key individuals) and reflect an understanding of anger as a natural reaction to the injustices observed by many of the participants. Assessment was conducted at pretreatment, posttreatment, and 1-month follow-up and included measures of DSM-IV IED diagnostic criteria, anger and anger expression (STAXI-2), overall distress, and PTSD criteria.

Overall, dropout rates were as might be expected in this population, with seven participants (18%) in the TF-CBT condition dropping out during the treatment and seven participants (18%) in the wait-list condition dropping out between posttreatment and 1-month follow-up. Baseline assessment showed that the TF-CBT group reported greater anger expression-out than the wait-list group ($P=.04$), suggesting that the TF-CBT group may have been somewhat more aggressive. Notably, both groups reported 13–14 potentially traumatic events and approximately one-fourth of the sample (TF-CBT = 33.3%, wait-list = 20.5%) met full criteria for PTSD. Ultimately, the TF-CBT group displayed significant reductions in anger expression and significant increases in anger control. This was superior to the wait-list group, who showed nonsignificant increases in anger expression and little change in anger control. Furthermore, at study's end, no participant in the TG-CBT met for current IED or PTSD at posttreatment or 1-month follow-up (vs. 79.5%–71.8% for IED and 7.7%–15.4% for PTSD in the wait-list group). These results suggest large treatment effects for TF-CBT in the treatment of IED.

Some limitations of the study should be noted, however. Changes in frequency and severity of aggressive acts were only indirectly assessed via the IED interview used in the study. In addition, it is difficult to know how current IED was defined because there was no specifier for current vs. past IED in the DSM-IV, nor a clear delineation of then frequency and severity threshold for DSM-IV. While this is more a limitation of the DSM-IV IED criteria set, the lack of reported operational definitions for these criteria, as well as a reduction from 100% current IED to 0% in the treatment group (and 80% in the wait-list group despite increases in anger expression out) in only 1 month raises questions about how current IED was defined. There is also the issue of comorbid trauma/PTSD. Past trauma was a requirement for the study despite it not being a part of the IED criteria set. Furthermore, there was a very high level of trauma across participants, partly owing to the conditions in Timor-Leste, with about one-fourth of all participants meeting full criteria for current PTSD and likely many other participants meeting for subclinical and/or past PTSD. Even the treatment, itself, was trauma focused and there was a reduction in current PTSD from 33% to 0% in the TF-CBT group. Thus it is possible that for several of the IED participants, aggression may have been better accounted for by their trauma/PTSD symptoms rather than IED. While the authors reported excluding individuals for which PTSD was primary, they did not specify how this was determined and/or if the treatment worked by reducing their trauma symptoms. Finally, the intervention was administered by a single, highly experienced therapist, leaving questions about its generalizability to other treatment providers. Despite these limitations, this study was an ambitious investigation in of IED treatment in a low-income postconflict country that provides further evidence that psychosocial interventions can be effective in treating IED/dysregulated affective aggression.

Summary

Research on psychosocial interventions for IED is still in its infancy. Cognitive-behavioral interventions have been shown to be effective in treating anger and aggression; however, little research has been conducted assessing the efficacy of CBT (or any psychosocial intervention) in treating the severe anger dysregulation and aggression characteristic of IED. The few published studies that have examined CBT for IED, though all somewhat methodologically limited, have been consistent in showing that CBT can reduce anger and aggressive tendencies and increase anger control. This improvement appears to be in excess of wait-list/self-monitoring controls and early data suggests the improvement from CBT exceeds that of more nondirective, client-centered therapy. However, more well-controlled studies are needed including studies using more rigorous comparison conditions (e.g., treatment as usual) as well as investigations of other treatment modalities both separate from, and in combination with, CBT.

References

American Psychiatric Association. (2013). *Diagnostic and statistical manual of mental disorders* (5th ed.). Washington, DC: American Psychiatric Association.

Beck, R., & Fernandez, E. (1998). Cogntive-behavioral therapy in the treatment of anger. *Cognitive Therapy and Research, 22*, 62–75.

Best, M., Williams, J. M., & Coccaro, E. F. (2002). Evidence for a dysfunctional prefrontal circuit in patients with an impulsive aggressive disorder. *Proceedings of the National Academy of Sciences of the United States of America, 99*(12), 8448–8453.

Biaggio, A. (2003). *Manual do Inventário de Expressão de Raiva como Estado e Traco (STAXI)*. São Paulo: Vetor.

Bowman-Edmondson, C., & Cohen-Conger, J. (1996). A review of treatment efficacy for individuals with anger problems: conceptual, assessment and methodological issues. *Clinical Psychology Review, 16*, 251–275.

Coccaro, E. F., Fanning, J. R., Keedy, S. K., & Lee, R. J. (2016). Social cognition in Intermittent Explosive Disorder and aggression. *Journal of Psychiatric Research, 83*, 140–150.

Coccaro, E. F., Harvey, P. D., Kupsaw-Lawrence, E., Herbert, J. L., & Bernstein, D. P. (1991). Development of neuropharmacologically based behavioral assessments of impulsive aggressive behavior. *The Journal of Neuropsychiatry and Clinical Neurosciences, 3*(2), S44–S51.

Coccaro, E. F., Noblett, K. L., & McCloskey, M. S. (2009). Attributional and emotional responses to socially ambiguous cues: validation of a new assessment of social/emotional information processing in healthy adults and impulsive aggressive patients. *Journal of Psychiatric Research, 43*(10), 915–925.

Costa, A. M., Medeiros, G. C., Redden, S., Grant, J. E., Tavares, H., & Seger, L. (2018). Cognitive-behavioral group therapy for intermittent explosive disorder: description and preliminary analysis. *Revista Brasileira de Psiquiatria, 40*(3), 316–319.

Davidson, K., Tyrer, P., Tata, P., Cooke, D., Gumley, A., Ford, I., et al. (2009). Cognitive behaviour therapy for violent men with antisocial personality disorder in the community: an exploratory randomized controlled trial. *Psychological Medicine, 39*(4), 569–577.

Deffenbacher, J., Filetti, L., Lynch, R., Dahlen, E., & Oetting, E. (2001). Cognitive-behavioral treatment of high anger drivers. *Behaviour Research and Therapy, 40*, 895–910.

Deffenbacher, J. L., & McKay, M. (2000). *Overcoming situational and general anger*. Oakland, CA: New Harbinger Publications.

Del Vecchio, T., & O'Leary, K. D. (2004). Effectiveness of anger treatments for specific anger problems: a meta-analytic review. *Clinical Psychology Review, 24*(1), 15–34.

DiGuiseppe, R., & Tafrate, R. C. (2003). Anger treatment for adults: a meta-analytic review. *Clinical Psychology: Science and Practice, 10*(1), 70–84.

Fettich, K. C., McCloskey, M. S., Look, A. E., & Coccaro, E. F. (2014). Emotion regulation deficits in intermittent explosive disorder. *Aggressive Behavior, 41*(1), 25–33.

Galovski, T., & Blanchard, E. B. (2002). The effectiveness of a brief psychological intervention on court-referred and self-referred aggressive drivers. *Behaviour Research and Therapy, 40*(12), 1385–1402.

Hazaleus, S. L., & Deffenbacher, J. L. (1986). Relaxation and cognitive treatments of anger. *Journal of Consulting and Clinical Psychology, 54*(2), 222–226.

Hewage, K., Steel, Z., Mohsin, M., Tay, A. K., De Oliveira, J. C., Da Piedade, M., et al. (2018). A wait-list controlled study of a trauma-focused cognitive behavioral treatment for intermittent explosive disorder in Timor-Leste. *The American Journal of Orthopsychiatry, 88*(3), 282–294.

Karakurt, G., Whiting, K., van Esch, C., Bolen, S. D., & Calabrese, J. R. (2016). Couples therapy for intimate partner violence: a systematic review and meta-analysis. *Journal of Marital and Family Therapy, 42*(4), 567–583.

Kulper, D. A., Kleiman, E. M., McCloskey, M. S., Berman, M. E., & Coccaro, E. F. (2015). The experience of aggressive outbursts in Intermittent Explosive Disorder. *Psychiatry Research, 225*(3), 710–715.

Lee, A. H., & DiGuiseppe, R. (2018). Anger and aggression treatments: a review of meta-analyses. *Current Opinion in Psychology, 19*, 65–74.

McCloskey, M. S., Noblett, K. L., Deffenbacher, J. L., Gollan, J. K., & Coccaro, E. F. (2008). Cognitive-behavioral therapy for intermittent explosive disorder: a pilot randomized clinical trial. *Journal of Consulting and Clinical Psychology, 76*(5), 876–886.

Michie, S., Whittington, C., Hamoudi, Z., Zarnani, F., Tober, G., & West, R. (2012). Identification of behaviour change techniques to reduce excessive alcohol consumption. *Addiction, 107*(8), 1431–1440.

National Collaborating Centre for Mental Health. (2010). *Antisocial personality disorder. Vol.* 77. Leicester: The British Psychological Society and The Royal College of Psychiatrists.

Onyut, L. P., Neuner, F., Schauer, E., Ertl, V., Odenwald, M., Schauer, M., et al. (2005). Narrative Exposure Therapy as a treatment for child war survivors with posttraumatic stress disorder: two case reports and a pilot study in an African refugee settlement. *BMC Psychiatry, 5*, 7.

Silove, D. (2013). The ADAPT model: a conceptual framework for mental health and psychosocial programming in post conflict settings. *Intervention, 11*, 237–248.

Snyder, C. R., Crowson, J. J., Houston, B. K., Kurylo, M., & Poirier, J. (1997). Assessing hostile automatic thoughts: development and validation of the HAT scale. *Cognitive Therapy and Research, 21*(4), 477–492.

Spielberger, C. D. (1999). *STAXI-2: State trait anger expression inventory-2, professional manual.* Lutz, FL: Psychological Assessment Resources, Inc.

Index

Note: Page numbers followed by *f* indicate figures and *t* indicate tables.

B

C

K

L

M

N

O

P

Q

R

S

T

U

V

W

Z

Made in the USA
Monee, IL
13 September 2026

62977021R00151